CW01082563

Marx's Theory of A...........

By the same author (dates are of first publication):

Szatíra és valóság (Satire and Reality), SzKK, Budapest, 1955
La rivolta degli intellettuali in Ungheria, Einaudi, 1958
Attila József e l'arte moderna, Lerici, 1964
The Necessity of Social Control, The Merlin Press, 1971
Lukács's Concept of Dialectic, The Merlin Press, 1972
The Work of Sartre: Search for Freedom, Harvester
Wheatsheaf, 1979
Philosophy, Ideology and Social Science, Harvester
Wheatsheaf, 1986
The Power of Ideology, Harvester Wheatsheaf, 1989
Beyond Capital: Towards a Theory of Transition, The Merlin
Press, 1995
*Socialism or Barbarism: From the "American Century" to the
Crossroads,* Monthly Review Press, 2001
A Educação Para Além do Capital, Boitempo Editorial, 2005

MARX'S THEORY
OF ALIENATION

István Mészáros
Emeritus Professor of Philosophy, University of Sussex

MERLIN PRESS

© István Mészáros
The author asserts the right to be identified
as the author of this work

Published by
The Merlin Press Ltd.
99 Wallis Road
London E9 5LN
www.merlinpress.co.uk

ISBN: 0850365546

First published May 1970
Second Edition November 1970
Third Edition 1972
Fourth Edition 1975
Reprinted 1978, 1979, 1982, 1986
Fifth Edition, with new preface, 2005

British Library Cataloguing in Publication Data
is available from the British Library

Printed in Great Britain by Lightning Source

Contents

Part II: Aspects of Alienation

Part III: **Contemporary Significance of Marx's Theory of Alienation**

Preface to the Fifth Edition

In the Introduction to the First Edition of *Marx's Theory of Alienation*, completed in May 1969, I argued – in contrast to the false opposition between 'young Marx' and 'mature Marx' – that the structuring core of the Marxian system *in statu nascendi*, as powerfully and irreversibly spelled out in the *Economic and Philosophic Manuscripts of 1844*, is the 'transcendence of labour's self-alienation' (p. 19). I also stressed at the same time that 'the critique of alienation has acquired a new historical urgency' (p. 11). For toward the end of the 1960s and in the early 1970s the unfolding events and developments 'dramatically underlined the intensification of the *global structural crisis of capital*' (Preface to the Third Edition, November 1971).

What was at stake already then with regards to the qualitatively different – i.e. no longer *partial* and *localizable* – structural crisis of our social order, and remains more so today, is that 'in the contemporary world situation it is no longer possible to conceive even the immediate tasks of socialist movements in terms of the political conquest of power ... but in terms of *strategic socio-economic alternatives, with far-reaching global implications, ... involving all existing social systems*' (p. 21). Accordingly, 'the self-evidently *global* character of the socio-economic crisis of our time requires *global remedies*, i.e. the "*positive transcendence* of labour's self-alienation" in all its many-sidedly conditioning complexity' (p. 22).

Today, thirty-five years later, when there is much talk about 'globalization', no one would wish to deny the global character of our predicament. However, the believers in capitalist globalization uncritically assume it is the permanent solution to all our problems, wishfully projecting also a 'global government' as its unproblematic corollary. Naturally, they reject the very idea of a serious crisis with its inextricable links to the grave condition of alienation.

Yet, the uncomfortable truth of the matter is that the structural crisis of the capital system, in evidence by now for too many decades to fit into even the most optimistic theories of the 'long cycle', shows absolutely no sign of lifting. On the contrary, it deepens as time goes by, bringing with it destructiveness in every vital domain. Such as the revealing shift from capital's once real, even if unhistorically idealized, *'productive destruction'* to ever more wasteful *destructive production*, and from the most irresponsible encroachment on *nature* – the irreplaceable basis of human existence itself – to the ultimately suicidal unleashing of the most destructive course of action in the form of illimitable 'preventive' and 'pre-emptive' wars, now aggressively imposed under blatantly false pretences, in a vain attempt to secure the system's survival at any cost.

The alienation of humankind, in the fundamental sense of the term, means the *loss of control*: its embodiment in an *alien force* which confronts the individuals as a *hostile* and *potentially destructive* power. When Marx analysed alienation in his *Economic and Philosophic Manuscripts of 1844*, he indicated four principal aspects of it: the alienation of human beings (1) from *nature*; (2) from their own *productive activity*; (3) from their 'species being', as members of the human species; and (4) from *each other*. He forcefully underlined that all this is not some 'fatality of nature' – as indeed the structural antagonisms of capital are characteristically misrepresented, so as to leave them in their place – but a form of *self-alienation*. In other words, not the deed of an all-powerful outside agency, natural or metaphysical, but the outcome of a determinate type of historical development which can be positively altered by a conscious intervention in the historical process, in order to 'transcend labour's self-alienation'.

In the ascending phase of the system's development the control of the social metabolism by capital resulted in a formerly unimaginable increase in the powers of production. But the other side of all such increase in productive powers is the dangerous multiplication of the powers of destruction, unless a conscious control of the whole process prevails in the service of a positive human design. The trouble is that capital is incompatible with an alternative mode of control, no matter how devastating the consequences of imposing its own fetishistic design of uncontrollable capital-expansion.

In the course of the last century in which we suffered the destruction of two world wars, the once productively beneficial alienation of control has become overwhelmingly negative, due to the end of the system's historical ascendancy. So much so, in fact, that today – as the conceivably most extreme form of self-imposed alienation – nothing less than the very survival of humankind is threatened both militarily and by the destruction of nature. This is why it is imperative to face up to the great challenge of capital's global uncontrollability in our time, before it becomes too late to do so. The historical urgency of the critique of alienation, in the Marxian spirit, could not be greater than it is today.

Rochester, June 2005

Preface to the Fourth Edition

Apart from minor corrections, the fourth edition remains unchanged.

Brighton, August 1974

Preface to the Third Edition

The need for a third edition, eighteen months after the publication of the first, is gratifying to any author. More important is, however, that the interest readers have shown in this work helps confirm the suggestion made in the Introduction: namely that "the critique of alienation seems to have acquired a new historical urgency". Recent events – from the collapse of the long cherished politics of blockading China to the dollar crisis, and from the eruption of major contradictions of interest among the leading capitalist countries to the revealing necessity of invoking Court Orders and other special measures against defiant strikers with increasing frequency even in the United States of America: the very land of the allegedly "integrated" working class – have all dramatically underlined the intensification of the global structural crisis of capital. It is precisely in relation to such crisis that the Marxian critique of alienation maintains its vital socio-historical relevance today more than ever before.

As to our volume itself, friends and critics have made the point that some of the major issues of present-day social-economic development – discussed especially in the last chapters – would require a somewhat more systematic analysis. While I believe that the framework of *Marx's Theory of Alienation* did not allow for much more than a rather summary treatment of these topical issues, my agreement with the substance of the criticism could not be fuller. In fact I have been working now for a number of years on a detailed investigation of such topics – a study I hope to complete and publish before long. In the meantime I can only point to two partial results belonging to this complex of problems: *The Necessity of Social Control* (Isaac Deutscher Memorial Lecture, Merlin Press, 1971) and a contribution to the volume: *Aspects of History and Class Consciousness* (Routledge & Kegan Paul, 1971) on "Contingent and Necessary Class Consciousness".

Sussex University, Brighton, November 1971

Preface to the Second Edition

I took the opportunity of this new edition for providing English translation – in an Appendix at the end of the volume – for some quotations which appeared in the first edition, on pages 67, 243-4 and 259, in German or French only. In addition, I have also corrected a few printing errors. Otherwise the new edition is unchanged.

Preface to the First Edition

I am indebted to friends and colleagues who offered helpful suggestions many of which have been incorporated in some form in the final draft.

Particular thanks are due to my friends, Arnold Hauser and Cesare Cases whose criticism and encouragement proved invaluable.

My greatest indebtedness is to my old teacher and friend George Lukács, who influenced in more ways than one my mode of thinking.

Sussex University, May 1969

Introduction

THE problems of alienation have been debated for a long time but interest in them is by no means diminishing. On the contrary: judging by some recent historical events and the ideological orientation of many of their participants, the critique of alienation seems to have acquired a new historical urgency.

Much discussion has been centred around Marx's *Economic and Philosophic Manuscripts of 1844* in the last forty years. The first—though incomplete—edition appeared in Russian in 1927 and was followed, in 1932, by complete German, Russian and French editions which made possible their diffusion in philosophical and literary circles all over the world. The key concept of these *Manuscripts* is the concept of alienation.

The number of books and articles written about, or referring to, the *Manuscripts of 1844* is countless. They are unquestionably the most talked about philosophical work in this century. In the discussions, however, it is often not realized that they also happen to be one of the most complex and difficult works of philosophical literature.

Their difficulties are by no means obvious at first sight. The enormous complexity of the closely interrelated theoretical levels is often hidden by formulations which look deceivingly simple. Paradoxically enough, Marx's great powers of expression—his almost unparalleled ability to formulate his ideas in a graphic style; his unique gift of producing "quotable" (but in fact multidimensional) aphorisms, etc.—make an adequate understanding of this work more, rather than less, difficult. For it is tempting to abstract, as many commentators do, from the complicated interconnections in order to concentrate on the apparent simplicity of the point most sharply in focus. However, unless the aphoristic formulations are grasped in their manifold philosophical interconnections, the dangers of misinterpretation are acute. The narrow "literal" reading of isolated passages (not to speak of the ideologically motivated misreadings[1] of similarly isolated aphorisms and passages) can only produce theories—like the "radically new Marx" of many writings

11

that one-sidedly concentrated on certain passages of the *Paris Manuscripts*, taken out of context and opposed to the rest of Marx's monumental work—based on the methodology of turning isolated quotations into sensationalistic slogans.

Marx's youthful works have been fittingly described as *"enigmatically clear"*.[2] In point of fact Marx has no youthful work to which this description could better apply than the *Manuscripts of 1844*. The reader who wants to get beyond the deceptive simplicity, in order to achieve a deeper understanding of this "enigmatic clarity", has to wrestle with several difficulties. Let us have a brief look at them.

1. *Fragmentariness*. As is well known, this work is incomplete. The *Manuscripts of 1844* range from extracts from books, with brief comments on them, through loosely connected notes and reflections on various topics, to a more or less comprehensive assessment of the Hegelian philosophy. While it is relatively easy to understand the particular texts and passages, it is by no means easy to see the guiding line of the work as a whole. The particular passages, however, only acquire their full meaning in relation to the general significance of the work as a whole.

2. *Language and terminology*. Here three kinds of problems arise of which the first does not apply, of course, to the German original:

(a) *Complexities of translation*. Some of the key terms— e.g. "Aufhebung"—have very different connotations in the original text. Thus "Aufhebung" in German means simultaneously: "transcendence", "suppression", "preserving", and "overcoming (or superseding) by raising it to a higher level". Clearly, no translator can solve difficulties of this kind in a completely satisfactory way. Even at the price of sounding extremely clumsy, he cannot couple-up more than two, or at the most three, of these complementary meanings, and in the vast majority of cases he must rely on selecting *one* term only. An ideal of conceptual accuracy which linguistically violates the text is self-defeating. All that one can hope to achieve is a reasonable approximation to the original. However, the reader himself can do something more. He can complete the reading of "transcendence" or "supersession", etc. with those missing ramifications of the original term which, for linguistic reasons, had to be left out.

(b) *Inadequacy of conceptual framework*. For the past few decades philosophy has been dominated—especially in English speaking countries—by various trends of positivistic empiricism and formalism. Consequently, numerous concepts used by Marx— perhaps most of his key concepts—must sound extremely odd, if not altogether meaningless or self-contradictory, to all those who are used to the misleading "common-sense simplicity" of positivistic empiricism or to the neat schematic straightforwardness of philosophical formalism, or both. The difficulties of understanding, due to this condition, cannot be sufficiently stressed. For, in view of the fact that the whole structure of Marx's theory is dialectical, his key concepts simply cannot be understood at all except in their dialectical —and often apparently self-contradictory—interrelatedness. "Transcendence", for instance, is not a transference into another realm, nor is it either "suppression" or "preservation" alone, but both at the same time. Or, to take another example : in contradistinction to so many philosophical conceptions, in Marx's view man is neither "human" nor "natural" alone but both : i.e. "*humanly* natural" and "*naturally* human" at the same time. Or again, at a higher level of abstraction, "specific" and "universal" are not *opposites* to each other, but they constitute a dialectical *unity*. That is to say : man is the "*universal* being of nature" only because he is the "*specific* being of nature" whose unique specificity consists precisely in its unique universality as opposed to the limited partiality of all the other beings of nature. At the level of both empiricism and formalism the notion of a unity of such opposites is self-contradictory. Only at the dialectical level of discourse can these notions acquire their full meaning without which it is impossible to understand the central ideas of Marx's theory of alienation. This is why the reader must constantly remember the fact that he is dealing with the complexities of a dialectical framework of discourse and not with the neat one-dimensionality of philosophical formalism, nor with the artificial simplicity of commonplace-mongering neo-empiricism.

(*c*) *Terminological ambiguity.* A relatively simple problem, provided the previous two points are kept in mind. Here the issue is that Marx, in his efforts to enter into a dialogue with his radical philosophical contemporaries like Feuerbach, has retained certain terms of their discourse which were at times in conflict with his own meaning. An example is "self-estrangement" which in Marx's *Manuscripts* stands for a greatly modified content that would call for an accordingly modified terminology, with more concrete expressions in specific contexts. An even more striking example is "human essence". As we shall see later, Marx categorically rejected the idea of a "human essence". Yet he kept the term, transforming its original meaning beyond recognition. In this case his aim was not simply to add new dimensions to an important concept (like "self-estrangement") but to demonstrate the emptiness of this philosophical term, in its traditional sense. And yet, in the course of such demonstration he used the same term himself, mostly without polemical references, although with a radically different meaning. An attentive reading of the contexts in which such borrowed terms occur can, however, clear out of the way this difficulty. (This remedy applies not only to "human essence" and "self-estrangement" mentioned above, but also to terms like "humanism", "positive humanism", "self-mediation", "species-being", etc.)

3. *Complexity of key concept: alienation.*[3] This problem represents one of the greatest difficulties. Marx's concept of alienation has four main aspects which are as follows:

(*a*) man is alienated from *nature*;
(*b*) he is alienated from *himself* (from his own *activity*);
(*c*) from his *"species-being"* (from his being as a member of the human species);
(*d*) man is alienated from *man* (from other men).

The first of these four characteristics of "alienated labour" expresses the relation of the worker to the *product* of his labour, which is at the same time, according to Marx, his relation to the *sensuous external world*, to the objects of nature.

The second, on the other hand, is the expression of labour's relation to the *act of production* within the labour process, that is to say the worker's relation to his own activity as alien activity which does not offer satisfaction to him in and by itself, but only by the act of selling it to someone else. (This means that it is not activity itself which brings satisfaction to him, but an abstract property of it: its saleability under certain conditions.) Marx also calls the first characteristic "estrangement of the *thing*", whereas the second: "*self*-estrangement".

The third aspect—man's alienation from his species-being—is related to the conception according to which the object of labour is the *objectification of man's species life*, for man "duplicates himself not only, as in consciousness, intellectually, but also actively, in reality, and therefore he contemplates himself in a world that he has created". Alienated labour, however, turns "M a n 's s p e c i e s b e i n g, both nature and his spiritual species property, into a being alien to him, into a means to his individual existence. It estranges man's own body from him, as it does external nature and his spiritual existence, his human being" (76).*

The third characteristic is implied in the first two, being an expression of them in terms of *human relations,* and so is the fourth characteristic mentioned above. But whereas in formulating the third characteristic Marx has taken into account the effects of alienation of labour—both as "estrangement of the thing" and "self-estrangement"—with respect to the relation of *man to mankind* in general (i.e. the alienation of "humanness" in the course of its debasement through capitalistic processes), in the fourth he is considering them as regards man's relationship to *other men.* As Marx puts the latter: "An immediate consequence of the fact that man is estranged from the product of his labour, from his life-activity, from his species being is the estrangement of man from man. If a man is confronted by himself, he is confronted by the other man. What applies to man's relation to his work, to the product of his labour and to himself, also holds of man's relation to the other man, and to the other man's labour and object of labour. In fact, the proposition that man's species nature is estranged from him means that one man is estranged from the other, as each of them is from man's essential nature" (77).

Thus Marx's concept of alienation embraces the manifestations of "man's estrangement from-*nature* and from *himself*" on the one hand, and the expressions of this process in the relationship of *man–mankind* and *man and man* on the other.

4. *Structure of Paris Manuscripts.* Despite the modest length—only about 50,000 words—the *Economic and Philosophic Manuscripts of 1844* are a great work of synthesis, of a particular kind: a *synthesis in statu nascendi* (more about that in a moment). We are witnessing in them the emergence of this unique synthesis as we follow the outlines of a vast, comprehensive conception of human experience in all its manifestations; more comprehensive in fact than anything before it, including the grandiose Hegelian vision. Marx sketches in the *Paris Manuscripts* the main features of a revolutionary new "human science"—opposed by him to the alienated

* Numbers in brackets refer to page numbers of Marx's *Economic and Philosophic Manuscripts of 1844,* translated by Martin Milligan; Lawrence and Wishart Ltd., London, 1959.
Marx's stresses are indicated by spaced lettering, my own are italicized. Similarly with other quotations. Spaced and also italicized lettering indicates stresses both by the authors concerned and by myself.

universality of abstract philosophy on the one hand and the reified fragmentariness and partiality of "natural science" on the other— from the viewpoint of a great synthesizing idea: "the alienation of labour" as the root cause of the whole complex of alienations.

Nobody should be deceived by the first impression of reading, in addition to extracts from books, fragmentary remarks, summary hints and paradoxical formulations, expressed in an aphoristic style. For a more attentive look would reveal that the *Paris Manuscripts* are much more closely argued than the first impression would suggest. As has been mentioned, the particular idea- of the *Manuscripts* only acquire their full meaning in relation to the general significance of the work as a whole. To put it in another way, the points made by Marx on widely ranging issues cannot be fully understood except as closely interrelated parts of a coherent *system* of ideas. The *Manuscripts of 1844* constitute Marx's first comprehensive system. In this system every particular point is "multidimensional": it links up with all the other points of the Marxian system of ideas; it implies them just as much as it is implied by them. (The problem of the relationship between *alienation and consciousness*, for instance, is never considered in isolation but—in sharp contrast to other philosophical approaches to the problem—as something occupying a determinate place within the system of human activities; as based upon the socio-economic basis and being in constant interplay with it.)

No system is conceivable, of course, without an internal structure of its own. It will be the task of Part I to go into the details of this problem. Here we can only indicate, very briefly, those character- istics which are essential for understanding the complex structure of Marx's first great work of synthesis.

In the *Economic and Philosophic Manuscripts of 1844* Marx asks two—complementary—sets of questions. The first set investigates *why* is there an antagonistic contradiction (or "hostile opposition", as sometimes he puts it):

> between different philosophical trends (of the same age as well as of different ages);
> between "Philosophy" and "science";
> between "Philosophy" (Ethics) and "Political Economy";
> between the theoretical and the practical sphere (i.e. between Theory and Practice).

The second set is concerned with the question of "transcendence" (Aufhebung), by asking *how* is it possible to supersede the existing state of affairs, the prevailing system of alienations, from the estrangements manifest in everyday life to the alienated conceptions of philosophy. Or, expressed in a positive form : *how* is it possible to achieve the *unity of opposites* in place of the antagonistic oppositions that characterize alienation. (The opposition between "doing and thinking", between "being and having", between "means and end", between "public life and private life", between "production and consumption", between "Philosophy and Science", between "Theory and Practice" etc.) The ideal of a *"human science"*, in place of alienated science and philosophy, (not to be confused with the vague and woolly notion of an "anthropological philosophy" or "humanist Marxism", nor with the equally vague and illusory "scientism" of some neo-Marxist writings) is a concrete formulation of this task of "transcendence" in the field of theory while the *"unity of theory and practice"* is the most general and comprehensive expression of the Marxian programme.

It goes without saying that the first set of questions is unthinkable without the second that animates and structures (or articulates) the former. Thus the problems of "transcendence" represent the "übergreifendes Moment" ("overriding factor")—to use Marx's expression—in this dialectical interrelationship of the two sets of questions. If there is an ultimately "irreducible" element in the philosophical discourse, it is the philosopher's "prise de position" to the supersession of the contradictions he perceives. But of course "irreducible" only ultimately, or "in the last analysis" (Engels), i.e. in the dialectical sense of a relative priority within a reciprocal determination. This means that while the philosopher's approach to "Aufhebung" certainly determines the limits of his insight into the nature of the contradictions of his age, it is also determined, in its concrete articulation, by the latter, i.e. by the sensitivity and depth of the philosopher's insight into the complex problematics of the world in which he lives.

Marx was by no means the first philosopher to raise some of the questions mentioned above. (The greatest of his immediate predecessors, Hegel, was in fact the originator of the concept of "Aufhebung" as a "unity of opposites".) But he was the first to raise the whole range of questions we have seen, while his predecessors, unable to formulate the aim of unifying theory and practice, abandoned their inquiry at the crucial point. The abstractness of their conception of "Aufhebung" kept their questioning within very narrow conceptual limits. Their diagnosis of problems was vitiated by the—merely conceptual—solutions they could envisage to them.

For Marx, by contrast, the question of "transcendence" was—starting with the earliest formulations of his philosophical outlook—inseparable from the programme of achieving the "unity of theory and practice". Prior to the *Manuscripts of 1844*, however, this ‧ principle remained rather abstract because Marx could not identify the "Archimedean point" through which it would be possible to translate the programme into reality. The introduction of the concept of "alienated labour" into Marx's thought has fundamentally changed all this. As we shall see later, as soon as the problem of transcendence has been concretized—in the *Manuscripts of 1844*—as the negation and supersession of "labour's self-alienation", Marx's system was born.

In this sense can we call the *Paris Manuscripts* a system *in statu nascendi*. For it is in these *Manuscripts* that Marx systematically explores for the first time the far-reaching implications of his synthesizing idea—"the alienation of labour"—in every sphere of human activity. The discovery of the "missing link" of his earlier reflections throws new light on all his ideas and particular points of criticism—some of them already formulated years before 1844—which now naturally fit together into an all-embracing conception. As Marx proceeds with his critical inquiry in the *Paris Manuscripts*, the depth of his insight and the unparalleled coherence of his ideas become more and more evident. There is an air of excitement about the whole enterprise—manifest also in the greatly heightened, often solemn, style of exposition—as Marx repeatedly spells out his great historical discovery, namely that the most varied forms of alienation which he surveys can be brought to a common denominator, in the field of *social practice*, through the tangibly concrete and strategically crucial concept of "alienated labour": the common focus of both sets of questions, i.e. both "why" (diagnosis) and "how" (transcendence).

In this context it is worth comparing Marx's criticisms of Hegel before and after the introduction of this synthesizing concept into his thought. Prior to its appearance, his critique of the Hegelian philosophy, however meticulous, remained *partial*, although the intent was, from the earliest stage of Marx's philosophical development, unmistakably that of a frontal attack on the Hegelian system as a whole. In the *Manuscripts of 1844*, however, we find a "Critique of the Hegelian Dialectic and Philosophy as a Whole"

(142–171). Thanks to the concept of "labour's self-alienation" the Hegelian philosophy is set into its proper perspectives : both its great historical achievements and limitations are revealed and made to seem self-evident in the light of Marx's fundamental synthesizing idea. Once in possession of this key that opens the doors of the Hegelian system as a whole, exposing to a comprehensive social criticism all its "secrets" and "mystifications", the laboriously detailed analysis of particular fields of this philosophy—e.g. the earlier attempted "Critique of the Hegelian Philosophy of Right"— becomes superfluous. (At any rate uninteresting for Marx, for it could now merely exemplify a general point towards which his earlier critical investigations of the Hegelian philosophy were striving.) In fact Marx never resumed his interrupted work on the Hegelian Philosophy of Right and his later projects concerning Hegel's thought—an investigation of his works on Logic and Aesthetic in particular—aimed at summarizing Hegel's achievements as well as sketching Marx's own ideas in these fields, rather than at a systematic criticism of the Hegelian philosophy as a whole. As far as the latter was concerned, Marx has done his reckoning with it for good, in the form of "a critical settling of accounts" (20), in the *Manuscripts of 1844*.

To sum up then, the core of the *Paris Manuscripts* that structures the whole work is the concept of the "transcendence of labour's self-alienation". This Marxian system *in statu nascendi* is simultaneously a kind of "stock-taking" as well as the formulation of a monumental programme for future investigations. While rethinking all the major problems that occupied him prior to the sketching of the *Manuscripts of 1844* Marx tries out his synthesizing idea in many directions, becoming fully aware of both the necessity of venturing into the most varied fields and of the difficulties and dangers involved in such an enterprise. This is why he writes in his *Preface* to the *Paris Manuscripts* (though, not surprisingly, only after the completion of the rest of the *Manuscripts*): "the wealth and diversity of the subjects to be treated, could have been compressed into one work only in a purely aphoristic style; whilst an aphoristic presentation of this kind, for its part would have given the impression of arbitrary systematizing. I shall therefore issue the critique of law, ethics, politics, etc., in a series of distinct, independent pamphlets, and at the end try in a special work to present them again as a connected whole showing the interrelationship of the separate parts, and finally, shall make a critique of the speculative elaboration of that material. For this reason it will be found that the interconnection between political economy and the state, law, ethics, civil life, etc., is touched on in the present work only to the extent to which political economy itself *ex professo* [particularly] touches on these subjects" (15). Thus in the course of writing the *Paris Manuscripts* Marx realizes the immensity of his undertaking as he beco..nes aware of the fact that his praxis-oriented general approach, unlike the method of aphoristic summariness he also practised to some extent, must proceed everywhere "by means of a *wholly empirical analysis*" (16), by submitting to the strictest scrutiny even the smallest details. It is not surprising, therefore, that the programme of issuing "the critique of law, ethics, politics, etc." took him a lifetime to accomplish and that this work had to assume a form very different indeed from the originally projected "independent pamphlets". For even the latter method would have been far too "aphoristic" and unjustifiably summary. The *Manuscripts of 1844* had to be left unfinished—it could not be otherwise with a flexible and open system *in statu nascendi* which should not be confused with some premature youthful synthesis. But their significance, despite their fragmentary character, is enormous, both in terms of what they have actually achieved and as regards the range and mode of inquiry they have opened up. Far from requiring subsequent major reversals or revisions, the *Manuscripts of 1844* have adequately anticipated the later Marx by grasping in a synthetic unity the problematics of a comprehensive, praxis-centred, radical reassessment of all facets of human experience "by means of a wholly empirical analysis based on a conscientious critical study of political economy" (16).

*   *   *

In accordance with the central characteristics of Marx's work, the ordering principle of the present study must be the focusing of attention on the various aspects and implications of Marx's concept of "Aufhebung" as they arise in the framework of his theory of alienation. In other words the key to understanding Marx's theory of alienation is his concept of "Aufhebung", and not the other way round. (This reversal of the structural relationship of concepts in assessing Marx's system has led astray all those commentators who tried to elucidate the Marxist world-view starting from the young Marx's concept of alienation as their ultimate point of reference: at best they ended up with some moralizing tautology—for clearly no concept can be elucidated by itself—and in many cases with grave distortions of Marx's system as a whole.[4]) The concept of "Aufhebung" must be in the centre of our attention for three main reasons :

(1) it is, as we have seen, crucial for the understanding of the *Economic and Philosophic Manuscripts of 1844* whose analysis constitutes the major part of this study;

(2) this concept of the "transcendence (Aufhebung) of labour's self-alienation" provides the essential link with the totality of Marx's work, including the last works of the so-called "mature Marx";

(3) in the development of Marxism after the death of its founders the issue was greatly neglected and, for understandable historical reasons, Marxism was given a more directly instrumental orientation. In the present phase of socio-historical development, however, when for the first time in history capitalism is being shaken to its foundations as a *world-system* (whereas all the past crises of capitalism, no matter how spectacular, were *partial* and *localizable*), the "transcendence of labour's self-alienation" is "on the order of the day". That is, in the contemporary world-situation it is no longer possible to conceive even the immediate tasks of socialist movements in terms of the political conquest of power—not as when the world-historical task was the breaking of the first and "weakest link of the chain"— but in terms of strategic socio-economical alternatives, with far-reaching global implications. This is why interest in certain aspects of Marx's conception which must have seemed rather remote to the working class movement at the turn of the century has been revived in the post-war period and attracts increasingly more attention over a widening range of the social spectrum, rather than being confined, as sectarian dogmatists would have it, to "isolated intellectuals". This phenomenon of revival is all the more significant because the problems at stake, as mentioned above, have global implications, involving all existing social systems, even if in very different ways. Precisely because the realization of these aspects of Marx's original programme could only be envisaged in a global frame-work, the concept of the "positive transcendence of labour's self-alienation" had to be pushed into the background at a time when Marxism embarked on the journey of its practical realization in the form of partial (national) socio-political movements, i.e. when Marxism was being turned from a global theory into organized movements which, for a long historical period—for the whole era of the defence of hardly won positions—had to remain partial and

limited. By contrast the self-evidently global character of the socio-economical crisis of our time requires global remedies: i.e. the "*positive transcendence* of labour's self-alienation" in all its many-sidedly conditioning complexity. It is not suggested, of course, that in the present world-situation the problems first diagnosed by Marx could be solved overnight; far from it. Nor was indeed Marx's theory of alienation ever meant as a recipe for "Messianic solutions", as we shall see later. The point is that in our age it becomes historically possible—and increasingly more necessary as well—to tackle the everyday issues facing socialist movements all over the world in their proper perspectives: as directly or indirectly related to the fundamental task of "the positive transcendence of labour's self-alienation".

*   *   *

In discussing Marx's theory of alienation the centre of analysis must be, needless to say, the *Economic and Philosophic Manuscripts of 1844*. Accordingly, the bulk of the present study is dedicated to a close scrutiny of the various aspects of Marx's theory of alienation as they appear in the *Paris Manuscripts*. At the same time it must be emphasized that no attempt is made here at reconstructing Marx's work on the basis of the *Manuscripts of 1844*. On the contrary, the framework of interpretation and evaluation of the latter is the totality of Marx's work without which accounts of his first synthesis can amount to no more than a caricature, however unintended. Not only because the "enigmatic remarks" and aphoristic hints of the *Paris Manuscripts* cannot be deciphered without reference to his later works but mainly because assigning the concept of alienation exclusively to the youthful period grossly falsifies the "mature Marx"—as we shall see later—undermining the unity and internal coherence of his thought. (That in some cases this may be a conscious design is beside the point; the result is the same.)

All analysis and interpretation necessarily involves some reconstruction from a determinate temporal position which is inevitably different from that of its object. To deny this simple fact would condemn us to the acceptance of the illusions of "scientism". The "irreducible element" of a philosopher's general conception, mentioned above, does not—and cannot—coincide with that of its counterparts which lie at the core of later interpretations. And no interpretation is conceivable without an "irreducible element" of its own as its point of departure and fundamental organizing centre. This does not mean of course, that the question of objectivity must be dismissed and replaced by some form of relativism. For the criteria of the objective validity of interpretations are given in the *affinity* of the different "irreducible elements" on one hand and in their practical historical relevance on the other. In other words the object of interpretation cannot be reached unless the approach is made on the basis of an objective affinity of values relevant to the given historical situation. This is why Marx's bourgeois interpreters and opponents—whether "neutral Marxologues" or conservative political propagandists—are bound to miss their target. The "irreducible element" (i.e. the open or hidden value-commitment) that motivates both the programmatically "neutral Marxology"— related to matters which necessarily exclude all pretences of "detached neutrality"—and the less bashful forms of opposition to Marxism may at times yield partial insights and results but notoriously fail to comprehend the coherently interrelated system of Marxist ideas as a whole, because of the hostile clash between the reciprocally exclusive approaches to the crucial problems of the given socio-historical reality, and in particular to the issue of "Aufhebung". If an account of the limits of validity of rival interpretations on these or similar lines does not satisfy those who would not settle for anything short of a final "scientific objectivity" (advocating in fact a fetishism of natural science), that cannot be helped. In favour of our account, however, it should be remarked that at least it does not require the introduction of false polarities into Marx's system, such as the presumed opposition between his "scientific concepts" and his alleged "ideological concepts"; nor does it require the expurgation of the latter from Marx's philosophical conception as a whole. Without these alleged "ideological concepts" Marx's conception could appear, maybe, more "scientific"; but it would be incomparably poorer and far less in agreement with our needs. To us there seems to be no real alternative to recognizing and accepting the limitations of relating the meaning of Marx's theory of alienation to our own historical predicament in terms of which it must be read and understood.

The present study aims in the first place at representing the genesis and internal development of Marx's theory of alienation, focusing attention not only on the historical and intellectual background to his main ideas but, above all, on the inner dynamism of his structure of thought as a whole. In the framework of such a preliminary general assessment—in Part I—the subsequent chapters attempt a detailed analysis of the various aspects of the complex problematics of alienation, from the economic aspects to the ontological and moral ones, and from the political to the aesthetic aspects. These chapters—from IV to VII—are relatively "self-contained",[5] not only in order to facilitate the understanding of Marx's often very complicated and "dispersed" arguments but also because some of the much disputed points can be more easily cleared up by organizing the material around the focal points of the topics mentioned above. However, two notes of warning are necessary here. The first is that the method followed in Part II makes unfortunately unavoidable the repetition of some centrally important passages in different contexts for which the reader's indulgence is sought. More important is the second point, namely that such a "self-contained", relatively independent discussion of the various aspects of Marx's theory of alienation requires the separation of the partial complexes of problems from their manifold dialectical interconnections. Although the problematics of Marx's theory of alienation is discussed in its totality in the concluding chapters, for an adequate understanding of the separate aspects it is necessary to read them in close conjunction with each other, constantly keeping in mind their fundamental structural interconnections.

On the basis of the detailed account of Marx's views on alienation in Parts I and II, in Part III it becomes possible to embark on a discussion of the main controversies surrounding this subject, without entering too much into the more tedious details of polemics. (Throughout the manuscript the less central or more technical points are discussed in the notes, in order to avoid overcrowding and overcomplicating the main body of analysis.) The final chapters aim at relating Marx's theory of alienation as a whole to contemporary problems by means of the common key issue of the *"positive transcendence of alienation"* : Marx's concept of "education". For it is our strongly felt conviction that only the Marxian concept of education—which, in sharp contrast to currently prevailing, narrowly institution-centred conceptions, embraces the totality of both individual and social processes—can offer a way out of the contemporary social crisis which is becoming increasingly more acute not least in the field of institutionalized education itself.

PART I

ORIGINS AND STRUCTURE
OF THE MARXIAN THEORY

If man's feelings, passions, etc., are not merely anthropological phenomena in the narrower sense, but truly ontological affirmations of essential being (of nature), and if they are only really affirmed because their object exists for them as an object of sense, then it is clear :

(1) That they have by no means merely one mode of affirmation, but rather that the distinctive character of their existence, of their life, is constituted by the distinctive mode of their affirmation. In what manner the object exists for them, is the characteristic mode of their gratification.

(2) Wherever the sensuous affirmation is the direct annulment of the object in its independent form (as in eating, drinking, working up of the object, etc.), this is the affirmation of the object.

(3) In so far as man, and hence also his feelings, etc., are human, the affirmation of the object by another is likewise his own enjoyment.

(4) Only through developed industry—i.e. through the medium of private property—does the ontological essence of human passion come to be both in its totality and in its humanity; the science of man is therefore itself a product of man's establishment of himself by practical activity.

(5) The meaning of private property—liberated from its estrangement—is the existence of essential objects for man, both as objects of enjoyment and as objects of activity.

—Economic and Philosophic Manuscripts of 1844

I. Origins of the Concept of Alienation

As is well known, Feuerbach, Hegel and English Political Economy exercised the most direct influence on the formation of Marx's theory of alienation. But we are concerned here with much more than simple intellectual influences. The concept of alienation belongs to a vast and complex problematics, with a long history of its own. Preoccupations with this problematics—in forms ranging from the Bible to literary works as well as treatises on Law, Economy and Philosophy—reflect objective trends of European development, from slavery to the age of transition from capitalism to socialism. Intellectual influences, revealing important continuities across the transformations of social structures, acquire their real significance only if they are considered in this objective framework of development. If so assessed, their importance—far from being exhausted in mere historical curiosity—cannot be stressed enough: precisely because they indicate the deep-rootedness of certain problematics as well as the *relative* autonomy of the forms of thought in which they are reflected.[6]

It must be made equally clear, however, that such influences are exercised in the dialectical sense of "continuity in discontinuity". Whether the element of continuity predominates over discontinuity or the other way round, and in what precise form and correlation, is a matter for concrete historical analysis. As we shall see, in the case of Marx's thought in its relation to antecedent theories discontinuity is the "übergreifendes Moment", but some elements of continuity are also very important.

Some of the principal themes of modern theories of alienation appeared in European thought, in one form or another, many centuries ago. To follow their development in detail would require copious volumes. In the few pages at our disposal we cannot attempt more than an outline of the general trends of this development, describing their main characteristics insofar as they link up with Marx's theory of alienation and help to throw light on it.

1. *The Judeo-Christian Approach*

The first aspect we have to consider is the lament about being *"alienated from God"* (or having "fallen from Grace") which belongs to the common heritage of Judeo-Christian mythology. The divine order, it is said, has been violated; man has alienated himself from "the ways of God", whether simply by "the fall of man" or later by "the dark idolatries of *alienated Judah*",[7] or later again by the behaviour of *"Christians alienated from the life of God".*[8] The messianic mission consists in rescuing man from this state of self-alienation which he had brought upon himself.

But this is as far as the similarities go in the Judeo-Christian problematics; and far-reaching differences prevail in other respects. For the form in which the messianic transcendence of alienation is envisaged is not a matter of indifference. "Remember"—says Paul the Apostle—"that ye were without Christ, being aliens from the commonwealth of Israel, and strangers from the covenant of promise, having no hope, and without God in the world : But now in Christ Jesus ye who sometimes were far off are made nigh by the blood of Christ. . . . Now therefore ye are no more strangers and foreigners, but fellow-citizens with the saints, and of the household of God; And are built upon the foundation of the apostles and prophets, Jesus Christ himself being the chief corner stone; In whom all the building fitly framed together groweth unto an holy temple in the Lord : In whom ye also are builded together for an habitation of God through the Spirit."[9] Christianity thus, in its universality, announces the imaginary solution of human self-alienation in the form of "the mystery of Christ".[10] This mystery postulates the reconciliation of the contradictions which made groups of people oppose each other as "strangers", "foreigners", "enemies". This is not only a reflection of a specific form of social struggle but at the same time also its mystical "resolution" which induced Marx to write : "It was only in appearance that Christianity overcame real Judaism. It was too r e f i n e d, too spiritual to eliminate the crudeness of practical need except by raising it into the ethereal realm. Christianity is the sublime thought of Judaism. Judaism is the vulgar practical application of Christianity. But this practical application could only become universal when Christianity as perfected religion had accomplished, in a t h e o r e t i c a l fashion, the alienation of man from himself and from nature."[11]

Judaism in its "crude" realism reflects with a much greater immediacy the actual state of affairs, advocating a virtually endless continuation of the extension of its worldly powers—i.e. settling for a "quasi-messianic" solution on earth : this is why it is in no hurry whatsoever about the arrival of its Messiah—in the form of two, complementary, postulates :

(1) the softening of *internal* class conflicts, in the interest of the cohesion of the national community in its confrontation with the outside world of the "strangers" : "For *the poor shall never cease out of the land* : therefore I command thee, saying, Thou shalt open thy hand wide unto *thy brother*, to *thy* poor, and to *thy* needy, in *thy* land."[12]

(2) the promise of readmission into the grace of God is partly fulfilled in the form of granting the power of domination over the "strangers" to Judah : "And strangers shall stand and feed your flocks, and the sons of the alien shall be your plowmen and your vinedressers."[13]

The formidable practical vehicle of this expanding domination was the weapon of "usury" which needed, however, in order to become really effective, its suitable counterpart which offered an unlimited outlet for the power of this weapon : i.e. the metamorphosis of Judaism into Christianity. For "Judaism attains its apogee with the perfection of civil society; but civil society only reaches perfection in the Christian world. Only under the sway of Christianity, which objectifies all national, natural, moral and theoretical relationships, could civil society separate itself completely from the life of the state, sever all the species-bonds of man, establish egoism and selfish need in their place, and dissolve the human world into a world of atomistic, antagonistic individuals."[14]

The ethos of Judaism which stimulated this development was not confined to the general assertion of the God-willed superiority of the "chosen people" in its confrontation with the world of strangers, issuing in commands like this : "Ye shall not eat any thing that dieth of itself : thou shalt give it unto the *stranger* that is in thy gates, that he may eat it; or thou mayest *sell it* unto an *alien* : for thou art an holy people unto the Lord thy God."[15] Far more important was in the practical sense the absolute prohibition imposed on the exploitation of the sons of Judah through *usury* : "If thou lend money to any of my people that is poor by thee, *thou shalt not be to him an usurer*, neither shalt thou lay upon him usury."[16] Usury was only allowed in dealings with *strangers*, but not with "brethren".

Christianity, by contrast, which refused to retain the discrimination between "any of my people" and "strangers" (or "aliens") postulating in its place the "universal brotherhood of mankind", not only deprived itself of the powerful weapon of "usury" (i.e. of "interest" and the accumulation of capital coupled with it) as the most important vehicle of early economic expansion but at the same time also became an easy prey to the triumphant advance of the "spirit of Judaism". The "crude and vulgar practical principle of Judaism" discussed by Marx—i.e. the effectively self-centred, internally cohesive, practical-empirical partiality—could easily triumph over the abstract theoretical universality of Christianity established as a set of "purely f o r m a l rites with which the world of self-interest encircles itself".[17] (On the importance of "usury" and the controversies related to it at the time of the rise of early capitalism, see p. 132.)

It is very important to emphasize here that the issue at stake is not simply the empirical reality of Jewish communities in Europe but "the spirit of Judaism"; i.e. the *internal* principle of European social developments culminating in the emergence and stabilization of capitalistic society. "The spirit of Judaism", therefore, must be understood, in the last analysis, to mean "the spirit of capitalism". For an early realization of the latter Judaism as an empirical reality only provided a suitable vehicle. Ignoring this distinction, for one reason or another, could lead—as it did throughout the ages—to scapegoat-hunting anti-semitism. The objective conditions of European social development, from the dissolution of pre-feudal society to the universal triumph of capitalism over feudalism, must be assessed in their comprehensive complexity of which Judaism as a sociological phenomenon is a part only, however important a part it may have been at certain stages of this development.

Judaism and Christianity are complementary aspects of society's efforts to cope with its internal contradictions. They both represent attempts at an imaginary transcendence of these contradictions, at an illusory "reappropriation" of the "human essence" through a fictitious supersession of the state of alienation. Judaism and Christianity express the contradictions of "partiality versus universality" and "competition versus monopoly" : i.e. *internal* contradictions of what has become known as "the spirit of capitalism". In this framework the success of partiality can only be conceived in contradiction to and at the expense of universality—just as this "universality" can only prevail on the basis of the suppression of partiality—and *vice versa*. Similarly with the relationship between competition and monopoly : the condition of success of "competition" is the negation of monopoly just as for monopoly the condition of extending its power is the suppression of competition. The partiality of Judaism : the "chimerical nationality of the Jew is the nationality of the trader, and above all of the financier"[18]—writes Marx, repeatedly emphasizing that "the social emancipation of the Jew is the emancipation of society from Judaism",[19] i.e. from the partiality of the financier's "nationality", or, expressed in more general terms, from "the Jewish narrowness of society".[20] "Jewish narrowness" could triumph in "civil society" because the latter required the dynamism of the "supremely practical Jewish spirit" for its full development. The metamorphosis of Judaism into Christianity carried with it a later metamorphosis of Christianity into a more evolved, less crudely partial form of—secularized—Judaism : "The Jew has emancipated himself in a Jewish manner, not only by acquiring the power of money, but also because money had become, through him and *also apart from him,* a world power, while the practical Jewish spirit has become the *practical spirit of the Christian nations.* The Jews have emancipated themselves in so far as the Christians have become Jews."[21] Protestant modifications of earlier established Christianity, in various national settings, had accomplished a relatively early metamorphosis of "abstract-theoretical" Christianity into "practical-Christian-Judaism" as a significant step in the direction of the complete *secularization* of the whole problematics of alienation. Parallel to the expanding domination of the spirit of capitalism in the practical sphere, the ideological forms have become more and more secular as well; from the various versions of "deism" through "humanistic atheism" to the famous declaration stating that "God is dead". By the time of the latter even the illusions of "universality" (with which "the world of self-interest encircles itself")—retained and at times even intensified by deism and humanistic atheism—have become acutely embarrassing for the bourgeoisie and a sudden, often cynical, transition had to be made to the open cult of partiality.

As has been mentioned, under the conditions of class society—because of the inherent contradiction between the "part" and the "whole", due to the fact that partial interest dominates the whole of society—the principle of partiality stands in an insoluble contradiction to that of universality. Consequently it is the crude relation of forces that elevates the prevailing form of partiality into a bogus universality, whereas the ideal-oriented negation of this partiality—e.g. the abstract-theoretical universality of Christianity, before its metamorphosis into "practical-Christian-Judaism"—must remain illusory, fictitious, impotent. For "partiality" and "universality" in their reciprocal opposition to each other are two facets of the same, alienated, state of affairs. Egoistic partiality must be elevated to "universality" for its fulfilment: the underlying socio-economic dynamism is both "self-centred" and "outer-directed", "nationalist" and "cosmopolitan", "protectionist-isolationist" and "imperialist" at the same time. This is why there can be no room for genuine universality, only for the bogus universalization of the crudest partiality, coupled with an illusory, abstract-theoretical *postulate* of universality as the—merely ideological—negation of effective, practically prevailing partiality. Thus the "chimerical nationality of the Jew" is all the more chimerical because—insofar as it is "the nationality of the trader and of the financier"—it is in reality the only effective universality: partiality turned into operative universality, into the fundamental organizing principle of the society in question. (The mystifications of anti-semitism become obvious if one realizes that it turns against the mere sociological phenomenon of Jewish partiality, and not against "the Jewish narrowness of society"; it attacks partiality in its limited immediacy, and thus not only does it not face the real problem: the partiality of capitalist self-interest turned into the ruling universal principle of society, but actively supports its own object of attack by means of this disorienting mystification.)

For Marx, in his reflections on the Judeo-Christian approach to the problems of alienation, the matter of central concern was to find a solution that could indicate a way out of the apparently perennial impasse: the renewed reproduction, in different forms, of the same contradiction between partiality and universality which characterized the entire historical development and its ideological reflections. His answer was not simply the double negation of crude partiality and abstract universality. Such a solution would have remained an abstract conceptual opposition and no more. The historical novelty of Marx's solution consisted in defining the problem in terms of the concrete dialectical concept of "partiality prevailing as universality", in opposition to genuine universality which alone could embrace the manifold interests of society as a whole and of man as a "species-being" (Gattungswesen—i.e. man liberated from the domination of crude, individualistic self-interest). It was this specific, socially concrete concept which enabled Marx to grasp the problematics of capitalist society in its full contradictoriness and to formulate the programme of a *practical* transcendence of alienation by means of a genuinely universalizing fusion of ideal and reality, theory and practice.

Also, we have to emphasize in this context that Marx had nothing to do with abstract "humanism" because he opposed right from the outset—as we have seen in the quotations taken from *On the Jewish Question*, written in 1843—the illusions of *abstract universality* as a *mere postulate*, an impotent "ought", a *fictitious* "reappropriation of non-alienated humanness". There is no trace, therefore, of what might be termed "ideological concepts" in the thought of the young Marx who writes *On the Jewish Question*, let alone in the socio-economically far more concrete reflections contained in the *Economic and Philosophic Manuscripts of 1844*.

2. Alienation as "Universal Saleability"

The secularization of the religious concept of alienation had been accomplished in the concrete assertions concerning "saleability". In the first place this secularization progressed within the religious shell. Nothing could withstand this trend of converting everything into a saleable object, no matter how "sacred" it may have been considered at some stage in its "inalienability" sanctioned by an alleged divine command. (Balzac's *Melmoth* is a masterfully ironical reflection on the state of a totally secularized society in which "even the Holy Spirit has its quotation on the Stock Exchange".) Even the doctrine of the "fall of man" had to be challenged—as it had been done by Luther, for instance—in the name of man's "liberty".[22] This advocacy of "liberty", however, in reality turned out to be nothing more than the religious glorification of the secular principle of "universal saleability". It was this latter which found its—however utopian—adversary in Thomas Münzer who complained in his pamphlet against Luther, saying that it was intolerable "that every creature should be *transformed into property*—the fishes in the water, the birds of the air, the plants of the earth".[23] Insights like this, no matter how profoundly and truthfully they reflected the inner nature of the transformations in course, had to remain mere utopias, ineffective protests conceived from the perspective of a hopeless anticipation of a possible future negation of commodity-society. At the time of the triumphant emergence of capitalism the prevalent ideological conceptions had to be those which assumed an affirmative attitude towards the objective trends of this development.

In the conditions of feudal society the hindrances which resisted the advance of "the spirit of capitalism" were, for instance, that "the vassal could not alienate without the consent of his superior" (Adam Smith),[24] or that "the bourgeois cannot alienate the things of the community without the permission of the king" (thirteenth century).[25] The supreme ideal was that everyone should be able "to give and to alienate that which belongs to him" (thirteenth century).[26] Obviously, however, the social order which confined to "The Lord" the power to "sell his Servant, or alienate him by Testament" (Hobbes)[27] fell hopelessly short of the requirements of "*free* alienability" of everything—including one's person—by means of some *contractual* arrangement to which the person concerned would be a party. Land too, one of the sacred pillars of the outdated social order, had to become alienable[28] so that the self-development of commodity society should go on unhampered.

That alienation as universal saleability involved *reification* has been recognized well before the whole social order which operated on this basis could be subjected to a radical and effective criticism. The mystifying glorification of "liberty" as "contractually safeguarded freedom" (in fact the *contractual abdication* of human freedom) played an important part in delaying the recognition of the underlying contradictions. Saying this does not alter, however, the fact that the connection between alienation and reification has been recognized—even though in an uncritical form—by some philosophers who far from questioning the contractual foundations of society idealized it. Kant, for instance, made the point that "such a contract is not a mere reification [or "conversion into a thing"— Verdingung] but the transference—by means of hiring it out—of one's person into the property of the Lord of the house".[29] An object, a piece of *dead* property could be simply alienated from the original owner and transferred into the property of someone else without undue complications: "the transference of one's property to someone else is its alienation" (Kant).[30] (The complications, at an earlier stage, were of an "external", political nature, manifest in the taboos and prohibitions of feudal society which declared certain things to be "inalienable"; with the successful abolition of such taboos the complications vanished automatically.) The *living* person, however, first had to be *reified*—converted into a thing, into a mere piece of property for the duration of the contract—before it could be mastered by its new owner. Reified in the same sense of "verdingen" in which Kant's younger contemporary Wieland uses the word in translating a line from Homer's Odyssey: "Fremdling, willst du dich wohl bei mir *zum Knechte verdingen?*"; "Stranger, will you become *my thing, my servant?*" (The current English translation, by contrast, characteristically reads like this: "Stranger," he said, "I wonder how you'd like to work for me if I took you on as *my man*, somewhere on an upland farm, *at a proper wage of course.*"[31])

The principal function of the much glorified "contract" was, therefore, the introduction—in place of the rigidly fixed feudal relations—of a new form of "fixity" which guaranteed the right of the new master to manipulate the allegedly "free" human beings as things, as objects without will, once they have "freely elected" to enter into the contract in question by *"alienating at will* that which belonged to them".

Thus human alienation was accomplished through turning everything "into a l i e n a b l e, saleable objects in thrall to egoistic need and huckstering. Selling is the practice of alienation. Just as man, so long as he is engrossed in religion, can only objectify his essence by an a l i e n and fantastic being; so under the sway of egoistic need, he can only affirm himself and produce objects in practice by subordinating his products and *his own activity* to the domination of an alien entity, and by attributing to them the significance of an alien entity, namely *money.*"[32] Reification of one's person and thus the "freely chosen" acceptance of a new servitude—in place of the old feudal, politically established and regulated form of servitude—could advance on the basis of a "civil society" characterized by the rule of money that opened the floodgates for the universal "servitude to egoistic need" (Knechtschaft des egoistischen Bedürfnisses).[33]

Alienation is therefore characterized by the universal extension of "saleability" (i.e. the transformation of everything into commodity); by the conversion of human beings into "things" so that they could appear as commodities on the market (in other words: the "reification" of human relations); and by the fragmentation of the social body into "isolated individuals" (vereinzelte Einzelnen) who pursued their own limited, particularistic aims "in servitude to egoistic need", making a virtue out of their selfishness in their cult of privacy.[34] No wonder that Goethe protested: "alles vereinzelte ist verwerflich", "all isolated particularity is to be

rejected",[35] advocating in opposition to "selfish isolationism" some
form of "community with others like oneself" in order to be able
to make a common "front against the world".[36] Equally no wonder
that in the circumstances Goethe's recommendations had to remain
utopian postulates. For the social order of "civil society" could
sustain itself only on the basis of the conversion of the various areas
of human experience into "saleable commodities", and it could
follow relatively undisturbed its course of development only so long
as this universal marketing of all facets of human life, including
the most private ones, did not reach its point of saturation.

3. Historicity and the Rise of Anthropology

"Alienation" is an eminently historical concept. If man is
"alienated", he must be alienated *from* something, as a result of
certain *causes*—the interplay of events and circumstances in relation
to man as the subject of this alienation—which manifest themselves
in a *historical* framework. Similarly, the "transcendence of alienation" is an inherently historical concept which envisages the successful accomplishment of a process leading to a qualitatively different
state of affairs.

Needless to say, the historical character of certain concepts is no
guarantee whatsoever that the intellectual edifices which make use
of them are historical. Often, as a matter of fact, mystifications set
in at one stage or another of the analysis. Indeed, if the concept of
alienation is abstracted form the concrete socio-economical process,
a mere *semblance* of historicity may be substituted for a genuine
understanding of the complex factors involved in the historical
process. (It is an essential function of mythologies to transfer the
fundamental socio-historical problems of human development to
an atemporal plane, and the Judeo-Christian treatment of the
problematics of alienation is no exception to the general rule.
Ideologically more topical is the case of some twentieth century
theories of alienation in which concepts like "world-alienation" fulfil
the function of negating the genuine historical categories and of
replacing them by sheer mystification.)

Nevertheless it is an important characteristic of intellectual
history that those philosophers achieved the greatest results in
grasping the manifold complexities of alienation—before Marx:
Hegel above all the others—who approached this problematics in
an adequate historical manner. This correlation is even more

significant in view of the fact that the point holds the other way round as well: namely those philosophers succeeded in elaborating a historical approach to the problems of philosophy who were aware of the problematics of alienation, and to the extent to which they were so. (It is by no means accidental that the greatest representative of the Scottish "historical school", Adam Ferguson[37] had at the centre of his thought the concept of "civil society" which was absolutely crucial for a socio-historically concrete understanding of the problematics of alienation.) The ontological determinants of this intellectual interrelationship need to retain our attention here for a moment.

It goes without saying, the development in question is by no means a simple linear one. At certain points of crisis in history when the possible socio-historical alternatives are still *relatively* open—a relative openness which creates a temporary "ideological vacuum" that favours the appearance of utopian ideologies—it is relatively easier to identify the objective characteristics of the emerging social order than at a later stage by which time the needs that bring into life in the field of ideology the "uncritical positivism" we are all too familiar with have produced a self-perpetuating uniformity. We have seen the profound but hopelessly "premature" insights of a Thomas Münzer into the nature of developments hardly perceivable on the horizon, and he did not stand alone, of course, in this respect. Similarly, at a much earlier age, Aristotle gave a surprisingly concrete historical analysis of the inherent interconnection between religious beliefs and politico-social as well as family-relations: "The family is the association established by nature for the supply of man's every day wants, and the members of it are called by Charondas 'companions of the cupboard', and by Epimenides the Cretan, 'companions of the manger'. But when several families are united, and the association aims at something more than the supply of daily needs, the first society to be formed is the village. And the most natural form of the village appears to be that of a colony from the family, composed of the children and grandchildren, who are said to be 'sucked with the same milk'. And this is the reason why Hellenic states were originally governed by kings; because the Hellenes were under royal rule before they came together, as the barbarians still are. Every family is ruled by the eldest and therefore in the colonies of the family the kingly form of government prevailed because they were of the same blood. As Homer says: 'Each one gives law to his children and to his wives.'

For they lived dispersedly, as was the manner in ancient times. *Wherefore men say that the Gods have a king, because they themselves either are or were in ancient times under the rule of a king. For they imagine, not only the forms of the Gods, but their ways of life to be like their own."*[38]

Many hundreds of years had to pass by before philosophers could reach again a similar degree of concreteness and historical insight. And yet, Aristotle's insight remained an isolated one: it could not become the cornerstone of a coherent philosophy of history. In Aristotle's thought the concrete historical insights were embedded in a thoroughly ahistorical general conception. The main reason for this was an overriding ideological need which prevented Aristotle from applying a historical principle to the analysis of society as a whole. In accordance with this ideological need it had to be "proved" that *slavery* was a social order in complete conformity with *nature* itself. Such a conception—formulated by Aristotle in opposition to those who challenged the established social relations— carried with it bogus concepts like "freedom by nature" and "slavery by nature". For, according to Aristotle, "there is a great difference between the rule over freemen and the rule over slaves, as there is between *slavery by nature* and *freedom by nature*".[39]

The introduction of the concept of "slavery by nature" has far-reaching consequences for Aristotle's philosophy. History in it is confined to the sphere of "freedom" which is, however, restricted by the concept of "freedom by nature". Indeed, since slavery must be fixed eternally—a need adequately reflected in the concept of "slavery *by nature*"—there can be no question of a genuine historical conception. The concept of "slavery by nature" carries with it its counterpart: "freedom *by nature*", and thus the fiction of slavery determined by nature destroys the historicity of the sphere of "freedom" as well. The partiality of the ruling class prevails, postulating its own rule as a hierarchial-structural superiority determined (and sanctioned) by nature. (The partiality of Judaism—the mythology of the "chosen people" etc.—expresses the same kind of *negation* of history as regards the fundamental structural relations of class society.) The principle of historicity is therefore inevitably degraded into pseudo-historicity. The model of a *repetitive cycle* is projected upon society as a whole : no matter what happens, the fundamental structural relations—determined by "nature"—are said to be always reproduced, not as a matter of empirical fact, but as that of an *apriori necessity*. Movement, accordingly, is confined to an increase in "size" and "complexity" of the communities analysed by Aristotle, and changes in both "size" and "complexity" are circumscribed by the concepts of "freedom by nature" and "slavery by nature", i.e. by the postulated apriori necessity of reproducing the same structure of society. Thus the insoluble social contradictions of his days lead even a great philosopher like Aristotle to operate with self-contradictory concepts like "freedom by nature", imposed on him by the entirely fictitious concept of "slavery by nature", in direct agreement with the prevailing ideological need. And when he makes a further attempt at rescuing the historicity of the sphere of "freedom by nature", declaring that the slave is not a man but a mere *thing*, a *"talking tool"*, he finds himself right in the middle of another contradiction: for the tools of man have a historical character, and certainly not one fixed by nature. Because of the partiality of his position, the dynamic, dialectically changing laws of social totality must remain a mystery to Aristotle. His postulate of a natural *"duality"*—directly rooted, as we have seen, in the ideological need of turning *partiality* into *universality*—make it impossible for him to perceive the manifold varieties of social phenomena as specific manifestations of an inherently interconnected, dynamically changing socio-historical totality.

The interrelationship between an awareness of alienation and the historicity of a philosopher's conception is a *necessary* one because a fundamental ontological question: the "nature of man" ("human essence", etc.) is the common point of reference of both. This fundamental ontological question is: what is in agreement with "human nature" and what constitutes an "alienation" from the "human essence"? Such a question cannot be answered ahistorically without being turned into an irrational mystification of some kind. On the other hand, a historical approach to the question of "human nature" inevitably carries with it some diagnosis of "alienation" or "reification", related to the standard or "ideal" by which the whole issue is being assessed.

The point of central importance is, however, whether or not the question of "human nature" is assessed within an implicitly or explicitly "egalitarian" framework of explanation. If for some reason the fundamental equality of all men is not recognized, that is *ipso facto* tantamount to negating historicity, for in that case it becomes necessary to rely on the magic device of "nature" (or, in religious conceptions, "divine order" etc.) in the philosopher's explanation of historically established inequalities. (This issue is quite distinct from

40 MARX'S THEORY OF ALIENATION

the question of the ideological justification of existing inequalities. The latter is essential for explaining the socio-historical determinants of a philosopher's system but quite irrelevant to the logically necessary interrelationship of a set of concepts of a particular system. Here we are dealing with the structural relations of concepts which prevail *within* the general framework of a system *already* in existence. This is why the "structural" and the "historical" principles cannot be reduced into one another—except by vulgarizers—but constitute a dialectical unity.) The philosopher's specific approach to the problem of equality, the particular limitations and shortcomings of his concept of "human nature", determine the intensity of his historical conception as well as the character of his insight into the real nature of alienation. This goes not only for those thinkers who—for reasons already seen—failed to produce significant achievements in this regard but also for positive examples, from the representatives of the Scottish "historical school" to Hegel and Feuerbach.

"Anthropological orientation" without genuine historicity—as well as the necessary conditions of the latter, of course—amounts to nothing more than mystification, whatever socio-historical determinants might have brought it into existence. The "organic" conception of society, for instance, according to which every element of the social complex must fulfil its "proper function"— i.e. a function predetermined by "nature" or by "divine providence" in accordance with some rigid hierarchial pattern—is a totally ahistorical and inverted projection of the characteristics of an established social order upon an alleged "organism" (the human body, for instance) which is supposed to be the "natural model" of all society. (A great deal of modern "functionalism" is, *mutatis mutandis*, an attempt at liquidating historicity. But we cannot enter here into the discussion of that matter.) In this regard it is doubly significant that in the development of modern thought the concept of alienation acquired an increasing importance parallel to the rise of a genuine, historically founded philosophical anthropology. On the one hand this trend represented a radical opposition to the mystifications of medieval pseudo-anthropology, and on the other it provided the positive organizing centre of an incomparably more dynamic understanding of the social processes than had been possible before.

Well before Feuerbach recognized the distinction between *"true: that is anthropological and false: that is theological essence of religion*",[40] religion was conceived as a historical phenomenon and the assessment of its nature was subordinated to the question of the historicity of man. In such a conception it became possible to envisage the *supersession* of religion insofar as mythology and religion were assigned only to a *particular stage*—though a necessary one—of the *universal history* of mankind, conceived on the model of man progressing from childhood to maturity. Vico distinguished three stages in the development of humanity (of humanity making its own history): (1) the age of Gods; (2) the age of heroes; and (3) "the age of men in which all men recognized themselves as *equal in human nature*".[41] Herder, at a later stage, defined mythology as "personified nature or dressed-up wisdom"[42] and spoke of the "childhood", "adolescence" and "manhood" of mankind, limiting even in poetry the possibilities of myth-creation under the circumstances of the third stage.[43]

But it was Diderot who spelled out the socio-political secret of the whole trend by emphasizing that once man succeeded in his critique of "the majesty of heaven" he will not shy away for long from an assault on the other oppressor of mankind: "the worldly sovereignty", for these two stand or fall together.[44] And it was by no means accidental that it was Diderot who reached this degree of clarity in political radicalism. For he did not stop at Vico's remarkable but rather abstract statement according to which "all men are equal in human nature". He went on asserting, with the highest degree of social radicalism known among the great figures of French Enlightenment, that *"if the day-worker is miserable, the nation is miserable".*[45] Not surprisingly, therefore, it was Diderot who succeeded to the highest degree in grasping the problematics of alienation, well ahead of his contemporaries, indicating as basic contradictions "the distinction of y o u r s and m i n e" ("distinction du t i e n et du, m i en"), the opposition between "one's own particular utility and the general good" ("ton utilité particulière et le bien général") and the subordination of the "general good to one's own particular good" ("le bien général au bien particulier").[46] And he went even further, emphasizing that these contradictions result in the production of *"superfluous wants"* ("besoins superflus"), *"imaginary goods"* ("biens imaginaires") and *"artificial needs"* ("besoins factices")[47]—almost the same terms as those used by Marx in describing the *"artificial needs and imaginary appetites"* produced by capitalism. The fundamental difference was, however, that while Marx could refer to a specific social movement as the

"material force" behind his philosophical programme, Diderot had
to content himself—because of his "premature situation"—with the
viewpoint of a far-away utopian community in which such contradictions as well as their consequences are unknown. And, of
course, in accordance with his utopian standpoint related to the
wretched working conditions of his day, Diderot could not see any
solution except the *limitation of needs* which should enable man to
liberate himself from the crippling *tedium of work*, allowing him to
stop ("de s'arrêter"), to *rest* ("reposer") and to *finish working*
("quand finirons-nous de travailler").[48] Thus an appeal is made to
the utopian fiction of a *"natural"* limitation of wants because the
type of labour which predominates in the given form of society is
inherently anti-human, and "fulfilment" ("jouissance") appears as
an *absence* of activity, not as enriched and enriching, humanly
fulfilling activity, not as self-fulfilment *in* activity. That which is
supposed to be "natural" and "human" appears as something idyllic
and *fixed* (by nature) and consequently as something to be jealously
protected against corruption from "outside", under the enlightening
guidance of "reason". Since the "material force" that could turn
theory into social practice is missing, theory must convert itself
into its own solution: into an utopian advocacy of the power of
reason. At this point we can clearly see that even a Diderot's
remedy is a far cry from the solutions advocated and envisaged by
Marx.

Marx's radical superiority to all who preceded him is evident in
the coherent dialectical historicity of his theory, in contrast to the
weaknesses of his predecessors who at one point or another were all
forced to abandon the actual ground of history for the sake of some
imaginary solution to the contradictions they may have perceived
but could not master ideologically and intellectually. In this context
Marx's profound insight into the true relationship between *anthropology* and *ontology* is of the greatest importance. For there is one
way only of producing an all-embracing and in every respect
consistent historical theory, namely by positively situating anthropology within an adequate general ontological framework. If,
however, ontology is subsumed under anthropology—as often
happened not only in the distant past but in our own time as well—
in that case one-sidedly grasped anthropological principles which
should be historically explained become self-sustaining axioms of
the system in question and undermine its historicity. In this respect
Feuerbach represents a retrogression in relation to Hegel whose philo-

sophical approach avoided on the whole the pitfall of dissolving
ontology within anthropology. Consequently Hegel anticipated to
a much greater extent than Feuerbach the Marxian grasp of
history, although even Hegel could only find "the *a b s t r a c t*,
l o g i c a l, *s p e c u l a t i v e* expression for the movement of history"
(146).

In contrast to both the Hegelian abstractness and the Feuerbachian retrogression in historicity Marx discovered the dialectical
relationship between materialist ontology and anthropology,
emphasizing that "man's *f e e l i n g s*, passions, etc., are not *merely
anthropological* phenomena in the [narrower] sense, but *truly
o n t o l o g i c a l* affirmations of essential being (of *nature*). . . .
Only through developed industry i.e. through the medium of private
property—does the *ontological essence* of human passion come to
be both in its *totality* and in its *humanity*; the *science of man* is
therefore itself a product of man's establishment of himself by
practical activity. The meaning of private property—liberated from
its estrangement—is the *e x i s t e n c e o f e s s e n t i a l o b j e c t s* for
man, both as objects of *enjoyment* and as objects of *activity*" (136–
137). We shall discuss some aspects of this complex of problems later
in this chapter, as well as in chapter IV, VI, and VII. What is
particularly important to stress at this point is that the *specific*
anthropological factor ("humanity") cannot be grasped in its
dialectical historicity unless it is conceived on the basis of the
historically developing *ontological totality* ("nature") to which it
ultimately belongs. A failure to identify the adequate dialectical
relationship between ontological totality and anthropological
specificity carries with it insoluble contradictions. In the first place
it leads to postulating some fixed "human essence" as the philosopher's "original datum", and consequently to the ultimate liquidation of all historicity (from Feuerbach to some recent theories of
"structuralism"). Equally damaging is another contradiction which
means that pseudo-historical and "anthropological" considerations
are applied to the analysis of certain social phenomena whose
comprehension would require a non-anthropomorphic—but of
course dialectical—concept of causality. To give an example : no
conceivable "anthropological hypothesis" could in the least help to
understand the "natural laws" which govern the productive processes of capitalism in their long historical development; on the
contrary, they could only lead to sheer mystifications. It might
seem to be inconsistent with Marx's historical materialism when we

are told in *Capital* that *"The nature of capital is the same in its developed as in its undeveloped form"*.[49] (Some people might even use this passage in support of their interpretation of Marx's as a "structuralist" thinker.) A more careful reading would, however, reveal that, far from being inconsistent, Marx indicates here the ontological ground of a coherent historical theory. A later passage, in which he analyses capitalist production, makes this clearer:

> "The principle which it [capitalism] pursued, of resolving each process into its constituent movements, *without any regard to their possible execution by the hand of man*, created the new modern science of technology. The varied, apparently unconnected, and petrified forms of the industrial processes now resolved themselves into so many conscious and *systematic* applications of natural science to the attainment of given useful effects. Technology also discovered the few main *fundamental forms of motion*, which, despite the diversity of the instruments used, are *necessarily* taken by *every productive action of the human body*. . . ."[50]

As we can see, the whole issue turns on understanding the *natural basis* (the general laws of causality, etc.) of *specifically human* historicity. Without an adequate grasp of this natural basis the "science of man" is simply inconceivable because everything gets ultimately dissolved into relativism. The "anthropological principle", therefore, must be put in its proper place, within the general framework of a comprehensive historical ontology. In more precise terms, any such principle must be transcended in the direction of a complex dialectical social ontology.

If this is not achieved—if, that is, the anthropological principle remains narrowly anthropological—there can be no hope whatsoever of understanding a process, for instance, which is determined by *its own* laws of movement and imposes on human beings *its own* patterns of productive procedure "without any regard to their possible execution by the hand of man". Similarly, nothing can be understood about the alienating "nature of capital" in terms of the fictitious postulates of an "egoistic human nature" so dear to the heart of the political economists. For the "sameness" of capital in both its "undeveloped" and "developed form"—a sameness which applies only to its "nature" and not to its form and mode of existence—must be explained in terms of the most comprehensive laws of a historical ontology founded on nature. The socially dominating rôle of capital in modern history is self-evident. But only the fundamental laws of social ontology can explain how it is possible that under certain conditions a given "nature" (the nature of capital) should unfold and fully realize itself—in accordance with its objective nature—by following its own inner laws of development, from its undeveloped form to its form of maturity, *"without any regard to man"*. Anthropological hypotheses, no matter how subtle, are apriori non-starters in this respect. Equally, a simple socio-historical hypothesis is of no use. For the issue at stake is precisely to explain what lies at the roots of historical development as its ultimate ground of determination, and therefore it would be sheer circularity to indicate the changing historical circumstances as the fundamental cause of development of capital itself. Capital, as everything else in existence, has—it goes without saying—its historical dimension. But this historical *dimension* is categorially different from an ontological *substance*.

What is absolutely essential is not to confound *ontological continuity* with some imaginary *anthropological fixity*. The ultimate ground of persistence of the problematics of alienation in the history of ideas, from its Judeo-Christian beginnings to its formulations by Marx's immediate predecessors, is the relative ontological continuity inherent in the unfolding of capital in accordance with its inner laws of growth from its "undeveloped" to its "developed form". To turn this relative ontological continuity into some fictitious characteristic of "human nature" means that an elucidation of the actual processes which underlie these developments is apriori impossible. If, however, one realizes that the ontological continuity in question concerns the "nature of capital", it becomes possible to envisage a *transcendence* (Aufhebung) of alienation, provided that the issue is formulated as a radical *ontological* transformation of the social structure as a *whole*, and not confined to the partial measure of a political expropriation of capital (which is simply a necessary first step in the direction of the Marxian transcendence of alienation). Only if some basic conditions of an ontological transcendence are satisfied and to the extent to which they are so— i.e. insofar as there is an effective *break* in the objective ontological continuity of capital in its broadest Marxian sense—can we speak of a *qualitatively* new phase of development: the beginning of the "true history of mankind". Without this ontological frame of reference there can be no consistent historical theory;—only some form of historical relativism instead, devoid of an objective measure of advance and consequently prone to subjectivism and voluntarism, to the formulation of "Messianic programmes" coupled with an arbitrary anticipation of their realization in the form of idealistic postulates.

Here we can clearly see the historical importance of the young Marx's discovery concerning the dialectical relationship between ontology and anthropology : it opened up the road to the elaboration of Marx's great theoretical synthesis and to the practical realization of the revolutionary programmes based on it. His predecessors, as a rule, turned their limited ontological insights into elements of a curious mixture of anthropological-moral-ideological preaching. Henry Home (Lord Kames), for instance—not a negligible figure but one of the greatest representatives of the Scottish historical school of Enlightenment—wrote the following lines : "*Activity is essential to a social being* : to a *selfish being* it is of no use, after procuring the means of living. A *selfish man*, who by his opulence has all the luxuries of life at command, and dependents without number, has no occasion for activity. Hence it may fairly be inferred, that were man destined by providence to be *entirely* selfish, he would be disposed by his constitution to rest, and never would be active when he could avoid it. The *natural activity of man*, therefore, is to me evidence, that his Maker did not intend him to be *purely a selfish being*."[51] Since the social grounds of this criticism cannot be spelled out—because of the contradiction inherent in it, i.e. because of the "selfishness" necessarily associated with the social class represented by Henry Home—everything must remain abstract-anthropological; worse : even this abstract criticism in the end must be watered down by the terms "*entirely*" and "*purely* selfish". A new form of conservatism appears on the horizon to take the place of the old one, appealing to the anthropological model of "Enlightened Man" : this "natural" realization of Triumphant Reason. "Even those who are most prone to persecution, begin to hesitate. *Reason*, resuming her sovereign authority, will banish it [i.e. persecution] altogether . . . within the next century it will be thought *strange*, that persecution should have prevailed among social beings. It will perhaps even be doubted, whether it ever was seriously put into practice."[52] And again : "*Reason at last prevailed, after much opposition* : the absurdity of a whole nation being slaves to a weak mortal, remarkable perhaps for no valuable qualification, *became apparent to all*."[53] But the unhistorical and categorical criteria of "rational" *v.* "absurd" rebound on this approach when it has to face some new problems. This is when its

conservatism comes to the fore : "It was not difficult to foresee the
consequences [of the general assault on the old order] : down fell
the *whole fabric*, the *sound parts* with the *infirm*. And man now
laugh currently at the *absurd notions* of their forefathers, without
thinking either of being patriots, or of being *good subjects*."[54] So
just as much as one's own selfishness had to be distinguished from
the "purely selfish" and "entirely selfish" behaviour of one's
opponents, now the "legitimately" used criterion of "absurdity" has
to be opposed to its "abuse" by those who carry it "too far",
endangering the "sound parts" of the "social fabric". "Reason" is
turned into a blank cheque, valid not only retrospectively but time-
lessly, sustaining the partial interest of its bearers, and destroying
the earlier historical achievements. The insoluble dilemma of the
whole movement of the Enlightenment is expressed in this mode
of arguing, well before it assumes a dramatic political form in
Burke's violent attacks on the French Revolution in the name of the
continuity of the "sound social fabric". A dilemma determined by
the objective contradiction of subordinating the general interest to
the partial interest of a social class.

Thus no sooner are the achievements of the Enlightenment
realized than they are liquidated. Everything must fit the narrowly
and ambiguously defined model of "Rational Man". Only those
aspects of alienation are recognized which can be classified as "alien
to Reason", with all the actual and potential arbitrariness involved
in such an abstract criterion. Historicity reaches only as far as is
compatible with the social position that requires these vague and
abstract criteria as its ground of criticism, for the acknowledgement
of human equality is, on the whole, confined to the abstract legal
sphere. The same goes for the achievements in anthropology : old
taboos are successfully attacked in the name of reason, but the
understanding of the objective laws of movement, situating the
specifically human factor within a dialectically grasped comprehensive natural framework, is hampered by the preconceived ideas
expressed in the self-idealizing model of "Rational Man".

The reasons for this ultimate failure were very complex. Its
ideological determinants, rooted in a social position dense with social
contradictions that had to remain veiled from the thinkers concerned, have been mentioned already. Equally important was the
fact that the underlying economic trends were still far from their
point of maturity, which made it virtually impossible to gain an
adequate insight into their real nature. (Marx could conceive his

theory from the position of a qualitatively higher historical vantage point.) But the crucial point was that the philosophers of the Enlightenment could only take—at best—some tentative first steps in the direction of the elaboration of a dialectical method but were unable to grasp the fundamental laws of a materialist dialectic: their social and historical position prevented them from doing so. (On the other hand Hegel succeeded later in identifying the central concepts of dialectics, but in an "abstract, speculative, idealist fashion".) This meant that they could not solve the dilemma inherent in historicized anthropology and anthropologically oriented history. For, paradoxically, history and anthropology helped one another up to a point, but turned into fetters for each other beyond that critical point. Only a materialist dialectic could have shown a way out of the impasse of this rigid oppositition. For the want of such a dialectic, however, the historical principle was either dissolved into the pseudo-historicity of some repetitive cycle, or tended towards its own absolutization in the form of historical relativism. The only possible solution which could have *transcended* both the "anthropological principle" and relativistic "historicism" would have been a synthesis of history and anthropology in the form of a comprehensive, materialist, dialectical *ontology*—having the concept of "self-developing human labour" (or "man's establishment of himself by practical activity" (136)) for its centre of reference. The revolutionizing idea of such a synthesis, however, did not appear in the history of human thought before the sketching of Marx's *Economic and Philosophic Manuscripts of 1844.*

4. *The End of "Uncritical Positivism"*

The middle of the eighteenth century marked a turning point in the various approaches to the problems of alienation. As the contradictions of the emerging new society started to become more visible, the earlier "uncritical positivism" that characterized not only the school of "Natural Law" but also the first classics of Political Economy, ran into insurmountable difficulties. In the previous period the concept of alienation has been used in regard to socio-economic and political phenomena in a thoroughly positive sense, insisting on the desirability of the alienation of land, political power, etc., on the positivity of "profit upon alienation", on the rightfulness of procuring interest without alienating capital, on selling one's labour, on reifying one's person, and so on. This one-sided positivism could not be maintained, however, once the crippling effects of the capitalistic mode of production—based on the general diffusion of alienation—started to erupt also in the form of social unrest that did not shy away from the violent destruction of the much glorified and idealized "rational" machinery of increasingly larger scale manufacture.

The crisis in the middle of the eighteenth century which brought into life the various critical theories was not, it goes without saying, an internal crisis of rising capitalism. It was, rather, a social crisis caused by a drastic transition from the antiquated feudal-artisan mode of production to a new one which was very far indeed from reaching the limits of its productive capabilities. This explains the essentially uncritical attitude towards the central categories of the new economic system even in the writings of those who criticized the social and cultural aspects of capitalistic alienation. Later on, when the inherent connection between the social and cultural manifestations of alienation and the economic system became more evident, criticism tended to diminish, instead of being intensified. The bourgeoisie which in the writings of its best representatives subjected some vital aspects of its own society to a devastating criticism, could not go, of course, as far as extending this criticism to the totality of capitalistic society. The social standpoint of criticism had to be radically changed first for that and, as we all know, a century had to elapse before this radical reorientation of social criticism could be accomplished.

There is no space here for a detailed systematic survey of the rise of social criticism. Our attention, again, must be confined to a few central figures who played an important rôle in identifying the problematics of alienation before Marx. We have already seen Diderot's achievements in this respect. His contemporary, Rousseau was equally important, though in a very different way. Rousseau's system is dense with contradictions, more so perhaps than any other in the whole movement of the Enlightenment. He himself warns us often enough that we should not draw premature conclusions from his statements, before carefully considering, that is, all the facets of his complex arguments. Indeed an attentive reading amply confirms that he did not exaggerate about the complexities. But this is not the full story. His complaints about being systematically misunderstood were only partially justified. One-sided though his critics may have been in their reading of his texts (containing as they did numerous qualifications that were often ignored), the fact remains that no reading whatsoever, however careful and sympathetic, could eliminate the inherent contradictions of his system. (Needless to say, we are not talking about logical contradictions. The *formal* consistency of Rousseau's thought is as impeccable as that of any great philosopher's, considering the non-abstract character of his terms of analysis. The contradictions are in the social substance of his thought, as we shall see in a moment. In other words, they are *necessary* contradictions, inherent in the very nature of a great philosopher's socially and historically limited standpoint.)

There are very few philosophers before Marx who would stand a comparison with Rousseau in social radicalism. He writes in his *Discourse on Political Economy*—in a passage he later repeats, stressing its central importance, in one of his *Dialogues*—that the advantages of the "social confederacy" are heavily weighed down on the side of the rich, against the poor :

"for this [the social confederacy] provides a powerful protection for the immense possessions of the rich, and hardly leaves the poor man in quiet possession of the cottage he builds with his own hands. Are not all the advantages of society for the rich and powerful? Are not all lucrative posts in their hands? Are not all privileges and exemptions reserved for them alone? Is not the public authority always on their side? If a man of eminence robs his creditors, or is guilty of other knaveries, is he not always assured of impunity? Are not the assaults, acts of violence, assassinations, and even murders committed by the great, matters that are hushed up in a few months, and of which nothing more is thought? But if a great man himself is robbed or insulted, the whole police force is immediately in motion, and woe even to innocent persons who chance to be suspected. If he has to pass through any dangerous road, the country is up in arms to escort him. If the axle-tree of his chaise breaks, everybody flies to his assistance. If there is a noise at his door, he speaks but a word, and all is silent. . . . Yet all this respect costs him not a farthing : it is the rich man's right, and not what he buys with his wealth. How different is the case of the poor man! *The more humantiy owes him, the more society denies him* . . . he always bears the burden which his richer neighbour has influence enough to get exempted from . . . all gratuitous assistance is denied to the poor when they need it, just because they cannot pay for it. I look upon any poor man as totally undone, if he has the misfortune to have an honest heart, a fine daughter and a powerful neighbour. Another no less important fact is that the losses of the poor are much harder to repair than those of the rich, and that the difficulty of acquisition is always greater in proportion as there is more need for it. 'Nothing comes out of nothing', is as true of life as in physics : *money is the seed of money*, and the first guinea is sometimes more difficult to acquire than the second million. . . . The terms of the social compact between these two estates of man may be summed up in a few words : 'You have need of me, because I am rich and you are poor. We will therefore come to an agreement. I will permit you to have the honour of serving me, on condition that you bestow on me the little you have left, in return for the pains I shall take to command you.' "[55]

If this is the case, it cannot be surprising that the menacing shadow of an inevitable revolution appears in Rousseau's thought :

"Most peoples, like most men, are docile only in youth; as they grow old they become *incorrigible*. When once customs have become established and prejudices inveterate, it is *dangerous and useless to attempt their reformation*; the people, like the foolish and cowardly patients who rave at sight of the doctor, can no longer bear that any one should lay hands on its faults to remedy them. There are indeed times in the history of States when, just as some kinds of illness turn men's heads and make them forget the past, *periods of violence and revolutions do to people what these crises do to individuals*: horror of the past takes the place of forgetfulness, and *the State, set on fire by civil wars, is born again, so to speak, from its ashes*, and takes on anew, fresh from the jaws of death, the vigour of youth. . . . The empire of Russia will aspire to conquer Europe, and will itself be conquered. The Tartars, its subjects or neighbours, will become its masters and ours, by *a revolution which I regard as inevitable*. Indeed, *all the kings of Europe are working in concert to hasten its coming*."[56]

Yet the same Rousseau also asserts, talking about himself, in his *Third Dialogue*, that "he always insisted on the *preservation of the existing institutions*".[57] And when he sets out the terms of his educational experiment, he writes : "*The poor man has no need of education*. The education of his own station is *forced upon him, he can have no other*; the education received by the rich man from his own station is least fitted for himself and for society. Moreover, a natural education should fit a man for any position. . . . Let us choose our scholar among the rich; we shall at least have made another man; *the poor may come to manhood without our help*."[58] (Accordingly, in the utopian community of his *Nouvelle Héloïse* there is no education for the poor.) The idealization of nature thus, paradoxically, turned into an idealization of the poor man's wretched conditions: the established order is left unchallenged; the poor man's subjection to the well-to-do is maintained, even if the *mode* of "commanding" becomes more "enlightened". Thus in the end Rousseau is justified in his assertion about his insistence "on the preservation of the existing institutions", notwithstanding his statements about social injustice and on the inevitability of a violent revolution.

But this idealization of nature is not some intellectual "original cause". It is the expression of a contradiction unknown to the philosopher himself, carrying with it a stalemate, a static conception in the last analysis: a purely imaginary transference of the problems perceived in society onto the plane of the moral "ought" which envisages their solution in terms of a "moral education" of men. The fundamental contradiction in Rousseau's thought lies in his incommensurably sharp perception of the *phenomena of alienation* and the glorification of their *ultimate cause*. This is what turns his philosophy in the end into a monumental moral sermon that reconciles all contradictions in the ideality of the moral sphere. (Indeed the more drastic the cleavage between ideality and reality, the more evident it becomes to the philosopher that moral "ought" is the only way of coping with it. In this respect—as in so many others as well—Rousseau exercises the greatest influence on Kant, anticipating, not in words but in general conception, Kant's principle of the "primacy of Practical Reason".)

Rousseau denounces alienation in many of its manifestations:

(1) he insists—in opposition to the traditional approaches to the "Social Contract"—that man cannot alienate his *freedom*. For "to alienate is to give or to sell . . . but for what does a people sell itself? . . . Even if each man could alienate himself, he could not alienate his children: they are born man and free; their liberty belongs to them, and no one but they has the right to dispose of it."[59] (Moreover, he qualifies this statement by adding that there can be only one rightful way of disposing of one's inalienable right to liberty: "each man, in giving himself to all, gives himself to nobody"[60] and therefore "in place of the individual personality of each contracting party, this act of association creates a *moral* and collective body, composed of as many members as the assembly contains voters, and receiving from this act its *unity*, its *common identity*, its life, and its will".[61] Which means, in Rousseau's eyes, that the individual has not lost anything by contracting out of his

"natural liberty"; on the contrary, he gains "*civil liberty* and the *proprietorship* of all he possesses".[62] Furthermore, man also "acquires in the civil state, *moral liberty*, which alone makes him truly *master of himself*; for the mere impulse of appetite is *slavery*, while *obedience to a law which we prescribe to ourselves is liberty*".[63]) As we can see, the argument progresses from reality to morality. By the time we reach the point of the Social Contract, we are confronted—in the shape of the much idealized "assembly"—with a *moral construction.*[64] The collective "moral body", its "unity and common identity" etc., are *moral postulates* of a would-be legitimization of the bourgeois system. The moral construction of the "assembly" is necessary precisely because Rousseau cannot envisage any real (i.e. effective material) solution to the underlying contradictions, apart from appealing to the idea of an "obedience to a law which we prescribe to ourselves" in the general political framework of the "assembly" which radically transcends, in an ideal fashion, the "bad reality" of the established order while leaving it intact in reality.

(2) A corollary of the previous point is the insistence on the *inalienability* and *indivisibility of Sovereignty.* According to Rousseau Sovereignty "being nothing less than the exercise of the general will, can never be alienated, and the Sovereign, who is no less than a collective being, cannot be represented except by himself".[65] Again it is clear that we are confronted with a *moral postulate* generated in Rousseau's system by the recognition that "the *particular* will tends, by its very nature, to *partiality*, while the *general will* tends to *equality*",[66] and by the philosopher's inability to envisage a solution in any other terms than those of a moral "ought". For while the particular will's tendency towards partiality is an ontological reality, the "general will's tendency to equality" is, in the given historical situation, a mere postulate. And only a further moral postulate can "transcend" the contradiction between the actual, ontological "is" and the moral "ought" of an equality inherent in the "general will". (Of course in Rousseau's structure of thought this insoluble contradiction is hidden beneath the self-evidence of a dual tautology, namely that "the particular will is partial" and "the general will is universal". Rousseau's greatness, however, breaks through the crust of this dual tautology paradoxically by defining "universality"—in an apparently inconsistent form—as "equality". The same "inconsistency" is retained by Kant, *mutatis mutandis*, in his criterion of moral universality.)

(3) A constantly recurring theme of Rousseau's thought is *man's alienation from nature*. This is a fundamental synthesizing idea in Rousseau's system, a focal point of his social criticism, and has many aspects. Let us briefly sum up its crucial points.

(*a*) "Everything is good when it leaves the hands of the Creator of things; everything degenerates in the hands of man"[67]—writes Rousseau in the opening sentence of *Émile*. It is civilization which corrupts man, separating him from nature, and introducing *"from outside"* all the vices which are *"alien to man's constitution"*. The result is the destruction of the *"original goodness of man"*.[68]

(*b*) In this development—away from nature by means of the vehicle of civilization—we can see a "rapid march towards the perfection of society and towards the deterioration of the species",[69] i.e. this alienated form of development is characterized by the grave contradiction between *society* and the human *species*.

(*c*) Man is dominated by his *institutions* to such an extent that the sort of life he leads under the conditions of institutionalization cannot be called by any other name than *slavery*: "Civilized man is born into slavery and he lives and dies in it: . . . he is *in the chains of our institutions*."[70]

(*d*) Vice and evil flourish in large towns and the only possible antidote to this alienation, country life, is increasingly under the dominion of the big towns: *"industry and commerce* draw all the money from the country into the capitals . . . *the richer the city the poorer the country*."[71] Thus the dynamic vehicles of capitalistic alienation—industry and commerce—bring under their spell nature and country life, ever intensifying the contradiction between *town* and *country*.

(*e*) The acquisition of *artificial needs* and the forced growth of "useless desires" characterizes the life of both the individuals and the modern State. "If we ask how the needs of a State grow, we shall find they generally arise, like the wants of individuals, less from any real necessity than from the *increase of useless desires*."[72] Corruption in this sense starts at an early age. The natural impulses and passions of the child are suppressed and replaced by artificial modes of behaviour. The result is the production of an *"artificial being"*[73] in place of the natural, "original" human being.

As we can see, in all these points the penetrating diagnosis of prevailing social trends is mixed with an idealization of nature as the necessary premise of the Rousseauian form of criticism. We shall return to the complex determinants of this approach in a moment.

(4) In his denunciation of the roots of alienation, Rousseau attributes to *money* and *wealth* the principal responsibility "in this *century of calculators*".[74] He insists that one should not *alienate oneself* by *selling oneself*, because this means turning the human person into a *mercenary*.[75] We have already seen that according to Rousseau "to alienate is to *give* or to *sell*". Under certain special conditions—e.g. in a patriotic war when one is involved in defending one's own country—it is permissible to alienate oneself in the form of *giving* one's life for a noble purpose, but it is absolutely forbidden to alienate oneself in the form of *selling* oneself : "for all the victories of the early Romans, like those of Alexander, had been won by brave citizens, who were ready, at need, to give their blood in the service of their country, but would *never sell it*."[76] In accordance with this principle Rousseau insists that the first and absolute condition of an adequate form of education is that the laws of the market should not apply to it. The good tutor is someone who is "not a *man for sale*" and he is opposed to the prevailing practice that assigns the vitally important function of education "to *mercenaries*".[77] Human relations at all levels, including the intercourse of nations with each other, are subordinated to the only criterion of deriving *profit* from the other, and consequently they are impoverished beyond recognition : "Once they know the profit they can derive from each other, what else would they be interested in ?"[78]

As we can see even from this inevitably summary account, Rousseau's eye for the manifold phenomena of alienation and dehumanization is as sharp as no one else's before Marx. The same cannot be said, however, of his understanding of the causes of alienation. In order to explain this paradox we have now to turn our attention to questions that directly concern the historical novelty of his philosophical answers as well as their limitations. In other words, we have to ask what made possible Rousseau's great positive achievements and which factors determined the illusory character of many of his answers and suggestions.

As we have seen in the previous section, the philosophers' concept of equality was indicative, in the age of the Enlightenment, of the measure of their achievements as regards both a greater historical concreteness and a more adequate understanding of the problematics of alienation. The validity of this general point is clearly displayed in Rousseau's writing. His concept of equality is uncompromisingly radical for his age. He writes in a footnote to *The Social Contract* : "Under bad governments, this equality is only *apparent and illusory*; it serves only *to keep the pauper in his poverty and the rich man in the position he has usurped.* In fact, laws are always of use to those who possess and harmful to those who have nothing : from which it follows that the social state is advantageous to men only *when all have something and none too much*."[79] Since, however, the actual social relations stand, as Rousseau himself recognizes, in a hostile opposition to his principle of equality, the latter has to be turned into a mere *moral postulate* "on which the whole social system *should* (doit) rest". In a categorical opposition to the actual state of affairs Rousseau stipulates that "the fundamental compact substitutes, for such physical inequality as nature may have set up between men, an equality that is *moral* and *legitimate*, and that men, who may be unequal in strength or intelligence, become every one *equal by convention and legal right*".[80] Thus the terms of transcendence are abstract. There does not appear on the horizon a material force capable of superseding the relations in which the pauper is kept "in his poverty and the rich man in the position he has usurped". Only a vague reference is made to the desirability of a system in which "all have something and none too much", but Rousseau has no idea how it could be brought into being. This is why everything must be left to the power of ideas, to "education"— above all : "moral education"—and to the advocacy of a legal system which presupposes in fact the effective diffusion of Rousseau's moral ideals. And when Rousseau, being the great philosopher he is who does not evade the fundamental issues even if they underline the problematic character of his whole approach, asks the question "how can one adequately educate the educator", he confesses in all sincerity that he does not know the answer. But he emphasizes that the characteristics of the good educator *ought* to be determined by the nature of the functions he *ought* to fulfil.[81] Thus, again and again, Rousseau's analysis turns out to be an uncompromising reassertion of his radical moral postulates.

However uncompromising is Rosseau's moral radicalism, the fact that his concept of equality is basically a moral-legal concept, devoid of references to a clearly identifiable system of social relations as its material counterpart (the vision of a system in which "all have something and none too much" is not only hopelessly vague but also far from being egalitarian) carries with it the abstract and often rhetorical character of his denunciation of alienation. Thus we can see that while his grasp of the necessity of equality enables him to open many a door that remained closed before him, the limitations of his concept of equality prevent him from pursuing his enquiry to a conclusion that would carry with it the most radical *social negation* of the whole system of inequalities and dehumanizing alienations, in place of the *abstract moral radicalism* expressed in his postulates.

The same point applies to the rôle of anthropological references in Rousseau's system. As we have seen, his conception of "healthy man" as a model of social development enables him to treat revolution as the only possible "reinvigorating force" of society under certain conditions. But such an idea is totally inadequate to explain the complexities of the historical situations in which revolutions occur. This we can see from the continuation of Rousseau's analysis of revolutions : "But such events are rare; they are exceptions, the cause of which is always to be found in the particular constitution of the State concerned. They cannot even happen *twice* to the same people, for it can make itself free as long as it remains barbarous, but not when the *civic impulse* has lost its vigour. Then disturbances may destroy it, but revolutions cannot mend it : it needs a master, not a liberator. *Free peoples, be mindful* of this maxim : 'Liberty may be gained, but can never be recovered'."[82] The anthropological model, therefore, paradoxically helps to nullify Rousseau's insight into the nature of social development, by confining revolutions—on the analogy of man's cycle of life—to a non-repeatable historical phase. Again it is clear that the ultimate reference is to the sphere of the moral "ought" : the whole point about violence and revolutions is made in order to shake men out of their callous indifference so that (by becoming "mindful of his maxim") they can save themselves from the fate of "disturbances and destruction".[83]

But all this does not quite explain Rousseau's system of ideas. It simply shows why—given his concept of equality as well as his anthropological model of social development—Rousseau cannot go beyond a certain point in his understanding of the problematics of alienation. The ultimate premises of his system are : his assumption of *private property* as the sacred foundation of civil society on the one hand, and the *"middle condition"* as the only adequate *form of distribution* of property on the other. He writes : "It is certain that *the right of property is the most sacred of all the rights* of citizenship, and even *more important* in some respects *than liberty itself*; . . . property is the true foundation of civil society, and the real guarantee of the undertakings of citizens : for if property were not answerable for personal actions, nothing would be easier than to evade duties and laugh at the laws."[84] And again : "the general administration is established only to secure individual property, which is antecedent to it."[85] As to the "middle condition", according to Rousseau it "constitutes the genuine strength of the State".[86] (Also, we ought to remember in this connection his insistence that "all ought to have something and none too much", as well as his thundering against the "big towns" which undermine the type of property relations he idealizes in many of his writings.) His justification for maintaining this type of private property is that "nothing is more fatal to morality and to the Republic than the continual shifting of rank and fortune among the citizens : such changes are both the proof and the source of a thousand disorders, and overturn and confound everything; for those who were brought up to one thing find themselves destined for another".[87] And he dismisses in a most passionate tone of voice the very idea of abolishing "mine" and "yours" : "Must *meum* and *tuum* be annihilated, and must we return again to the forests to live among bears? This is a deduction in the manner of my adversaries, which I would as soon anticipate as let them have the shame of drawing."[88]

These ultimate premises of Rousseau's thought determine the concrete articulation of his system and set the limits to his understanding of the problematics of alienation. He recognizes that law is made for the protection of private property and that everything else in the order of "civil society"—including "civil liberty"—rests on such foundation. Since, however, he cannot go beyond the horizon of this idealized civil society, he must maintain not only that law is made for the benefit of private property but also that private property is made for the benefit of the law as its sole guarantee.[89] Thus the circle is irrevocably closed; there can be no escape from it. Only those features of alienation can be noticed which are in agreement with the ultimate premises of Rousseau's system. Since private property is taken for granted as the absolute condition of civilized life, only its form of distribution is allowed to be queried, the complex problematics of alienation cannot be grasped at its *roots* but only in some of its *manifestations*. As to the question : which of the multifarious manifestations of alienation are identified by Rousseau, the answer is to be sought in the *specific form* of private property he idealizes.

Thus he denounces, for instance, the corruption, dehumanization, and alienation involved in the cult of money and wealth, but he grasps only the *subjective* side of the problem. He insists, rather naïvely, that the wealth which is being produced is *"apparent and illusory*; a lot of money and little effect".[90] Thus he displays no real understanding of the immense *objective power* of money in the "civil society" of expanding capitalism. His dissent from the alienated manifestations of this power is confined to noticing its subjective effects which he believes to be able to neutralize or counteract by means of the *moral education* he passionately advocates. The same goes for his conception of the "social contract". He repeatedly stresses the importance of offering a *"fair exchange"*[91] and an *"advantageous exchange"*[92] to the people involved. The fact that human relations in a society based on the institution of "exchange" cannot conceivably be "fair" and "advantageous" to all, must remain hidden from Rousseau. In the end what is considered to be "fair" is the maintenance of a hierarchical system, a social order "in which every person being equal to his occupation" the rulers rule and the ruled ones "will animate the zeal of their deserving rulers, by showing them, without flattery or fear, the importance of their office and the severity of their duty."[93]

What Rousseau opposes is not the alienating power of money and property as such, but a particular mode of their realization in the form of the *concentration* of wealth and all that goes with *social mobility* produced by the dynamism of expanding and concentrating capital. He rejects the *effects* but gives his full support, even if unknowingly, to their *causes*. Since his discourse, because of the ultimate premises of his system, must be confined to the sphere of effects and manifestations, it must become sentimental, rhetorical and, above all, moralizing. The various manifestations of alienation he perceives must be opposed in such a discourse—which necessarily abstracts from the investigation of the ultimate causal determinants —at the level of mere *moral postulates*: the acceptance of the system of *"meum* and *tuum"* together with its corollaries leaves no alternative to this. And precisely because he is operating from the standpoint of the same material base of society whose manifestations he denounces—the social order of private property and "fair and advantageous exchange"—the terms of his social criticism must be intensely and abstractly moralizing. Capitalistic alienation as perceived by Rousseau in its particular manifestations—those, that is, which are harmful to the "middle condition"—is considered by him contingent, not necessary, and his radical moral discourse is supposed to provide the non-contingent alternative so that the people, enlightened by his unmasking of all that is merely "apparent and illusory", would turn their back on the artificial and alienated practices of social life.

These moralizing illusions of Rousseau's system, rooted in the idealization of a way of life allegedly appropriate to the "middle condition" in opposition to the actuality of dynamically advancing and universally alienating large-scale capitalistic production, are necessary illusions. For if the critical enquiry is confined to devising alternatives to the dehumanizing effects of a given system of production while leaving its basic premises unchallenged, there remains nothing but the weapon of a moralizing—"educational"—appeal to individuals. Such an appeal directly invites them to oppose the trends denounced, to resist "corruption", to give up "calculating", to show "moderation", to resist the temptations of "illusory wealth", to follow the "natural course", to restrict their "useless desires", to stop "chasing profit", to refuse "selling themselves", etc., etc. Whether or not they *can* do all this, is a different matter; in any case they *ought* to do it. (Kant is truer to the spirit of Rousseau's philosophy than anyone else when he "resolves" its contradictions by asserting with abstract but bold moral radicalism : *"ought implies can".*) To free the critique of alienation from its abstract and "ought-ridden" character, to grasp these trends in their objective ontological reality and not merely in their subjective reflections in the psychology of individuals, would have required a new social standpoint : one free from the paralysing weight of Rousseau's ultimate premises. Such a radically new socio-historical standpoint was, however, clearly unthinkable in Rousseau's time.

But no matter how problematic are Rousseau's solutions, his approach dramatically announces the inevitable end of the earlier generally prevailing "uncritical positivism". Helped by his standpoint rooted in the rapidly disintegrating "middle condition" at a time of great historical transformation, he powerfully highlights the various manifestations of capitalistic alienation, raising alarm about their extension over all spheres of human life, even if he is unable to identify their causes. Those who come after him cannot ignore or sidestep his diagnoses, though their attitude is often very different from his. Both for his own achievements in grasping many facets of the problematics of alienation and for the great influence of his views on subsequent thinkers Rousseau's historical importance cannot be sufficiently stressed.

There is no space here to follow in any detail the intellectual history of the concept of alienation after Rousseau.[94] We must confine ourselves to a very brief survey of the main phases of development leading to Marx.

The historical succession of these phases can be described as follows:

(1) The formulation of a critique of alienation within the framework of general moral postulates (from Rousseau to Schiller).

(2) The assertion of a necessary supersession of capitalistic alienation, accomplished speculatively ("Aufhebung" = "a second alienation of human existence = an alienation of alienated existence", i.e. a merely imaginary transcendence of alienation), maintaining an uncritical attitude towards the actual material foundations of society (Hegel).

(3) The assertion of the historical supersession of capitalism by socialism expressed in the form of moral postulates intermingled with elements of a realistic critical assessment of the specific contradictions of the established social order (the Utopian Socialists).

The moralizing approach to the dehumanizing effects of alienation seen in Rousseau persists, on the whole, throughout the eighteenth century. Rousseau's idea of "moral education" is taken up by Kant and is carried, with great consistency, to its logical conclusion and to its highest point of generalization. Towards the end of the century, however, the sharpening of social contradictions, coupled with the irresistible advancement of capitalistic "rationality", bring out into the open the problematic character of a direct appeal to the "voice of conscience" advocated by the propounders of "moral education". Schiller's efforts at formulating his principles of an "aesthetic education"—which is supposed to be more effective as a floodgate against the rising tide of alienation than a direct moral appeal—reflect this new situation, with its ever intensifying human crisis. (We shall return to a discussion of Schiller's idea of an "aesthetic education" in Chapter X.)

Hegel represents a qualitatively different approach, insofar as he displays a profound insight into the fundamental laws of capitalistic society.[95] We shall discuss Hegel's philosophy and its relation to Marx's achievements in various contexts. At this point let us briefly deal with the central paradox of the Hegelian approach. Namely that while an understanding of the *necessity* of a supersession of the capitalistic processes is in the foreground of Hegel's thought, Marx finds it imperative to condemn his "uncritical positivism", with full justification, needless to say. The moralizing criticism of alienation is fully superseded in Hegel. He approaches the question of a transcendence of alienation not as a matter of *moral "ought"* but as that of an *inner necessity*. In other words the idea of an "Aufhebung" of alienation ceases to be a moral postulate: it is considered as a necessity inherent in the dialectical process as such. (In accordance with this feature of Hegel's philosophy we find that his conception of equality has for its centre of reference the realm of "is", not that of a moral-legal "ought". His "epistemological democratism"—i.e. his assertion according to which all men are *actually* capable of achieving true knowledge, provided that they approach the task in terms of the categories of the Hegelian dialectic —is an essential constituent of his inherently historical conception of philosophy. No wonder, therefore, that later the radically ahistorical Kierkegaard denounces, with aristocratic contempt, this "omnibus" of a philosophical understanding of the historical processes.) However, since the socio-economic contradictions themselves are turned by Hegel into "thought-entities", the necessary "Aufhebung" of the contradictions manifest in the dialectical process is in the last analysis nothing but a merely *conceptual* ("abstract, logical, speculative") supersession of these contradictions which leaves the actuality of capitalist alienation completely un-challenged. This is why Marx has to speak of Hegel's "uncritical positivism". Hegel's standpoint always remains a bourgeois stand-point. But it is far from being an unproblematical one. On the contrary, the Hegelian philosophy as a whole displays in the most graphic way the gravely problematic character of the world to which the philosopher himself belongs. The contradictions of that world transpire through his categories, despite their "abstract, logical speculative" character, and the message of the *necessity* of a trans-cendence counteracts the *illusory* terms in which such a transcen-dence is envisaged by Hegel himself. In this sense his philosophy as a whole is a vital step in the direction of a proper understanding of the roots of capitalistic alienation.

In the writings of the Utopian Socialists there is an attempt at changing the social standpoint of criticism. With the working class a new social force appears on the horizon and the Utopian Socialists as critics of capitalistic alienation try to reassess the relation of forces from a viewpoint which allows them to take into account the existence of this new social force. And yet, their approach *objectively* remains, on the whole, within the limits of the bourgeois horizon, though of course *subjectively* the representatives of Utopian Socialism negate some essential features of capitalism. They can only project a supersession of the established order of society by a socialist system of relations in the form of a largely imaginary model, or as a moral postulate, rather than an ontological necessity inherent in the contradictions of the existing structure of society. (Characteristically enough : educational utopias, oriented towards the "workman", form an essential part of the conception of Utopian Socialists.) What makes their work of an enormous value is the fact that their criticism is directed towards clearly identifiable material factors of social life. Although they do not have a *comprehensive* assessment of the established social structures, their criticism of some vitally important social phenomena—from a critique of the modern State to the analysis of commodity production and of the rôle of money—greatly contributes to a radical reorientation of the critique of alienation. This criticism, however, remains *partial*. Even when it is oriented towards the "workman", the proletarian social position appears in it only as a directly given sociological immediacy and as a mere negation. Thus the Utopian critique of capitalist alienation remains—however paradoxical this may sound—within the orbit of capitalistic partiality which it negates from a partial standpoint. Because of the inescapable partiality of the critical standpoint the element of "ought", again, assumes the function of constructing "totalities" both negatively—i.e. by producing the overall object of criticism in want of an adequate comprehension of the structures of capitalism—and positively, by providing the utopian counter-examples to the negative denunciations.

And this is the point where we come to Marx. For the central feature of Marx's theory of alienation is the assertion of the historically necessary supersession of capitalism by socialism freed from all the abstract moral postulates which we can find in the writings of his immediate predecessors. The ground of his assertion was not simply the recognition of the unbearable dehumanizing effects of alienation—though of course subjectively that played a very important part in the formation of Marx's thought—but the profound understanding of the objective ontological foundation of the processes that remained veiled from his predecessors. The "secret" of this elaboration of the Marxian theory of alienation was spelled out by Marx himself when he wrote in his *Grundrisse* :

"this process of *objectification* appears in fact as a process of *alienation* from the *standpoint of labour* and as *appropriation* of alien labour from the *standpoint of capital*."[96]

The fundamental determinants of capitalistic alienation, then, had to remain hidden from all those who associated themselves— knowingly or unconsciously, in one form or in another—with "the standpoint of capital".

A radical shift of the standpoint of social criticism was a necessary condition of success in this respect. Such a shift involved the critical adoption of the standpoint of labour from which the capitalistic process of *objectification* could appear as a process of *alienation*. (In the writings of thinkers before Marx, by contrast, "objectification" and "alienation" remained hopelessly entangled with one another.)

But it is vitally important to stress that this adoption of labour's standpoint had to be a critical one. For a simple, uncritical identification with the standpoint of labour—one that saw alienation only, ignoring both the *objectification* involved in it, as well as the fact that this form of *alienating-objectification* was a *necessary* phase in the historical development of the objective ontological conditions of labour—would have meant hopeless *subjectivity* and *partiality*.

The *universality* of Marx's vision became possible because he succeeded in identifying the problematics of alienation, from a critically adopted standpoint of labour, in its complex ontological totality characterized by the terms "objectification", "alienation", and "appropriation". This critical adoption of the standpoint of labour meant a conception of the proletariat not simply as a sociological force diametrically opposed to the standpoint of capital— and thus remaining in the latter's orbit—but as a *self-transcending* historical force which cannot help superseding *alienation* (i.e. the historically given *form* of *objectification*) in the process of realizing its own immediate ends that happen to coincide with the "reappropriation of the human essence".

Thus the historical novelty of Marx's theory of alienation in relation to the conceptions of his predecessors can be summed up in a preliminary way as follows :

(1) the terms of reference of his theory are not the categories of

"Sollen" (ought), but those of *necessity* ("is") inherent in the objective ontological foundations of human life;

(2) its point of view is not that of some *utopian partiality* but the *universality* of the critically adopted standpoint of labour;

(3) its framework of criticism is not some abstract (Hegelian) "speculative totality", but the *concrete totality* of dynamically developing society perceived from the material basis of the proletariat as a necessarily self-transcending ("universal") historical force.

II. *Genesis of Marx's Theory of Alienation*

1. *Marx's Doctoral Thesis and His Critique of the Modern State*

ALREADY in his Doctoral Thesis Marx tackled some of the problems of alienation, though in a quite peculiar form, analysing the Epicurean philosophy as an expression of a historical stage dominated by the "privatization of life" (Privatisierung des Lebens). The "isolated individuality" (die isolierte Individualität) is representative of such a historical stage, and philosophy is characterized by the simile of the "moth" that seeks "the lamplight of the private realm" (das Lampenlicht des Privaten) after the universal sunset. These times which are also characterized by a particular intensity of a "hostile schism [estrangement] of philosophy from the world" (feindliche Diremption der Philosophie mit der Welt) are, however, "Titanic" (Titanenartig) because the cleavage within the structure of the given historical stage is tremendous ("riesenhaft ist der Zwiespalt"). From this viewpoint Lucretius—the Epicurean poet—must be considered, according to Marx, the true heroic poet of Rome. A poet who "celebrates in song the substance of the Roman Spirit; in place of Homer's joyful, robust, total characters here we have hard, impenetrably armoured heroes lacking in all other qualities; the *war of all against all* (bellum omnium contra omnes), the rigid form of being-for-itself, nature that lost its god and god who lost its world".[97]

As we can see, Marx's analysis serves to throw into relief a principle—*bellum omnium contra omnes*—which has a fundamental bearing on alienation. Later on, in connection with the Hobbesian philosophy, he refers to the same principle, in opposition to the romantic and mystifying approach of his contemporaries, the "true socialists" : "The true socialist proceeds from the thought that the dichotomy of life and happiness (der *Zwiespalt von Leben und Glück*) must cease. To prove this thesis, he summons the aid of nature and assumes that in it this dichotomy does not exist; from this he deduces that since man, too, is a natural body and possesses all the general properties of such a body, no dichotomy should exist for him either. Hobbes had much better reasons for invoking nature as a proof of his *bellum omnium contra omnes*. Hegel, on whose construction our true socialist depends, actually perceives in nature the *cleavage*, the dissolute period of the absolute idea and even calls the animal the concrete anguish of God."[98]

The *contradictory* character of the world is already in the centre of Marx's attention when he analyses the Epicurean philosophy. He emphasizes that Epicurus is principally interested in contradiction, that he determines the nature of the atom as inherently contradictory. And this is how the concept of alienation appears in Marx's philosophy, stressing the contradiction between "existence alienated from its essence" : "Durch die Qualitäten erhält das Atom eine Existenz, die seinem Begriff widerspricht, wird es als *entäussertes*, von seinem Wesen unterschiedenes Dasein gesetzt."[99] And again: "Erstens macht Epikur den *Widerspruch* zwischen Materie und Form zum Charakter der erscheinenden Natur, die so das Gegenbild der wesentlichen, des Atoms, wird. Dies geschieht, indem dem Raum die Zeit, der passiven Form der Erscheinung die aktive entgegengesetzt wird. Zweitens wird erst bei Epikur die Erscheinung als Erscheinung aufgefasst, d. h. als eine *Entfremdung des Wesens*, die sich selbst in ihrer Wirklichkeit *als solche Entfremdung betätigt*."[100] Marx also emphasizes that this "externalization" and "alienation" is a "Verselbstständigung", i.e. an independent, autonomous mode of existence, and that the "absolute principle" of Epicurus' atomism —this "natural science of self-consciousness"—is "abstract individuality".[101]

Marx's next step towards a more concrete formulation of the problematics of alienation was closely connected with his enquiries into the nature of the *modern state*. The historical tendency described earlier by Marx in its generic form with the terms "isolated individuality" and "abstract individuality" appeared now not in its negativity but as a positive force (positive as synonymous with "real" and "necessary", and not as predicative of moral approval). This historical tendency is said to give rise to the "self-centred" modern state, in contradistinction to the polis-state in which the "isolated individuality" is an unknown phenomenon. Such a modern state, whose "centre of gravity" was discovered by modern philosophers "within the state itself", is thus the natural condition of this "isolated individuality".

Viewed from the standpoint of this "self-centred" modern state

the principle of *bellum omnium contra omnes* can be formulated
as if it possessed the elemental force, eternal validity, and
universality of the laws of nature. It is significant that in Marx's
discussion of the "Copernican law" of the modern state the name
of Hobbes appears again in company of those philosophers who
greatly contributed to the elaboration of the problematics of alienation. "Immediately before and after the time of Copernicus's great
discoveries on the true solar system the law of gravitation of the
state was discovered : the centre of gravity of the state was found
within the state itself. As various European governments tried to
apply this result with the initial superficiality of practice to the
system of equilibrium of states, similarly Macchiavelli and
Campanella began before them and Hobbes, Spinoza, and Hugo
Grotius afterwards down to Rousseau, Fichte and Hegel, to consider the state with the eye of man and to develop its natural laws
from reason and experience, not from theology, any more than
Copernicus let himself be influenced by Joshua's supposed command
to the sun to stand still over Gideon and the moon over the vale of
Ajalon."[102]

In this period of his development Marx's attention is focused
primarily on the problems of the state. His early evaluation of the
nature and function of religion appears in this connection. Criticizing those who held the view according to which the downfall of the
old religions brought with it the decadence of the States of Greece
and Rome, Marx emphasizes that on the contrary it was the downfall of these states that caused the dissolution of their respective
religions.[103] This kind of assessment of religion has, of course, its
predecessors, but it reaches its climax in Marx's theory of alienation.
At the time of writing the article just referred to, Marx's sphere of
reference is still confined to politics. Nevertheless his radical reversal
of his opponents' approach—which he calls "history upside down"[104]
—is a major step in the direction of a comprehensive materialist
conception of the complex totality of capitalist alienation.

The most important work for the understanding of the development of Marx's theory of alienation up to the Autumn of 1843 is
his *Critique of the Hegelian Philosophy of Right*. We shall discuss
later in a more detailed form Marx's criticism of the Hegelian view
of alienation. At this point, however, it is necessary to quote a very
important passage from this work, in order to show some characteristic features of this phase of Marx's intellectual development. It
reads as follows :

"The present condition of society displays its difference from the earlier state of civil society in that—in contrast to the past—it does not integrate the individual within its community. It depends partly on chance, partly on the individual's effort etc. whether or not he holds on to his estate; to an e s t a t e which, again, determines the individual merely e x t e r n a l l y. For his station is not inherent in the individual's labour, nor does it relate itself to him as an objective community, organized in accordance with constant laws and maintaining a permanent relationship to him. . . . The principle of the bourgeois estate—or of bourgeois society—is e n j o y m e n t and the a b i l i t y t o e n j o y. In a political sense the member of bourgeois society detaches himself from his estate, his real private position; it is only here that his characteristic of being human assumes its significance, or that his determination as a member of an estate, as a communal being, appears as his h u m a n deter-mination. For all his other determinations a p p e a r in bourgeois society as i n e s s e n t i a l for man, for the individual, as merely e x t e r n a l determinations which may be necessary for his existence in the whole—i.e. as a tie with the whole—but they constitute a tie which he can just as well cast away. (The present bourgeois society is the consistent realization of the principle of i n d i v i d u a l i s m; individual existence is the ultimate end; activity, labour, content etc. are o n l y means.)[105] . . . The r e a l m a n is the p r i v a t e i n d i v i d u a l of present-day political constitution. . . . Not only is the e s t a t e founded on the d i v i s i o n of society as its ruling law, it also divorces man from his universal being; it turns him into an animal that directly coincides with his determination. The Middle Ages constitute the a n i m a l h i s t o r y of mankind, its Zoology. The modern age, our c i v i l i z a t i o n commits the opposite error. It divorces from man his o b j e c t i v e being as something merely e x t e r n a l and material."[106]

As we can see, many elements of Marx's theory of alienation, developed in a systematic form in the *Manuscripts of 1844*, are already present in this *Critique of the Hegelian Philosophy of Right*. Even if Marx does not use in this passage the terms "Entfremdung", "Entäusserung", and "Veräusserung", his insistence on the "d i v i s i o n of society" ("T r e n n u n g der Sozietät") and on the merely "e x t e r n a l determination of the individual" ("ä u s s e r-l i c h e Bestimmung des Individuums"), with their direct reference to the "divorce of man from his o b j e c t i v e being" ("Sie trennt das g e g e n s t ä n d l i c h e Wesen des Menschen von ihm") in the age of "c i v i l i z a t i o n"—i.e. in modern capitalistic society—take him near to the basic concept of his later analysis.

Moreover, we can note in our quotation a reference to the mere *"externality of labour"* as regards the individual (*"Tätigkeit, Arbeit, Inhalt etc. sind nur Mittel"* etc.): an idea that some ten months later is going to occupy a central place in Marx's theory of alienation. Here, however, this phenomenon is considered basically from a legal-institutional standpoint. Accordingly, capitalism is characterized as "the consistent realization of the principle of i n d i v i d u a l i s m" ("das durchgeführte Prinzip des Individualismus"), whereas in Marx's later conception this "principle of individualism" is put in its proper perspective: it is analysed as a manifestation *determined* by the *alienation of labour*, as one of the principal aspects of labour's self-alienation.

2. *The Jewish Question and the Problem of German Emancipation*

The Autumn of 1843 brought certain changes in Marx's orientation. By that time he was already residing in Paris, surrounded by a more stimulating intellectual environment which helped him to draw the most radical conclusions from his analysis of contemporary society. He was able to assess the social and political anachronism of Germany from a *real* basis of criticism (i.e. he could perceive the contradictions of his own country from the perspective of the actual situation of a historically more advanced European state) and not merely from the standpoint of a rather *abstract ideality* that characterized German philosophical criticism, including, up to a point, the earlier Marx himself.

Philosophical generalizations always require some sort of *distance* (or "outsider-position") of the philosopher from the concrete situation upon which he bases his generalizations. This was evidently the case in the history of philosophy from Socrates to Giordano Bruno, who had to die for being radical outsiders. But even later, "outsiders" played an extraordinary part in the development of philosophy: the Scots with respect to the economically much more advanced England; the philosophers of the backward Naples (from Vico to Benedetto Croce) in relation to the capitalistically more developed Northern Italy; and similar examples can be found in other countries as well. A great number of philosophers belong to this category of outsiders, from Rousseau and Kierkegaard down to Wittgenstein and Lukács in our century.

To Jewish philosophers a particular place is to be assigned in this context. Owing to the position forced upon them by virtue of being social outcasts, they could assume an intellectual standpoint *par excellence* which enabled them, from Spinoza to Marx, to accomplish some of the most fundamental philosophical syntheses in history. (This characteristic becomes even more strikin; if one compares the significance of these theoretical achievements with the artistic products of Jewish painters and musicians, sculptors and writers. The outsider's viewpoint that was an advantage in theoretical efforts became a drawback in the arts, because of the inherently *national* character of the latter. A drawback resulting— apart from a very few exceptions, such as the quite peculiar, intellectualistic-ironical, poems of Heine—in somewhat rootless works, lacking in the suggestiveness of representational qualities and therefore generally confined to the secondary range of artistic achievements. In the twentieth century, of course, the situation greatly changes. Partly because of a much greater—though never complete—national integration of the particular Jewish communities accomplished by this time thanks to the general realization of the social trend described by Marx as the "reabsorption of Christianity into Judaism".[107] More important is, however, the fact that parallel to the advance of this process of "reabsorption"—i.e. parallel to the triumph of capitalistic alienation in all spheres of life—art assumes a more abstract and "cosmopolitan" character than ever before and the experience of rootlessness becomes an all-pervasive theme of modern art. Thus, paradoxically, the earlier drawback turns into an advantage and we witness the appearance of some great Jewish writers—from Proust to Kafka—in the forefront of world literature.)

The outsider position of the great Jewish philosophers was doubly accentuated. In the first place, they were standing in a necessary opposition to their discriminatory and particularistic national communities which rejected the idea of Jewish emancipation. (e.g. "The German Jew, in particular, suffers from the general lack of political freedom and the pronounced Christianity of the state."[108]) But, in the second place, they had to emancipate themselves also from Judaism in order not to paralyse themselves by getting involved in the same contradictions at a different level, i.e. in order to escape from the particularistic and parochial positions of Jewry differing only in some respects but not in substance from the object of their first opposition. Only those Jewish philosophers could achieve the comprehensiveness and degree of universality that characterize the systems of both Spinoza and Marx who were able to grasp the issue of Jewish emancipation in its paradoxical duality, as inextricably intertwined with the historical development of mankind. Many others, from Moses Hess to Martin Buber, because of the particularistic character of their perspectives—or, in other words, because of their inability to emancipate themselves from "Jewish narrowness"—formulated their views in terms of second rate, provincialistic Utopias.

It is highly significant that in Marx's intellectual development a most important turning point, in the Autumn of 1843, coincided with a philosophical *prise de conscience* with regard to Judaism. His articles *On the Jewish Question*,[109] written during the last months of 1843 and in January 1844, sharply criticized not only German backwardness and political anachronism that rejected Jewish emancipation, but at the same time also the structure of capitalistic society in general as well as the rôle of Judaism in the development of capitalism.

The structure of modern bourgeois society in relation to Judaism was analysed by Marx on both the social and political plane in such terms which would have been unthinkable on the basis of acquaintance with the German—by no means typical—situation alone. During the last months of 1842 Marx had already studied the writings of French Utopian Socialists, e.g. Fourier, Étienne Cabet, Pierre Leroux and Pierre Considérant. In Paris, however, he had the opportunity of closely observing the social and political situation of France and to some extent even getting personally involved in it. He was introduced to the leaders of the democratic and socialist opposition and often frequented the meetings of the secret societies of workers. Moreover, he intensively studied the history of the French Revolution of 1789 because he wanted to write a history of the Convention. All this helped him to become extremely well acquainted with the most important aspects of the French situation which he was trying to integrate, together with his knowledge and experience of Germany, into a general historical conception. The contrast he drew, from the "outsider's" viewpoint, between the German situation and French society—against the background of modern historical development as a whole—proved fruitful not only for realistically tackling the Jewish question but in general for the elaboration of his well-known historical method.

Only in this framework could the concept of *alienation*—an eminently historical concept, as we have seen—assume a central place in Marx's thought, as the converging point of manifold socio-economic as well as political problems, and only the notion of alienation could assume such a rôle within his conceptual framework. (We shall return to a more detailed analysis of the conceptual structure of Marx's theory of alienation in the next chapter.)

In his articles *On the Jewish Question* Marx's starting point is, again, the principle of *bellum omnium contra omnes* as realized in bourgeois society ("bürgerliche Gesellschaft") that splits man into a public citizen and a private individual, and separates man from his "communal being" (Gemeinwesen), from himself, and from other men. But then Marx goes on to extend these considerations to virtually every aspect of this extremely complex "bürgerliche Gesellschaft"; from the interconnections between religion and the state—finding a common denominator precisely in a mutual reference to alienation—to the economic, political and family-relations which manifest themselves, without exception, in some form of alienation.

He uses a great variety of terms to designate the various aspects of alienated bourgeois society, such as "Trennung" (divorce or separation), "Spaltung" (division or cleavage), "Absonderung" (separation or withdrawal), "verderben" (spoil, corrupt), "sich selbst verlieren, veräussern" (lose and alienate oneself), "sich isolieren und auf sich zurückziehen" (isolate and withdraw oneself into oneself), "äusserlich machen" (externalize, alienate), "alle Gattungsbände des Menschen zerreissen" (destroy or disintegrate all the ties of man with his species), "die Menschenwelt in eine Welt atomistischer Individuen auflösen" (dissolve the world of man into a world of atomistic individuals), and so on. And all these terms are discussed in specific contexts which establish their close interconnections with "Entäusserung", "Entfremdung", and "Veräusserung".[110]

Another important study from this period of Marx's intellectual development, written simultaneously with the articles *On the Jewish Question*, is entitled: *Critique of the Hegelian Philosophy of Right. Introduction.*[111] In this work the primary task of philosophy is defined as a radical criticism of the "non-sacred" forms and manifestations of self-alienation, in contrast to the views of Marx's contemporaries—including Feuerbach—who confined their attention to the critique of religious alienation. Marx insists, with great passion, that philosophy should transform itself in this spirit. "It is the task of history, therefore once the other-world of truth has vanished, to establish the truth of this world.

The immediate task of philosophy, which is in the service of history, is to *unmask human self-alienation in its secular form* now that it has been unmasked in its sacred form. Thus the criticism of heaven is transformed into the criticism of earth, the criticism of religion into the criticism of law, and the criticism of theology into the criticism of politics."[112]

In this study one cannot fail to perceive the "outsider's" standpoint in relation to the German situation. Marx points out that merely opposing and negating German political circumstances would amount to nothing more than an anachronism, because of the enormous gap that separates Germany from the up-to-date nations of Europe. "If one were to begin with the *status quo* itself in Germany, even in the most appropriate way, i.e. negatively, the result would still be an anachronism. Even the negation of our political present is already a dusty fact in the historical lumber room of modern nations. I may negate powdered wigs, but I am still left with unpowdered wigs. If I negate the German situation of 1843 I have, according to French chronology, hardly reached the year 1789, and still less the vital centre of the present day."[113] The contrast between German anachronism and the historically "up-to-date nations" of Europe points, in Marx's view, towards a solution that with respect to Germany is rather more of a "categorical imperative" than an actuality: the *proletariat* that has yet to develop itself beyond the Rhine.[114]

In complete agreement with the line of thought characteristic of the articles *On the Jewish Question*—in which Marx emphasized, as we have seen, that the complete emancipation of Judaism is inconceivable without the universal emancipation of mankind from the circumstances of self-alienation—he repeatedly stresses the point that "The emancipation of the German coincides with the emancipation of man".[115] Moreover, he emphasizes that "It is not radical revolution, universal human emancipation which is a Utopian dream for Germany, but rather a *partial, merely political* revolution which leaves the pillars of the building standing"[116] and that "In Germany complete [universal] emancipation is a *conditio sine qua non* for any *partial* emancipation".[117] The same applies to the *Jewish Question*; for no degree of *political* emancipation can be considered an answer when "the Jewish narrowness of society" is at stake.

The importance of these insights is enormous, not only methodologically—insofar as they offer a key to understanding the nature of Utopianism as the inflation of *partiality* into *pseudo-universality* —but also practically. For Marx clearly realizes that the practical supersession of alienation is inconceivable in terms of politics alone, in view of the fact that politics is only a *partial* aspect of the totality of social processes, no matter how centrally important it may be in specific historical situations (e.g. late eighteenth century France).

But the limits are also in evidence in these articles. The opposition between "partiality" and "universality" is grasped in its rather abstract generality and only one of its aspects is concretized, negatively, in Marx's rejection of *"political* partiality" as a possible candidate for bringing about the supersession of alienation. Its positive counterpart remains unspecified as a general *postulate of "universality"* and thus assumes the character of a "Sollen" (ought). The identification of "universality" with the ontologically funda- mental sphere of *economics* is a later achievement in Marx's thought. At this stage his references to political economy are still rather vague and generic. Although he sees intuitively that "the relation of industry, of the world of wealth in general, to the political world is a major problem of modern times",[118] his assessment of the specific contradictions of capitalism is still rather unrealistic : "While in France and England," he writes, "the problem is put in the form : political economy or the rule of society over wealth; in Germany it is put in the form : national economy or the rule of private property over nationality. Thus, in England and France it is a question of abolishing monopoly, which has developed to its final consequences; while in Germany it is a question of proceeding to the final consequences of monopoly."[119] It is, therefore, not surprising that the element of "ought"—in want of a concrete demonstration of the fundamental economic trends and contradictions which objectively point to the necessary supersession of alienation—plays such an important part in Marx's thought at this stage of his development. In 1843 Marx is still forced to conclude that the critique of religion ends "with the *categorical imperative* to overthrow all those con- ditions in which man is an abased, enslaved, abandoned, contemptible being",[120] and his first assessment of the rôle of the proletariat is in full agreement with this vision. In the *Economic and Philosophic Manuscripts of 1844*, however, Marx makes a crucial step forward, radically superseding the "political partiality" of his own orientation and the limitations of a conceptual framework that characterized his development in its phase of "revolutionary democratism".

3. Marx's Encounter with Political Economy

The *Economic and Philosophic Manuscripts of 1844* are evidently the work of a genius; considering the monumentality of this synthesis and the depth of its insights it is almost unbelievable that they were written by a young man of 26. There may appear to be a contradiction here, between acknowledging the "work of a genius" and the Marxist principle according to which great men, just as much as great ideas, arise in history "when the time is ripe for them". In fact "Dr. Marx's genius" was noticed by Moses Hess and others well before the publication of any of his great works.

And yet, we are not involved in any contradiction whatsoever. On the contrary, Marx's own development confirms the general principle of Marxism. For "genius" is but an abstract potentiality before it is articulated in relation to some specific *content* in response to the objective requirements of a historically given situation. In the abstract sense—as "phenomenal brain-power" etc. —"genius" is always "around", but it is wasted, unrealized, or whittled away in activities and products which leave no mark behind them. The unrealized "genius" of Dr. Marx that mesmerized Moses Hess is a mere historical curiosity as compared with its full realization in Marx's immense works which not only did not in the least impress the same Moses Hess but succeeded only in arousing his narrow-minded hostility.

In the concrete realization of the potentiality of Marx's genius his grasp of the concept of "labour's self-alienation" represented the crucial element: the "Archimedean point" of his great synthesis. The elaboration of this concept in its complex, Marxian comprehensiveness—as the philosophical synthesizing point of the dynamism of human development—was simply inconceivable prior to a certain time, i.e. prior to the relative maturation of the social contradictions reflected in it. Its conception also required the perfection of the intellectual tools and instruments—primarily through the elaboration of the categories of dialectics—which were necessary for an adequate philosophical grasp of the mystifying phenomena of alienation, as well as, of course, the intellectual power of an individual who could turn to a proper use these instruments. And last, but not least, the appearance of this "Archimedean concept" also presupposed the intense moral passion and unshakeable character of someone who was prepared to announce a "w a r by all means"[121] on the "conditions in which man is an abased, enslaved, abandoned, contemptible being"; someone who could envisage his *personal* fulfilment, the realization of his intellectual aims, in the "realization through abolition" of philosophy in the course of fighting that war. The simultaneous fulfilment of all these conditions and prerequisites was necessary indeed for the Marxian elaboration of the concept of "labour's self-alienation"—at a time when the conditions were "ripe for it".

It is well known that Marx started to study the classics of political economy at the end of 1843, but they only served to give, in both *On the Jewish Question* and his *Introduction to a Critique of the Hegelian Philosophy of Right*, a background lacking in definition to a primarily *political* exposition, in the spirit of his programmatic utterance according to which the criticism of religion and theology must be turned into the criticism of law and politics.

In accomplishing the transformation of Marx's thought mentioned above, the influence of a work entitled *Outlines of a Critique of Political Economy* (Umrisse zu einer Kritik der Nationalökonomie; written by the young Engels in December 1843 and January 1844 and sent to Marx in January for publication in *Deutsch-Französischen Jahrbüchern*) was very important. Even in 1859 Marx wrote about these *Outlines* in terms of the highest praise.

Alienation, according to this early work of Engels, is due to a particular mode of production which "turns all natural and rational relations upside-down". It can be called, therefore, the "unconscious condition of mankind". Engels' alternative to this mode of production is formulated in the concrete programme of socializing private property : "If we abandon private property, then all these unnatural divisions disappear. The difference between interest and profit disappears; capital is nothing without labour, without movement. The significance of profit is reduced to the weight which capital carries in the determination of the costs of production; and profit thus remains inherent in capital, in the same way as capital itself reverts to its original unity with labour."[122]

The solution conceived in these terms would also show a way out from the contradictions of the "unconscious conditions of mankind", defined in this connection as economic crises : "Produce with consciousness as human beings—not as *dispersed atoms* without *consciousness of your species*—and you are beyond all these *artificial and untenable antitheses*. But as long as you continue to produce in the present unconscious, thoughtless manner, at the *mercy of chance*—for just as long *trade crises* will remain" (196).

Stimulated by this work of the young Engels, Marx intensified his study of the classics of political economy. (A few months later he also met Engels who was just returning from England and could recall his observations in the industrially most advanced country.) The outcome of Marx's intensive study of political economy was his great work known by the title *Economic and Philosophic Manuscripts of 1844*. They show a fundamental affinity of approach with the work of the young Engels but their scope is incomparably broader. They embrace and relate all the basic philosophical problems to the fact of labour's self-alienation, from the question of freedom to that of the meaning of life (see CHAPTER VI), from the genesis of modern society to the relationship between individuality and man's "communal being", from the production of "artificial appetites" to the "alienation of the senses", and from an assessment of the nature and function of Philosophy, Art, Religion and Law to the problems of a possible "reintegration of human life" in the real world, by means of a "positive transcendence" instead of the merely conceptual "Aufhebung" of alienation.

The converging point of the heterogeneous aspects of alienation is the notion of "labour" (Arbeit). In the *Manuscripts of 1844* labour is considered both in general—as "productive activity": the fundamental ontological determination of "humanness (*"menschliches* Dasein", i.e. really *human* mode of existence)—and in particular, as having the form of capitalistic "division of labour". It is in this latter form—capitalistically structured activity—that "labour" is the ground of all alienation.

"Activity" (Tätigkeit), "division of labour" (Teilung der Arbeit), "exchange" (Austausch) and "private property" (Privateigentum) are the key concepts of this approach to the problematics of alienation. The ideal of a "positive transcendence" of alienation is formulated as a necessary socio-historical supersession of the *"mediations"*: PRIVATE PROPERTY—EXCHANGE—DIVISION OF LABOUR which interpose themselves between man and his activity and prevent him from finding fulfilment in his labour, in the exercise of his productive (creative) abilities, and in the human appropriation of the products of his activity.

Marx's critique of alienation is thus formulated as a rejection of these *mediations*. It is vitally important to stress in this connection that this rejection does not imply in any way a negation of *all* mediation. On the contrary : this is the first truly dialectical grasp of the complex relationship between mediation and immediacy in the history of philosophy, including the by no means negligible achievements of Hegel.

A rejection of all mediation would be dangerously near to sheer mysticism in its idealization of the *"identity* of Subject and Object"*. What Marx opposes as alienation is not mediation in general but a set of *second order* mediations (PRIVATE PROPERTY—EXCHANGE—DIVISION OF LABOUR), a "mediation of the mediation", i.e. a *historically specific* mediation of the *ontologically fundamental* self-mediation of man with nature. This "second order mediation" can only arise on the basis of the ontologically necessary "first order mediation"—as the specific, *alienated form* of the latter. But the "first order mediation" itself—productive activity as such—is an absolute ontological factor of the human predicament. (We shall return to this problematics under both its aspects—i.e. both as "first order mediation" and as alienated "mediation of the mediation"— in a moment.)

Labour (productive activity) is the one and only absolute factor in the whole complex : LABOUR—DIVISION OF LABOUR—PRIVATE PROPERTY—EXCHANGE. (Absolute because the human mode of existence is inconceivable without the transformations of nature accomplished by productive activity.) Consequently any attempt at overcoming alienation must define itself in relation to this absolute as opposed to its manifestation in an alienated form. But in order to formulate the question of a positive transcendence of alienation in the actual world one must realize, from the earlier mentioned standpoint of the "outsider", that the *given form* of labour (WAGE LABOUR) is related to *human activity* in general as the *particular* to the *universal*. If this is not seen, if "productive activity" is not differentiated into its radically different aspects, if the ontologically absolute factor is not distinguished from the historically specific form, if, that is, activity is conceived—because of the absolutization of a particular form of activity—as a homogeneous entity, the question of an actual (practical) transcendence of alienation cannot possibly arise. If PRIVATE PROPERTY and EXCHANGE are considered absolute—in some way "inherent in human nature"—then DIVISION OF LABOUR, the capitalistic form of productive activity as WAGE

LABOUR must also appear as absolute, for they reciprocally imply each other. Thus the second order mediation appears as a first order mediation, i.e. an absolute ontological factor. Consequently the negation of the alienated manifestations of this mediation must assume the form of nostalgic moralizing postulates (e.g. Rousseau).

The study of political economy provided Marx with a most detailed analysis of the nature and functioning of the capitalistic form of productive activity. His negation of alienation in his previous writings was centred, as we have seen, on the critique of the existing institutions and legal-political relations and "labour" appeared only *negatively*, as a missing determination of the individual's position in "bürgerliche Gesellschaft". In other words : it appeared as an aspect of a society in which the *political* and *social* spheres are divided in such a way that the individual's position in society is *not inherent in his labour*. Before the *Manuscripts of 1844* the economic factor appeared only as a vaguely defined aspect of socio-political relations. Even the author of the articles *On the Jewish Question* and on the *Hegelian Philosophy of Right* did not realize the fundamental ontological importance of the sphere of *production* which appeared in his writings in the form of rather generic references to "needs" (Bedürfnisse) in general. Consequently Marx was unable to grasp in a comprehensive way the complex hierarchy of the various kinds and forms of human activity : their reciprocal *interrelations* within a *structured* whole.

All this is very different in the *Manuscripts of 1844*. In this work Marx's ontological starting point is the self-evident fact that man, a specific part of *nature* (i.e. a being with *physical* needs historically prior to all others) must *produce* in order to sustain himself, in order to satisfy these needs. However, he can only satisfy these primitive needs by *necessarily* creating, in the course of their satisfaction through his productive activity, a complex hierarchy of *non-physical* needs which thus become necessary conditions for the gratification of his original physical needs as well. Human activities and needs of a "spiritual" kind thus have their ultimate ontological foundation in the sphere of material production as specific expressions of human interchange with nature, mediated in complex ways and forms. As Marx puts it : *"the entire so-called history of the world is nothing but the begetting of man through human labour, nothing but the coming-to-be [Werden] of nature for man"* (113). Productive activity is, therefore, the *mediator* in the "subject-object relationship" between man and nature. A mediator that enables man to lead a *human* mode of existence, ensuring that he does not fall back into nature, does not dissolve himself within the "object". "Man lives on nature", writes Marx, "—means that nature is his body, with which he must remain in continuous intercourse if he is not to die. That man's physical *and spiritual* life is linked to nature means simply that nature is linked to itself, for man is a part of nature" (74).

Productive activity is hence the source of consciousness and "alienated consciousness" is the reflection of alienated activity or of the alienation of activity, i.e. of labour's self-alienation.

Marx uses the expression: "man's *inorganic* body", which is not simply that which is given by nature, but the concrete expression and embodiment of a historically given stage and structure of productive activity in the form of its products, from material goods to works of art. As a result of the alienation of labour, "man's inorganic body" appears to be merely external to him and therefore it can be turned into a commodity. Everything is "reified", and the fundamental ontological relations are turned upside down. The individual is confronted with mere objects (things, commodities), once his "inorganic body"—"worked-up nature" and externalized productive power—has been alienated from him. He has no consciousness of being a "species being". (A "Gattungswesen"— i.e. a being that has the consciousness of the species to which it belongs, or, to put it in another way, a being whose essence does not coincide directly with its individuality. Man is the only being that can have such a "species-consciousness"—both subjectively, in his conscious awareness of the species to which he belongs, and in the objectified forms of this "species-consciousness", from industry to institutions and to works of art—and thus he is the only "species being".)

Productive activity in the form dominated by capitalistic isolation —when "men produce as dispersed atoms without consciousness of their species"—cannot adequately fulfil the function of *mediating* man with nature because it "reifies" man and his relations and reduces him to the state of animal nature. In place of man's "consciousness of his species" we find a cult of privacy and an idealization of the abstract individual. Thus by identifying the human essence with mere individuality, man's biological nature is confounded with his proper, specifically human, nature. For mere individuality requires only *means* to its *subsistence*, but not specifically human—humanly-natural and naturally-human, i.e. *social*—forms

of self-fulfilment which are at the same time also adequate manifestations of the life-activity of a "Gattungswesen", a "species
being". "*Man is a species being* not only because in practice and in
theory he adopts the species as his object (his own as well as those
of other things) but—and this is only another way of expressing it—
but also because he treats himself as the actual, living species;'
*because he treats himself as a u n i v e r s a l and therefore a free
being*" (74). The mystifying cult of the abstract individual, by
contrast, indicates as man's nature an attribute—mere individuality—which is a *universal* category of nature in general, and by
no means something *specifically human*. (See Marx's praise of
Hobbes for having recognized in nature the dominance of individuality in his principle of *bellum omnium contra omnes*.)

Productive activity is, then, *alienated activity* when it departs
from its proper function of humanly *mediating* in the subject-object
relationship between man and nature, and tends, instead, to make
the isolated and reified individual to be reabsorbed by "nature".
This can happen even at a highly developed stage of civilization if
man is subjected, as the young Engels says, to "a natural law based
on the unconsciousness of the participants" (195). (Marx has
integrated this idea of the young Engels into his own system and
more than once referred to this "natural law" of capitalism not only
in the *Manuscripts of 1844* but in his *Capital* as well.[123])

Thus Marx's protest against alienation, privatization and
reification does not involve him in the contradictions of an idealization of some kind of a "natural state". There is no trace of a
sentimental or romantic nostalgia for nature in his conception. His
programme, in the critical references to "artificial appetites" etc.,
does not advocate a return to "nature", to a "natural" set of
primitive, or "simple", needs but the "full realization of *man's
nature*" through an adequately *self-mediating* human activity.
"Man's nature" (his "specific being") means precisely *distinctiveness*
from nature in general. The relationship of man with nature is "self-
mediating" in a twofold sense. First, because it is nature that
mediates itself with itself in man. And secondly, because the
mediating activity itself is nothing but man's attribute, located in a
specific part of nature. Thus in productive activity, under the first
of its dual ontological aspects, *nature mediates itself with nature*,
and, under its second ontological aspect—in virtue of the fact that
productive activity is inherently *social* activity—*man mediates himself with man.*

The second order mediations mentioned above (institutionalized in the form of capitalistic DIVISION OF LABOUR—PRIVATE PROPERTY —EXCHANGE) disrupt this relationship and subordinate productive activity itself, under the rule of a blind "natural law", to the requirements of commodity-production destined to ensure the reproduction of the isolated and reified individual who is but an appendage of this system of "economic determinations".

Man's productive activity cannot bring him fulfilment because the institutionalized second order mediations interpose themselves between man and his activity, between man and nature, and between man and man. (The last two are already implied in the first, i.e. in the interposition of capitalistic second order mediations between man and his activity, in the subordination of productive activity to these mediations. For if man's self-mediation is further mediated by the capitalistically institutionalized form of productive activity, then nature cannot mediate itself with nature and man cannot mediate himself with man. On the contrary, man is confronted by nature in a hostile fashion, under the rule of a "natural law" blindly prevailing through the mechanisms of the market (EXCHANGE) and, on the other hand, man is confronted by man in a hostile fashion in the antagonism between CAPITAL and LABOUR. The original interrelationship of man with nature is transformed into the relationship between WAGE LABOUR and CAPITAL, and as far as the individual worker is concerned, the aim of his activity is necessarily confined to his self-reproduction as a mere individual, in his physical being, Thus means become ultimate ends while human ends are turned into mere means subordinated to the reified ends of this institutionalized system of second order mediations.)

An adequate negation of alienation is, therefore, inseparable from the radical negation of capitalistic second order mediations. If, however, they are taken for granted—as for instance in the writings of political economists as well as of Hegel (and even in Rousseau's conception as a whole)—the critique of the various manifestations of alienation is bound to remain partial or illusory, or both. The "uncritical positivism" of political economists needs no further comment, only the remark that its contradictions greatly helped Marx in his attempts at clarifying his own position. Rousseau, despite his radical opposition to certain phenomena of alienation, could not break out from a vicious circle because he reversed the actual ontological relationships, assigning priority to the second order mediations over the first. Thus he found himself trapped by an insoluble contradiction of his own making : the idealization of a fictitious "fair exchange" opposed, sentimentally, to the ontologically fundamental first order mediations, i.e. in Rousseau's terminology, to "civilization". As far as Hegel is concerned, he identified "objectification" and "alienation" partly because he was far too great a realist to indulge in a romantic negation of the ontologically fundamental self-mediation (and self-genesis) of man through his activity (on the contrary, he was the first to grasp this ontological relationship, although in an "abstract, speculative" manner), and partly because, in virtue of his social standpoint, he could not oppose the capitalistic form of second order mediations. Consequently he fused the two sets of mediations in the concept of "objectifying alienation" and "alienating objectification" : a concept that *apriori* excluded from his system the possibility of envisaging an actual (practical) supersession of alienation.

It was Marx's great historical achievement to cut the "Gordian knot" of these mystifyingly complex sets of mediations, by asserting the absolute validity of the ontologically fundamental first order mediation (in opposition to romantic and Utopian advocates of a *direct* unity) against its alienation in the form of capitalistic DIVISION OF LABOUR—PRIVATE PROPERTY and EXCHANGE. This great theoretical discovery opened up the road to a "scientific demystification" as well as an actual, practical negation of the capitalistic mode of production.

4. Monistic Materialism

In elaborating a solution to the complex issues of alienation much depends on the "Archimedean point" or common denominator of the particular philosophical system. For Marx, in his *Economic and Philosophic Manuscripts of 1844* this common denominator was, as already mentioned, the concept of a capitalistic "alienation of labour". He emphasized its importance as follows: "The examination of d i v i s i o n o f l a b o u r a n d e x c h a n g e is of extreme interest, because these are p e r c e p t i b l y a l i e n a t e d expressions of human a c t i v i t y and of e s s e n t i a l h u m a n p o w e r as a s p e c i e s activity and power" (134).

If, however, one's centre of reference is "religious alienation", as in Feuerbach's case, nothing follows from it as regards actual, practical alienation. For "*Religious estrangement* as such occurs only in the realm of c o n s c i o u s n e s s, of man's inner life, but *economic estrangement* is that of r e a l l i f e; *its transcendence therefore embraces both aspects*" (103). Feuerbach *wanted* to tackle the problems of alienation in terms of real life (this programmatic affinity explains Marx's attachment to Feuerbach in a certain period of his development), in opposition to the Hegelian solution, but because of the abstractness of his viewpoint: idealized "man" ("human essence" taken generically, and not as "the ensemble of social relations"[124]), his position remained basically *dualistic*, offering no real solution to the analysed problems.

The main importance of the classics of political economy for Marx's intellectual development was that by throwing light on the palpable sphere of economics (analysed by them, as regards the capitalistic stage of production, in the most concrete terms) they helped him to concentrate on the "perceptibly alienated expressions of human activity" (134). His awareness of the importance of productive activity enabled Marx to identify, with utmost clarity, the contradictions of a non-mediated, undialectical, "dualistic materialism".

It is significant that Marx's intense study of political economy sharpened his criticism of Feuerbach and, at the same time, pushed into the foreground the affinities of Marxian thought with certain characteristics of the Hegelian philosophy. It may seem paradoxical at first that, in spite of the *materialistic* conception shared by both Marx and Feuerbach, and in spite of the much closer *political affinity* between them than between Marx and Hegel, the relationship of the historical materialist Marx and the *idealist* Hegel is incomparably more deeply rooted than that between Marx and Feuerbach. The first embraces the totality of Marx's development whereas the second is confined to an early, and transitory, stage.

The reason is to be found in the basically *monistic* character of the Hegelian philosophy in contrast to Feuerbach's *dualism*. In the famous passage in which Marx distinguishes his position from the Hegelian dialectic he also emphasizes the deep affinity, insisting on the necessity of turning "right side up again" that which in Hegel's philosophy is "standing on its head".[125] But it would be impossible to turn the Hegelian conception "right side up again", in order to incorporate its "rational kernel" into Marx's system, if there did not lie at the basis of their "opposite" philosophical approaches the common characteristics of two—ideologically different, indeed opposite—*monistic* conceptions. For dualism remains dualism even if it is turned "the other way round".

By contrast, we can see in Marx's *Theses on Feuerbach* his complete rejection of Feuerbach's ontological and epistemological *dualism*: "The chief defect of all hitherto existing materialism—that of Feuerbach included—is that the thing (Gegenstand), reality, sensuousness is conceived only in the form of the o b j e c t (Objekt) or of c o n t e m p l a t i o n (Anschauung), but not as h u m a n s e n s u o u s activity, practice, not subjectively. Hence it happened that the a c t i v e side, in contradistinction to materialism, was developed by idealism—but only abstractly, since of course, idealism does not know real, sensuous activity as such. Feuerbach wants sensuous objects, really differentiated from thought-objects, but he does not conceive human activity itself as o b j e c t i v e (gegenständliche) activity. Hence, in the *Essence of Christianity*, he regards the theoretical attitude as the only genuinely human attitude, while practice is conceived and fixed only in its dirty-judaical form of appearance."[126]

This reference to "practice" is very similar to Goethe's principle concerning *Experiment as Mediator between Object and Subject* (Der Versuch als Vermittler von Objekt und Subjekt),[127] and the second thesis on Feuerbach emphasizes this similarity even more strongly. Now the lack of such mediator in Feuerbach's philosophy means that its dualism cannot be overcome. On the contrary, it assumes at the level of social theory the sharpest possible form: "The materialist doctrine that men are products of circumstances and upbringing, forgets that it is men that change circumstances and that the educator himself needs educating. Hence this doctrine necessarily arrives at dividing society into two parts, of which one is superior to society."[128] This is why Feuerbach's system, in spite of the philosopher's materialistic approach, and in spite of his starting out "from the fact of religious self-alienation",[129] cannot be in a lasting agreement with the Marxian philosophy. For a kind of "materialistic dualism" is manifest in Feuerbach's philosophy at every level, with all the contradictions involved in it. (Cf. "abstract thinking" *v.* "intuition", "contemplation", "Anschauung"; "isolated individual" *v.* "human essence"; "abstract individual" *v.* "human species", and so on.)

The secret of Marx's success in radically transcending the limitations of dualistic, contemplative materialism is his unparalleled dialectical grasp of the category of mediation. For no philosophical system can be monistic without conceptually mastering, in one form or another, the complex dialectical interrelationship between mediation and totality. It goes without saying, this applies—*mutatis mutandis*—to the Hegelian philosophy as well. Hegel's idealistic monism has for its centre of reference his concept of "activity" as "mediator between Subject and Object". But, of course, the Hegelian concept of "activity" is "abstract mental activity" which can mediate only "thought-entities". ("Object", in Hegel's philosophy is "alienated Subject", "externalized World Spirit" etc., i.e. in the last analysis it is a pseudo-object.) In this characteristic of the Hegelian philosophy the inner contradictions of its concept of mediation come to the fore. For Hegel is not a "mystifier" because "he is an idealist" : to say this would amount to hardly more than an unrewarding tautology. Rather, he is an idealist mystifier because of the inherently contradictory character of his concept of mediation, i.e. because of the taboos he imposes upon himself as regards the second order mediations while he is absolutizing these—historically specific—forms of capitalistic "mediation of the mediation". The philosophical repercussions of such a step are far-reaching, affecting all his main categories, from the assumed identity of "alienation" and "objectification" to the ultimate identity of "subject" and "object", as well as to the conception of "Aufhebung" as a merely conceptual "reconciliation" of the subject with itself. (Even the *"nostalgia"* for the original direct unity appears—though in an "abstract, speculative, logical form"—in the conceptual opposition between "Ent-*äusserung*", alienation, and "Er-*innerung*", i.e. turning "inwards", remembering a past necessarily gone for ever.)

Only in Marx's monistic materialism can we find a coherent comprehension of "*objective* totality" as "sensuous reality", and a correspondingly valid differentiation between subject and object, thanks to his concept of mediation as ontologically fundamental productive activity, and thanks to his grasp of the historically specific, second order mediations through which the ontological foundation of human existence is alienated from man in the capitalist order of society.

5. *The Transformation of Hegel's Idea of "Activity"*

Activity appeared in the writings of the classics of political economy as something *concrete*, belonging to the palpable manifestations of real life. It was, however, confined in their conception to a *particular sphere* : that of manufacture and commerce, considered completely ahistorically. It was Hegel's great theoretical achievement to make *universal* the philosophical importance of activity, even if he 'did this in an *abstract* form, for reasons mentioned already.

Marx writes in his *Manuscripts of 1844* about the magnitude as well as the limitations of the Hegelian achievements : "Hegel's standpoint is that of modern political economy. He grasps l a b o u r as the e s s e n c e of man—as man's essence in the act of proving itself : he sees only the positive, not the negative side of labour. Labour is man's c o m i n g - t o - b e f o r h i m s e l f within a l i e n a t i o n, or as a l i e n a t e d man. The only labour which Hegel knows and recognizes is *a b s t r a c t l y m e n t a l labour*" (152). Thus with Hegel "activity" becomes a term of crucial importance, meant to explain human genesis and development in general. But the Hegelian concept of "activity" acquires this universal character at the price of losing the sensuous form "labour" had in political economy. (That the political economist conception of "labour" was one-sided, partial, and ahistorical, does not concern us here where the point at stake is the relative historical significance of this conception.)

Marx's concept of "activity" as *practice* or "productive activity" —identified both in its *positive* sense (as human objectification and "self-development", as man's necessary self-mediation with nature) and in its *negative* sense (as alienation or second order mediation)— resembles the political economist's conception in that it is conceived in a sensuous form. Its theoretical function is, however, radically different. For Marx realizes that the non-alienated foundation of that which is reflected in an alienated form in political economy as a *particular* sphere is the *fundamental ontological sphere* of human existence and therefore it is the ultimate foundation of all kinds and forms of activity. Thus *labour*, in its "sensuous form", assumes its universal significance in Marx's philosophy. It becomes not only the key to understanding the determinations inherent in all forms of alienation but also the centre of reference of his practical strategy aimed at the actual supersession of capitalistic alienation.

To accomplish the Marxian formulation of the central issues of alienation, a critical incorporation of Hegel's achievements into Marx's thought was of the greatest importance. By becoming aware of the universal philosophical significance of productive activity Marx made a decisive step forward with respect to the writings of political economy and thus he was enabled to work out certain objective implications of the latter which could not be realized by the political economists themselves because of the partial and unhistorical character of their approach. We can see this clearly expressed in the following words of Marx: "To assert that division of labour and exchange rest on private property is nothing short of asserting that labour is the essence of private property—an assertion which the political economist cannot prove and which we wish to prove for him. Precisely in the fact that division of labour and exchange are embodiments of private property lies the twofold proof, on the one hand that human life required private property for its realization, and on the other hand that it now requires the supersession of private property" (134). Thus political economy cannot go to the roots of the matter. It conceives a *particular* form of activity (capitalistic division of labour) as the *universal* and *absolute* form of productive activity. Consequently in the reasoning of political economists the ultimate point of reference cannot be *activity itself* in view of the fact that a particular form of activity— the historically established socio-economic practice of capitalism—is absolutized by them.

Political economy evidently could not assume as its ultimate point of reference activity in general (i.e. productive activity as such: this absolute condition of human existence) because such a step would have made impossible the absolutization of a *particular form* of activity. The only type of "absolute" which enabled them to draw the desired conclusions was a *circular* one: namely the assumption of the basic characteristics of the specific form of activity whose absoluteness they wanted to demonstrate as being *necessarily inherent* in *"human nature"*. Thus the historical *fact* of capitalistic EXCHANGE appeared in an idealized form on the absolute plane of "human nature" as a *"propensity* to exchange and barter" (Adam Smith) from which it could be easily deduced that the "commercial" form of society, based on the capitalistic division of labour, is also the *"natural"* form of society.

If the absolute factor is identified with private property (or with some fictitious "propensity to exchange and barter", which is only another way of saying the same thing), then we are confronted with an insoluble contradiction between *natural* and *human*, even if this contradiction is hidden beneath the rhetorical assumption of a harmonious relationship between "human nature" and capitalistic mode of production. For if one assumes a fixed human nature (e.g. a "propensity to exchange and barter"), then the really *natural* and *absolute* necessity (expressed in the self-evident truth of the words: "man must *produce* if he is not to die") is subordinated to a *pseudo-natural* order. (The proposition equivalent to the Marxian self-evident truth, according to the alleged "natural order" of "human nature", should read: *"man must exchange and barter if he is not to die"*, which is by no means true, let alone self-evidently true.) Thus the ontologically fundamental dimension of human existence is displaced from its natural and absolute status to a *secondary* one. This is, of course, reflected in the scale of values of the society which takes as its ultimate point of reference the system of exchange and barter: if the capitalistic order of things is challenged, this appears to the "political economists" as though the very existence of mankind is endangered. This is why the super-session of alienation cannot conceivably be included in the pro-gramme of political economists, except perhaps in the form of illusorily advocating the cure of some *partial effects* of the capitalistic alienation of labour which is idealized by them, as a system, as man's "necessary" and "natural" mode of existence.[130] And this is why the attitude of political economists to alienation must remain, on the whole, one that cannot be called other than "uncritical positivism".

Hegel supersedes, to some extent, this contradiction of political economy, by conceiving activity in general as the absolute condition of historical genesis. Paradoxically, however, he destroys his own achievements, reproducing the contradictions of political economy at another level. Insofar as he considers "activity" as the absolute condition of historical genesis, logically prior to the form of externalization, he can—indeed he *must*—raise the question of an "Aufhebung" of alienation; for the latter arises in opposition to the original direct unity of the "Absolute" with itself. Since, how-ever, he cannot distinguish, as we have seen, between the "external-ized" form of activity and its "alienated" manifestations, and since it is inconceivable to negate "externalization" without negating the absolute condition: activity itself, his concept of "Aufhebung" cannot be other than an abstract, *imaginary* negation of alienation as objectification. Thus Hegel, in the end, assigns the same characteristic of untranscendable absoluteness and universality to the alienated form of objectification as to activity itself and there-fore he conceptually nullifies the possibility of an actual supersession of alienation. (It goes without saying that a form, or *some* form of *externalization*—i.e. objectification itself—is as absolute a condition of development as activity itself : a non-externalized, non-objectified activity is a non-activity. In this sense *some kind* of mediation of the absolute ontological condition of man's interchange with nature is an equally absolute necessity. The question is, however, whether this mediation is in *agreement* with the objective ontological character of productive activity as the fundamental condition of human existence or *alien* to it, as in the case of capitalistic second order mediations.)

Marx draws the conceptual line of demarcation between LABOUR as "Lebensäusserung" (manifestation of life) and as "Lebensentäusserung" (alienation of life). LABOUR is "Lebensentäusserung" when "I work in order to live, in order to produce a means to living, but my work itself is not living", i.e. my activity is forced upon me "by an external necessity" instead of being motivated by a need corresponding to an "inner necessity".[131]

In the same way, Marx makes the distinction between an *adequate* mediation of man with man on the one hand and "*alienated* mediation" of human activity through the intermediary of things on the other hand. In the second type of mediation—"in the alienation of the *mediating activity itself*" (indem der Mensch diese *vermittelnde Tätigkeit selbst* entäussert)—man is active as a "dehumanized man" (entmenschter Mensch). Thus human productive activity is under the rule of "an *alien mediator*" (fremder Mittler)—"instead of *man himself* being the *mediator for man*" (statt dass der Mensch selbst der Mittler für den Menschen sein sollte) and consequently labour assumes the form of an "*alienated mediation*" (entäusserte Vermittlung) of human productive activity.[132]

Formulated in these terms, the question of "Aufhebung" ceases to be an imaginary act of the "Subject" and becomes a concrete, practical issue for real man. This conception envisages the super-session of alienation through the abolition of "alienated mediation" (i.e. of capitalistically institutionalized second order mediation), through the liberation of labour from its reified subjection to the power of things, to "external necessity", and through the conscious enhancing of man's "inner need" for being humanly active and finding fulfilment for the powers inherent in him in his productive activity itself as well as in the human enjoyment of the non-alienated products of his activity.[133]

With the elaboration of these concepts—which fully master the mystifying complexity of alienation that defeated no less a dialectician than Hegel himself—Marx's system *in statu nascendi* is virtually brought to its accomplishment. His radical ideas concerning the world of alienation and the conditions of its supersession are now coherently synthesized within the general outlines of a monumental, comprehensive vision. Much remains, of course, to be further elaborated in all its complexity, for the task undertaken is "Titanenartig". But all further concretizations and modifications of Marx's conception—including some major discoveries of the older Marx—are realized on the conceptual basis of the great philosophical achievements so clearly in evidence in the *Economic and Philosophic Manuscripts of 1844.*

III. *Conceptual Structure of Marx's Theory of Alienation*

1. *Foundations of the Marxian System*

LEGENDS are easily invented and difficult to dispose of. An empty balloon (sheer ignorance of all the relevant evidence) and a lot of hot air (mere wishful thinking) is enough to get them off the ground, while the persistence of wishful thinking amply supplies the necessary fuel of propulsion for their fanciful flight. We shall discuss at some length, in the chapter which deals with *The Controversy about Marx*, the main legends associated with the *Economic and Philosophic Manuscripts of 1844*. At this point, however, we have to deal, briefly, with a legend that occupies a less prominent place in the various interpretations in an explicit form, but which has, none the less, a major theoretical importance for an adequate assessment of Marx's work as a whole.

The *Manuscripts of 1844*, as we have seen, lay down the foundations of the Marxian system, centred on the concept of alienation. Now the legend in question claims that Lenin had no awareness of this concept and that it played no part in the elaboration of his own theories. (In the eyes of many dogmatists this alleged fact itself is, of course, ample justification for labelling the concept of alienation "idealist".)

If Lenin had really missed out Marx's critique of capitalistic alienation and reification—his analysis of "alienation of labour" and its necessary corollaries—he would have missed out the core of Marx's theory: the *basic* idea of the Marxian system.

Needless to say, nothing could be further from the truth than this alleged fact. Indeed the very opposite is the case: for in Lenin's development as a Marxist his grasp of the concept of alienation in its true significance played a vital role.

It is an irrefutable fact that *all* of Lenin's important theoretical works—including his critique of *Economic Romanticism* as well as his book on *The Development of Capitalism in Russia*—postdate his detailed *Conspectus of The Holy Family*, written in *1895*. The central ideas expressed in this *Conspectus* in the form of comments remained in the centre of Lenin's ideas in his subsequent writings. Unfortunately there is no space here to follow the development of Lenin's thought in any detail. We must content ourselves with focusing attention on a few points which are directly relevant to the subject of discussion.

It is of the greatest significance in this connection that in his *Conspectus of The Holy Family* Lenin quotes a long passage from this early work and comments upon it as follows :

> "This passage is highly characteristic, for it shows how Marx approached the *basic idea of his entire 'system'*, sit venia verbo, namely *the concept of the social relations of production*".[134]

Little matters whether or not one puts, half-apologetically, in inverted commas the word "system". (Lenin, understandably, had to do this because of the customary polemical references to "system-building", associated, in Marxist literature, with the Hegelian philosophy. Besides, he was writing the *Conspectus* of a book highly critical of the Hegelian system and of the uses to which it had been put by the members of "The Holy Family".) What is vitally important in this connection is the fact that "the basic idea of Marx's entire system"—"the concept of the social relations of production"— is precisely his concept of alienation, i.e. the Marxian critical demystification of the system of "labour's self-alienation", of "human self-alienation", of "the practically alienated relation of man to his objective essence", etc., as Lenin correctly recognized it. This we can clearly see if we read the passage to which Lenin's comment refers :

> "Proudhon's desire to abolish non-owning and the old form of owning is exactly identical to his desire to abolish the *practically alienated relation of man to his o b j e c t i v e   e s s e n c e*, to abolish the p o l i t i c a l - e c o n o m i c expression of *human self-alienation*. Since, however, his criticism of political economy is still bound by the premises of political economy, the reappropriation of the objective world is still conceived in the political-economic form of p o s s e s s i o n. Proudhon indeed does not oppose owning to non-owning, as Critical Criticism makes him do, but p o s s e s s i o n to the old form of owning, to p r i v a t e   p r o p e r t y. He declares possession to be a 's o c i a l   f u n c t i o n'. In a function, 'interest' is not directed however toward the 'exclusion' of another, but toward setting into operation and realizing my own powers, the powers of my being. Proudhon did not succeed in giving this thought appropriate development. The concept of 'e q u a l possession' is a political-economic one

and therefore itself still an *alienated expression* for the principle that the o b j e c t   as   b e i n g   f o r   m a n, as the o b j e c t i v e   b e i ŋ g   o f m a n, is at the same time the e x i s t e n c e   o f   m a n   f o r   o t h e r m e n, *his   h u m a n   r e l a t i o n   t o   o t h e r   m e n, t h e   s o c i a l   b e - h a v i o u r   o f   m a n   i n   r e l a t i o n   t o   m a n.* Proudhon `abolishes political-economic   *estrangement*   w i t h i n   political-economic *estrangement.*"[185]

Those who are sufficiently acquainted with the *Economic and Philo- sophic Manuscripts of 1844* will not fail to recognize that these ideas come from the *Paris Manuscripts.* In fact not only these pages but many more in addition to them had been transferred by Marx from his *1844 Manuscripts* into *The Holy Family.* The Russian Com- mittee in charge of publishing the collected works of Marx, Engels and Lenin—the same Committee which finds "idealist" the *Manu- scripts of 1844*—acknowledged in a note to Lenin's *Conspectus of The Holy Family* that Marx "considerably increased the initially conceived size of the book by incorporating in his chapters parts of his economic and philosophical manuscripts on which he had worked during the spring and summer of 1844".[136] Lenin could not read, of course, Marx's *Manuscripts of 1844*, but in his *Conspectus of The Holy Family* he quoted a number of important passages, in addition to the one on Proudhon, which originated in the *Economic and Philosophic Manuscripts of 1844* and which deal with the prob- lematics of alienation.[137]

If, then, Marx's *Manuscripts of 1844* are idealistic, so must be Lenin's praise of their central concept—incorporated from them into *The Holy Family*—as "the basic idea of Marx's entire system". And this is not the worst part of the story yet. For Lenin goes on praising this work (see his article on Engels) not only for containing *"the foundations of revolutionary materialist socialism"* but also for being written *"in the name of a real, human person".*[138] Thus Lenin seems to "capitulate" not only to "idealism", confounding it with "revolutionary materialist socialism", but—*horribile dictu*—to "humanism" as well.

Needless to say, this "humanism" of writing "in the name of a real, human person" is simply the expression of the "standpoint of labour" that characterizes the *Manuscripts of 1844.* It expresses— in explicit polemics against the fictitious entities of idealist philosophy —the critically adopted standpoint of "the worker, trampled down by the ruling classes and the state";[139] the standpoint of the pro- letariat in its opposition to the "propertied class" which "feels happy

and confirmed in this self-alienation, it recognizes a s i t s o w n
p o w e r", whereas "the class of the proletariat feels annihilated in
its self-alienation; it sees in it its own powerlessness and *the reality
of an inhuman existence*".[140] This is what Lenin, and Marx, had in
mind when they spoke of the "real, human person". However, no
amount of textual evidence is likely to make an impression on those
who, instead of really "reading Marx" (or Lenin, for that matter),
prefer reading *into* the classics of Marxist thought their own legends,
representing—under the veil of a high-sounding verbal radicalism
—the sterile dogmatism of bureaucratic-conservative wishful thinking.

As Lenin had brilliantly perceived, the central idea of Marx's
system is his critique of the capitalistic reification of the social
relations of production, the alienation of labour through the reified
mediations of WAGE LABOUR, PRIVATE PROPERTY and EXCHANGE.

Indeed Marx's general conception of the historical genesis and
alienation of the social relations of production, together with his
analysis of the objective ontological conditions of a necessary supersession of alienation and reification, constitute a system in the best
sense of the term. This system is not *less* but *more* rigorous than the
philosophical systems of his predecessors, including Hegel; which
means that any omission of even one of its constituent parts is bound
to distort the *whole* picture, not just one particular aspect of it. Also,
the Marxian system is not *less* but far *more* complex than the Hegelian one; for it is one thing ingeniously to invent the logically appropriate "mediations" between "thought-entities", but quite another
to identify in reality the complex intermediary links of the multifarious social phenomena, to find the laws that govern their institutionalizations and transformations into one another, the laws that
determine their relative "fixity" as well as their "dynamic changes",
to demonstrate all this in reality, at *all* levels and spheres of human
activity. Consequently any attempt at reading Marx not in terms
of his own system but in accordance with some preconceived, plati-
tudinous "scientific model" fashionable in our own days, deprives
the Marxian system of its revolutionary meaning and converts it
into a dead butterfly-collection of useless pseudo-scientific concepts.

It goes without saying that Marx's system is radically different
from the Hegelian one. Not only as regards the opposition between
the actual social phenomena, depicted by Marx, and the Hegelian
"thought-entities", but also in that the Hegelian system—due to its

internal contradictions—had been *closed* and ossified by Hegel himself, whereas the Marxian system remains *open-ended*. We shall return to the discussion of this vitally important difference between a closed and an open system in the last section of this chapter. But first we have to consider the structure of the Marxian system as a whole, in order to gain a clearer understanding of its manifold complexities.

On the face of it, the *Economic and Philosophical Manuscripts of 1844* are critical commentaries on Hegel and on the theories of political economists. A closer look, however, reveals much more than that. For the critique of these theories is a vehicle for developing Marx's own ideas on a great variety of closely interconnected problems.

As has been mentioned, the system we can perceive in the *Economic and Philosophic Manuscripts of 1844* is a system *in statu nascendi*. This can be recognized, above all, in the fact that the basic ontological dimension of labour's self-alienation does not appear in its universality until the very end of this work, i.e. in the section on *money*. As a matter of fact this section had been written *after* Marx's critical examination of the Hegelian philosophy in the same manuscript, although in the published versions the latter is put to the end (in accordance with Marx's wishes). And this is by no means a negligible point of chronological detail. Indeed Marx's profound assessment of the Hegelian philosophy as a whole—made possible by his analysis of political economy which enabled him to recognize that "Hegel's standpoint is that of modern political economy" (152)—puts into Marx's hands the key to unlocking the ultimate ontological secret of the "money-system", thus enabling him to embark on a comprehensive elaboration of a materialist dialectical theory of value. (Compare this part of the *Manuscripts of 1844*, in concreteness as well as in comprehensiveness notwithstanding its limited size, with a work that tackles the same problematics: Marx's *Comments* on James Mill's *Elements of Political Economy*, written shortly before his *Critique of the Hegelian Dialectic and Philosophy as a Whole*, probably in May or June 1844.[141]) It is by no means accidental that a substantial part of these pages on *The Power of Money* had been subsequently incorporated by Marx in his *Capital*.

But even if this general ontological dimension of labour's self-alienation is not rendered explicit until the very end of the *Economic and Philosophic Manuscripts of 1844*, it is implicitly there, though of course at a lower level of generalization, almost right from the beginning. At first it is present in this system *in statu nascendi* only as a vague intuition and, accordingly, Marx's method of analysis is more *reactive* than *positive* and self-sustaining : he lets his hand be guided by the problematics of the immediate subject of his criticism, namely the writings of political economists.

As his insights accumulate (through his gradual realization that the partial aspects : "worker as a commodity", "abstract labour", "one-sided, machine-like labour", "earth estranged from man", "stored-up human labour = dead capital", etc. point in the same direction) the originally adopted framework proves to be hopelessly narrow and Marx casts it aside.

From the discussion of *Estranged Labour* (67) onwards Marx follows a different plan : the centre of reference of every single issue is now the concept of "alienated labour" as the "essential connection" between the whole range of estrangements "and the m o n e y-system" (68). And yet, although this programme is there in the last section of the *first* manuscript, it is not fully realized until the very end of the *third* manuscript. In this latter Marx is able at last to demystify the "money-system"—this ultimate mediator of all alienated mediations, this "p i m p between man's need and the object, between his life and his means of life" (137), this "visible divinity" (139)—as "the alienated a b i l i t y o f *m a n k i n d*" (139), as "the external, common m e d i u m and f a c u l t y of turning an i m a g e into r e a l i t y and r e a l i t y into a mere i m a g e (a faculty not springing from man as man or from human society as society)" (140), as "the existing and *active concept of value . . . the general c o n f o u n d i n g and c o m p o u n d i n g of all things—* the world upside down . . . the *fraternization of impossibilities"* which *"makes contradictions embrace"* (141). And all this in the context of explaining the "truly o n t o l o g i c a l affirmations of essential being (of nature)" (136), "the *ontological* essence of human passion" (136), and "the e x i s t e n c e of e s s e n t i a l o b j e c t s for man, both as objects of *enjoyment* and as objects of *activity"* (137).

Thus Marx's system *in statu nascendi* is accomplished when he clearly realizes that although the money-system reaches its climax with the capitalistic mode of production, its innermost nature cannot be understood in a limited historical context but in the broadest ontological framework of man's development through his labour, i.e. through the ontological self-development of labour via the necessary intermediaries involved in its necessary self-alienation and reification at a determinate stage (or stages) of its process of self-realization.

2. Conceptual Framework of Marx's Theory of Alienation

The difficulties of Marx's discourse in his *Manuscripts of 1844* are not due merely to the fact that this is a system *in statu nascendi* in which the same problems are taken up over and over again, at an increasingly higher level of complexity, in accordance with the emergence and growing concretization of Marx's vision as a whole—though of course this is one of the main reasons why people often find this work prohibitively complicated. Some of its major difficulties, however, are inherent in Marx's method in general and in the objective characteristics of his subject of analysis.

Marx investigates both the *historical* and the *systematic-structural* aspects of the problematics of alienation in relation to the dual complexities of "real life" and its "reflections" in the various forms of thought. Thus he analyses :

(1) the manifestations of labour's self-alienation in reality, together with the various institutionalizations, reifications and mediations involved in such a practical self-alienation, i.e. WAGE LABOUR, PRIVATE PROPERTY, EXCHANGE, MONEY, RENT, PROFIT, VALUE, etc., etc.;

(2) the reflections of these alienations through religion, philosophy, law, political economy, art, "abstractly material" science, etc.;

(3) the interchanges and reciprocities between (1) and (2); for "the gods in the beginning are not the cause but the effect of man's intellectual confusion. Later this relationship becomes reciprocal" (80);

(4) the inner dynamism of any particular phenomenon, or field of enquiry, in its development from a lesser to a higher complexity;

(5) the structural interrelations of the various social phenomena with each other (of which the reciprocity between (1) and (2) is only a specific type) as well as the historical genesis and renewed dialectical transformation of this whole system of manifold interrelations;

(6) a further complication is that Marx analyses the particular theories themselves in their concrete historical embeddedness, in addition to investigating their structural relations to each other at

a particular time (e.g. Adam Smith the political economist compared to Adam Smith the moral philosopher; at the same time the types of answers given by Adam Smith—both as an economist and as a moralist—are situated historically, in relation to the development of capitalism in general).

As we can see, then, the main difficulties we experience in reading the *Economic and Philosophic Manuscripts of 1844*, with the exception of those due to their being a system *in statu nascendi*, are expressions of Marx's efforts directed at adequately dealing with the mystifying complexities of his subject of analysis on the basis of concrete empirical enquiry in place of mere philosophical abstraction.

In the course of his analysis of the various theoretical reflections of actual human self-alienation Marx makes the general point that :

> "It stems from the very nature of estrangement that each sphere applies to me a *different and opposite yardstick*—ethics one and political economy another; for each is a specific estrangement of man and focuses attention on a *particular round of estranged essential activity,* and each stands in an *estranged relation* to the other. Thus M. Michel Chevalier reproaches Ricardo with having abstracted from ethics. But Ricardo is allowing political economy to speak its own language, and if it does not speak ethically, this is not Ricardo's fault" (121).

Thus he emphasizes that the contradictions we encounter in these fields are necessarily inherent in the structural relation of the various disciplines of thought to each other and to a common determinant which paradoxically makes them oppose each other. But how is such a paradoxical relationship possible? How does this double alienation come about?

Before we can make an attempt at elucidating Marx's enigmatic answers to these far from easy questions, we have to embark on a journey back to some fundamentals of Marx's discourse.

Marx's immediate problem is : why is there such a gulf between philosophy and the natural sciences? Why does philosophy remain as alien and hostile to them as they remain to philosophy? This opposition is absurd because :

> "natural science has invaded and transformed human life all the more p r a c t i c a l l y through the medium of industry; and has prepared human emancipation, however directly and much it had to

consummate dehumanization. I n d u s t r y is the actual historical relation of nature, and therefore of natural science, to man. If, therefore, industry is conceived as the e x o t e r i c revelation of man's e s s e n t i a l p o w e r s, we also gain an understanding of the h u m a n essence of nature or the n a t u r a l essence of man. In consequence, natural science will lose its *abstractly material*—or rather, its *idealistic*—tendency, and will become the *basis of h u m a n science*, as it has already become the basis of actual human life, albeit in an estranged form. O n e basis for life and another basis for s c i e n c e is *a priori* a lie. The nature which comes to be in human history—the genesis of human society—is man's r e a l nature; hence *nature* as it comes to be *through industry*, even though in an e s t r a n g e d *form*, is true a n t h r o p o l o g i c a l *nature*" (110-111).

From this quotation it becomes clear that in his criticism of philosophy Marx is not led by some misconceived ideal of remodelling philosophy on *natural* science. Indeed he sharply criticizes both philosophy and the natural sciences. The first for being "speculative" and the latter for being "abstractly material" and "idealistic". In Marx's view both philosophy and the natural sciences are manifestations of the same estrangement. (The terms "abstractly material" and "idealistic" indicate that natural science is now "in an estranged form" the basis of "actual human life", because of the fact that it is necessarily interconnected with an alienated form of industry, corresponding to an alienated mode of production, to an alienated form of productive activity.) This is why Marx opposes to *both* "speculative philosophy" and to "abstractly material, idealistic natural science" his ideal of a *"h u m a n science"*.

What Marx means by "h u m a n science" is a science of concrete synthesis, integrated with real life. Its standpoint is the ideal of non-alienated man whose *actual human*—as opposed to both "speculatively invented" and to practically dehumanized, "abstractly material"—needs determine the line of research in every particular field. The achievements of the particular fields—guided right from the beginning by the common frame of reference of a non-fragmented "human science"—are then brought together into a higher synthesis which in its turn determines the subsequent lines of investigations in the various fields.

This conception of "human science", in its opposition to "abstractly material and idealistic" natural science, is obviously directed against the fragmentation and "unconscious", alienated determination of science. Many instances of the history of science testify that the extent to which certain fundamental lines of research are carried out are greatly determined by factors which lie, strictly speaking, far beyond the boundaries of natural science itself. (To take a topical example: there can be no doubt whatever that *automation* is at least as fundamentally a *social* problem as a *scientific* one.) The lines of research actually followed through in any particular age are necessarily *finite* whereas the lines of *possible* research are always virtually *infinite*. The rôle of social needs and preferences in scaling down the infinite to the finite is extremely important. However—and this is the point Marx is making—in an alienated society the process of scaling down itself, since it is "unconsciously" determined by a set of alienated needs, is bound to produce further alienation : the subjection of man to increasingly more powerful instruments of his own making.

The structure of scientific production is basically the same as that of fundamental productive activity in general (all the more because the two merge into one another to a considerable extent): a lack of control of the productive process as a whole; an "unconscious" and fragmented mode of activity determined by the inertia of the institutionalized framework of the capitalistic mode of production; the functioning of "abstractly material" science as a mere *means* to predetermined, external, alienated ends. Such an alienated natural science finds itself between the Scylla and Charibdis of its "autonomy" (i.e. the idealization of its "unconscious", fragmentary character) and its subordination as a mere *means* to external, alien ends (i.e. gigantic military and quasi-military programmes, such as lunar flights). Needless to say, the subjection of natural science as a mere means to alien ends is by no means accidental but necessarily connected with its fragmented, "autonomous" character, and, of course, with the structure of alienated productive activity in general. Since science develops in a fragmented, compartmentalized framework, it cannot conceivably have overall aims which, therefore, have to be imposed on it from outside.

Philosophy, on the other hand, expresses a twofold alienation of the sphere of speculative thinking (1) from all practice—including the, however alienated, practice of natural science—and (2) from other theoretical fields, like political economy, for instance. In its speculative "universality" philosophy becomes an "end in itself" and "for itself", fictitiously opposed to the realm of means : an abstract reflection of the institutionalized alienation of means from ends. As a radical separation from all other modes of activity philosophy appears to its representatives as the only form of "species-activity", i.e. as the only form of activity worthy of man as a "universal being". Thus instead of being a universal dimension of all activity, integrated in practice and in its various reflections, it functions as an independent ("verselbständigt") "alienated universality", displaying the absurdity of this whole system of alienations by the fact that this fictitious "universality" is realized as the most esoteric of all esoteric *specialities*, strictly reserved for the alienated "high priests" (the "Eingeweihten") of this intellectual trade.

If the "abstractly material" character of the particular natural sciences is linked to a productive activity fragmented and devoid of perspectives, the "abstractly contemplative" character of philosophy expresses the radical divorce of theory and practice in its alienated universality. They represent two sides of the same coin: labour's self-alienation manifest in a mode of production characterized by Marx and Engels as "the unconscious condition of mankind".

This takes us back to our original problem. Why is it that the different theoretical spheres apply "a different and opposite yardstick" to man? How is it possible that though both philosophy and political economy express the same alienation, their "language" is so different that they cannot communicate with each other?

In order to simplify these matters to some extent, let us try and illustrate, however schematically, the structural interrelationship of the principal concepts involved in Marx's theory of alienation. (Schematic illustrations of this kind are always problematical because they have to express in a fixed, "two-dimensional" form the complexity of dynamic interchanges. It must be stressed, therefore, that they are not meant to be substitutes for an adequate conceptual understanding but merely a visual aid towards it.)

The fundamental terms of reference in Marx's theory of alienation are "man" (M), "nature" (N), and "industry" or "productive activity" (I). For an understanding of "the h u m a n essence of nature or the n a t u r a l essence of man" (110) the concept of "productive activity" (or "industry"—used from now on for the sake of brevity) is of a crucial importance. "Industry" is both the *cause* of the growing complexity of human society (by creating new needs while satisfying old ones: "the first historical act is the *production of new needs*"[142]) and the *means* of asserting the supremacy of man—as "universal being" who is at the same time a unique "specific being"—over nature. In considering Marx's views we have to remember that when he applies the term "actual" (*wirklich*) to man he either equates it with "historical" (110), or simply implies historicity as a necessary condition of the human predicament. He wants to account for every aspect of the analysed phenomena in inherently historical terms, which means that nothing can be taken for granted and simply assumed as an ultimate datum. On the contrary, the whole theory hinges on the proof of the historical *genesis* of all its basic constituents. Accordingly, Marx pictures the relationship between "man" (M), "nature" (N), and "industry" (I) in the form of a *threefold interaction* between its constituent parts. This can be illustrated as follows:

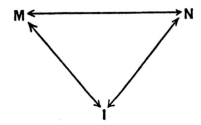

As we can see, here we have a dialectical *reciprocity* (indicated by the double-ended arrows) between all three members of this relationship which means that "man" is not only the *creator* of industry but also its *product*. (Similarly, of course, he is both product and creator of "truly anthropological nature"—above all in himself, but also outside him, insofar as he leaves his mark on nature. And since man's relation to nature is mediated through an alienated form of productive activity, "anthropological nature" outside man bears the marks of this alienation in an ever-extending form, graphically demonstrated by the intensity of *pollution* that menaces the very existence of mankind.)

Talking about this process of reciprocal interaction, Marx calls it the "genesis of human society". At the same time he designates the two main aspects of industry's fundamental (first order) mediating function by the expressions "n a t u r a l essence of man" and "h u m a n essence of nature" (110). His expression: "man's r e a l nature"—as opposed to man's biological or animal nature—is meant to embrace both aspects and thus to define *human nature* in terms of a necessarily *threefold* relationship of dialectical reciprocity. Man's biological or animal nature, by contrast, can only be defined in terms of a *twofold* relationship, or, to put it the other way round, picturing the basic ontological situation merely in terms of a two-fold relationship, between "Man" and "Nature", would only account for the characteristics of man's biological-animal nature. For human consciousness implies already a specific human relation to "industry" (taken in its most general sense as "productive activity"). One of the basic contradictions of theories which idealize the *unmediated* reciprocity between "Man" and "Nature" is that they get themselves into the impasse of this animal relationship from which not a single feature of the dynamism of human history can be derived. Then, in an attempt to get rid of this contradiction—in order to be able to account for the specifically human character-istics—they are forced to assume a "ready-made human nature", with all the *apriorism* and *theological teleologism* that necessarily go with such a conception of philosophy.

Rousseau's conception, *mutatis mutandis*, belongs to the latter category, though in a paradoxical way. For in the most generic terms Rousseau is aware of the ludicrous character of idealizing nature. He stresses that : "he who wants to preserve, in civil society, the primacy of natural feelings, has no idea of what he wants. Always standing in contradiction to himself, always oscillating between his inclinations and his duties, he will be neither a man nor a *citoyen*; he will be good neither for himself nor for others. He will be one of those people of our age; a Frenchman, an English-man, a *bourgeois* : a *nothing*."[143] And yet, this insight never induces Rousseau to elaborate a genuinely historical account of man and his relationships. On the contrary, despite his insights he continues to operate with the fictitious notion of "preserving man's original constitution".[144] (It must be emphasized that his idealization of a—hierarchical—*family* as the *anthropological model* of "natural" relations—opposed to the system which produces an "artificial being"—proves to be a major drawback in his analyses.) Even if he recognizes the irrevocable remoteness of the "original" direct unity—in Hegelian terms the inherently *past* character of "Er-*innerung*" as opposed to the *present* actuality of "Ent-*äusserung*"—he continues, unlike Hegel, to postulate it, often in a negative form, in his senti-mental negation of "civilization". In Rousseau's conception "industry" (civilization) exercizes an essentially *disruptive* function, by putting an end to a "natural" relationship. Such an interpretation may enable the philosopher to grasp certain contradictions of a given stage of society, but it does not allow him to indicate a solution that could stand the test of actual historical development. "Industry" (civilization) comes into the picture as something *"evil"*, even if Rousseau recognizes, nostalgically, that it cannot be done away with. Thus his system, at its very foundations, is profoundly *ahistorical*. It can be illustrated in contrast to Marx's conception as follows:

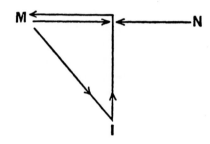

As we can see, there is a kind of "short circuit" in this account, and the one-sided interaction between man and industry results in the tragic negativity of divorcing or alienating man from nature. (It would be interesting to inquire into the relationship between Rousseau's conception of man and nature and the Kantian notion of *"das Böse"*—"evil"—and in general the Kantian philosophy of history, its tragic vision of man.) Since the fundamental ontological relations are pictured by Rousseau in these terms, his educational ideal of preserving the "original" substance of humanness by cultivating the "naturally good" in man, is bound to remain not only utopian but also tragically hopeless. The "short-circuit" produces a "vicious circle" which cannot be broken except by the unwarranted assumption of a "ready-made" educator. Rousseau himself is conscious of the problematic character of such a construction but, given his fundamental concepts, he cannot do anything against it. "The more we reflect the more we recognize the growing difficulties. For the educator *ought to have been* educated for his pupil; the servants ought to have been educated for their masters, so that all those who are in the pupil's vicinity would communicate to him the right things; one should go backwards from education to education up to I do not know which point. Otherwise how could one expect the proper education of a child from someone who himself had not been properly educated? Is it impossible to find such a rare mortal? [An adequately educated educator.] I do not know. In this age of moral decadence who knows the height of virtue of which the human soul is still capable? But *let us assume* that we have found this prodigy. From considering what he *ought* to do we can find out what he *ought to be* like."[145]

Being is thus derived from *ought* in order to serve as the pivotal point of this whole system of postulates opposed to the actuality of "civilization". Since the foundation of all historicity—which is also the only possible ground of an "education of the educator"—is negated, the educator must be fictitiously assumed and assigned the unreal function of protecting the "natural being" from the temptations of civilization, money, sophistication, etc., thus educationally rescuing him from the perspectives of becoming an "artificial being". The tragic utopianism of this whole approach is manifest in the all-pervasive contradiction that while Rousseau *negates* the ontologically fundamental mediation of man and nature through "industry" (not only in his explicit polemics against "civilization" but primarily by postulating "natural man") he positively *affirms* the alienated mediations of this mediation (1) by idealizing the alleged anthropological primacy of a rigidly hierarchical family; (2) by postulating an—equally hierarchical—system of education in which "the servant is educated for the master", and "everyone is educated for his own station" etc., and in which the educator is miraculously "set above" the rest of society; and (3) by asserting the atemporal nature and ideal necessity of the capitalistically institutionalized second order mediations—"fair and advantageous exchange", the eternal permanence of "meum" and "tuum", etc.— as we have seen already. No wonder, therefore, that the overall impression of Rousseau's conception is a *static* one, adequately expressed in the tragic pathos of a revolt condemned to inertia and impotence. A pathos expressing the unfavourable configuration of a set of contradictions, perceived and depicted from a specific socio-historical standpoint by this great philosopher and writer.

Marx's approach is radically different. He is not talking simply about man's alienation from "nature" as such, but about man's alienation from *his own* nature, from "anthropological nature" (both within and outside man). This very concept of "man's own nature" *necessarily implies* the ontologically fundamental self-mediation of man with nature through his own productive (and self-producing) activity. Consequently "industry" (or "productive activity") as such, acquires an essentially *positive* connotation in the Marxian conception, rescuing man from the theological dilemma of "the fall of man".

If such an essentially positive rôle is assigned to "industry" in the Marxian conception, how then can we explain "alienation" as "self-alienation", i.e. as the "alienation of labour", as the "alienation of human powers from man through his own productive activity".

To anticipate, briefly, the central topic of the next chapter insofar as is necessary in this connection, let us draw up a comparative diagram. Let (M) stand for "man", (P) for "private property and its owner", (L) for "wage labour and the worker", (AN) for "alienated nature",[146] and (AI) for "alienated industry" or "alienated productive activity", then we can illustrate the changed relationships as follows :

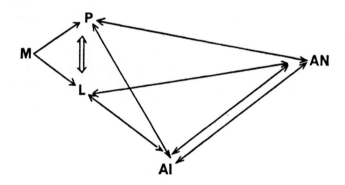

Here, as a result of "labour's self-alienation"—the objectification of productive activity in the form of "alienated labour" (or "estranged essential activity", to use another of Marx's expressions)—we have a multiplicity of basic interrelations :

(1) (M) is split into (P) and (L);

(2) (P) and (L) antagonistically oppose each other;

(3) the original (M) ↔ (I) ↔ (N) reciprocity is transformed into the alienated interrelationships between :

(a) (P) ↔ (AI) ↔ (AN) and
(b) (L) ↔ (AI) ↔ (AN).

Furthermore, since now everything is subordinated to the basic antagonism between (P) and (L), we have the additional alienated interrelations of :

(4) (P) ↔ (L) ↔ (AI) and
(5) (P) ↔ (L) ↔ (AN).

In these sets of relationships in which the second order mediations of (P) and (L) have taken the place of "man" (M), the concepts of "man" and "mankind" may appear to be mere philosophical abstractions to all those who cannot see beyond the direct immediacy of the given alienated relations. (And they are indeed abstractions if they are not considered in terms of the socio-historically concrete forms of alienation which they assume.) The disappearance of "man" from the picture, his practical suppression through the second order mediations of (P) and (L)—(we had to omit the other institutionalized second order mediations, e.g. EXCHANGE, MONEY, etc., partly because they are already implied in (P) and (L), and partly in order to simplify the basic interrelations as far as possible) —means not only that there is a *split* now at every link of these alienated relationships but also that LABOUR can be considered as a mere *"material fact"*, instead of being appreciated as the *human* agency of production.

The problem of the reflection of this "reification" in the various theoretical fields is inseparable from this double mediation, i.e. from the "mediation of the mediation". The political economist gives a "reified", "fetishistic" account of the actual social relations of production when, from the standpoint of idealized PRIVATE PROPERTY (P) he treats LABOUR (L) as a mere material fact of production and fails to relate both (P) and (L) to "man" (M). (When Adam Smith, as Marx observes, starts to take "man" into account, he leaves immediately the ground of political economy and shifts to the speculative viewpoint of ethics.)

Now we are in a better position for understanding Marx's assertion according to which each theoretical sphere applies a different, indeed opposite yardstick to man, and "each stands in an estranged relation to the other". For if the foundation of theoretical generalizations is not the fundamental ontological relationship of (M) ↔ (I) ↔ (N) but its *alienated form*: the reified "mediation of the mediation"—i.e. (M) ↔ (P) ↔ (L) ↔ (AI) ↔ (AN)—then political economy, for instance, which *directly* identifies itself with the standpoint of private property, is bound to formulate its discourse in terms of (P) and (L), whereas ethics, in accordance with its own position which coincides only *indirectly* with "the standpoint of political economy" (i.e. the standpoint of private property), will speculatively oppose the abstract concept of "Man" to (P) and (L). The fact that both disciplines approach, from different— though only methodologically, not socially different—points of view, the same complex phenomenon, remains hidden from the representatives of both speculative, moralizing philosophy and empiricist political economy.

We could illustrate the respective positions of Ethics, Political Economy, and the "abstractly material" Natural Sciences in relation to the alienated and reified social relations of production like this :

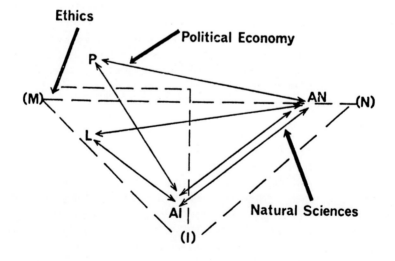

As we can see, the "language" of Political Economy and Ethics— not to mention the Natural Sciences—cannot be common because their central points of reference are far from being the same.[147] Political Economy's points of reference are (P) ↔ (AN) ↔ (L) and (P) ↔ (AI) ↔ (AN), whereas Ethics (and, *mutatis mutandis*, speculative philosophy in general) has for its centre of reference abstract "Man" (or its even more abstract versions, like "World Spirit" etc.), depicted in his relations with "Nature" and "Industry" or "Civilization" more often than not in a Rousseau-like fashion, with all the apriorism and transcendentalism involved in it. (The points of reference of the Natural Sciences are, of course, (AN) and (AI), in their dual orientation towards nature, or "basic research", on the one hand, and towards productive technology, or "applied science", on the other. Intensified "alienation of nature"—e.g. *pollution*—is unthinkable without the most active participation of the Natural Sciences in this process. They receive their tasks from "alienated industry", in the form of capitalistic "targets of production"— i.e. targets subordinated to the "blind natural laws" of the market— irrespective of the ultimate human implications and repercussions of the realization of such tasks.)

Moreover, as Marx emphasizes, the idealization of abstract "Man" is nothing but an alienated, speculative expression of the (P) ↔ (L) relationship. The nature of the actual relationships is such that adequately to comprehend them it is necessary to assume a radically critical attitude towards the system of alienations which "externalizes" (or "objectifies") man in the form of "alienated labour" and "reified private property". "Real man"—the "real, human person"—does not actually exist in a capitalist society except in the alienated and reified form in which we encounter him as "Labour" and "Capital" (Private Property) antagonistically opposing each other. Consequently the "affirmation" of "man" must proceed via the *negation* of the alienated social relations of production. Speculative philosophy, however, does not *negate* the (P) ↔ (L) ↔ (AI) ↔ (AN) relationship but merely *abstracts* from it. And through its abstract concept of "Man" which ignores the basic antagonism of society: the actuality of (P) ↔ (L), speculative philosophy depicts the alienated social relations of production—in accordance with its own specific ideological function—in a "sublimated" fashion, transforming the "palpable reality" of actual social contradictions into a fictitious, and *apriori* insoluble, opposition between the "realm of here and now" and its "transcendental" counterpart.

It is clear from the Marxian account that the various theoretical spheres reflect—in a necessarily alienated form, corresponding to a set of specific alienated needs—the actual alienation and reification of the social relations of production. They all focus attention "on a particular round of estranged essential activity" (i.e. political economy on the reproduction of the economic cycle of production; speculative philosophy on "spiritual activity" and on the norms regulating human behaviour, in its most general terms; and the "abstractly material" natural sciences on the conditions of a direct interchange between man and nature) and they stand "in an estranged relation to each other".

Since neither political economy nor speculative philosophy have a real awareness of the social dynamism inherent in the antagonism between private property and labour—and precisely because they cannot possibly recognize the objective character of this antagonism as one "hastening to its annulment"—their systems must remain *static*, corresponding to the necessarily ahistorical standpoint of private property which they represent, directly or indirectly. Viewed from such a standpoint they can only perceive—at best— the *subjective* aspect of this basic contradiction : the direct clash of individuals over "goods" or "property", but they cannot grasp the *social necessity* of such clashes. Instead they either interpret them as manifestations of "egoistic *human nature*"—which amounts to an actual defence of the position of private property under the semblance of a "moral condemnation" of "human egoism"—or, more recently, treat these clashes as problems of a "lack of communication", as tasks for a "human engineering", aiming at devising methods for a minimization of "conflicts about property", in order to ensure the continued existence of the alienated social relations of production.

Marx, by contrast, grasps this whole complexity of interrelated concepts at their strategic centre : the *objective* social dynamism of the contradiction between PROPERTY and LABOUR. He recognizes that "human life required private property for its realization" (134) because "only through developed industry—i.e. through the *medium* of private property—does the *ontological essence* of human passion come to be both in its totality and in its humanity" (136). Alienation, reification, and their alienated reflections are therefore socio-historically *necessary* forms of expression of a fundamental ontological relationship. This is the "positive aspect" of labour's self-alienation.

At the same time Marx emphasizes the negative aspect as well. The latter is directly displayed in the social contradiction between PRIVATE PROPERTY and LABOUR : a contradiction which, however, cannot be perceived from the standpoint of private property, nor from that of a spontaneous identification with labour in its partiality, but only from the critically adopted standpoint of labour in its self-transcending universality. In Marx's eyes the increasing evidence of an irreconcilable social antagonism between private property and labour is a proof of the fact that the ontologically necessary phase of labour's self-alienation and reified self-mediation—"through the medium of private property" etc.—is drawing to its close. The intensification of the social antagonism between private property and labour demonstrates the innermost contradiction of the given productive system and greatly contributes to its disintegration. Thus human self-objectification in the form of self-alienation loses its relative historical justification and becomes an indefensible social anachronism.

Ontological necessity cannot be realistically opposed except by another ontological necessity. Marx's line of reasoning—in stressing the *relative* (historical) necessity of self-alienation as well as the disruptive *social anachronism* of self-objectification as self-alienation at a later stage of development—establishes "Aufhebung" (the transcendence of alienation) as a concept denoting *ontological necessity*. Marx argues that what is at stake is the *necessity* of an *actual* supersession of the earlier indispensable but by now increasingly more paralysing (therefore historically untenable) reification of the social relations of production. In this respect, too, his theory brings a radical break with the views of his predecessors who could picture "transcendence" either as a mere *moral postulate* (a "Sollen") or as an abstract *logical requirement* of a speculative scheme devoid of practical relevance.

As to the transcendence of alienation in the theoretical fields, it must be clear from what has been said so far that Marx's ideal of a "human science" is not meant to be a programme of remodelling philosophy and the humanities on the natural sciences. Not only because the latter are also specific forms of alienation but, above all, because we are concerned here with a practical, not with a theoretical issue. For whatever model we may have in mind as our ideal of philosophical activity, its applicability will depend on the totality of social practice which generates, in any particular socio-

historical situation, the practicable intellectual needs not less than
the material ones. The realization of Marx's ideal of a "human
science" presupposes, therefore, the "self-sustaining" (*"positive"*)
existence of such—non-alienated—needs in the social body as a
whole. Marx's formulation of the ideal itself, by contrast, corresponds to the needs of *negating*—under their theoretical aspects—
the totality of the existing social relations of production. "Human
science", therefore, becomes a reality to the extent to which
alienation is *practically* superseded and thus the totality of social
practice loses its fragmented character. (In this fragmentation
theory is opposed to practice and the particular fields of "estranged
essential activity"—both theoretical and practical—oppose each
other.) In other words, in order to realize "human science" philosophy, political economy, the "abstractly material" natural sciences,
etc., must be *reciprocally integrated* among themselves, as well as
with the totality of a social practice no longer characterized by the
alienation and reification of the social relations of production. For
"human science" is precisely this *dual integration*—in transcendence
of the earlier seen *dual alienation*—of the particular theoretical
fields (1) among themselves and (2) with the totality of a non-
alienated social practice.

The "übergreifendes Moment" (overriding factor) of this complex
is, of course, the supersession of alienation in social practice itself.
Since, however, alienated social practice is already integrated, in an
"inverted" and alienated form, with "abstractly material" science
and speculative philosophy, the actual transcendence of alienation
in social practice is inconceivable without superseding at the same
time the alienations of the theoretical fields as well. Thus Marx
conceives the actual process of "Aufhebung" as a *dialectical interchange* between these two poles—the theoretical and the practical—
in the course of their *reciprocal reintegration*.

3. *Alienation and Teleology*

As we have seen, both "alienation" and its "Aufhebung" denote
an ontological necessity in the Marxian system. What we have to
consider now is the kind of *teleology* which is at work in the developments depicted by Marx.

Marx is often accused of "economic determinism". He is
supposed to hold the naïve idea according to which economy

determines, mechanically, every aspect of development. Such accusations, needless to say, cannot be taken seriously. For—as has been mentioned already—in Marx's view the first historical act of man is the *creation* of his first new need, and no mechanical determination can conceivably account for that. In Marx's dialectical conception the key concept is "human productive activity" which *never* means simply "economic production". Right from the beginning it is much more complex than that, as Marx's references to *ontology* in fact indicate. We are concerned here with an extremely complicated structure and Marx's assertions about the ontological significance of economics become meaningful only if we are able to grasp the Marxian idea of manifold specific *mediations*, in the most varied fields of human activity, which are not simply "built upon" an economic basis but also actively *structure* the latter through the immensely intricate and relatively *autonomous* structure of their own. Only if we succeed in dialectically grasping this multiplicity of specific mediations can we really understand the Marxian notion of economics. For if economics is the "ultimate determinant", it is also a "determined determinant" : it does not exist outside the always concrete, historically changing complex of concrete mediations, including the most "spiritual" ones. If the "demystification" of capitalistic society, because of the "fetish-character" of its mode of production and exchange, has to start from the analysis of economics, this does not mean in the least that the results of such economic enquiry can be simply transferred to other spheres and levels. Even as regards the culture, politics, law, religion, art, ethics, etc. of capitalistic society one has still to find those complex mediations, at various levels of historico-philosophical generalization, which enable one to reach reliable conclusions both about the specific ideological forms in question and about the given, historically concrete form of capitalistic society as a whole. And this is even more evident if one tries to transfer the enquiry to a more general level, as becomes in fact necessary in the course of the structural analysis of any particular form of society, or of any specific form of human activity. One cannot grasp the "specific" without identifying its manifold interconnections with a given system of complex mediations. In other words : one must be able to see the "atemporal" (systematic) elements in temporality, and the temporal elements in the systematic factors.

"Economic determinism", it goes without saying, negates the

MARX'S THEORY OF ALIENATION

dialectical interrelationship between temporality and atemporality, discontinuity and continuity, history and structure. It opposes to the Marxian dialectical conception a mechanical model in which an atemporal structure of determinations prevails. (Some so-called "structuralist Marxists", with their anti-dialectical rejection of "historicism", are representatives of "vulgar economic determinism", dressed in a culturally fashionable "structuralist" cloth. It was this old trend of "vulgar economic determinism" which made Marx say a long time ago : "I am not a Marxist".) The concept of complex *mediations* is missing from the vision of economic determinists who —however unconsciously—capitulate to "blind economic necessity" which seems to prevail through the fetish-character of capitalism, through the alienation and reification of the social relations of production under capitalism. (The *Geisteswissenschaften* ["sciences of the Spirit"] and—*mutatis mutandis*—their modern structuralist versions are, as regards their fundamental conceptual structure, a mystified form of economic determinism "upside down", insofar as the crucial concept of *mediation* is missing from them. They mirror the immediacy of capitalistic reification, even if in an inverted fashion, asserting the same kind of direct mechanical determinations under "spiritualized" names. Consequently they either display a rigid negation of all historicity, or invent a pseudo-history of the "Spirit", devoid of the objective dialectical transitions and media- tions which characterize a genuine historical account. Significantly enough some "Marxist structuralists" can switch with the greatest ease to and fro between the categories of the *Geisteswissenschaften* and their own pseudo-Marxist—i.e. vulgar economic determinist— concepts.)

Since both "alienation" and "Aufhebung" must be understood, according to Marx, in terms of ontological necessity, a correct historical conception depends on the interpretation of such necessity. Economic determinism as a historical hypothesis is a contradiction in terms because it implies the ultimate negation of history. If history means anything at all, it must be "open-ended". An adequate historical conception must be, therefore, open to the idea of a break of the chain of—"reified", "fetishistic", "blind", etc.—economic determinations. (Indeed a transcendence of alienation is incon- ceivable without the break of this chain.) Such an idea is, needless to say, inadmissible from the view point of economic determinism which must therefore negate history, by taking its own—ahistorical

—standpoint for granted and by turning it into an alleged "permanent structure".

At this point the paradoxical character of Hegel's achievements proves to be particularly instructive. Lukács, in his essay on *Moses Hess*, emphasizes that: "Hegel's tremendous intellectual contribution consisted in the fact that he made *theory* and *history* dialectically relative to each other, grasped them in a dialectical, reciprocal penetration. Ultimately, however, his attempt was a failure. He could never get as far as the genuine unity of theory and practice; all that he could do was either to *fill the logical sequence* of the categories with rich historical material, or *rationalize history*, in the shape of a succession of forms, structural changes, epochs, etc., which he raised to the level of categories by *sublimating and abstracting them*."[148]

What Lukács could not see at the time of writing *History and Class-Consciousness* was the fact that the Hegelian historical conception as a whole—conceived from the necessarily ahistorical "standpoint of political economy" which carried with it the identification of "alienation" and "objectification"—had to be thoroughly ahistorical or, more exactly, pseudo-historical. For no matter how fine and sensitive were Hegel's particular historical insights, because of his ahistorical *assumptions*—i.e. "objectification" = "alienation", etc.—he had to negate history in its totality by assigning to it an "end", in accordance with an *apriori* "goal". It was not the case, therefore, that—in order to complete his system—Hegel inconsistently left the ground of his historical conception but right from the beginning his conception was inherently ahistorical. This is why he *had* to operate with the method of rationalizing history and relativizing the logical sequence of categories. And this is why he had to "deduce" a sublimated human history from the categories of thought, instead of elucidating the latter in terms of the former. (The recognition of a "humanly natural and naturally human" agent of history—necessarily carrying with it a specific objectivity which can only be grasped in terms of a dialectical social ontology—would have prevented him from conveniently putting an end to history at the point of the "reconciliation of the World Spirit" with capitalistic reality anticipated by the Hegelian system from the very moment of its conception.) Thus—however paradoxical this may sound—despite his (abstract) programmatic criticism of "immediacy" Hegel ended up by idealizing the immediacy of the fetishism of capitalism manifest in the *historically determinate* identity of capitalistic objectification and capitalistic alienation.

Human actions are not intelligible outside their socio-historical framework. But human history in its turn is far from being intelligible without a *teleology* of some kind. If, however, the latter is of a "closed", *aprioristic* kind—i.e. all varieties of *theological teleology*—the philosophical system which makes use of such a conception of teleology must be itself a "closed system".

The Marxian system, by contrast, is organized in terms of an inherently historical—"open"—teleology which cannot admit "fixity" at any stage whatsoever. This we can illustrate, briefly anticipating some main points of the subsequent chapters, with reference to two Marxian assertions in particular :

(1) According to Marx all necessity is "*historical* necessity", namely "a *disappearing* necessity" ("eine *verschwindende* Notwendigkeit"[149]). This concept not only makes intelligible the multiple transformations and transitions of social phenomena in terms of historical *necessity* but at the same time it leaves the doors wide open as regards the future development of human society. (More about this in CHAPTER VIII.)

(2) The "goal" of human history is defined by Marx in terms of the *immanence* of human development (as opposed to the *apriori transcendentalism* of theological teleology), namely as the realization of the "human essence", of "humanness", of the "specifically human" element, of the "universality and freedom of man", etc. through "man's establishment of himself by practical activity" (136) first in an alienated form, and later in a positive, self-sustaining form of life-activity established as an "inner need". Man as the "self-mediating being of nature" must develop—through the objective dialectics of an increasingly higher complexity of human needs and aims—in accordance with the most fundamental objective laws of ontology of which—and this is vitally important—man's own active mediatory rôle is an essential part. Thus the Marxian system remains open because in this account the very "goal" of history is defined in inherently historical terms, and not as a fixed target. In Marx's account history remains open in accordance with the specific ontological necessity of which self-mediating human teleology is an integral part : for there can be no way of predetermining the forms and modalities of human "*self*-mediation" (whose complex teleological conditions can only be satisfied in the course of this self-mediation itself) except by arbitrarily reducing the complexity of

human actions to the crude simplicity of mechanical determinations. Nor can there be a point in history at which we could say : "now the human substance has been fully realized". For such a fixing would deprive the human being of his essential attribute : his power of "self-mediation" and "self-development".[150]

PART II

ASPECTS OF ALIENATION

But the exercise of labour power, labour, is the worker's own life-activity, the manifestation of his own life. And this life-activity he sells to another person in order to secure the necessary means of subsistence. Thus his life-activity is for him only a means to enable him to exist. He works in order to live. He does not even reckon labour as part of his life, it is rather a sacrifice of his life. It is a commodity which he has made over to another. Hence, also, the product of his activity is not the object of his activity. What he produces for himself is not the silk that he weaves, not the gold that he draws from the mine, not the palace that he builds. What he produces for himself is wages, and silk, gold, palace resolve themselves for him into a definite quantity of the means of subsistence, perhaps into a cotton jacket, some copper coins and a lodging in a cellar. And the worker, who for twelve hours weaves, spins, drills, turns, builds, shovels, breaks stones, carries loads, etc.— does he consider this twelve hours' weaving, spinning, drilling, turning, building, shovelling, stone-breaking as a manifestation of his life, as life? On the contrary, life begins for him where this activity ceases, at table, in the public house, in bed. The twelve hours' labour, on the other hand, has no meaning for him as weaving, spinning, drilling, etc., but as earnings, which bring him to the table, to the public house, into bed. If the silk worm were to spin in order to continue its existence as a caterpillar, it would be a complete wage-worker.

—Wage-Labour and Capital

IV. *Economic Aspects*

1. *Marx's Critique of Political Economy*

THE general character of a work is determined by its writer's standpoint. It is important to ask, therefore, what is Marx's standpoint when he analyses the various aspects of alienation. It is relevant here, that Marx had reproached Proudhon with having criticized political economy from the standpoint of political economy, thus ending up with the contradiction of abolishing political-economic estrangement *within* political-economic estrangement.[151] Likewise Marx characterized Hegel as having the standpoint of modern political economy (154).

The problem of the philosopher's standpoint, as regards alienation, is identical, in the final analysis, to the problem of his attitude towards the *supersession* (Aufhebung) of alienation. To share "the standpoint of political economy" means to be unable to work out in concrete terms the conditions of an actual supersession. And to supersede alienation "w i t h i n political-economic alienation" means not to supersede it at all.

When Marx writes about alienation, he is careful to distinguish his position from the utopian criticism of political economy. In fact he had criticized Proudhon as early as the eighteen forties for his inability to detach himself from the utopian approach to the category of property of the French socialists like Saint-Simon and Fourier.[152] We shall soon see the concrete economic problems involved in Proudhon's utopianism as criticized in Marx's *Manuscripts of 1844*. It was Proudhon's inability to solve these problems that made him adopt contradictorily, in spite of his explicit programmatic intentions, the standpoint of political economy "in a roundabout way".[153]

Why had Marx to oppose the standpoint of political economy?

Basically because it was in contradiction to the historical approach that could envisage the supersession of alienation.

Marx characterizes the position of political economy as one based on a "fictitious primordial condition". This fictitious primordial condition is a fallacious line of reasoning: in this case it exhibits

123

the characteristic of a *petitio principii*. The political economist "*assumes* in the form of fact, of an event, what he is supposed to *deduce*—namely the necessary relationship between two things—between, for example, division of labour and exchange. Theology in the same way explains the origin of evil by the fall of man; that is, it *assumes as a fact*, in historical form, *what has to be explained*" (68–69). Fallacies of this kind pervade the history of thought. Their varieties are determined by the particular character of the disregarded concrete historical interconnections. (Some neglect or ignore the existing relations; others assert non-existing connections; others again reverse the order of the actual interrelations, etc.)

Here we see a good example of a basic characteristic of Marxian thought; namely that the historical approach to everything is at the same time a substantiation of the categories of logic in concrete, historical terms. In this sense *petitio principii* is nothing but a *relational determination* which excludes the question of the concrete historical *becoming* (Werden) by *assuming* an a priori being (Sein), in order to explain away the difficulties and contradictions of a *determinate being* (bestimmtes Dasein).

On this account no relation or social fact—which is, by definition, a relation—can be accepted as given. Everything specific, everything that has a form (since every particular form expresses a specific *relation* to its *content*) must be explained in terms of *becoming*, and so no primordial condition can be assumed. This is why Marx starts out by defining the historically primary relationship between man and nature as *nature's relation to itself*, on the grounds that man is a specific part of nature. Even as regards nature itself, without a concrete historical reference nothing more can be asserted than that it is identical with itself, whereas the assertion of the part-whole relationship (man as a specific part of the totality of nature) requires an inherently historical conception.

In order to define man as a specific part of nature, one must have not only a comprehensive historical conception of nature itself, which accounts for the possibility, indeed necessity, of differentiation within nature (a necessity dependent on the generation of conditions incompatible with the previous state of affairs), but also a particular factor which necessitates a *peculiar form of differentiation* that results in the intrinsic man-nature relationship.

The factor that involves this peculiar form of differentiation (that is the one which reformulates the part-whole relationship in this way: man, a specific part of nature) is "industry", "purposive activity", "essential life-activity". In this sense the concept of activity (labour) is logically (and historically) *prior* to the concept of man. But this priority is, of course, a *relative* one, for all three members of this dialectical relationship belong to the same complex whole, and none of them can be abstracted from it without destroying this specific relationship as such.

Marx opposes to the approach of the political economist,[154] which has at its point of departure the logical structure of a *petitio principii*, a method of proceeding "from an a c t u a l economic fact". And this fact is that "Labour produces not only commodities: *it produces itself and the worker as a c o m m o d i t y*—and does so in the proportion in which it produces commodities generally" (69).

This point about labour producing itself and the worker as a commodity is of the utmost importance for the understanding of Marx's position on the question of supersession. Since the very foundation of human existence and of all human attributes is the purposive productive activity which has, as we have seen, a relative priority over the concept of man, if one cannot present labour in a historical framework, showing the actual process in which purposive productive activity *becomes* wage-labour (or "alienated labour"), one has no ground for envisaging a supersession.

Marx formulates this point very clearly in *Capital* when he writes: "It is clear that capital presupposes labour as wage-labour. But it is just as clear that *if labour as wage-labour is taken as the point of departure*, so that the identity of labour in general with wage-labour appears to be self-evident, then capital and monopolized land must also appear as the *natural* form of the conditions of labour in relation to labour in general. To be capital, then, appears as the natural form of the means of labour and thereby as the purely real character arising from their function in the labour-process in general. *Capital and produced means of production thus become identical terms.* . . . Labour as such, in its simple capacity as *purposive productive activity, relates to the means of production, not in their social determinate form*, but rather in their concrete substance, as material and means of labour; . . ."[155]

As we see, Marx's concept of "alienated labour" (or wage-labour) is inseparable from his idea that the *social determinate form* of the productive activity which obtains the "i n c r e a s i n g v a l u e of the world of things" at the price of the "d e v a l u a t i o n of the world of men" is one that can be superseded.

Marx's interest in problems of political economy is directly related to this question of supersession. He emphasizes that "the entire revolutionary movement necessarily finds both *its empirical and its theoretical basis* in the movement of p r i v a t e p r o p e r t y—in that of *economy*, to be precise" (102), and most of the criticism the young Marx directs against his political comrades concerns their relation to the problem of a practical transcendence of human alienation.

One of the most important passages on this point, in the *Manuscripts of 1844*, reads as follows: "This m a t e r i a l, immediately s e n s u o u s private property is the material sensuous expression of e s t r a n g e d h u m a n life. Its movement—production and consumption—is the s e n s u o u s revelation of the movement of all production hitherto—i.e. the realization or the reality of man. Religion, family, state, law, morality, science, art, etc., are only p a r t i c u l a r modes of production, and fall under its general law. The positive transcendence of p r i v a t e p r o p e r t y as the appropriation of h u m a n life is, therefore, the positive transcendence of all estrangement—that is to say, the return of man from religion, family, state, etc., to his h u m a n, i.e. s o c i a l mode of existence. Religious estrangement as such occurs only in the realm of c o n s c i o u s n e s s, of man's inner life, but economic estrangement is that of r e a l l i f e; its transcendence therefore embraces both aspects" (102–103).

It is self-evident that one cannot fight estrangement of real life— that is, economic estrangement—without mastering in theory the complex economico-social problems involved in it. But the kind of economic investigations that Marx envisages make no sense whatsoever unless one's attitude to the question of "practice" is essentially the same as his. Thus Marx's criticism here is directed not only against the representatives of speculative philosophy, but also against those who, like Feuerbach, are only capable of conceiving practice in its "dirty-judaical form of appearance".[156]

On the other hand the attempts of the *"piecemeal reformers"* (30) at formulating their views in economico-institutional form is also condemned to futility, because the reformer aims at an improvement *within* the given structure, and by the means of the same structure, and is therefore subject to the very contradictions which he intends to counteract or neutralize.

To Marx, in contradistinction to the reformer, economic investigations do not serve as theoretical grounds of an *economic* action, but of a *political* one. He is interested in problems of economy only insofar as they reveal the complex hierarchy of the structure that he wants to see positively transcended. He wants to unveil not the *"weak"* points of the capitalist system (which were anyway quite obvious, because of their striking human repercussions, to many moralist critics well before Marx), but its *strong* ones. Those which converge into the outcome he calls *"movable property's civilized victory"* (91) i.e. the victory of early capitalism over feudalism.

Marx's economic investigations helped him to discover the internal contradictions of the economic force that resulted in this "civilized victory", and so to open up the field for action of a quite different kind. Different, because an *economic action* could only alleviate the contradictions of a dynamic force—the one behind movable property's civilized victory—which is itself *economic* in character.

This is why Marx objects so strongly, already in the *Manuscript of 1844*, to Proudhon's approach to the matter. He writes: "The diminution in the interest on money, which Proudhon regards as the annulling of capital and as the tendency to socialize capital, is really and immediately . . . only a symptom of the victory of working capital over extravagant wealth—i.e. the transformation of all private property into industrial capital. It is a total victory of private property over all those of its qualities which are still in a p p e a r a n c e human, and the complete subjection of the owner of private property to the essence of private property—l a b o u r. . . . The decrease in the interest-rate is therefore a symptom of the annulment of capital only inasmuch as it is a symptom of the rule of capital in the process of perfecting itself—of the estrangement in the process of becoming fully-developed and therefore of hastening to its annulment. This is indeed the only way in which that which exists affirms its opposite" (127–128).

As we see, the standpoint of this economic analysis is not an economic but a *political* one, and everything culminates in the reference to the "process of becoming fully-developed", interpreted as a hastening of estrangement to the point at which it is annulled.

Indeed the question of a positive transcendence can only be put in *political* terms so long as the society which is thought of as an actual supersession of the one criticized is still to be born. It is a characteristic of politics (and, naturally, of aesthetics, ethics, etc.,) to *anticipate* (and thus to further) future social and economic developments. Politics could be defined as the *mediation* (and, with its institutions, as a means of this mediation) between the *present and future* states of society. Its categories, accordingly, exhibit the character appropriate to this mediating function, and references to the future are therefore an integral part of its categories. (Conservative politics exhibits just as much as radical politics the characteristics of this mediating function. Only its categories are less explicit and the positive stress is, of course, on defining its relation to the present. The conservative kind of political mediation tries to maximize the element of continuity in its attempts at linking the present with the future whereas radical politics, of course, lays the emphasis on discontinuity.)

Economics, by contrast, has no such function of mediation and therefore cannot operate with categories of the future. If it does, it necessarily becomes *utopian politics* (or utopian social philosophy) disguised as political economy.

From this it follows that "supersession" cannot be envisaged in purely economic terms but in *politically, morally, aesthetically,* etc. qualified categories. Marx's treatment of the subject is by no means an exception in this respect. He can only use economic categories when he analyses the existing social form of productive activity. When it comes to the question of "positive transcendence", "supersession" etc., he uses expressions like "the complete e m a n c i p a t i o n of all human senses and attributes" (106). We can note not only that the point has very strong *moral* overtones, but also the fact that the key word—*emancipation*—underlined by Marx himself, is a specifically political term.

The term—applied by Marx to characterize "supersession"—which comes the nearest to the categories of economics is "association" (63–64). But precisely because of its comprehensive, all-embracing character, it cannot be other than a general political principle envisaged as the centre of reference of a future socialist economy. And to define its character as a *socialist* economic principle it must be related to specifically political and moral issues. (Such as "equality", "emancipation of all human senses and attributes", "earth as personal property of man" etc.) "Association" can be of various kinds and in its economic references, as used by Marx indicates only :

(1) something that already belongs to the existing economic structure (e.g. "economic advantage of large-scale landed property");

(2) a *negativity* (i.e. that "association" is a guarantee against economic crises).

It is through the references to political and moral issues that the category of "association" acquires its Marxian meaning—in sharp contrast to the possible corporative interpretation and application of the term—which makes it suitable to become the basic principle of socialist economics. (This is one of the main reasons behind the Marxian method of analysis which closely relates the economic issues to the political, moral, etc., ones. Even the aesthetic problems, as we shall see in Chapter VII, are analysed in a manner that puts into relief their interconnections with the most general economic and political issues, and thus help to substantiate the specifically socialist character of the solutions envisaged to these general formulations.) However if one disrupts the link between the political, moral and economical aspects of these issues then in view of the above-mentioned reasons they lose their Marxian socialist character, and their relevance to a positive transcendence of alienation becomes extremely doubtful.

Marx's procedure is, thus, to start out from an *economic analysis* conceived as the theoretical basis of an envisaged *political action*. This does not mean, however, that he identifies "transcendence" with this political action. On the contrary, he often emphasizes that the alienation of productive activity can only be ultimately overcome in the *sphere of production*. Political action can only create the general conditions which are not identical with, but are a necessary *prerequisite to* the actual supersession of alienation. The concrete process of supersession itself lies in the future, well ahead of the period of political action that establishes the conditions which are necessary for the process of positive transcendence to get started. How far that process lies in the future, cannot be said, because it depends upon so many conditions, including that of scientific development. Anyway there can be little doubt about it that the old Marx located this process of positive transcendence in an even more distant future than the young one.[157]

If we compare this conception to that of Proudhon, it becomes clear that what is missing from the latter is the *intermediary link* necessary to create the prerequisites of a positive transcendence. The *utopian* character of Proudhon's philosophy is determined by the lack of this intermediary link, just as the theological character of Rousseau's concept of man is determined by his negative attitude to the necessary mediation (Industry, or "civilization") between man and nature, that is, by the lack of this mediating link in his concept of the "natural state".

Proudhon envisages a direct *economic measure* to tackle the negative aspects of the given situation, and thus in the final analysis he dissolves politics into utopian economics. Because of this identification of politics with economic action he must locate the process of supersession in the present or immediate future, and also must operate with the categories of political economy.

This is what Marx calls "abolishing political-economic estrange-ment w i t h i n political-economic estrangement". Since in the wages of labour "labour does not appear as an end in itself but as the servant of the wage", Proudhon's idea of "forcing-up of wages", Marx argues, solves nothing. For "even the e q u a l i t y o f w a g e s demanded by Proudhon only transforms the relationship of the present-day worker to his labour into the relationship of all men to labour. *Society is then conceived as an abstract capitalist.* Wages are a direct consequence of estranged labour, and estranged labour is the direct cause of private property. The downfall of the one aspect must therefore mean the downfall of the other" (81).

This whole criticism leads later to the conclusion that the appropriation of capital by the community does not mean an end to alienation. For even if the community owns capital and the principle of equality of wages is carried through, insofar as the community is no more than a community of *labour* (that is, wage-labour), the whole relation of estrangement survives in a different form. In this new form, labour is raised to an "i m a g i n e d universality" (100), but does not conquer the human status and dignity, "does not appear as an end in itself", because it is con-fronted by another imagined universality: "the c o m m u n i t y as the universal capitalist". Only if this relation of being confronted by a power outside oneself, which is the same thing as not being an end in oneself, is superseded, may one speak of a positive transcendence of alienation.

2. *From Partial to Universal Alienation*

As we have already mentioned, the young Marx wants to find out the secret of "movable property's civilized victory". Political economy guides him in this enterprise. He often acknowledges and praises the merits of classical political economy, because he sees in it a successful attempt at investigating the actual relations of production in modern society. In *Capital*, Marx calls the categories of political economy "forms of thought expressing with social validity the conditions and relations of a definite, historically determined mode of production, viz., the production of commodities",[158] and this judgment is in complete agreement with his assessment of political economy in the *Economic and Philosophic Manuscripts of 1844.*

The point about movable property's civilized victory refers both to the actual socio-economic development and to political economy, as conceptualizing the laws of this development. According to Marx the important achievement was to treat *human labour* as "the source of wealth" (91). He describes the development of political economy in terms of its degree of awareness of the fact that labour is the source of wealth. In this sense he distinguishes four stages in the development of political economy, the first two of which are very closely connected:

(1) monetary system;
(2) mercantile system;
(3) physiocracy;
(4) liberal political economy.

Following the young Engels, he calls Adam Smith the Luther of Political Economy (93–94) and, in contradistinction, the adherents of the monetary and mercantile system are called "idolators, fetishists, Catholics" (93), and elsewhere "fetish-worshippers of metal-money" (123). Physiocracy provides a link between the first two and the fourth stage in the development of political economy, insofar as it achieves "the dissolution of feudal property in political economy", while at the same time it accomplishes feudal property's "metamorphosis and restoration in political economy, save that now its language is no longer feudal but economic" (95–96).

The fourth stage, identified in the first place with the work of Adam Smith, not only unveils the fetishism of the monetary and mercantile system, but also supersedes the inconsistencies and the one-sidedness of physiocracy, by extending to the entire field of economy the principle of labour as the universal source of wealth. To use Marx's words in characterizing the achievement of liberal political economy as contrasted with physiocracy, "labour appears

at first only as a g r i c u l t u r a l labour; but then asserts itself as
l a b o u r in general" (97).

What does all this mean with respect to alienation?

The answer is given at once when we consider that one cannot
even discuss alienation if one remains in the realm of fetishism.
Fetishism, in Marx's use of the term, means in this connection
simply to view wealth as something outside man and independent
of him : as something that possesses the character of absolute
objectivity.

If it does possess this character of absolute objectivity, then it is
of course "sacrosanct". It is important to remember in this context
that the first great controversial issues, connected with alienation,
at the end of the Middle Ages, were "alienability of land" and
interest obtained through lending money without the "alienation of
capital". If the source of wealth—in this case land—possesses such
absolute objectivity, then obviously it cannot be alienated And
"movable property's civilized victory" could not become real without
defeating this view. On the other hand movable property also
needed a kind of stability, although an entirely different one from
the "non-alienability of land". This new kind of *dynamic* stability
was asserted by pressing for the legitimacy of profit "*without* the
alienation of capital" : an essential condition of accumulation. As
a consequence, many heretics were condemned, or even burned by
the Catholic Church for maintaining that profit upon lending without alienation of capital was not a sin, let alone a capital sin.
Significantly enough a representative of physiocracy, the French
politician and economist Turgot, as late as the sixties of the
eighteenth century, had to defend the adherents of this "heretical"
view.[159]

To consider wealth only as an external object, and not as a
specific manifestation of human relations, means that the problem
of alienation cannot even be raised beyond the generality—and at
the same time the absoluteness—of "the fall of man". And it is only
appropriate that once wealth (the product of human efforts) acquires
this character of absolute objectivity, then the other side of the
relationship—human nature as manifest in the various kinds of
human activity—also appears under the aspect of absoluteness and
metaphysical eternity. This is graphically expressed in the concept
of the fall of man, often implicitly assumed as the foundation of
theoretical explanations related to this matter.

Physiocracy represents a stage in the development of political economy when this appearance of absoluteness is questioned as regards both sides of the relationship. Human activity is considered as the source of wealth, for it is recognized that land has no value in and by itself but only in connection with human labour. (This is what is meant by the rather obscure Marxian expression that "the subjective essence of wealth has already been transferred to labour" (96).) On the other hand activity is defined in concrete terms, as *agriculture*, and only in this specific form is acknowledged as the source of value.

However in a definition of wealth-producing activity in this *specific* form, as Marx says, "*labour is not yet grasped in its generality and abstraction*: it is still bound to a particular n a t u r a l   e l e m e n t   a s   i t s   m a t t e r, and it is therefore only recognized in a   p a r t i c u l a r   m o d e   o f   e x i s t e n c e   d e t e r- m i n e d   b y   n a t u r e. It is therefore still *only a s p e c i f i c, particular alienation of man*, just as its product is conceived only as a specific form of wealth, due more to nature than to labour itself. The land is here still recognized as a phenomenon of nature independent of man—not yet as capital, i.e. as an aspect of labour itself. Labour appears, rather, as an aspect of the l a n d. But since the *fetishism* of the old external wealth, of wealth existing only as an object, has been reduced to a very simple natural element, and since—even if only partially and in a particular form—its essence has been recognized within its subjective existence, there is the necessary step forward in that *the g e n e r a l   n a t u r e   o f wealth has been revealed* and that l a b o u r has therefore in its total absoluteness (i.e. its abstraction) been raised and established as the p r i n c i p l e" (96).

This revelation of the general nature of wealth and the establish- ing of labour "in its total absoluteness and abstraction" (that is to say, irrespective of its specific forms within the given mode of production) as the universal principle of production and develop- ment, nevertheless, has not been accomplished by the representatives of physiocracy, but by those of the next stage: liberal political economy.

Physiocracy could not realize that *agriculture*, as the particular form, has to be subsumed under the universal one: *industry* (that is, productive activity in general), and its comprehensive manifesta- tion at the given historical stage, *wage-labour*. This is why physiocracy, unlike liberal political economy, could not completely detach itself from the old fetishism.

Obviously the fact that the major representatives of physiocracy are to be found in France, and not in England, is inseparable from the general state of French economy in the eighteenth century, characterized by the young Marx as the economy of a "not yet fully developed money-nation". And here we can see again a concrete instance of Marx's method of grasping in a unity the socio-historical and systematic-structural elements.

It is in the context of fetishism—taken as an example to illustrate a general point—that Marx emphasizes the intimate interrelation between theory and social practice. After contrasting a France "still dazzled by the sensuous splendour of precious metals" with the fully developed money-nation, England, he writes that "the extent to which the solution of theoretical riddles is the task of practice, just as true practice is the condition of a real and positive theory, is shown, for example, in fetishism" (123). And he analyses in the same spirit the previous stages of socio-economical and theoretical development.

Alienation, in his account, is already inherent in feudal relations, for landed property is the basis of the dominion of private property. Feudal landed property is considered as a particular manifestation of alienation because the fact that land is possessed by a few great lords means that earth is estranged from man in general and confronts him as an alien power.

Once land is monopolized then, from the point of view of developing industry, the great issue is obviously the alienability of land. But in this general sense in which earth is the first condition of man's existence, land is, of course, absolutely *inalienable* from *man*. In fact feudal ideology (contemporary to conditions in which land is already alienated by a *group* of men), could not assert its standpoint in terms of "man", but only in terms of its own *partiality*. This partiality then had to be elevated above the rest of society, by the claim of *divine* ascendancy. The claimed divine ascendancy gave it a form of legitimacy, even if a fictitious one. Since, however, the claim of divine ascendancy directly justified the absolute rule of a *partial* position, there was no need for an appeal to the concept of "man" in feudal ideology. Nor was there any room for it.

The concept of "man" was popularized by those who fought feudal power and its ideology. What is paradoxical, however, is that in the writings of these anti-feudal thinkers the concept of man is not put forward to *negate* alienation, but to *affirm* and sustain it, although in a different form. They affirmed and sustained the principle of alienation and alienability in a *universal* form, extending its realm over every aspect of human life, including *"self-alienation"* and *"self-alienability"*. And this they did in the name of "man".

This universalization of the principle of alienation and alienability carries with it, naturally, the notion of *equality*, in the sense that follows.

We have to remember here that according to Marx the original tendency inherent in the division of land is equality (64). And elsewhere he says that "The political economist reduces everything (just as does politics in its *Rights of Man*) to man i.e. to the individual whom he strips of all determinateness so as to class him as capitalist or worker" (129). This concept of man, in its political or economic form, is, of course, not short of asserting, even if only abstractly, the principle of equality. Land is alienable because we all belong to the general class of "man", and in this sense we are all equal. (If, however, possession of land were of divine ascendancy, nobody could advocate its alienability. Nor could they challenge the social hierarchy that goes with the dogma of non-alienability of land.)

Yet no sooner is this equality asserted, it is already denied, because the concept of alienation and alienability implies *exclusion*. In fact the form in which land can be alienated is necessarily one that transfers the *rights of possession*—though not in principle, as in feudal ideology, but *de facto*—to a limited number of people. At the same time—again not in principle, but in a practice necessarily implied in the notion of alienability—the rest of the population is *excluded* from the possession of land.

Thus the concrete form in which the principle of equality is realized is formal-legalistic: the possession of equal rights to have the Rights of Man. That is to say, if the idea of equality is related to the *right of possession* it is necessarily transformed into the abstract formal principle of *possession of rights*. In other words: it is deprived of its content.

The abstractness and formal-legalistic character of "The Rights of Man" is determined by the irreconcilable contradiction between content and form: the new *partiality* of motivating content and the formal *universality* of ideological appeal. This is not a conceptual abstractness that could be removed or improved upon. It is an objectively necessary abstractness, determined by the internal contradictions of a concrete historical situation. It is quite impossible to "demystify" this abstract structure without exposing the contradiction between actual partial content and formally universal ideological appeal. But to do this one needs a socio-historical standpoint very different from that of the original champions of "The Rights of Man".

This is why the assertion of equality as a content (that is, a theory that wants to go beyond the point marked by the abstract formalism of the Rights of Man) must set out from denying alienation and alienability. And for the same reason, this assertion of equality must also oppose all forms of individualistic possession that may imply exclusion.

3. *From Political to Economic Alienation*

In feudal landed property the ties between land and its proprietor are not yet reduced to the status of mere material wealth. As Marx puts it, "The estate is *individualized* with its lord : it has his rank, is baronial or ducal with him, has his privileges, his jurisdiction, his political position, etc. It appears as the *inorganic body* of its lord. Hence the proverb *nulle terre sans maître*, which expresses the fusion of nobility and landed property. Similarly the rule of landed property does not appear directly as the rule of mere capital. For those belonging to it, the estate is more like their fatherland. It is *a constricted sort of nationality*" (61).

This kind of individualization and personification also means that the relation between the owner of land and those working on the estate—his serfs—is predominantly *political*. Consequently its negation must also first take an essentially political form. Accordingly, at the beginning of its development, modern economic thought is still an integral part of politics. Only later, when feudal landed property is defeated and the new mode of production well established, does economic thought acquire the form of an independent science. Then it finds a *specifically economic* equivalent to what was *politically* formulated in the manifestos of the Rights of Man.

The development of political economy, in its reference to the concept of man, takes the course of negating this "constricted sort of nationality". It becomes increasingly clear that political economy aims at a universality, first on a national scale, and then on a cosmopolitan one. Mercantilism has still a predominantly national character. Liberal political economy, however, makes amply clear that its most general laws know no frontiers, and are subject to no limitations.

In this development from partiality to universality, from personification to impersonalization, from political limitations and mediations to economic freedom and immediateness, political economy gradually supersedes the old fetishism and clearly formulates the conditions of unhampered alienation. Thus the development from political partiality to economic universality means that particular or "specific" alienation is turned into one that is universal.

At the beginning of this development we find feudal property, which conceals the fact that the original unity : Man (M) had split in the course of historical development into Property (P) and Labour (L). Feudal property relations conceal this split by means of a *political* mediation. This political mediation creates the false appearance of a unity that historically disappeared ages ago.

Marx, after analysing feudal individualization and personification, as opposed to the later state when "a man is bound to his land, not by his character, but only by his purse-strings", says that it is necessary that the false appearance of unity be abolished, "that landed property, the root of private property, be dragged completely into the movement of private property and that it become a *commodity*; that the rule of the proprietor appear as the *undisguised* rule of private property, of *capital, freed of all political tincture*" (62).

When this is accomplished, the medieval proverb *nulle terre sans maître* automatically loses its validity, and thus the basic relations become characterized, as Marx says, by the newly adopted proverb : *l'argent n'a pas de maître*. It is quite obvious that the proverb *nulle terre sans maître* expresses a directly political relationship, in contradistinction to the later stage when the relationship between (P) and (L) is an essentially *economic* one. It is freed not only of all *political tincture*, but also of all remnants of *personification*.

However, at the beginning of these developments the facts, on one hand, that land is *individualized* and, on the other, that the serf (L) *belongs* to the feudal lord (P), make it appear as if there existed a *unity* of the two. But this "unity" is only an external one. It is not kept alive by an internal cohesive force of a positive economic nature, but by the strength of a political institution, and by the absence (or weakness) of an economic force that could effectively challenge it.

Later, when this economic force becomes stronger within the feudal system, the split appears more and more marked, and the relatively short distance of (P) and (L) from the "political axis" that originally created the impression of a real unity, increases considerably. This could be illustrated as follows:

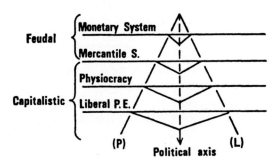

The more this distance increases, the more the old politics loses its mediating power and leaves this function to *money*. Or, to put it in another way: the more money overtakes the mediating function of politics, the more evident becomes the split between property and labour, and the more the power and range of direct politics decreases. (Of course we are talking about a *trend*, and therefore it must be emphasized that direct politics *never* loses completely its mediating power and function.)

In this process of transferring the mediating power of politics to an economic factor landed property is opposed by movable private property, and the liberation of the labourer from his political bonds is accomplished by an alliance between labour and industrial capital. When Marx makes this point, he also points out that the opposition between landed and movable property is not a basic opposition, because they belong to the same category. Landed property in its continuing opposition to capital is nothing but "*private property—capital*—still afflicted with l o c a l and political prejudices; it is capital which has not yet regained itself from its entanglement with the world—*capital not yet f u l l y d e v e l o p e d*. It must in the course of its w o r l d - w i d e d e v e l o p m e n t achieve its abstract, that is its *p u r e expression*" (91).

As we see, Marx's analysis sets out from defining private property as capital, and from this standpoint contrasts one form of private property (landed property) to another (movable property or industrial capital). Only if industrial capital is grasped as the "pure expression" of capital, can private property be defined as capital, and landed property—in its contrast to industrial capital—as "capital not yet fully-developed". Here, again, we can note that the degrees of *logical* complexity and abstraction (from the limited validity of the locally affected form to the universal validity of the "pure expression") correspond to degrees of *historical* maturity.

But why does the development of capital (private property) follow this course, characterized by the well-known contradiction between movable and landed property that eventually leads to movable property's civilized victory? What makes necessary the development of labour as alienated labour in this form?

We would seek in vain for an answer to this question in the *Manuscripts of 1844*. The key to an answer, nevertheless, can be found in a passage of *Capital*, where Marx says that all production of surplus-value has for its *natural basis* the productiveness of *agricultural labour*.[160]

It is self-evident, that no society of even limited complexity can come into existence without the production of basic foodstuffs that exceed the individual requirements of the labourers. But it is equally self-evident that the existence of agricultural surplus-product does not contain any *economic* determination as to the manner of its appropriation. It can be appropriated by a limited group of people, but it can also be distributed on the basis of the strictest equality. Now the point is that the most elementary requirements of the capitalistic mode of production (competition, growth, accumulation, etc.,) prescribe by *economic* necessity a *fixed* relation between production and appropriation (i.e. private ownership).

To render stable the relation between production and appropriation when agricultural surplus-product first becomes available, and to secure in this way the accumulation of wealth as well as to increase the power of the given society, one must have a *political* determination as the fundamental regulative principle of the society in question. What brings this political determination into existence may be, of course, enormously varied, from an outside challenge menacing the life of the community to a favourable geographical location furthering a speedier accumulation of wealth, and its discussion does not belong here. What matters in this connection is :

(1) that the first stage in the development of the alienation of labour must have a *political* form;

(2) that an absolute prerequisite of the genesis of a capitalistic society based on an inherent *economic* principle is the previous existence of a *politically fixed relation* between property and labour, regulating the distribution or allocation of all surplus-product and making accumulation possible. (Without the existence of such a relation—as in the case of egalitarian natural societies—there can be no accumulation and the society is bound to remain a stagnating one.) In other words : an essential prerequisite of *universal* (economic) alienation is the realization of *specific* (politically affected) alienation. Universal alienation logically implies partial alienation, and as we see, also historically alienation first must be political-partial before becoming economic-universal.

4. *Division and Alienation of Labour, Competition and Reification*

The question of alienation is directly related to the issue of surplus-product and surplus-value, and the various phases in the development of political economy are characterized by Marx according to their positions as regards the origin and nature of surplus-value. Here is a comparative table to illustrate their inter-relations and development :

[SEE OPPOSITE PAGE]

Thus the development of political economy from the monetary system to liberal political economy corresponds to the historical development from feudal landed property to industrial capital, and from labour's complete political dependence (serfdom) to politically emancipated industrial labour.

As we can see, liberal political economy is the culmination of this development. Its superiority is recognized by Marx on the ground of the following considerations :

(1) it defines capital as "s t o r e d - u p   l a b o u r" (38);

(2) it points out that the accumulation of capital mounts with the division of labour and that the division of labour increases with the accumulation of capital (131);

Dominant form of property	Dominant form of labour	Corresponding stage of political economy	Its sphere of reference and its view on surplus-value
Landed property that has reached a relatively high degree of accumulation of wealth	Serfdom	Monetary system	Circulation; has no definite view on surplus-value
Commercially interested and colonially expanding— therefore nation-conscious— landed property	Feudally bound labour, making the first steps towards a political emancipation	Mercantile system	Circulation; surplus-value is identified with surplus-money, the balance of trade surplus
By the advancement of commercial capital and by the accomplishments of the manufacture system deeply affected, modernized landed property	Agricultural labour, still submitted to political determinations	Physiocracy	Agricultural production; surplus-value is grasped as the product of agricultural labour, set in motion by rent-yielding property
Industrial capital, freed of all political and natural determinations	Politically emancipated industrial labour (day-labour, wage-labour)	Liberal political economy	Production in general; surplus-value is defined as being produced by labour in general, set in motion by capital

(3) it develops sharply and consistently—however one-sidedly—the idea that labour is the sole essence of wealth (95);

(4) it demolishes the mysticism attached to rent;[161]

(5) it proves that the governing power of modern society is not political, but economic: the purchasing power of capital (37–38); and finally:

(6) it establishes itself as the sole politics and sole universality, making plain its own cosmopolitan character (94–95).

Needless to say that in all the above characteristics the problem of the alienation of labour, directly or indirectly, is involved.

But now we come to a turning-point in the analysis.

We have already seen that liberal political economy detaches itself from the old fetishism. However, according to Marx, it becomes powerless when facing fetishism in a new form, called the fetishism of commodities. This is the point where the historical limitations of liberal political economy come to light.

The main problems we have to consider in this context concern the division of labour and its relation to private property, money-system and the form of value, competition and monopoly.

Marx's principal objection to liberal political economy is that it is unable to prove the assertion that the essence of private property is labour (134). And this question is inseparably connected with the assessment of the nature of the division of labour. The correct assessment is vital to the whole issue of alienation. This is why Marx dedicates so much time to the analysis of the division of labour.

According to Marx the political economists are all in agreement not only in asserting the mutual interrelation between division of labour and accumulation of capital, but also in pointing out that only liberated private property could accomplish a really comprehensive and economically rewarding division of labour. The weakness, however, lies in their attempts at founding the division of labour in *human nature* ("propensity to exchange and barter" Adam Smith). At this point they contradict each other,[162] although in the final analysis all of them maintain that division of labour, based on exchange, is absolutely indispensable to a civilized society.

Marx cannot accept this kind of assessment of the relationship of private property—exchange—division of labour, for an acceptance would amount to admitting that alienation cannot be superseded in reality. He defines division of labour as an economic expression that only applies to the conditions of alienation. In Marx's view the political economists confuse "the social character of labour" (129)—an absolute condition of society—with the division of labour. One can think of superseding alienation precisely because it is possible to oppose the social character of labour to the alienating historical condition of the division of labour. According to Marx, once life-activity ceases to be regulated on the basis of private property and exchange, it will acquire the character of activity of man as a species-being. In other words: the social character of labour will manifest itself directly, without the alienating mediation of the division of labour. As things stand, however, division of labour makes the conditions and powers of life become independent of man and rule over him.[163]

The genesis of the division of labour, as conceived by the political economists, could be illustrated as follows :

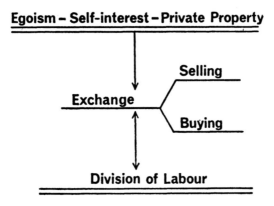

Egoism – Self-interest – Private Property

Selling

Exchange

Buying

Division of Labour

In this view egoism is an absolute condition, not a historical product. It is also identified with private property.[164] At the same time, the mutual interplay is confined to the sphere of exchange and the division of labour. It is recognized that value is produced in the sphere of this mutual interaction, but egoism (private property) is conceived as the absolute condition, indispensable to set in motion the other two.

By contrast, Marx's conception could be schematized like this :

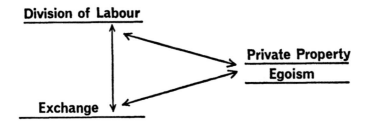

Division of Labour

Private Property
Egoism

Exchange

Here we have a three-way interaction, and egoism is rather the outcome of the interplay than the cause of it.

One of the most important categories of liberal political economy is *competition*, in its radical opposition to monopoly. The young Marx and Engels, however, point out that this opposition is hollow. It is hollow because competition presupposes monopoly: the basic monopoly of private property. On the other hand they also show that only one side of the coin is that competition presupposes monopoly. The other is that monopoly breeds competition and competition turns into monopoly. They distinguish two kinds of competition. *Subjective* competition is between workers and workers on one hand, and capitalists and capitalists on the other. *Objective* or fundamental competition is between workers and property owners.

Competition based on the monopoly of private property[165] goes with a mode of production that appears to be governed by a *natural law*, not the will of the people involved. In this characteristic can one recognize the new type of *fetishism*. (The term fetishism is used in the same sense as before, meaning that the phenomenon in question appears as something outside man, confronting him as an alien power.)

The most important aspects of this mode of production directly relevant to our problem are "reification", "abstract labour", and "imaginary appetites".

Marx quotes with approval the following words of E. Buret, the French economist: "Poverty is not so much caused by men as by the *power of things*" (49). But the power of things to cause poverty is only one aspect of reification. The most important of them is that the worker is made into a *commodity* (69). Marx also points out that the law of supply and demand governs the production of men just as much as of every other commodity (22), and that the worker as a "living Capital" is a special sort of commodity that has the misfortune to be "a capital with needs". But, as a result of the law of supply and demand, the worker's "human qualities only exist in so far as they exist for capital alien to him" (84). This means that human needs can only be gratified to the extent to which they contribute to the accumulation of wealth. The labourer is a commodity because he is reproduced only as a *worker*, and it is in accordance with the needs of private property—needs asserted in the form of the above-mentioned "natural law"—that this reproduction takes place.

Abstract labour is one-sided, machine-like labour, and, of course, it is the result of the division of labour under conditions of competition. Marx defines the factory-system as "the essence of industry—of labour—brought to its maturity" (97). But the price of this maturity is the "reduction of the greater part of mankind to abstract labour" (30), because the conditions of competition under which this maturity is accomplished are alienating. Competition carries with it a rationalization of the production process—in the sense of breaking up complex processes into their simplest elements so that they can be easily executed through competitively advantageous large-scale production—irrespective of its human consequences. The outcome is the duffusion of industrial machinery and the mechanization of human labour.[166] For the worker this means not only that he finds no human satisfaction in his labour because he is "depressed spiritually and physically to the condition of a machine and from being a man becomes an *abstract activity and a stomach*" (25), but also that, since he has "sunk to the level of the machine he can be *confronted by the machine as a competitor*" (26). Paradoxically, the greater the bargaining-power of labour and the higher its price is, the more deeply is it affected by the competitive power of the machine. In the diffusion of automation this is just as important as the technological virtues of the scientific discoveries that made automation possible. Although this last point is not made by Marx, clearly it offers a topical support to his idea that it is impossible to supersede "political-economic alienation within political-economic alienation", i.e. by simply improving the competitive power of labour, by "forcing-up wages", etc.

The question of *"imaginary appetites"* is, of course, very closely connected with the previous two. For, if everything is subordinated to the need of the accumulation of wealth, it is irrelevant whether the needs thus created are properly human, or indifferent, or even dehumanizing needs. Marx writes that "every person speculates on creating a *n e w need* in another, so as to drive him to a fresh sacrifice, to place him in a *new dependence*" and that "the extension of products and needs falls into c o n t r i v i n g and ever-c a l c u l a t i n g subservience to inhuman, refined, unnatural and *i m a g i n a r y appetites*" (115–116).

So, division of labour turns into the opposite of its original sense and function. Instead of liberating man from his dependence on nature, it continues to create new and artificial, unnecessary limitations. Thus, paradoxically, because of the "natural law based on the unconsciousness of the participants", the more private property

—obeying the law of competition—extends its power and realm, supplying commodity-man with a great abundance of commodities, the more everything becomes subjected to a power outside man. And, to make the contradiction even sharper, this applies not only to the worker but also to the owner of private property (126).

5. *Alienated Labour and "Human Nature"*

The whole economic argument culminates in a new concept of man. For, in discussing the crucial problems of the division of labour, Marx radically challenges the account of *human nature* given by the political economists.

We may remember that he praised liberal political economy for having abstracted from the individual appearances of human inter-relations, for having developed sharply and consistently, though one-sidedly, the idea of labour as the sole essence of wealth, and for having incorporated private property in man himself. He praised them because in these achievements they have effectively overcome the limitations of "idolators, fetishists, Catholics". However, these achievements have another side too. Abstracting consistently from the individual appearances carried with it a further estrangement from man. And incorporating private property in man himself amounted to bringing man within the orbit of private property and alienation (94).

Marx is passionately opposed to the attitude of political economy which does not consider the worker "when he is not working, as a *human being*; but leaves such consideration to criminal law, to doctors, to religion, to the statistical tables, to politics and to the workhouse beadle" (30). He objects to the acceptance of reification by political economy under the form of considering labour "in the abstract *as a thing*" (34). He objects to the practice of carrying to the extremes a virtue which first resulted in the supersession of the old fetishism, but then necessarily implied a submission to a new type of fetishism : to fetishism brought to its maturity in its highest, most abstract and universal form (95).

The political economists often emphasize that there is a mutual interaction between the division of labour and the accumulation of capital. However, since they are not interested in the worker as a human being, they are unable to grasp this interrelation in its complexity. Instead of considering all of its main aspects :

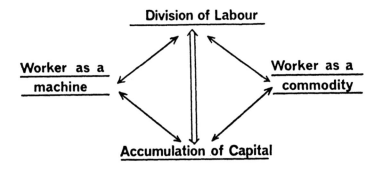

they confine their attention to the division of labour-accumulation of capital relationship. Similarly, they do not consider that labour does not simply produce commodities and value, but also produces itself as a commodity (84–85), as well as the devaluation of the world of men (69).

This abstraction from the human side of these interrelations follows from the basic conception of political economy that *assumes* private property as an essential attribute of human nature. Consequently, political economy cannot "grasp the essential connection between private property, avarice, and the separation of labour, capital and landed property; between exchange and competition, value and the devaluation of men, monopoly and competition, etc.; the connection between this whole estrangement and the m o n e y-system" (68).

Marx indicates *alienated labour* as the essential connection between the whole estrangement and the money-system. Private property is considered only as the *product*, the necessary consequence of alienated labour, that is, "of the external relation of the worker to nature and to himself" (80).

This conclusion is reached on the ground that the worker could not come to face the product of his own activity as a stranger if he were not alienating himself from himself in the very *act of production*. Activity cannot be unalienated activity if its product is alienation; for the product is nothing but the sum of activity, of production (72).

Political economy cannot reach this conclusion. From the standpoint of economics as a special science what matters is, of course, not the assessment of the *human* implications of an objective economic process, but the analysis of the necessary conditions of an undisturbed functioning and reproduction of the given process. This is why the political economist is interested in the conditions of the worker only in so far as these conditions are necessary to production in general, that is to say, in so far as they are the conditions of the *worker*. The political economist, therefore, is only interested in social reforms either because they are necessary to the undisturbed functioning of the cycle of reproduction, or because, as Adam Smith for instance does in some of his works, he writes from the standpoint of moral philosophy, provided it does not conflict with the standpoint of economics. (The idea that egoism is the ultimately decisive factor in human interactions is obviously common to liberal political economy and the leading trend of moral philosophy of the epoch.)

Marx's whole approach is characterized by a constant reference to man as opposed to wage-labourer. This is made possible only because his approach is based on a conception of human nature radically opposed to that of political economy. He denies that man is an essentially *egoistic* being, for he does not accept such a thing as a *fixed* human nature (or, indeed, a fixed anything). In Marx's view man is by nature neither egoistic nor altruistic. He is *made*, by his own activity, into what he is at any given time. And so, if this activity is transformed, today's egoistic human nature will change in due course.

And here we can see how crucially important is the fact that in Marx's theory there is no static element. The complex manifestations of human life, including their objectified and institutional forms, are explained in an ultimate reference to a dynamic principle: *activity* itself. This is in sharp contrast to the conceptions that tried to *deduce* the various characteristics of the given form of society, including private property, from an arbitrarily *assumed* static conception of a fixed human nature. In Marx's view private property and its human consequences have to be historically explained, not assumed or deduced from an assumption. According to Marx private property is called into existence by alienated activity, and then in its turn it does, of course, profoundly affect human aspirations. As Marx writes: "Private property made us so stupid and one-sided that an object is only o u r s when we have it—when it exists for us as capital, or when it is *directly possessed*, eaten, drunk, worn, inhabited, etc.—in short, when it is utilized by us" (106).

This condemnation of "having", as opposed to "being", was not, of course, first voiced by Marx. His approach was directly influenced by the Utopian Socialists, and by Proudhon and Moses Hess. But with him what is new is a coherent insistence on the ultimate foundations of human interrelations, developing in detail the implications of an approach first attempted by the young Engels in his *Outlines of a Critique of Political Economy*.[167]

This approach—whose centre of reference is productive activity or *praxis*—carries with it that what emerges as the "essence of human nature" is not *egoism*, but *sociality*. (i.e. "the *ensemble* of social relations", as Marx puts it in his sixth thesis on Feuerbach.) "Sociality" as the defining characteristic of human nature is radically different from those criticized by Marx. Unlike "egoism", it cannot be an abstract quality inherent in the single individual. It can only exist in the relations of individuals with each other.

By implication, the adequate fulfilment of human nature cannot be *competition*—this "unconscious condition of mankind" that corresponds to egoism and to the Hobbesian *bellum omnium contra omnes*—but *conscious association*. "Activity and consumption"— writes Marx—"both in their content and in their mode of existence, are social: social activity and social consumption; the human essence of nature first exists only for social man; for only here does nature exist for him as a bond with man—as his existence for the other and the other's existence for him—as the life-element of the human world; only here does nature exist as the foundation of his own human existence. Only here has what is to him *his natural existence become his human existence*, and nature become man for him. Thus society is the consummated oneness in substance of man and nature—the true resurrection of nature—the naturalism of man and the humanism of nature both brought to fulfilment" (103–104).

Thus it is expected that human nature ("sociality") liberated from institutionalized egoism (the negation of sociality) will supersede "reification", "abstract labour", and "imaginary appetites". It is not difficult to see that so long as competition is the governing power of production, or in other words, so long as "cost-effectiveness" is the overriding principle of productive activity, it is quite impossible to consider the worker *as a man* at the various stages and phases of the cycle of production. Human activity under the conditions of competition is bound to remain wage-labour, a commodity submitted to the "natural law" of the objective, independent needs of competition. Similarly, it is easy to see the relevance of the supersession of competition to the achievement of the human requirements of self-fulfilling activity (as opposed to "abstract labour", the negation of sociality), and to the elimination of "imaginary appetites".

At this point several problems could be raised as regards the nature of the developments envisaged by Marx. Since, however, the moral and political as well as the aesthetic aspects of Marx's theory of alienation have to be systematically explored before we can tackle such problems, their analysis must be left to later chapters.

V. Political Aspects

1. Property Relations

As we have seen in the previous chapter the first stage in the development of the alienation of labour had to have a *political* form, because the existence of an agricultural surplus-product does not contain any *economic* determination as to the manner of its appropriation. An economic principle of appropriation and redistribution can only operate at a fairly high level of development and it presupposes a relation, already fixed, politically, between production and appropriation.

The question arises : if the surplus-product is not distributed on the basis of the strictest equality, what kind of measures ought to be taken in order to ensure the normal functioning of the given society? Two conditions have to be kept in mind :

(1) The smaller the amount of surplus-product, the more *exclusive* the appropriating group or class must be if the purpose of *accumulation* is to be reached, that is if the society is to be saved from being a stagnating one, like the egalitarian natural societies.

(2) If, for similar reasons, one wants to avoid violent conflicts (and the waste of goods necessarily associated with them) in determining which group is going to appropriate the available surplus-product on any particular occasion, one must find a regulative principle or institution capable of establishing and safeguarding continuity.

But where can one find such a regulative principle? If it were only to safeguard continuity on an established basis one could immediately enumerate a number of possible candidates. But the fundamental question is : how is this continuity *established* in the first place? The point of departure must be discriminative appropriation itself. Any other approach would presuppose some kind of totally unjustified, ahistorical assumption. To set out from discriminative appropriation itself does not involve unwarranted assumptions. Yet it can provide a framework of explanation. For the original appropriation of a given surplus-product, under the conditions it generates, is bound to function as a self-asserting and self-perpetuating power.

And yet,·the question remained unanswered : how did the change that resulted in the establishment of a politically fixed appropriation—private property—occur? We could only show that there is a necessary relationship between original appropriation and the later politically fixed, continuous appropriation.

Obviously, the answer to our question can only be provided by the most detailed historical analysis, which is greatly handicapped by the scarcity of available data. What we are, however, concerned with here is that one cannot simply assume a stereotyped original private property, in view of the fact that historical research has recorded a great variety of forms.

Every form of original private property is *sui generis* and there is no reason to presuppose that this specific character has nothing to do with the specific form of the previous property on whose basis it had originated. Differentiations in later stages of development are determined, at least to some extent, by the particular set of conditions that characterize the earlier stages. This means that we have to dismiss the naïve idea of an idyllic and homogeneous original communal property. Communal property itself must be conceived as of very different types. This will help to explain the specific character of the original private property which grew out of it.[168]

This, of course, does not solve the problem of how the various forms of primitive communal property originated. It is indeed doubtful whether such problems can ever be solved. For our purpose it is sufficient to emphasize the *specific* character of *all* property-relations, whether communal or private.

This applies not only to the remote past but also to the present and future. To posit a homogeneous communal property as the supersession of the alienating capitalistic property-relations is unhistorical. "Property-relations" is obviously a key-concept in the analysis of alienation; but it would be naïve to suppose that the direct negation of those specific property-relations will not produce something equally specific. Thus the question of alienation is not settled once and for all by simply negating the capitalistic property-relations. We should not forget that we are dealing with a complex set of interrelations of which "property-relations" is a part only.

All the same, the analysis of property-relations is very important in connection with alienation because the fundamental problems of human *freedom* are closely related to them. Marx asks the question :

how does man emancipate himself from being subjected to the blind forces of natural necessity? The answer: "by his productive activity" directly involves property-relations. For, by necessity, all production—primitive and feudal, capitalistic and socialistic alike— must be regulated in the framework of specific property-relations.

Thus the original problem of freedom—man's relation to nature— is modified. Now one has to ask: in what way and to what extent does a specific form of property impose limitations upon human freedom? A further complication is that these limitations may or may not also appear as direct political-legal restrictions. Therefore the problem of freedom has to be discussed in a *threefold* relation:

(1) The degree of *freedom from natural necessity* achieved by a given stage of human development. Property-relations must be evaluated here in respect of their contribution to this achievement.

(2) Forms of property are expressions of determinate human relations. Therefore the question must arise: how is the amount of freedom achieved in sense (1)—i.e. freedom from natural necessity—*distributed* among the various groups brought together in the existing property-relations? Under certain conditions it may be the case that the condition of *any* degree of freedom in sense (1) deprives the vast majority of the population from any enjoyment of it, which is reserved to small sections of the society. Freedom in this essentially *negative* sense, as contrasted to the positive character of sense (1), does not refer directly to the relationship between man and nature but between *man and man*. It is freedom *from* the interfering power of other men. (One must, however, emphasize that there is an inherent interrelationship between the negative and positive senses of freedom. Thus already sense (2)—this essentially negative sense—of freedom has a positive aspect, insofar as it necessarily contains a reference to sense (1).)

(3) The third relation concerns "freedom *to* exercise man's essential powers". It is *positive* in character, and therefore it needs something other than legal sanctions for its realization. (It goes without saying that one cannot legislate about freedom in sense (1).) In fact legality is completely powerless beyond the point of providing a favourable framework for positive developments. One can only legislate about the essentially negative sense (2), to remove anachronisms and to put up safeguards against their re-erection.

Even if freedom is realized in sense (2)—i.e. if it is legally distributed according to the principle of equality—the question remains: how far is man free in the positive sense? Marx described this sense as freedom to exercise man's "essential powers". Political-legal restriction can obviously interfere with this free exercise of man's essential powers. But even if this interference is removed, positive freedom is not brought to its fulfilment so long as there may be other factors to interfere with it. Nor can one hope for a legislative solution to the problem: the difficulties inherent in positive freedom must be solved at the level where they arise. Property-relations in this respect are to be evaluated according to the criterion of how much (or little) they promote the free exercise of man's essential powers.

Thus the political aspects of Marx's theory of alienation can be summed up in this threefold relation of freedom to the existing property-relations. The central question is then: how much does a given form of property-relations contribute to render man more free:

(1) from natural necessity;
(2) from the interfering power of other men; and
(3) in relation to a fuller exercise of his own essential powers.

The question of alienation, in this context, concerns a process that negatively affects freedom in this threefold relations of man to *nature*, to the *"other man"*, and *"to himself"*, i.e. to his own essential powers. In other terms: alienation in this respect is the negation of human freedom in its negative and positive senses.

2. *Capitalistic Objectification and Freedom*

Marx's answer to the question: do capitalistic property-relations render man more free in the above senses, is a historically qualified and substantiated No.

At first glance it might seem as if his answer as regards the first two aspects were Yes, whereas with respect to man's relation to his own essential powers a categorical No. However, a closer look reveals that this cannot be so. Marx conceives these three aspects as inseparable from one another. Inseparable not only in a conceptual sense in which negative characteristics cannot be defined without some reference to the positive ones. Rather: this conceptual inseparability is interpreted as a reflection of their necessary inter-relatedness in reality.

Consequently if the analysis of capitalistic property-relations reveals an advancement in sense (1), if, that is, we find that as a result of the productive powers inherent in these relations man is less dependent upon natural necessity than before, this carries with it positive implications both for senses (2) and (3). Equally: the extension of freedom in sense (2) liberates some human powers and energies which were previously subjugated and which now contribute to the advancement of freedom as man's relation to nature. So it is not difficult to see that the unhampered exercise of man's essential powers for Marx must also mean that the problem of freedom in senses (1) and (2) is solved adequately to the high degree of development of the society in question.

This stage can only be postulated by Marx. Talking about the future, he defines it as the *"positive transcendence of private property"*, as "fully developed naturalism", and "fully developed humanism". This stage of development where man's essential powers are fully exercised—this is why it is called "fully developed humanism"—is described as "the genuine resolution of the strife between existence and essence, between objectification and self-confirmation, between freedom and necessity, between the individual and the species" (102). All this needs two qualifications:

1. Man's freedom from natural necessity must always remain a relative achievement, however high a degree it may reach.

2. By implication, man's essential powers can only be exercised insofar as it is made possible by the greater or lesser extent of limitations imposed by the given degree of human freedom in relation to nature.

The various aspects of freedom are elements of a dialectical reciprocity. Therefore, to return to the original question, if the analysis of capitalistic property-relations shows that man cannot exercise his essential powers, the restrictions and limitations of this kind are bound to have their negative repercussions on the degree of freedom achieved by capitalistic society in senses (1) and (2). And this goes for all three members of this reciprocity in relation to each other.

Thus if we consider the first aspect of freedom, in contrasting capitalistic property-relations to feudal ones, it becomes obvious that the tremendous increase in society's productive powers potentially advances human freedom to a very great extent. And yet, Marx argues, this great positive potentiality is counteracted by two major factors:

First: the ever increasing productive forces are not governed by the principle of "conscious association", but they are subjected to a "natural law" which blindly prevails over the individuals involved.

Secondly: while the increasing productive forces could indeed satisfy the real human needs, because of the irrational character of the process as a whole (termed by the young Engels "the unconscious condition of mankind"), *partial* needs of private property—the abstract needs of expanding production and gain—prevail over real human needs. To give Marx's own words: "The increase in the quantity of objects is accompanied by an *extension* of the realm of the alien powers to which man is subjected, and every new product represents a new potency of mutual swindling and mutual plundering" (115).

So the potential liberating force of the new productive powers is frittered away. The realm of alien powers to which man is subjected, as Marx puts it, is *extended* instead of being reduced.

Already in the Kantian philosophy of history the question appeared: what is the relationship between satisfying human needs and morality, and the moral tone of Marx's analysis is self-evident. We shall deal in the next chapter with the moral aspects of these problems. What we have to underline here is that because of the artificiality of a large number of needs created by capitalistic property-relations the question whether man advanced his freedom in relation to nature had to be answered by Marx in the negative.

As regards the second aspect of freedom, the paradoxical result of capitalistic developments was already mentioned in the previous chapter, in connection with Marx's criticism of the "Rights of Man". We have seen that freedom from political bonds and restrictions of a certain kind was an elementary condition of the new social development: both in the sense of setting free all men to enable them to enter into *contractual* relations, and as regards the "alienability of land" and the legitimacy of profit without the "alienation of capital". But as soon as the right of equality has been applied to acquisition and possession, it has necessarily become abstract (equality as mere possession of rights), because it is impossible both to possess something individualistically (exclusively) and at the same time also to share it in the same respect with someone else.

On this account as soon as negative freedom (on the ruins of feudal legality) is achieved, the new legal system has to start legislating in order to codify actual inequalities, maintaining its flexibility only at the above-mentioned abstract level.

Politically-legally sanctioned lack of freedom in this sense directly manifests itself as "the antithesis of propertylessness and property" (98). Marx goes, however, further than this. He emphasizes that so long as this antithesis is not comprehended as an *antagonism* between *labour* and *capital*, it "remains an antithesis of indifference, not grasped in its active connection, its internal relation—an antithesis not yet grasped as a contradiction" (98).

This latter consideration brings us to the third, most complex aspect of freedom. But before starting to discuss it, we have to mention that according to Marx within the general framework of the capitalistic State and legal system human activity is carried on as an "alien, a coerced acivity" (78), as *"forced labour"* (72), as an activity which is "under the domination, the coercion and the yoke of another man" (79). Thus although the fundamental governing principle of the new society is *economic* (as opposed to the essentially *political* regulative principle of feudal society), it cannot be divorced from the political framework in which it operates. Therefore the task of "universal human emancipation" must be formulated "in the *political* form of the emancipation of the workers" (82), which implies a "practically critical attitude" towards the state. In other words,[169] a radical transformation, and ultimate abolition, of the state is an essential condition of the realization of the Marxian programme.

The third aspect of freedom may be described as the synthesis of the first two. For man's relation to his own essential powers is at the same time his relation to nature and to the "other man".

The first question is then: what are man's "essential powers"? Only after answering this question can one ask the second, which is specifically related to capitalistic property-relations: how does alienation affect the exercise of man's essential powers?

In Marx's view man's essential powers are the specifically human powers and characteristics, i.e. those which distinguish man from other parts of nature.

"*Labour* is man's active property" (28), and as such it is supposed to be an internal property that should manifest itself in a "spontaneous activity" (73). Labour is thus specific in man as a free activity and is contrasted with the "animal functions—eating, drinking, procreating" (73) which belong to the realm of necessity.

The power of man to *objectify* himself through his labour is also a specifically human power. Again, it is supposed to manifest itself as the "objectification of man's specific life" : objectification bearing the inherently human characteristics insofar as it enables man to "contemplate himself in a world that he has created" (76) and not only in thought.

Marx describes man as "a *u n i v e r s a l* and therefore a free being" (74), and the power which enables man to be such a being is derived from *sociality*. This means that there is a direct connection between freedom as man's universality, and sociality. As we know, according to Marx "The h u m a n essence of nature first exists only for social man" (103), and he adds that true individuality cannot be grasped in abstraction from sociality. Not even if the form of individuality one has in mind is scientific,[170] or indeed artistic, creative activity.

No doubt, Hegel is right in saying that it is an essential power of man to "duplicate himself intellectually". But in Marx's view this can only arise on the basis of the previously mentioned essential human powers. This second—intellectual—duplication is closely related to the human powers objectified in reality, whether the individual concerned is conscious of this interrelation or not.

The common denominator of all these human powers is sociality. Even our five senses are not simply part of our animal heritage. They are humanly developed and refined as a result of social processes and activities. Therefore the crucial question is : do the new property-relations further or hinder the advancement of sociality as the basis of all specifically human powers?

The young Engels answers this question with an emphatic No in these words: "private property isolates everyone in his own crude solitariness",[171] and Marx's answer is an equally emphatic No.

Labour that should be an *internal*, active property of man as a result of capitalistic alienation becomes *external* to the worker ("labour is e x t e r n a l to the worker, i.e. it does not belong to his essential being; . . . The worker therefore only feels himself outside his work, and in his work feels outside himself."—72). Not "life-activity", in which man "affirms himself", but mere "m e a n s to his i n d i v i d u a l   e x i s t e n c e", self-denial which "mortifies his body and ruins his mind". Alienation transforms spontaneous activity into "coerced labour", an activity which is a mere means to obtain essentially animal ends (eating, drinking, procreating), and thus "what is animal becomes human and what is human becomes animal" (72–77). To make things worse, even this alienated form of activity—necessary though for mere survival—is often denied to the worker because "labour itself becomes an object which he can get hold of only with the greatest effort and with the most irregular interruptions" (69). (To remedy this, in socialist constitutions there is a clause which legally entitles man to work. This may seem to contradict the point I made that one cannot realize by legislative means the positive criteria of freedom. However, this socialist right can only refer to work as *external* to man and as a *means* to his existence. Legislation could never make labour into an *internal need* of man. Positive social—and moral—processes are necessary to achieve this result.)

Objectification under conditions when labour becomes external to man assumes the form of an alien power that confronts man in a hostile manner. This external power, private property, is "the product, the result, the necessary consequence, of a l i e n a t e d l a b o u r, of the external relation of the worker to nature and to himself" (80). Thus if the result of this kind of objectification is the production of a hostile power, then man cannot "contemplate himself in a world that he has created", in reality, but, subjected to an external power and deprived of the sense of his own activity, he invents an unreal world, he subjects himself to it, and thus he restricts even further his own freedom.

If man is alienated from other men and from nature then the powers that belong to him as a "universal being" obviously cannot be exercised. Universality is abstracted from man and transformed into an impersonal power which confronts him in the form of money; this "bond of all b o n d s", "the universal a g e n t of d i v o r c e", "the true b i n d i n g agent—the universal g a l v a n o-c h e m i c a l power of Society" (139).

3. Political "Negation of the Negation" and Emancipation

The picture that emerges from the details of Marx's criticism is that of a fragmented society and of an impoverished individual. How could such a state of affairs be positively transcended? This is a question which must underlie Marx's analysis. For without attempting to give an answer to it the criticism itself would remain at least hopelessly abstract, if not altogether devoid of meaning.

Would the destruction of the capitalistic State and the elimination of the legal restrictions imposed by it solve the problem? Obviously not, because according to Marx even the *annulment of the State* (of any State) would still leave parts of the task unsolved (101).

To conceive the task of transcendence simply in political terms could result in "the re-establishing of 'Society' as an abstraction *vis-à-vis* the individual" (104), against which Marx gave his warning. And this would re-establish alienation in a different form.

The great difficulty lies in this, that positive transcendence must start with political measures because in an alienated society there are no social agencies which could effectively restrict, let alone supersede, alienation.

If, however, the process starts with a political agency which must establish the preconditions of transcendence, its success will depend on the self-consciousness of this agency. In other words, if this agency, for one reason or another, cannot recognize its own limits and at the same time restrict its own actions to these limits, then the dangers of "re-establishing 'Society' as an abstraction *vis-à-vis* the individual" will be acute.

Politics in this sense must be conceived as an activity whose ultimate end is *its own annulment* by means of fulfilling its determinate function as a necessary stage in the complex process of positive transcendence. This is how Marx describes communism as a *political* principle. He emphasizes its function as the *negation of the negation,* and therefore confines it to the *"next stage* of historical development", calling it "the dynamic principle of the *immediate future"* (114).

According to some interpreters, "Marx here means crude, equalitarian communism, such as that propounded by Babeuf and his followers" (114). But this interpretation is not at all convincing. Not only because Marx speaks with approval of this "crude equalitarian communism", but mainly because we can find several other places in the Paris Manuscripts where Marx, in different contexts (98–99, 101, 103, 123–124, 164), makes the same point.

His position is that communism "of a political nature" (101) is still affected by the estrangement of man. As a negation of private property, it is a form of *mediation.* (That is, it sustains a position by means of negating its opposite. And it is a "negation of a negation" because it negates private property which is itself a "negation of human essence".) It is not a *"self*-originating position but rather a position originating from private property" (124), which means that so long as this mediation remains, some kind of alienation goes with it.

The most important passage of the *Manuscripts* relevant to this point reads as follows: ". . . atheism is humanism mediated with itself through the annulment of religion, whilst communism is humanism mediated with itself through the annulment of private property. Only through the *annulment of this mediation* which is itself, however, a *necessary premise*—does positively *self-deriving* humanism, *p o s i t i v e h u m a n i s m* come into being" (164).

Now how could this "humanism mediated with itself" be a "necessary premise of positively self-deriving humanism", i.e. something highly objective, if it were "crude egalitarian communism", which is a subjective, voluntaristic image? This interpretation obviously cannot be maintained without contradicting Marx.

When communism transforms itself into "positively self-deriving humanism" it necessarily ceases to be politics. The crucial Marxian distinction is that between communism as a *political movement*—which is confined to a particular historical stage of human development—and communism as comprehensive *social practice*. This second sense is referred to when Marx writes that "this communism, as fully-developed naturalism, equals humanism, and as fully-developed humanism equals naturalism" (102).

All politics is bound to a greater or lesser extent to partiality. This is clearly implied by Marx when he says that the emancipation of society from private property is expressed in the *political* form of the *emancipation of the worker* (82). To expect, therefore, from *partiality* to accomplish the *universality* of positive transcendence would be as a practical attitude at least naïve and as a theory self-contradictory.

Positive transcendence thus simply cannot be envisaged as the "negation of the negation", i.e. in merely political terms. Its realization can only be conceived in the universality of social practice as a whole. At the same time, however, it ought to be emphasized that as a necessary intermediary link the rôle of a politics conscious of its limits as well as of its strategic functions in the totality of social practice, is crucial for the success of a socialist transformation of society.

VI. *Ontological and Moral Aspects*

1. *The "Self-mediating Being of Nature"*

The central theme of Marx's moral theory is: how to realize *human freedom*. This means that he has to investigate not only the man-made—i.e. self-imposed—obstacles to freedom in the given form of society, but also the general question of the nature and limitations of freedom as *human* freedom. The problem of freedom arises in the form of practical tasks in the course of human development and only later, in fact much later, can philosophers make an abstraction out of it.

So the real issue is *human* freedom, not an abstract principle called "freedom". And since the *specific* character of everything is at the same time both the *"essence"* (power, potential, function) of that given thing and its *limit*, so it will be found that human freedom is not the *transcendence* of the limitations (specific character) of human nature but a *coincidence* with them. In other words: human freedom is not the *negation* of the specifically *natural* in the human being—a negation for the sake of what appears to be a *transcendental ideal*—but, on the contrary, its *affirmation*.

Transcendental ideals—in the sense in which transcendental means the supersession of inherently human limitations—have no place in Marx's system. He explains their appearance in earlier philosophical systems as a result of a socially motivated unhistorical assumption of certain absolutes. To take an example: if the eighteenth-century political economist founds his theories on "human nature", identified with *egoism*, his moral philosopher counterpart (who, as in the case of Adam Smith, may be the same person) will complete the picture by superimposing on this "egoist man" the image of a transcendental ideal. It is not without significance that Kant was influenced by Adam Smith. (See Kant's essay *On Perpetual Peace* in which *"Handelsgeist"*—"commercial spirit" —is a key concept.)

Criticizing this kind of approach Marx does not only object to transcendentalism. He also rejects the picture on which the trans-

162

cendental ideal is superimposed. i.e. the conception of man who is *by nature* egoistic. In Marx's view this kind of superimposition is only possible because we live in an alienated society where man is *de facto* egoistic. To identify the egoistic (alienated) man of a given historical situation with man in general and thus conclude that man is by nature egoistic is to commit the "ideological fallacy" of unhistorically equating the *part* (i.e. that which corresponds to a *partial* interest) with the *whole*. The outcome is, inevitably, a fictitious man who readily lends himself to this transcendental superimposition.

Thus a criticism of moral transcendentalism in Marx's view makes sense only if it is coupled with the demolition of the conception according to which "man is by nature egoistic". If this is not accomplished, transcendentalism—or some other form of ethical dualism—necessarily reappears in the system of the philosopher who is unable to grasp "egoism" historically, in the contradictions of a situation that produces alienated "commodity man". The criticism of transcendentalism must reveal the interdependence of the two-fold distortion which consists in inventing *abstract ideals* for man while depriving him not only of all ideality but of all humanness too. It must show that what disappears in this juxtaposition of the realms of "is" and "ought" (in the opposition of man reduced to a state of beast and an abstract spiritual being, or in the opposition of man's "lower self" to his "higher self") is precisely the real human being.

This real human being for Marx exists both as *actuality* (alienated "commodity man") and *potentiality* (what Marx calls: "the rich human being"). And thus we can see that the rejection of transcendentalism and ethical dualism does not carry with it the dismissal of *ideality* without which no moral system worthy of this name is conceivable. This rejection implies, however, that a natural basis must be found for all ideality.

Marx's ontological starting point is that man is a specific part of nature and therefore he cannot be identified with something abstractly spiritual. "A b e i n g only considers himself independent when he stands on his own feet; and he only stands on his own feet when he owes his e x i s t e n c e to himself" (112)—writes Marx. The ontological question of existence and its origin is a traditional question of both theology and philosophy. The framework in which Marx raises it—i.e. the definition of man as a specific part of nature, as "the self-mediated being of nature" (112)—radically transforms this question.

When it is formulated in a *theological* framework, assuming a wholly spiritual being as the creator of man, this brings with it a set of moral ideals (and corresponding rules) which aim at liberating man from his "animal nature". Thus human dignity is conceived as the *negation* of human nature, inspired by the *duty* (associated with a feeling of *gratitude* etc.) towards the being to whom man *owes* his own existence. And since *freedom* in this framework is divorced, by definition, from anything natural—nature appears only as an obstacle—and since man, equally by definition, cannot separate himself from nature, human freedom cannot possibly appear as *human*, but only in the form of an *abstract generality* ("free will"[172] etc.), as a mysterious or fictitious *entity*. This kind of freedom, needless to say, only exists by the grace of the transcendental being.

In Marx's formulation what exists by the grace of another being (what I *owe* him) is not freedom, but the *denial* of it. Only an "independent being" can be called a free being, and ties of "owing" necessarily imply dependence, i.e. the negation of freedom. If, however, man "owes" nature and himself (which is ultimately the same thing: this is what Marx rather obscurely calls "the self-mediated being of nature and of man") his own existence, he owes nobody anything. In this Marxian sense "owing his existence" simply means that "there is a particular *causal relation* in virtue of which man is a *specific* part of nature". Thus "owing" in the other sense—the one that carries with it the abstract idea of duty—is rejected. And with this rejection the abstract ideals and duties that could be externally imposed on man are excluded from Marx's moral system.

The Marxian "self-mediated being of nature and of man"—man who is not the animal counterpart of a set of abstract moral ideals—is by nature neither good, nor evil; neither benevolent nor malevolent; neither altruistic nor egoistic; neither sublime nor a beast; etc., but simply a natural being whose attribute is: "self-mediating". This means that he can *make* himself become what he is at any given time—in accordance with the prevailing circumstances—whether egoistic or otherwise.

Terms like malevolence, egoism, evil, etc., cannot stand on their own, without, that is, their positive counterpart. But this is equally true about the positive terms of these pairs of opposites. Therefore it does not matter which side is assumed by a particular moral philosopher in his definition of human nature as inherently egoistic and malevolent or altruistic and benevolent: he will necessarily end up with a thoroughly *dualistic* system of philosophy. One cannot avoid this unless one denies that either side of these opposites is inherent in human nature itself.

2. *The Limits of Freedom*

Does this mean that we should regard these opposites as worthless abstractions to get rid of by means of a conceptual reclassification? Certainly not. For they are not only abstractions but, unlike "free will", also facts of human life as we have known it so far. If the "self-mediating" being can turn himself into what he is under determinate circumstances and in accordance with them, and if we find that egoism is just as much a fact of human life as benevolence, then the task is to find out: what are the reasons why man made himself become a being who behaves egoistically.

The practical aim of such an investigation is, of course, to see in what way the process that results in the creation of egoistic human beings could be reversed. To insist that man is "by nature" egoistic necessarily implies the rejection of such an aim, whatever the motivation behind this negative attitude might be. To insist, on the other hand, that man is "by nature" benevolent amounts to attributing nothing less than mythical powers to "evil influences"— whether identified with the theological image of "evil" or with the alleged "irrationality of man", etc., in order to be able to account for the morally condemned deeds of men. This latter approach puts its holders, from the outset, in a position of defeat, even if this is not clear to the holders themselves, and even if they veil defeat as victory under the cloak of utopian wishful thinking. (Dualism is transparent in utopian conceptions: the idealized solution is rigidly opposed to the rejected reality. And since ideality and reality are not grasped as members of a dialectical interrelation, the abyss of dualistic, undialectical opposition has to be bridged by some arbitrary assumption, such as, for instance, the presumed benevolent nature of man.)

The only way to avoid transcendentalism and dualism (regarded by Marx as abdications of human freedom) is to take man, without prejudicial assumptions, simply as a natural being who is not dyed either pink or black by the various systems of moral philosophy.

This way Marx can also get rid of the notion of "original sin" by saying that man never lost his "innocence" simply because he never had it. Nor was he "guilty" to start with. Guilt and innocence are relative and *historical* terms that can only be applied under certain conditions and from a specific point of view, i.e. their assessment is subject to change.

Marx derides the theologians who try to explain the origin of evil by the fall of man (69), i.e. in the form of an ahistorical assumption. He also scorns the moral philosophers who do not explain the known characteristics of human behaviour in their historical genesis but simply *attribute* them to human nature, which means that what they are unable to account for they assume as *apriori* given and fixed. Marx could negatively describe "natural man" in a polemic against this practice of assumptions as man who has not been misrepresented by moral philosophers.

Positively though man must be described in terms of his needs and powers. And both are, equally, subject to change and development. Consequently there can be nothing fixed about him, except what necessarily follows from his determination as a natural being, namely that he is a being with *needs*—otherwise he could not be called a natural being—and *powers* for their gratification without which a natural being could not possibly survive.

The problem of freedom can only be formulated in these contexts, which means that there can be no other than *human* form of freedom. If we attribute, in religious alienation, absolute freedom to a being, we only project on a metaphysical plane and in an inverted form our own attribute: naturally and socially limited human freedom. In other words: by positing a non-natural being with absolute freedom we blind ourselves to the fact that freedom is rooted in nature. "Absolute freedom" is the absolute negation of freedom and can only be conceived as absolute chaos. To escape the contradictions involved in the concept of absolute freedom that manifests itself in the form of a strict order, theology either takes refuge in mysticism, or adds further human attributes to the image of the absolute—e.g. goodness and love for man—contradictorily determining thus the being who by definition cannot have determinations without being deprived of his absolute freedom.[178]

The "return from religious alienation" in Marx's view is only possible if we recognize the fictitious character of "absolute freedom" and if we *affirm* the specific human limitations, instead of vainly trying to *transcend* them for the sake of a fiction. Thus if man is a natural being with a multiplicity of needs, human fulfilment—the realization of human freedom—cannot be conceived as an abnegation or subjugation of these needs, but only as their properly human gratification. The only proviso is that they must be inherently human needs.

On the other hand if man as a part of nature must work "if he is not to die", and thus he is in this respect under the spell of necessity, human freedom cannot be realized by turning one's back on the realities of this situation. Transcendental references will be of no help whatsoever because they only transfer the problem to a different plane, assigning at the same time an inferior status to the "realm of necessity" (or "phenomenal world" as opposed to the "noumenal world", etc.).

Again, the solution lies in *affirming* this limitation as the source of human freedom. Productive activity, imposed upon man by natural necessity, as the fundamental condition of human survival and development thus becomes identical to human fulfilment, i.e. the realization of human freedom. Fulfilment, by logical necessity, implies limitations, for only that which is limited in some way or ways can be fulfilled. If a philosopher adopts a different view in this regard, he must end up with something like the Kantian notion of fulfilment in a transcendental infinity, i.e. he must end up with a theological structure of morality, whether he wants it or not.[174]

These problems indicate why it was necessary for Marx to introduce strong anti-theological polemics into his assessment of morality. The anti-theological references in Marx's philosophical works cannot be explained by pointing to the unquestionably significant impact of Feuerbach's *Essence of Christianity* on the radical young Hegelians. (The less so because Marx very soon became aware of the gap that separated him from Feuerbach.) The main reason why Marx had to dedicate so much effort to anti-theological polemics was that if he wanted to describe man as an "independent being", as the "self-mediated being of nature and of man", or in other words if he wanted to produce a coherent system of morality, based on a monistic ontology, he could not possibly avoid challenging the dualistic theological picture which is the direct *negation* of what he calls the "essentiality" and "universality" of man.

It is necessary to emphasize, however, that this anti-theological affirmation of human limitations, in order to derive from it the

168 MARX'S THEORY OF ALIENATION

picture of man as an "essential" and "universal" being is a "negation of the negation". And since the negation of the negation is still dependent on what it negates, one cannot speak of a truly natural, positive morality while theological references form an integral part of it. There is a parallel situation here with the negation of private property. (See section 3. of the previous chapter.) Both theology and private property are defined as negations of the essentiality of man in his "self-mediating" relation to nature. To define man as an essential being by negating theology and private property, i.e. in terms of anti-capitalist and anti-theological references, is a negation of the negation. Such a negation of the negation is by no means "self-mediating", because it asserts the essentiality and universality of man through negating its negation by both theology and private property. Thus the self-mediating relationship between man and nature is not reestablished, as both private property and theology remain in the picture, even if in a negated form. Consequently one cannot envisage in reality a truly natural morality before all references to theology and private property—including the negative references—have disappeared from the definition of man as an essential and universal being.

3. Human Attributes

As we have seen, in drawing the picture of the moral agent one cannot assume any human characteristics (like "egoism", etc.) as apriori given without committing oneself at the same time to a dualistic system of morality. One cannot take for granted anything more than the fact that man is a part of nature, and only on this basis may one ask the question: what is *specific* about man as part of nature. In this context two important questions have to be asked:

1. What are the *general* characteristics of a *natural being*?
2. What are the *specific* characteristics of a *human* natural being.

"M a n"—writes Marx—"is directly a n a t u r a l b e i n g". "As a natural being and as a living natural being he is on the one hand furnished with n a t u r a l p o w e r s o f l i f e—he is an active natural being. These forces exist in him as tendencies and abilities— as i m p u l s e s. On the other hand, as a natural, corporeal, sensuous, objective being he is a s u f f e r i n g, conditioned and limited creature, like animals and plants. That is to say, the o b j e c t s of his impulses exist outside him, as o b j e c t s independent of him; yet these objects are o b j e c t s of his n e e d—essential o b j e c t s, indispensable to the manifestation and confirmation of his essential powers" (156). Marx goes on to say that the concept of an *objective being* necessarily implies *another being* which is the *object* of that objective being. This relation is, however, by no means one-sided : the *object* in its turn has the objective being for *its object*. "As soon as I have an object, this object has me for an object" (157). That is to say, I am affected by this object, or in other words, I am in some specific way subjected to it. Considered at this level, my relation to my objects is the same as that between non-human natural objects. "The sun is the o b j e c t of the plant— an indispensable object to it, confirming its life—just as the plant is an object of the sun, of the sun's o b j e c t i v e essential power" (157).

But Marx carries this line of thought even further and emphasizes that *every* natural being has its nature *outside itself* : "A being which does not have its nature outside itself is not a n a t u r a l being and plays no part in the system of nature. A being which has no object outside itself is not an objective being. A being which is not itself an object for some third being has no being for its o b j e c t; i.e. it is not objectively related. Its be-ing is not objective. *An un-objective being is a n u l l i t y—an u n - b e i n g*" (157). From this two important conclusions follow :

(1) that the "nature" of *any* objective being is not some mysteriously hidden "essence", but something that naturally defines itself as the necessary relation of the objective being to its objects, i.e. it is a specific objective relation; (only "un-beings" or "nullities" need be "defined" in mystifying references to mysterious essences);

(2) that "having one's nature outside oneself" is the necessary mode of existence of *every* natural being, and is by no means specific about *man*. Thus if someone wants to identify *externalization* with *human alienation* (as Hegel did, for instance), he can only do this by confounding the whole with one specific *part* of it. Consequently "objectification" and "externalization" are relevant to alienation only insofar as they take place in an *inhuman* form. (As if the sun's "life-awakening power" turned *against* the sun under conditions when the sun could in principle prevent this from happening.)

As regards man's status as a *specific* part of nature, Marx writes : "But man is not merely a natural being, he is a h u m a n natural being. That is to say, he is a *being for himself*. Therefore he is a s p e c i e s b e i n g, and has to confirm and manifest himself as such both in his being and in his knowing. Therefore, h u m a n

objects are not natural objects as they *immediately* present themselves, and neither is h u m a n s e n s e as it immediately is as it
is objectively—h u m a n sensibility, human objectivity. Neither
nature objectively nor nature subjectively is directly given in a form
adequate to the h u m a n being. And as everything natural has to
have its b e g i n n i n g, m a n too has his act of coming-to-be—
h i s t o r y—which, however, is for him a known history, and hence
as an act of coming-to-be it is a *conscious self-transcending act of
coming-to-be*. History is the true natural history of man" (158).

To render clearer this passage let us contrast the views expressed
in it with Hume's assertion according to which "An affectation
betwixt the sexes is a passion evidently implanted in human
nature".[175] This assertion, even if it claims to have the truth-value
of self-evidence, is nothing more than an unhistorical *assumption*
that, on closer inspection, turns out to be false on two counts:

(1) insofar as this passion is "implanted in nature", it is not confined to human beings, i.e. it is not a *human* passion;

(2) insofar as it is a specifically human passion, it is not at all
"*implanted* in human nature", but it is a *human achievement*. The
essential characteristic of this passion as a *human* passion is that it
is inseparable from the consciousness of the "other sex" being a
particular *human being* and at the same time it is also inseparable
from the consciousness of the self as that of a *humanly* passionate
being. This human achievement is what Marx calls, rather obscurely,
"a conscious self-transcending act of coming-to-be" in which *nature
transcends itself* (or "mediates itself with itself") and becomes *man*,
remaining in this "self-transcendence", of course, a natural being.

Nothing is therefore "implanted in *human* nature". Human
nature is not something *fixed by nature*, but, on the contrary, a
"nature" which is *made by man* in his acts of "self-transcendence"
as a natural being. It goes without saying that human beings—due
to their natural-biological constitution—have *appetites* and various
natural propensities. But in the "conscious self-transcending act of
coming-to-be" they must become *human* appetites and propensities,
fundamentally changing their character by being transformed into
something *inherently historical*. (Without this transformation both
art and morality would be unknown to man: they are only possible
because man is the creator of his *human* appetites. And both art
and morality—both inherently historical—are concerned with the
properly human appetites and propensities of man, and not with
the direct, unalterable determinations of the natural being. Where

there is no—inherently historical—alternative, there is no room for either art or morality.) Therefore in only one sense may one speak of "human nature" : in the sense whose centre of reference is historical change and its foundation, human society. In Marx's words : "The nature which comes to be in human history—the genesis of human society—is man's r e a l nature; hence nature as it comes to be through industry, even though in an estranged form, is true a n t h r o p o l o g i c a l nature"(111).

Putting into relief the specifically human about all the natural needs of man, does not, of course, mean arguing for a new kind of "higher self" to sit in judgment over these natural needs. There is nothing wrong with man's natural appetites, provided they are stilled in a *human way*. This human way for satisfying one's natural appetites—which, as needs and appetites, are transformed in the process of "self-transcendence" and "self-mediation"—will depend on the actual degree of civilization, and the social practice that corresponds to it, to which one belongs.[176] And when one says that the primitive natural needs and appetites have become human, this is only to stress that they are now *specifically natural*.

This is why human fulfilment cannot be conceived in abstraction from, or in opposition to, nature. To divorce oneself from "anthropological nature" in order to find fulfilment in the realm of abstract ideas and ideals is just as inhuman as living one's life in blind submission to crude natural needs. It is by no means accidental that so many of the worst immoralities throughout the history of mankind were committed in the name of high-sounding moral ideals utterly divorced from the reality of man.[177]

In the same way, the fact that "self-consciousness" is an essential feature of human gratification cannot mean that self-consciousness alone may be opposed to the "world of estrangement", which happens to be the world of objects. "Self-consciousness" that divorces itself from the world of objects (i.e. a consciousness whose centre of reference is the object-less abstract self) does not *oppose* alienation but, on the contrary, *confirms* it. This is why Marx scorns the abstract philosopher who "sets up himself (that is, one who is himself *an abstract form of estranged man*) as the m e a s u r i n g - r o d for the estranged world" (149). The objectivity of this philosopher is false objectivity, because he deprives himself of all real objects.

We are not free to choose our self-consciousness. Human self-consciousness—the consciousness of a specific natural being—must be "sensuous consciousness", because it is the consciousness of a sensuous (sensible) natural being. However, "sensuous consciousness is not the abstractly sensuous consciousness but a *humanly sensuous consciousness*"(150). And since the activities of this specific natural being are necessarily displayed in a *social* framework, true self-consciousness of this being must be his consciousness of being a *social* being. Any abstraction from these basic characteristics could only result in an *alienated* self-consciousness.

Here we can see, why Marx had to correct the Hegelian ideas he incorporated in his picture of man the way he did :

(1) Starting from the fact that man is a specific part of nature, he could not confine *labour*—in his attempt to account for human *genesis*—to "abstractly mental labour". What is abstractly mental cannot generate on its own something inherently natural, whereas on the natural basis of reality one can account for the genesis of "abstractly mental labour".

(2) For the same reason he could not accept the identification of "objectifying" with "alienation". In relation to an *objective natural being* what is called "objectification" cannot be simply declared "alienation" (or "estrangement"), because this objectification is its *natural* and necessary mode of existence. On the other hand if we conceive an "abstractly spiritual being" whose adequate mode of existence would be of course merely spiritual, in relation to this being "objectification" and "estrangement" become identical. However, apart from this case—in which both "natural" and "objective" are excluded from the definition of this merely spiritual being— only two possibilities are open to the philosopher :

(*a*) to give up the *objectivity* of the *natural* being (in order to accept the necessity of alienation) and thus to end up with a contradiction in terms;

(*b*) to insist that *objectification* is the only possible mode of existence for a natural being (as we have seen, the sun too "objectifies itself" in the living plant; of course the sun cannot think of itself, but this is no reason for depriving it of its objective self—"life-giving power", etc.—and for denying its objectification), but *some forms* of objectification are *inadequate* to the "essence" = "nature outside it" = "social mode of existence" of the human being.

(3) Consequently : if it is the *inadequacy* of some forms of objectification that may properly be called alienation, it is not true that objectivity equals "estranged human relations", although it may be true that the objectivity of civilized society as we have known it

so far carried with it estranged human relations. By contrast, an adequate form of human objectification would produce social objectivity as *objectified* but *non-alienated* human relations.

(4) From the previous points it must follow that the "supersession" of alienation has to be envisaged in terms of the actual *social reality*, i.e. as a transcendence of alienation in social practice as opposed to mere imagination.

4. *The Alienation of Human Powers*

The foregoing considerations are essential to decide "what is human" and what should be rejected as alienation. They not only turn down the "measuring-rod" provided by the abstract philosopher, characterizing it as a particular embodiment of alienated activity, but also offer a new measure by saying that there can be no other *measure of humanness* than *man himself*.

It would be no use to try and answer the question that arises at this point, namely: "which man", by saying: "non-alienated man". Such an answer would amount to reasoning in a circle. What we are after is, precisely, to find out what is "non-alienated". The facts that one may refer to, as elements and stages of a possible definition, are:

(1) man is a *natural* being;

(2) as a natural being he has natural *needs* and natural *powers* for their gratification;

(3) he is a being who lives in a *society* and *produces* the conditions necessary for his existence in an inherently *social* way;

(4) as a productive social being he acquires *new needs* ("needs created through social partnership"[178]) and *new powers* for their gratification;

(5) as a productive social being, he transforms the world around him in a specific way, leaving *his* mark on it; nature thus becomes *"anthropological nature"* (111) in this man-nature relationship; everything now becomes at least potentially, a part of human relations; (nature in these relations appears in a great variety of forms ranging from material elements of utility to objects of scientific hypothesis and of aesthetic pleasure);

(6) by establishing on a natural basis his own conditions of life in the form of social-economic institutions and their products, man "duplicates himself" *practically*, thus laying the foundations of "contemplating himself in a world that he has created";

(7) by means of his new powers which are, just as his new needs, "created through social partnership" and interaction, and on the basis of the "practical duplication" just referred to, he also *duplicates himself intellectually*".

Considering these characteristics not in isolation, but in their manifold interrelatedness, it will be seen that the gratification of human needs takes place in an alienated form if this means either a submission to the *crude* natural appetites, or the *cult of the self*— whether this self is described as a creature who is by nature selfish or as an abstract self-consciousness.

The abstract philosopher's approach to the problem of alienation is itself an alienated one. Not only because it confines itself to man's ability to "duplicate himself intellectually", ignoring that only the conditions enumerated in points 1 to 6. make this duplication possible. And not only because he does not distinguish between *alienated* and *true* intellectual self-duplication, but also because he opposes an alienated intellectual self-duplication as true self-confirmation to those conditions (i.e. the objectified social reality) without which no self-confirmation is conceivable for a human (social) natural being.

On the other hand, the submission to the crude naturalness of a given appetite is alienation because it opposes itself, even if unconsciously, to *human* development.[179] It negates (practically or theoretically) the social changes by virtue of which the originally merely natural needs too are now *mediated* in a complex way, so that they have lost their primitive character. It is by no means a mere historical coincidence that the century that has achieved the highest degree of *sophistication* in every sphere has also produced the most remarkable *cult of the primitive*,[180] from philosophical and psychological theories to social and artistic practices.

When we come to consider "privatization" in the light of the formerly enumerated characteristics, its alienated nature becomes transparent, because "privatization" means abstracting (in practice) from the *social side* of human activity. If, however, the social activity of production is an elementary condition for the *human* existence of the individual (with his increasingly complex and socially embedded needs), this act of abstracting—whatever form it might take—is necessarily alienation, because it confines the individual to his "crude solitariness". Society is man's "second nature", in the sense in which the original natural needs are transformed by it, and at the same time integrated into an enormously more extensive network of needs which are all together the product of socially active man. To abstract therefore from this aspect of man in the *cult of the self* as opposed to social man amounts to the cult of an over-simplified alienated self, because the true self of the human being is necessarily a *social self*, whose "nature is outside itself", i.e. it defines itself in terms of specific and immensely complex interpersonal, social relations. Even the *potentialities* of the individual can only be defined in terms of relations of which the individual is but a part. For someone to be a "potentially great piano player" not only the existence of a—socially produced—musical instrument is necessary, but even more so the highly complex social activity of discriminative musical enjoyment.

In all these cases alienation appears as *divorcing* the individual from the social, the natural from the self-conscious. By contraposition it follows that in a non-alienated human relation individual and social, natural and self-conscious must belong together—and form a *complex unity*. And this brings us to another important question: what is the connection between alienation and those needs and powers which are the outcome of social intercourse, i.e. the product of society?

Here we have first to distinguish between two senses of both *natural* and *artificial* as used by Marx. In sense one, natural means simply "that which is a direct product of nature"; and in opposition to it artificial means "man-made". In sense two, however, what is not a direct product of nature but is generated through a *social intermediary* is "natural" insofar as it is identical with man's "second nature", i.e. his nature as created through the functioning of sociality. (It is important to distinguish between "sociality" and "society". The latter, as contrasted with the "sensuous" (sensible) immediateness of the particular individuals, is an abstraction: to grasp it one must transcend this immediateness of the individuals. "Sociality", however, is actually inherent in every single individual. This is why a society may never be justifiably called "natural", whereas sociality is rightly defined as man's second nature.) The opposite to this second sense of natural is clearly not "man-made"— it *is* man-made—but "that which opposes itself to human nature as sociality". Only this second sense of "artificial" is morally relevant. Man-made needs and appetites are not artificial in the second sense provided they are in *harmony* with the functioning of man as a *social* natural being. If, however, they are in disharmony with it, or may even carry it to a point of break-down, they must be rejected as *artificial needs*.

It is worth comparing the Marxian view with Hume's classification of human needs and powers : "There are three different species of goods which we are possessed of; the *internal* satisfaction of our minds; the *external* advantages of our body; and the enjoyment of such *possessions* as we have acquired by our industry and good fortune. We are perfectly secure in the enjoyment of the first. The second may be ravished from us, but can be of no advantage to him who deprives us of them. The last only are both exposed to the violence of others, and may be transferred without suffering any loss or alteration; while at the same time there is not a *sufficient quantity* of them to supply every one's *desires* and *necessities*. As the improvement, therefore, of these goods is the chief advantage of society, so the i n s t a b i l i t y of their possession, along with their s c a r c i t y, is the chief impediment".[181]

One should notice first of all that while Hume attaches the adjectives *internal* to class one, and *external* to class two, he is unable to attach any qualifying adjective to class three. And no wonder: beyond the "internal" and "external" there is only the realm of abstraction. To "abstract enjoyment" only an *abstract need* can correspond, e.g. the need of abstracting from the fact that what is for me only an abstract need of possession, in no connection with my actual human needs, to other people may well be essentials ("necessities") to the gratification of their actual human needs. (This consideration presents, if nothing else, a *prima facie* case for tackling the problem of justice and injustice on lines opposed to those of Hume.)

Furthermore, the question of necessary *scarcity* here arises only in relation to my abstract need of possession. Actual human needs and appetites, whether internal or external, can, in fact, be stilled, whereas there is nothing to limit an *abstract* need—e.g. if the objects of my appetite are not food or poetry, but the multiplication of my money—except the scarcity of the objects to which it is related. However, abstract appetites are *inherently* insatiable—i.e. there is nothing in their nature to limit them "from the inside", in contrast to my mental and bodily appetites—therefore their objects are just as "scarce" in relation to *one* person as to *any number* of them. In other words scarcity is no argument in favour of excluding other people from possession, let alone for establishing "natural justice" on the grounds of such an exclusion. All the less so, because in the only sense in which one may properly speak of a problem of scarcity, it is simply a correlation between the existing actual human needs and the available powers, goods, etc., for their gratification. But this is, of course, a historically changing *contingent* relation, and not a matter of some *apriori necessity* on whose ground one may erect a Humean or even Kantian structure of morality.[182]

As we see Hume, paradoxically, helps to confirm Marx's contention that the "need of possession" is an *abstract* and *artificial* need. Every abstract need—since it abstracts from man—is, by implication, artificial. And thus "abstract", "artificial" and "alienated" become equivalent, in relation to both *needs* and *powers*. The reason why this is so is because abstract (artificial) needs cannot generate powers that correspond to the essential (social) nature of man. They can only generate *abstract powers* which are divorced from the human being and even set up against him. Or the other way round : abstract powers can only generate abstract, artificial needs.

According to Marx in the course of self-alienation man "becomes an *abstract activity* and a *stomach*" (25). His natural functions : eating, drinking, procreating—which are *"genuinely human functions"*—now become *animal*, because *"in the abstraction* which separates them from the sphere of all other human activity and turns them into sole and ultimate ends, they are animal" (73). Or, to express this contradiction in stronger terms, as a result of alienation "man (the worker) no longer feels himself to be freely active in any but his animal functions . . . and in his human functions he no longer feels himself to be anything but animal. What is animal becomes human and what is human becomes animal". (73—The fact that Marx here—because of the particular context—names the worker only does not mean, of course, that this alienation only affects the worker and not the owner of capital. He often emphasizes that they are two sides to the *same* human alienation. Labour is *"objectless subject"*, whereas capital is *"subjectless object"*.)

The "a b s t r a c t existence of man as a mere w o r k m a n" (86) means, however, that even if labour remains a "subject", it cannot be the "human subject" because no "objectless subject" can be called properly human. (As we have seen, the "essence" or "nature" of the human being cannot be found *within* the subject, but *outside* it, in its objectified relations.) This "objectless subject", therefore, insofar as it is a natural being with real needs, can only be a *"p h y s i c a l   s u b j e c t"*: "The extremity of this bondage is that

178 MARX'S THEORY OF ALIENATION

it is only as a w o r k e r that he continues to maintain himself as
a p h y s i c a l s u b j e c t, and that it is only as a p h y s i c a l
s u b j e c t that he is a w o r k e r" (71).

On the other hand "the production of the object of human activity as c a p i t a l—in which all the natural and social determinateness of the object is e x t i n g u i s h e d; in which private property
has lost its natural and social quality" (86—i.e. it has lost its "subjective essence" or subject) is at the same time the production of a
need, however abstract it may be. This need is "The need for
money . . . the true need produced by the modern economic system,
and it is the *only need* which the latter produces" (116). This is a
very important observation because it indicates that if one merely
displaces the existing capitalists and transforms society into what
Marx calls the "universal capitalist", no basic change has taken place
as regards the substance of alienation. A society where this alienated "need for money" manifests itself in the aim of increasing
"public wealth" can be another form of alienated society, as compared to that in which this aim is confined to "private wealth".
There is nothing inherently human about the accumulation of
wealth. The aim should be, according to Marx, the "enrichment of
the human being", of his *"inner wealth"* (106), and not simply
the enrichment of the *"physical subject"*.

Needless to say, this does not mean that the problem of material
well-being should be ignored, but that it should not be formulated
in abstraction from the real individual. The principle of "accumulation of public wealth first", among other things, provides the
politician with an excuse for postponing measures aimed at meeting
important human needs. Besides : if the abstract need of "having"
is to be blamed, to a great extent, for alienation, the reformulation
of this principle of "having" cannot achieve the programme of
superseding alienation. What it may, however, achieve, is the unwanted transformation of an alienated practice into an alienated
aspiration. But even if a much larger slice of the public wealth
is distributed among individuals, this is beside the point. The real
aim is "inner wealth" which is not a kind of abstract contemplation,
but self-confirmation in the fullness of one's life-activity. That is to
say, it is the whole structure of life-activity that needs transformation—from everyday work to a real participation in the highest
levels of the policy-making that has a bearing on one's life—
and not merely the output-potential of a country's material production.

The enrichment of the physical subject only, is the enrichment of "commodity-man" who is a "spiritually and physically dehumanized being" (85). The fight against alienation in Marx's eyes is, therefore, a struggle for rescuing man from a state where "the extension of products and needs falls into contriving and ever-calculating subservience to inhuman, refined, unnatural and imaginary appetites" (116). This alienated state which is characterized not only by the artificial "refinement of needs" but also by "their artificially produced crudeness" (122), makes a mockery of man's desires to extend his powers in order to enable himself to realize human fulfilment, because this increase of power amounts to the "extension of the realm of the alien powers to which man is subjected" (115). Thus man *defeats his own purpose*.

What happened in this process of alienation to the genuinely human needs and senses? Marx's answer is that their place has been taken by the "sheer estrangement" of *all* physical and mental senses,—by *"the sense of having"* (106). This alienated sense finds a universal embodiment in *money*: this "alienated ability of mankind" (139), which means that man's "species-nature" now manifests itself in an alienated form: as the universality of money.

Money, thanks to the domination of the sense of having over everything else, sets itself between man and his object. "By possessing the property of buying everything, by possessing the property of appropriating all objects, money is thus the object of eminent possession. The universality of its property is the omnipotence of its being. It therefore functions as the almighty being. Money is the pimp between man's need and the object, between his life and his means of life" (137). In this *mediation* money replaces the real object and dominates the subject. In it *needs* and *powers* coincide in an abstract way: only those needs are recognized as real needs by an alienated society which can be bought by money, i.e. which are within the reach and power of money.

Under these conditions the personal characteristics and qualities of the individual are secondary. "The extent of the power of money is the extent of my power. Money's properties are my properties and essential powers—the properties and powers of its possessor. Thus, what I am and am capable of is by no means determined by my individuality"(138). Through its power of being the *common measure* of everything, it can "exchange every property for every other, *even contradictory*, property and object: it is the

fraternization of impossibilities."[183] "It transforms fidelity into in-
fidelity, love into hate, hate into love, virtue into vice, vice into
virtue, servant into master, master into servant, idiocy into intelligence, and intelligence into idiocy" (141).

What state of affairs could be more immoral than these conditions
of an alienated society? In such conditions what a labour of
Sisyphus is that of the abstract philosopher who confines his attention to the "ambiguities" of the concepts of "vice" and "virtue", not
realizing that the difficulties do not arise from *thought* but from
the *practical* "overturning power" of money. Before one can finish
the self-imposed task of finding exemplifications for one's own
definition of virtue, it is turned in practice into its opposite, and
countless contradictory examples can be found to refute any such
definition. Nothing, in these matters, is solved by definitions only.
The task, as Marx sees it, is *practical* : it consists in establishing a
society in which the human powers are not alienated from man,
and consequently they cannot turn themselves against him.

5. *Means and Ends, Necessity and Freedom: the Practical Pro-gramme of Human Emancipation.*

Since the task is practical, the solutions must be envisaged in
practical terms, indicating, that is, a practical power capable of
facing up to the task. When Kant wishfully appealed to "natural
scarcity" in envisaging the realization of his transcendental ideal of
morality, he was expecting a miracle from nature, although speculatively he was, of course, well aware of the "chain of natural
causality". Thus, if one wants to avoid a similar contradiction, one
must realize that the only power capable of practically ("positively")
superseding the alienation of human activity is self-conscious human
activity itself.

This may seem a vicious circle. If "alienation of self-consciousness" is due to alienated activity ("alienation of labour"), how can
one expect the supersession of alienated activity by *means* of "self-
conscious human activity", which is the "end in itself" and not
simply a "means to an end"? The contradiction is obvious and yet
only apparent. It arises from a rigid and mechanistic conception
of the relations between "means and ends", and from an equally
mechanistic view of causality as mere succession.

This problem is in more than one respect similar to the dilemma
expressed in one of Marx's theses on Feuerbach: *how to educate the*

educator. On a mechanistic account of causality if men, as products of an alienated society, need educating, this cannot be done except by those who stand "outside alienated society". But those who stand "outside alienated society" or "outside alienation" stand nowhere. In this sense the much publicised "outsider" is really an unintended caricature of the Feuerbachian "educator".

Thus if one tackles the problem of human self-alienation, one should not start with the self-defeating assumption that alienation is a homogeneous inert totality. If one pictures reality (or "being") as a homogeneous inert totality, the only thing one can oppose to this conceptual nightmare is an equally nightmarish "movement" and "negation" as "nothingness". This description of reality as "inert totality", in whatever form it may be expressed, is counter-productive. It arises from the assumption of abstract and rigid dualistic opposites—such as "absolute necessity" and "absolute freedom"—which, by their very definition, cannot possibly communicate or interact with each other. There is no genuine possibility of movement in such a picture of reality.

Were society an "inert totality of alienation", nothing could possibly be done about it. Nor could there be any problem of alienation, or awareness of it, for if consciousness were the consciousness of this "inert totality" it would be one with alienation. In other words: it would be simply the "consciousness of inert totality"— if there could be such a thing (strictly speaking: "the consciousness of inert totality" is a contradiction in terms)—and not the "consciousness of inert totality being alienation", i.e. not a consciousness which reveals and opposes—in however abstract a form—the alienated nature of this inert totality.

Alienation is an inherently *dynamic* concept: a concept that necessarily implies change. Alienated activity not only produces "alienated consciousness", but also the "consciousness of being alienated". This consciousness of alienation, in however alienated a form it might appear—e.g. envisaging self-confirmation in "being at home in unreason as unreason" (161)—not only contradicts the idea of an alienated inert totality, but also indicates the appearance of a *need* for the supersession of alienation.

Needs produce powers just as much as powers produce needs. Even if in the mind of the abstract philosopher this genuine human need is reflected, as it must be, in an alienated form, this does not alter the fact that the need itself is genuinely human in the sense that it is rooted in changing reality. The "educator", who also needs educating, is just as much a part of the alienated society as any-body else. His activity, consisting of a more or less adequate concep-tualization of an actual process, is not "non-alienated activity" by virtue of the fact that he is in his way aware of alienation. Insofar as he is a part of alienation he too, is, in need of being educated. Yet he is not an inert piece in an inert totality, but a human being, a specific part of an immensely complex and inherently dynamic *interpersonal totality*, however much or little alienated his self-consciousness may be. Hegel is not merely an "alienated educator",—which he certainly is, no less than Feuerbach—but he is at the same time also an "anti-alienation educator" (i.e. a practical, and not merely a conceptual, negator of alienation), even if this effect of his activity, realized through Feuerbach, Marx and others, is not an intended one. (On the contrary, it presupposed the direct *negation* of his solutions.)

These considerations apply, *mutatis mutandis*, also to Marx. As Marx himself says, if I have an object the object has me for an object. Consequently if I have an alienated object, this latter has me for an object, and thus I am necessarily subject to alienation. Marx as an educator is both product and negator of an alienated society: his teaching expresses a specific relation to a specific, his-torically concrete alienated object. The proposition according to which "an alienated reflection of self-alienation, is not self-conscious-ness, but alienated self-consciousness" implies its extrapolation: "a true reflection of self-alienation, however true, is not the self-con-sciousness of a non-alienated being, but true self-consciousness of a being in alienation". This is why Marx, being a specific part of the complex web of an alienated society, must define himself as a *practical* being in practical opposition to the actual trends of alien-ation in the existing society. As a non-alienated man, he is "true self-consciousness as a *practical programme*" of the supersession of the historically concrete content and form of alienation. But this *programme* should not be confused with non-alienated reality. It is in fact a "true reflection of an alienated reality". (One should not forget Marx's view on the "negation of the negation".) When the programme becomes reality, in the process of practical supersession, it ceases to be a programme, a reflection of a specific historical rela-tion, i.e. it ceases to be attached to the Marxian framework of nega-tion of the negation. "True self-consciousness" of a reality from which alienation has *entirely* disappeared, should not be confused with Marx's original programme, because the latter defined itself in a specific relation to alienation (as its negation) which is missing from the first. True self-consciousness of such a society cannot possibly be then its consciousness as that of a "non-alienated society", but simply the consciousness of a "human society". That is to say, this consciousness is not the consciousness of a *negation*—conditioned by its negated object—but a consciousness of *positivity*. If therefore one conceives a society in which alienation is *totally* superseded, there is no place for Marx in it. It would be, of course, in absolutely no need of "educators". To anticipate a *totally* non-alienated society as a *final* achievement would be, however, rather problematic. The framework of the right assessment of this problem of human development must be the dialectical conception of the relationship between continuity and discontinuity—i.e. "discontinuity in continuity" and "continuity in discontinuity"—even if the strongest possible emphasis is put on the *qualitative* differences between the contrasted stages.

The supersession of alienated activity through self-conscious human practice is not a static relation of a *means* to an *end*, with no possibility of interplay. Nor is it a *mechanistic causal chain* presupposing ready-made parts that could not possibly be altered in the relation,—only their respective position is subject to change, as that of two billiard balls after their collision. Just as much as alienation is not a *single act* (whether a mysterious "fall" or a mechanistic result), its opposite, the supersession of alienated activity through self-conscious enterprise, can only be conceived as a complex *process* of *interaction* that produces *structural* changes in *all* parts of the human totality.

Activity is alienated activity when it takes the form of a schism or opposition between "means" and "end", between "public life" and "private life", between "being" and "having", and between "doing" and "thinking". In this alienated opposition "public life", "being" and "doing" become subordinated as a mere means to the alienated end of "private life" ("private enjoyment"), "having", and "thinking".[184] Human self-consciousness, instead of attaining the level of true "species-consciousness", in this relation—where public life (the life-activity of man as a species-being) is subordinated, as a means to an end, to mere private existence—becomes an atomistic consciousness, the abstract-alienated consciousness of mere "having" as identified with private enjoyment. And in this way, since the mark of *free activity* that distinguishes man from the animal world is the *practical* (non-abstract) *consciousness* of man as a "self-mediating" (i.e. creative, not just passively "enjoying") human being,[185] the realization of human freedom as man's purpose becomes impossible because its ground—man's life-activity—has become a mere means to an abstract end.

For a solution one does not have to go to the realm of abstraction, because it is given as a *potential reality*—an *actual* potentiality—in the *potential unity* of the members of this practical opposition or contradiction. Thus the *negation* of alienation is not an "absolute" (empty) negativity, but, on the contrary, the *positive assertion* of a relation of unity whose members really exist in an *actual opposition* to each other.

From this it follows that if someone tries to get rid of only *one* side of the opposition, his "solution" must remain fictitious and alienated. And this applies, of course, to *both* sides taken *separately*. The mere abolition of the "private" is just as artificial and alienated as the "fragmentation", "atomization", "privatization" of the "public". The absolutization of any one of the two sides means either that man is deprived of his *individuality* and becomes an abstract "public producer", or that he is deprived of his *sociality* and is transformed into an equally abstract "private consumer". They are both "commodity men", with the difference that while one defines his own essence as "commodity-producer", the other finds self-confirmation in being a self-contained "commodity-consumer".

When Marx speaks of man's "inner wealth" in opposition to alienation, he refers to the "r i c h human being" and to "rich h u m a n n e e d". This being is rich because he is "the human being i n n e e d o f a totality of human life-activities—the man in whom *his own realization exists as an inner necessity, as need*" (111–112). This is the criterion that should be applied to the moral assessment of every human relation and there are no other criteria beside it. Any addition could only be of an "external" kind, i.e. abstractly superimposed on the real man. Thus if one wants to find out whether or not a particular form of the relation between *man* and *woman* is "moral" (human), Marx will answer him: "In this relationship . . . is s e n s u o u s l y m a n i f e s t e d, reduced to an observable f a c t, the extent to which the human essence has become nature to man, or to which nature has to him become the human essence of man. From this relationship one can therefore judge man's whole level of development. . . . In this relationship is revealed, too, *the extent to which man's n e e d has become a human need*; the extent to which, therefore, *the o t h e r person as a person* has become for him a need—the extent to which he in his *individual* existence is at the same time a *social being*" (101). Consequently if the other person is merely a cook, a maid and a whore for man, their relation only satisfies his dehumanized animal needs.

The same criterion of humanness—as inner need of a totality of life-activities—will decide what kind of relationships ought to be morally rejected and practically opposed. The tone of moral indignation is very strong when Marx speaks about capital as the "g o v e r n i n g p o w e r over labour". Yet its ground is not an abstract appeal to an abstract concept of "justice", but a reference to the fact that "the capitalist possesses this power, not on account of his personal or human qualities, but inasmuch as he is an o w n e r of capital. His power is the p u r c h a s i n g power of his capital, which nothing can withstand."[186]

What is in question here is not the Hume-type (or "political economist") treatment of justice (although the contrast is self-evident), but morality in general. In Marx's view nothing is worthy of moral approval unless it helps the realization of human life-activity as internal need. If, therefore, gratification is divorced from activity, and thus the individual qualities of man lose their significance, the obvious verdict is moral condemnation. This principle remains valid even if there is not a single capitalist to point at. If it is *position* that determines the importance (or significance) of the individual and not the other way round, the relationship is of an alienated character and consequently it is to be opposed.

Human gratification is inconceivable in abstraction from the *real individual*. In other words: "human sensuous appropriation" or "self-confirmation" is inconceivable without human individual enjoyment. Only the real human individual is capable of realizing the *unity of opposites* (public life—private life; production—consumption; doing—thinking; means—ends;) without which it is unjustifiable to speak of the supersession of alienation. This unity means not only that private life has to acquire the practical consciousness of its social embeddedness, but also that public life has to be personalized, i.e. become the natural mode of existence of the real individual; not only that passive consumption must change into creative (productive, man-enriching) consumption, but also that production must become enjoyment; not only that subjectless abstract "having" must acquire a concrete being, but also that the "physical subject" or being cannot transform itself into a real human being without "having", without acquiring the "non-alienated ability of mankind";[187] not only that thinking from abstraction must change into practical thinking, directly related to the real—and not imaginary or alienated—needs of man, but also that doing must lose its unconscious coercive character and become self-conscious free activity.

All this directly leads to the question of the resolution of the contradiction between *means* and *ends*, between *necessity* and *freedom*, as Engels puts it, "the reconciliation of mankind with nature and with itself". It is obvious that when human life-activity is only a means to an end, one cannot speak of freedom, because the human powers that manifest themselves in this kind of activity are *dominated* by a need *external* to them. This contradiction cannot be overcome unless work—which is a mere *means* in the present relation—becomes an *end in itself*. In other words: only if labour becomes an *internal need* for man, only then may one refer to work as "free activity".

This is what Marx means when he speaks of the "rich human being" for whom "his own realization exists *as an inner necessity, as n e e d*". His definition of *freedom as an "inner necessity"* does not call for an abstract conceptual "recognition of necessity",[188] but for a *positive need*. Only if this positive need as an *inner* necessity for work exists, only then will labour be able to lose its character as a necessity *external* to man.

Since only as positive need, as inner necessity is labour *enjoyment*, therefore self-realization, human fulfilment is inseparable from the emergence of this positive need. *Freedom* is thus the realization of man's own purpose: *self-fulfilment in the self-determined and externally unhindered exercise of human powers*. As self-determination, the ground of this free-exercise of man's powers is not an abstract "categorical imperative" that remains *external* to the real human being, but an actually existing positive need of self-realizing *human* labour. Thus means (labour) and ends (need) in this *process* of humanization mutually transform each other into truly human activity as enjoyment and self-realization, whereby power and purpose, and means and ends appear in a natural (human) unity.

6. *Legality, Morality and Education*

In all this the importance of morality is central. Morality in the Marxian sense is not a collection of abstract prescriptions and prohibitions, but a *positive function* of the society of the real individuals. "Legality" is tailored to fit the *"average man"*, i.e. the abstractly "public man", morality the particular *social individual*. Both correspond to specific needs of human society, and neither can fulfil the other's functions as we know them now.

Institutionalized legality can only externally relate itself to man as abstractly public man, but never *internally* to the real individual. Its function is fulfilled in :

(1) *formulating* certain *requirements* (e.g. educational) in connection with established *positions* and thus regulating the activities of the individual in a merely institutional framework (i.e. the individual as employee, taxpayer, etc.);

(2) *enforcing* the rules and norms laid down for the normal functioning of the existing social institutions by means of *punitive sanctions*. But legality does not make its own *norms*, it merely codifies them, and thus it is in an external relation even to its own content. Legality may therefore be defined as the codification and enforcement of previously established norms. (This definition does not conflict with the ability of legality to extrapolate from some basic norms and thus to formulate on its own their corollaries, as well as to eliminate, within limits well marked by these basic norms, existing inconsistencies.)

The norms themselves exist, well before any legal codification, as *needs* essential for the functioning of the society. Were they "inner needs" of man, there would be no need whatsoever for *enforcing* them *externally* (if all men happily paid their taxes— because of an "inner need" which should not be confused with an abstract appeal to the externally superimposed idea of a "moral duty" to do so—there would be no need for laws against tax-evasion, etc.). The existence of legality is thus the practical proof of the impotence of morality in this respect. It proves that the social needs of man as a particular member of society have not become internal needs for the real individual, but remained external to him as "needs of the society". (The notion of "moral duty", as used in the various forms of "Individualethik", is an abstract and alienated expression of this contradiction.) But the continued existence of ,legality is at the same time also a proof of its own impotence in this fundamental respect : it is totally incapable of transforming these external "needs of the society" into internal needs of the real individual. (Legality cannot create even "artificial needs" in man, like that of "keeping up with the Jones's". Advertising fulfils this function by appealing to an alienated "status—morality", creating thus the new artificial need by associating it with already established ones.)

Yet this reciprocally conditioning impotence should not lead us to draw pessimistic conclusions. On the contrary: it only shows that it is absurd to expect from any one of the two what it cannot do, and thus it makes us more aware of the real potentialities of *both*. The existence of legality is a constant challenge to morality to get rid of its own impotence. Morality can never achieve this in an *absolute* sense without completely abolishing itself. On the other hand, just as morality completely divorced from legality is deprived of its challenging real task and reduced into a dusty abstraction of philosophical books, so is legality separated from morality completely devoid of content and justification, and thus at least potentially an easy tool of the most arbitrary determinations. It is not enough to pin-point in legality the "reified" appearance of those "moral ideals" which have become *practical* possibilities, through the complex working of the manifold organs of morality, for the *vast majority* of society—which makes possible their codification. One must also underline that this "fixing", however reified, enables morality not to start again from point zero, but set out from beyond the codified average as its new starting point.

There could be no human advancement without this mutually conditioning interplay of the two. While morality without legality is Quixotic wishful thinking, or an abstract transcendental assumption, legality without its dynamic content is only an arbitrary framework that enables the substitution of voluntaristic, partial needs for those of the existing society. What is to be opposed is not the legal safeguarding of a certain level of moral attainment, but its divorce from man which results in a reified form of "fixing". (There may be many forms of legal institutions whose potentialities should be constantly explored with an increasing humanization of legality in view. One such form is what is called "direct democracy": virtually a "virgin land" for theoretical and practical efforts of this kind.)

Those who advocate the abolition of *all* norms and sanctions confuse "measure" with *external* measure. They forget about the natural-human and thus *internal* measure: man himself. Only in relation to this measure can one define human *progress* as a never-enough decrease in external legality and a corresponding increase in internal self-determination or morality proper.

One cannot repeat frequently enough: nothing is achieved by

mere institutional changes in these matters, because the abolition of existing institutions leaves behind a void that must be filled somehow; and it is certainly not filled by the legal establishment of new institutions which are in themselves only an empty framework in need of a content. In formalized institutional change there is no guarantee whatsoever against the reproduction, in a new form, of the contradictions of the old institutions.

No formalized institution can achieve the ideal of man "for whom his own realization exists as an inner necessity, as n e e d", because this would imply the contradiction of making *external* to man his own realization. Such a task which, to be self-realization in fact, cannot conceivably be external, but only *internal*. This task cannot be done for man except by man himself. Morality is a positive function of society : of man struggling with the task of his own realization. Morality, therefore, is not external to man only if, and to the extent to which, it is related to this task, but immediately becomes external to man when it abstracts from him. (Dualistic superimpositions.)

The organ of morality as man's self-mediation in his struggle for self-realization is *education*. And education is the *only possible* organ of human self-mediation, because education—not in a narrow institutional sense—embraces all activities that can become an internal need for man, from the most natural human functions to the most sophisticated intellectual ones. Education is an inherently personal, *internal* matter : nobody can educate us without our own *active* participation in the process. The good educator is someone who *inspires self-educating*. Only in this relation can one conceive the supersession of mere externality in the totality of life-activities of man, —including not the total abolition, but the increasing transcendence of external legality. But this supersession, because of the conditions necessary to it, cannot be conceived simply as a static *point* in history beyond which starts the "golden age", but only as a continuing *process*, with *qualitatively* different achievements at its various stages.

VII. *Aesthetic Aspects*

1. *Meaning, Value and Need: an Anthropomorphic Framework of Evaluation*

ALIENATION deeply affected, and continues to affect, both artistic creation and aesthetic enjoyment. There are very few artists today who would not acknowledge this, even if their attitudes towards it may greatly differ. Marx's contemporary influence among writers is closely linked with this fact. He was the first to raise the alarm about artistic alienation in his powerful analysis of the conditions which engulf the artist. He focused attention on certain characteristics of capitalistic development which for twentieth-century artists are inescapable facts of life, and he did this at a time when the signs of the underlying trend were hardly noticeable. To transfer the assessment of this trend from the *"Urnebel"* (primæval fog) of philosophical abstraction into the broad daylight of concrete social analysis, elaborating at the same time a practical programme for its reversal, was one of Marx's great achievements.

Others before him—especially Schiller and Hegel—had already discussed the opposition between the "rationalism" of capitalistic society and the requirements of art. Yet Schiller wanted to eliminate the negative effects of this opposition by means of an "aesthetic education of, mankind" as a mere educational appeal confined to the consciousness of the individuals—and Hegel, while avoiding Schiller's illusions, accepted this trend as necessarily inherent in the historical development of *"Weltgeist"* (world spirit).

Marx raised the issue in a qualitatively different way. He represented this anti-artistic trend as an indictment of capitalism, envisaging measures—a radical transformation of society—by means of which it should be brought to a halt.

Aesthetic considerations occupy a very important place in Marx's theory. They are so closely intertwined with other aspects of his thought that it is impossible adequately to understand even his economic conception without grasping its aesthetic links. This may sound odd to ears tuned to the key of utilitarianism. For Marx, however, art is not the sort of thing that ought to be assigned to the idle realm of "leisure" and therefore of little, if any, philosophical importance, but something of the greatest human and thus also theoretical significance.

Needless to say, just as it is not possible to appreciate Marx's economic thought and ignore his views on art, it is equally impossible to grasp the meaning of his utterances on aesthetic matters without constantly keeping in mind the economic interconnections. But they are *interconnections* and not one-sided *mechanistic determinations*. The *common* frame of reference is man as a *natural being* who is *active* in order to satisfy his needs, not only economically, but artistically too. Consequently, what we have to discuss first of all is Marx's conception of anthropology.

Aesthetic judgments are linked—directly or indirectly, explicitly or by implication—with the crucial evaluative question of "ought". But how does one justify value-assertions? If one wants to avoid arbitrariness and its pseudo-justification by an equally arbitrary assumption—i.e. by a categorical reference to the alleged dichotomy and unbridgeable rift between "is" and "ought"—one must find some basis for the asserted values.

In Marx's view this basis is man himself. Every single concept belongs to an anthropocentric system. This fact is often veiled by different patterns and grades of mediation by virtue of which instrumental concepts may appear altogether free from anthropocentric links and determinations. On the other hand concepts like "omnipotence", "omniscience", etc., must seem meaningless or self-contradictory if not considered in an anthropocentric framework. And there are, of course, innumerable concepts whose anthropocentric character is directly obvious. However mediated their links to human reality, all concepts acquire their meaning ultimately through these links.

There is, however, a further connection which we have to keep in mind: the interconnection between *meaning* and *value*. To understand it, one needs, again, an anthropocentric framework of reference. The structure of meaning, with all its patterns and degrees of mediation, is closely linked to the human structure of values, which in its turn is founded on the constitution of man as a *"self-mediating"* (self-constituting) *natural being*.

Thus the values we assert, with a simple gesture or by means of complicated philosophical arguments, have their *ultimate* foundation and *natural* basis in human *needs*. There can be no values without corresponding needs. Even an alienated value must be based on a—correspondingly alienated—need. Gold is a worthless metal without the need that transforms it into something greatly appreciated. The same consideration applies to all kinds and forms of value. Art, too, represents value only insofar as there is a human need that finds fulfilment in the creation and enjoyment of works of art.

Values are therefore *necessarily* linked to beings who have *needs*, and the nature of these needs determines the character of the values. The values of a natural being, however sophisticated they may be, must be rooted in nature. The so-called spiritual values of man are in fact aspects of the full realization of his personality as a natural being.

The dialectical interconnection between meaning, value and need—which will be discussed later under a different aspect— can only be grasped in the inherently *historical* concept of the "self-mediating self-constitution" of the human natural being. Such a conception, by accounting for the *genesis* of human values, dissolves the false dichotomy of "is" and "ought". To put it in another way : this dichotomy has to be *postulated* by abstract philosophers because of their historically conditioned inability to account for the *genesis* of human values. They simply *assume* the values, in a metaphysical form, and run away from the challenge of justification by *postulating* a dichotomy as well as a dualistic structure of reality that necessarily goes with it. Thus they "remedy" *petitio principii* by begging the question.

By contrast, Marx's approach which explains the emergence of values by the historical development of human needs, is free from assumptions and arbitrary postulates. It sets out from an irrefutable fact : man's constitution as a natural being. But Marx grasps this fact in its dialectical complexity, and therefore he does not have to end up with the contradiction of a dualistic superimposition. Mechanistically considered, there is nothing of "ought" about the fact that man, a natural being, has needs. The dialectical conception, however,—which identifies man as a *specific* part of nature : the *"self-mediating* natural being"—brings out into the open the *genesis of value* as human *"self-constitution"*. The primitive constitution of man is a "brute natural fact", and *as such* it has nothing to do with value. But this "as such" is a mere abstraction, linked to either a transcendental assumption (e.g. the Kantian "primacy of practical reason") or to a mechanistic disregard for the *specific* in nature as man, or indeed to both. For the so-called "brute natural facticity" in the primitive constitution of man is *at the same time*, at *any* stage of human development, a constitution as "self-constitution" too : a "self-mediatingly natural" or "naturally self-mediating self-constitution" of man. "Self-constitution" exists simultaneously as *need* ("is") and *value* ("ought") in man. (It also exists of course, as an observable fact, linked to the complex laws of nature and human history.) Self-constituting self-realization of man in the course of his historical confrontation with nature and with himself, is both man's need and value : and there can be no value whatsoever beyond it. All values and disvalues which were produced in the historical development of mankind are both *derivative* and *constitutive* of this fundamental value of humanness. Value is an inseparable dimension of reality ("is", "fact"), but—it goes without saying—only of *human* reality. And the potentialities of man—both for "good" and for "evil", i.e. for self-realization and self-destruction—cannot be projected back to some "original state", because human potentialities, too, are constituted in the unending course of humanly "self-mediating self-constitution".

It must be emphasized, however, that this self-constitution is inherently conditioned by nature. Man is free only insofar as the conditions of development are the result of self-constitution itself. This does not mean, however, that freedom can be opposed to nature in man. It would be a mistake to share the position adopted by many philosophers that *freedom* and *value* are not dimensions of nature. According to Marx they are; but they must be grasped as dimensions of *"humanly self-mediating* nature". One must always return to the natural basis of human development, otherwise one gets lost in the clouds of philosophical abstraction and relativism.

If there are ages in which philosophy postulates an opposition between nature and freedom, fact and value, "is" and "ought", the appearance of such oppositions must be explained in terms of concrete historical analysis which reaches down to the roots of these dichotomies. As we shall see, the Marxian principle that asserts the natural foundation of human self-realization is crucially important for the understanding of the nature of artistic experience—as regards both the artist and his public—and its increasing alienation with the advance of capitalism.

Characteristically, parallel to the extension of "rationalism" inherent in capitalistic development—or, to describe it more precisely, the growing abstraction from human needs in favour of the "needs" of the market—"nature" and "realism" become pejorative terms in every sphere. First—when this trend is not yet overpowering—

"nature" is taken up as a romantic ideal and it is opposed to the humanly impoverishing "rationalism of civilization" (Rousseau, Schiller). Later the once criticized trend is accepted and even idealized. While Adam Smith was still aware of the human impoverishment involved in the advantageous system of capitalistic "rationalization", his followers lose in the end all sensitivity for this side of the question. The more industry develops, the more one-sidedly the political economists describe the reduction of human activity to *mechanical motion* as the ideal state of things. Marx quotes in his *Manuscripts of 1844* a significant passage from James Mill's *Elements of Political Economy* which reads as follows: "The agency of man can be traced to very simple elements. He can, in fact, do nothing more than *produce motion*. He can move things towards one another, and he can separate them from one another: *the properties of matter perform all the rest.* . . . As men in general cannot perform many operations with the same quickness and dexterity with which they can by practice learn to perform a few, it is always an *advantage* to limit as much as possible the number of operations imposed upon each. For dividing labour, and distributing the powers of man and machinery, to the *greatest advantage*, it is in most cases necessary to operate upon a large scale; in other words to produce the commodities in greater masses. It is this *advantage* which gives existence to the great manufactories" (132). It does not even occur to James Mill that "advantage" could—and should— mean something else beside the competitive advantage of large-scale capitalistic factories for the market. An advantage which is, in fact, whittled away by the "natural law" of blind competition, leaving behind a maximized dehumanization inherent in the maximization of "rationalizing" (i.e. irrational, uncontrolled) mechanization and fragmentation.

By then the "rationality" of capitalism has got the upper hand, suppressing the awareness of man's inherent links to nature. No wonder, therefore, that the nature to be fitted into this revised picture is degraded, dehumanized nature. Utilitarianism that philosophically reflects this state of affairs operates, characteristically, with the concept of "pleasure" as its central category: it tries to explain human morality with reference to a phenomenon which is far from being specifically human. Thus the "naturalism" of the utilitarians expresses a conception of nature which is divorced and alienated from man. That such a conception must lead to a dualistic superimposition, in the form of an aristocratic and arbitrary classification of the "qualities of pleasure" expressed in the contemptuous motto : "better a Socrates dissatisfied than a pig satisfied", can be a surprise only to those who are unable to understand the underlying trend of dehumanization.

On the other hand, the "anti-naturalistic" criticisms of utilitarianism are not one whit better. What they oppose is not nature in man, but an *alienated* conception of nature—without the slightest awareness of this distinction, of course. Their criticism that "one cannot derive values from natural characteristics" applies only to a conception of "natural" which is divorced from the *specifically natural*, i.e. human. The framework of such a discourse is riddled with arbitrary assumptions and intuitionistic assertions and declarations. And the structure is, again, characterized by a dualistic superimposition of arbitrarily assumed "intrinsic values" over the crude naturalness of the world of man. Thus "naturalistic" and "anti-naturalistic" trends of philosophy—differing only in form from each other—are equally alienated expressions of the growing dehumanization. They are, both, unable to grasp the specifically natural as the human foundation of the asserted values.

2. *Marx's Concept of Realism*

In art we witness similar developments. If utilitarianism is a trivial and shallow philosophy, its artistic counterpart, "naturalism", is a graphic embodiment of disconnected triviality and utter shallowness. This is so because nature depicted by naturalistic artists, often in the most tediously detailed "faithful" manner, is dehumanized nature.

There is but one sense in which "faithfulness" is relevant to art : it is a faithfulness in representing the reality of man. Insofar as nature matters, it is already comprehended in the reality of man. Man's reality, however, is not given in a direct natural (phenomenal) immediacy, but only in an immensely complex dialectically structured, human totality. Consequently, there is a world of difference between the faithfulness of shallow naturalism and that of *realism* which aims at the comprehension of this dialectical totality of man.

In the realist work of art every represented natural or man-made object must be *humanized*, i.e. the attention must be focused on its human significance from a historically and socially specific point of view. (Van Gogh's chair is of great artistic significance precisely because of the artist's powerful humanization of an otherwise insignificant everyday object.) Realism, with regard to its means, methods, formal and stylistic elements, is necessarily subject to change, because it reflects a constantly changing, and not a static, reality.

What remains unchanged in realism and thus enables us to apply this general term to the aesthetic evaluation of works of many ages is this: realism reveals, with artistic adequacy, those fundamental trends and necessary connections which are often deeply hidden beneath deceptive appearances, but which are of a vital importance for a real understanding of the human motivations and actions of the various historical situations. This is why mere means and stylistic aptitudes could never make someone become a realist artist. For all such means, etc., change according to the general require-ments and characteristics of the particular age, and in accordance with the concrete needs of the given subject-matter, moulded by the artist in a concrete situation. What will determine whether he is a realist or not is what he *selects* from a mass of particular experi-ences to stand for the given, historically and socially specific, reality. If he is not able to select *humanly significant* particulars which reveal the fundamental trends and characteristics of the changing human reality, but—for one reason or another—satisfies himself with depicting reality as it *appears* to him in its *immediacy*, no "faithfulness of detail" will raise him above the level of superficial naturalism.

What is wrong with naturalism is precisely its reproduction of deceiving appearances. Naturalism takes it for granted that the human meaning of reality is given in the immediacy of the appearances, while it is in fact always, and in particular in an age so torn by contradictions as ours, concealed by pseudo-values and non-lasting stabilities. The violent rejection of the naturalistic picture by so many modern artists is therefore quite understandable. But in the various other "isms" we find a formally different adoption of the practice of taking things in their immediacy, only now associated with the strong suggestion that the reality of man is devoid of any meaning.

Thus the various "isms" (imagism, expressionism, dadaism, ana-lytic and synthetic cubism, futurism, surrealism, constructivism, etc.), just like the anti-naturalistic philosophical schools, do not make the situation one whit better. They fail to distinguish between humanized and dehumanized nature and thus reject nature altogether, only to be compelled in the end to readapt it in an equally dehumanized abstract form. They defeat themselves by accepting the false alternative of abstraction versus naturalism as the only possible opposition. Thus, ironically, they capitulate before the artistic alienation which they had set out to oppose.

It would be an error to say that these trends oppose *realism*. Yet, it would be worse not to see that, often even programmatically, they oppose themselves to what they *assume* to be realism. Their common denominator is in fact this indirect, or explicit, opposition. (Explicit in names like "surrealism", "constructivism", etc.). They assume to be realism what suits their need to establish their own identity through the adoption of purely formal and stylistic characteristics. In such a frame of reference realism is arbitrarily identified with a collection of rather pedestrian formal and stylistic features which, in fact, amount to nothing more than superficial naturalism. (Significantly, the investigation of the fundamental differences between realism and naturalism cannot find a place in theoretical writings which sympathize with the formalistic conception of both realism and "avantguard" as opposed to each other.) And pointing out the highly anachronistic character of this pedestrian "realism" serves to establish the "avantguard" character of their own efforts.

This artistic crisis is deeply rooted in the all-embracing power of alienation. As this power intensifies, the artist is increasingly denied the possibility of identifying himself with the fundamental trends of the historically given human reality. And what could be more damaging for art than this? For, as Keats wrote, "A poet is the most unpoetical of any thing in existence; because he has no Identity—he is continually filling some other Body. The Sun, the Moon, the Sea and Men and Women who are creatures of impulse are poetical and have about them an unchangeable attribute—the poet has none; no Identity—he is certainly the most unpoetical of all God's creatures."[189] Since true artistic character is born from the relationship between the poet of "no Identity" and reality of "permanent attributes"—permanent of course only in the dialectical sense of "continuity in discontinuity"—the progressive weakening of this relationship makes increasingly more problematic the artistic character and value of modern works of art. Artists become more and more entangled in abstract formal preoccupations. In their contradictory attempt to find a *formal* remedy to their difficulties, they only aggravate the situation, themselves contributing to the further weakening and ultimate break-up of the relationship which is the sole force that can confer value on a work of art.

As the artist's isolation intensifies, so multiply the difficulties of effective protest against it. Since the difficulties of establishing artistic identity through an intimate relationship with the given, however complex, human reality are enormous, (i.e. the difficulties of creating one's identity through a *socially significant content*) many artists desperately attempt to solve this problem by opposing the "traditional" form of artistic self-identification (tradition in the end becomes a dirty word) and confine themselves to external formal characteristics. But through defining their own identity in purely formal terms they become their own jailers, imposing upon every particular experience the same abstract scheme. Their prison is erected from self-imposed and often extremely cerebralized formal rules and stylistic patterns. Only the greatest of them are able to break out of this self-erected prison for whom, as for Picasso, belonging to an "ism" is never more than a transitory stage on the road of great realistic achievements.

Realism is the central notion of Marxian aesthetics, as has been made clear in more than one of Lukács' writings.[190] And no wonder that this concept occupies such a key position. It could not be otherwise, seeing that for Marx realism is not just one among the innumerable artistic trends, confined to one period or another (like "romanticism", "imagism", etc.), but the only mode of reflection of reality which is adequate to the specific powers and means at the disposal of the artist. The inimitable masters of Greek art are great realists, and so is Balzac. There is absolutely nothing *stylistically* common to them. But despite the centuries, social, cultural, linguistic barriers, etc., that separate them, they can be brought to a common denominator because, in accordance with the specific traits of their historical situations, they achieve an artistically adequate depiction of the fundamental human relations of their times. It is in virtue of this that they may be called great realists.

Thus "realism" is equivalent to "artistic adequacy", that is the artistically proper depiction of the manifold and constantly changing relations in which man finds himself. Consequently, any form of *"anti-realism"*—whether a programmatic effort or simply an unconscious practice—is necessarily an expression of alienation. (The formerly mentioned "rationalism" and "abstraction" of capitalistic society obviously nourish these anti-realistic trends and efforts. Characteristically enough, the artistic headlines of our century are captured by such trends.)

Marx's view of realism implies that:

(1) there *is* something significant—with characteristics *of its own*—to be depicted, and failure to grasp those characteristics through the specific potentialities and means of art counts as misrepresentation or distortion, and as such is aesthetically unacceptable;

(2) one must be able to apply certain standards to the *organs* of *depiction*, otherwise it would be impossible to raise the question of misrepresentation and distortion;

(3) similarly, one must be able to apply certain standards to the *organs* of aesthetic *experience*, otherwise there could be no aesthetic judgment;

(4) the standards of creative depiction, aesthetic experience and critical judgment must have some *common* denominator, otherwise there is no guarantee against internal contradiction that would inevitably make vacuous the concept of realism.

In other words: both the object of depiction and the artistic form in which it appears, just as much as the aesthetic experience itself under its various aspects, must have objective criteria of assessment.

But why depiction? The simple answer is: because man, as a natural, "sensuous" being, is constituted the way he is. As Marx puts it: "To be sensuous is to s u f f e r. Man as an objective, sensuous being is therefore a s u f f e r i n g being—and because he feels what he suffers, a p a s s i o n a t e being. Passion is the essential force of man energetically bent on its object" (158—In German: "Sinnlich sein ist l e i d e n d sein.")

Here we have the whole dialectic of *"mimesis"*, identified as anthropomorphically rooted in the objective constitution of man. As a natural being man "suffers" (senses) his own constitution (needs and powers in their inter-relations) as well as the manifold effects of nature and society on his social-individual being. Thus—to continue a point earlier discussed—all *meaning* is *"value-bound"*, because it originates through this complex suffering relationship of the human subject to its objects. But this relationship is qualitatively different from *passive registering*. This latter is a mechanical process and is absolutely unable to originate any meaning whatsoever. Meaning is only possible because "man feels what he suffers" (or senses), unlike a photographic plate which is totally indifferent towards the objects whose reflections affect it.

In this "feeling what man senses" are established the primitive *values* of man, and every single object that affects him, no matter in what way and form, occupies a definite place in the human system of values in which meaning and value are inseparably inter-related. Thus "suffering" as discussed by Marx is value-creating, and therefore *active*,—paradoxical as it might seem to some. There is no "suffering" without feeling, only mechanical registration. And also, there is no "feeling" without "passion", in its Marxian sense, because man, to be in relation at all with his objects, must be "energetically bent on them", which implies the presence of passion—although of various intensity—in all human relations, in-cluding the most mediated ones.

Suffering, feeling and passion, therefore, constitute a dialectical unity which is inherently active. Utilitarianism fails to grasp this unity and ends up with identifying human gratification with the passive enjoyment of "pleasure". The real situation is far more complex, "for *suffering, apprehended humanly, is an enjoyment of self in man*" (106). Enjoyment is, therefore, the individual's appre-hension of the human adequacy of its powers to their objects, even though this relation in many cases assume the form of intense suffer-ing. This view enables Marx to avoid the circularity of utilitarianism which explains pleasure in terms of enjoyment and enjoyment in terms of pleasure.

The inherently active character of the relationship between suffer-ing, feeling and passion makes the objections levelled against *mimesis*—which in fact confuse it with passive registration—grossly misplaced. Artistically specific and adequate *mimesis* is a condition *sine qua non* for art, because through it alone can works of art acquire a meaning. (Those who reject *mimesis* must at the same time also opt for the meaninglessness of art.) And the above-men-tioned dialectical unity of suffering-feeling-passion ensures the active, creative character of artistically proper *mimesis*. This, again, shows that the alternative between *naturalistic dehumanization of mimesis* and meaningless *abstractionism* is a false alternative, brought into being by the advance of alienation in the field of art.

3. The "Emancipation of the Human Senses".

Marx speaks of "*the complete e m a n c i p a t i o n of all human senses and attributes*" (106) and this sums up perhaps better than anything else his philosophical programme. The accent is on the adjective *human*, which throws new light on the endlessly debated philosophical question of what place does and ought the sensuous to occupy on the human scale of values. This question is, needless to say, crucial also for the assessment of the significance of art. It is enough to think of the views of numerous philosophers, from Plato to Hegel and beyond, to see the importance of this question.

Marx strongly opposes the idealist tradition that assigns an inferior place to the sensuous, and consequently also to art. "To the e y e"—he writes—"an object comes to be other than it is to the e a r. The peculiarity of each essential power is precisely its p e c u l i a r e s s e n c e, and therefore also the peculiar mode of its objectification, of its o b j e c t i v e l y a c t u a l living b e i n g. Thus *man is affirmed in the objective world* not only in the act of thinking, but *with a l l his senses*" (108).[191]

As we can see the task of emancipation of all human senses and attributes in philosophical terms is first of all a rehabilitation of the senses and their rescue from the inferior place assigned to them by idealist bias. It can be done because they are not just senses, but *human* senses. "It is obvious that the h u m a n eye gratifies itself in a way *different from the crude, non-human eye*; the human e a r different from the crude, non-human ear, etc." (107) "The s e n s e caught up in crude practical need has only a r e s t r i c t e d sense. For the *starving man* it is not the *human form* of food that exists, but only its *abstract being as food*; it could just as well be there in its crudest form, and it would be impossible to say wherein this feeding-activity differs from that of a n i m a l s. *The care-burdened man in need has no sense for the finest play*; the *dealer* in minerals sees only the *mercantile value* but not the *beauty* and the unique nature of the mineral : he has no *mineralogical sense*. Thus, the *objectification* of the human essence both in its *theoretical* and *practical* aspects is required *to make man's s e n s e h u m a n*, as well as to create the h u m a n s e n s e corresponding to the entire wealth of *human and natural* substance"(108–109).

Thus, human senses cannot be considered as simply given by nature. What is specifically *human* in them is a creation by man himself. As the world of nature becomes humanized—showing the marks of human activity—so do the senses, related to humanly more and more affected objects, become specifically human and increasingly more refined.[192]

This historical process of the refinement and humanization of the senses is an inherently *social* process. "The eye has become a human eye, just as its object has become *a social, human object*—an object emanating from man for man. The senses have therefore become directly in their practice *theoreticians*. They relate themselves to the thing for the sake of the thing, but the thing is an objective *human relation* to itself and to man, and vice versa. *Need and enjoyment* have consequently lost their *egoistical* nature, and nature has lost its *mere utility* by use becoming *human use*" (106–107).

Human senses, therefore, are of an immense variety and richness. They are *innumerable*: their number corresponds to the infinite wealth of objects to which human senses relate themselves. Examples like "musical ear", "mineralogical sense" indicate the manifold character of the objects to which they refer. The same object displays many features—e.g. the beauty of the mineral as contrasted with its exploitable physical properties or its mercantile value— which become real for the individual only if he possesses the sensitivity (i.e. "mineralogical sense", "musical ear", etc.) to grasp them.

The truly human senses are characterized by the highest complexity. The possession of eyes is not enough for grasping visual beauty. One must possess for that the sense of beauty. Human senses are intertwined not only among themselves but, also, every one of them with all the other human powers, including of course the power of reasoning. Only in virtue of these interconnections is the sense of beauty possible. "Man appropriates his total essence in a total manner, that is to say, as a whole man" (106). Separating senses—which have become "directly in their practice theoreticians"—from reasoning, in order to subordinate the former to the latter is, therefore, artificial and arbitrary. This is why the idealist picture of the senses must be rejected.

Yet the task of "emancipating all human senses and attributes" is far from being solved by the right apprehension of the complex interrelations of human powers. The problem is, as Marx sees it, that man, because of alienation, *does not* appropriate "his total essence as a *whole man*", but confines his attention to the sphere of mere *utility*. This carries with it an extreme impoverishment of the human senses.

If "the human essence of nature first exists only for social man" (103), *privatization* inherent in capitalistic development must mean that nature loses its *humanized* character, becomes alien to man. Objects that confront the isolated individual appear to him with their utilitarian sides only (e.g. commercial value and not mineralogical beauty), and this utility is not of human—social—but of narrowly individual use. Thus need and enjoyment, in a direct reversal of the original process of self-mediating humanization, acquire a new "egoistical nature" in the world of capitalistic fragmentation. And since the senses can only be called "theoreticians" in virtue of their "distance" from the immediacy of natural-animal need—i.e. in virtue of the fact that the primitive need has become a "self-mediated need"; a humanly mediated, humanly transformed need—seeing that now the *human* mediation of need is being suppressed in the process of egoistic privatization and fragmentation, the senses lose their "theoretician" character.

"*Human* enjoyment" implies a higher than narrowly individual level of gratification in the spontaneity of experience. Such level is attainable only because the *humanly* gratified sense is interrelated with all the other human senses and powers in the very act of enjoyment itself. (The foundation of this interrelatedness is the historical *genesis*—i.e. self-mediating socialization and humanization—of these senses and powers.) If, therefore, the complex social interrelatedness of the particular senses is disrupted by the "crude solitariness" of egoistic self-gratification, this means inevitably that enjoyment itself loses its general human significance—ceases to be *human* enjoyment, by becoming mere self-satisfaction of the isolated individual—and its level sinks into crude *immediacy* to which no *standard* can apply.

Significantly enough : this development goes hand in hand with a general crisis of aesthetic values and standards. And no wonder. for if the general significance of human enjoyment is replaced by the crude immediacy of private self-gratification, there can be no *common measure* or standard of evaluation. Its place is taken either by a superficial description of the mechanical constitutents and responses of the given process, or by a pretentious and often irrationalistic monologue of introspection concerning one's own isolated "aesthetic experience". They are both astronomical distances away even from the preconditions of aesthetic evaluation.

The two observed phenomena—the impoverishment of the senses and of their gratification on one hand, and the endless attacks on the objectivity of aesthetic standards and values on the other—are thus closely interlinked. Such attacks, in their sheer negativity and repetitiousness, become a substitute for aesthetic thinking, defending or even glorifying the types of aesthetic experience that characterize the conditions of privatization, fragmentation, "crude solitariness" and egoistic self-gratification.

All this is summed up in saying that the place of all physical and mental senses has been occupied by "the sheer estrangement of all the senses—*the sense of having*" (106). Needs that are developed in these conditions are those that directly correspond to the immediacy of private utility and private appropriation. The general outcome is human impoverishment on a massive scale running parallel to the material enrichment of the isolated individual.

As we can see the real situation amazingly resembles its idealistic depiction which was passionately rejected by Marx. The vital difference, however, which made his rejection necessary, will be evident if we remind ourselves that while the idealists described those objectionable features as being inherent in the *senses themselves*—excluding therefore the possibility of significant changes—Marx emphasized that we are dealing with a *historical* phenomenon: a dehumanized state of affairs due to capitalistic alienation. In this concrete historical definition of the problem he was able not only to assert the possibility of transcending the capitalistic dehumanization of the senses but also, positively, to identify in the "complete emancipation of all human senses and attributes" the *raison d'être* of socialism.

The negative effects on art of the formerly described development have to be considered in relation to: (1) the artist himself; (2) the subject-matter of his work; (3) the "public" of modern art.

(1) With the advance of alienation the artist's isolation increases. He has been set free from all the bonds against which the Renaissance artists had to fight, but only at the price of submitting himself to the impersonal power of the art market. Artists in pre-capitalist societies were, on the whole, integrated with the social body to which they belonged. By contrast, artists under capitalism have to experience the fate of being "outsiders" or even "outcasts". And the fact that the "universal galvano-chemical power of society" (money) rules over his work, means that the latter loses its direct sense and, subjected to the general laws of commercialization, becomes a mere means to an alien end. To reconquer the sense of his work the artist has to break through the paralysing intermediary of the art market and establish an inherently artistic relation with his public. The public itself is no less affected by all-

pervasive commercialization than the artist, which makes the latter's task doubly difficult.

(2) The artist has become free to choose in every respect the subject-matter of his works, but at the price of having to put up with constant doubts about their relevance. One of the central themes of modern art is in fact the problematic character of works that are created in a situation in which the artist is "the omega and the alpha"—and "measures himself with himself". Thus, ironically, the freedom of the artist to choose the subject-matter of his work turns out to be an extreme restriction that brings with it endlessly recurring themes and problems. And to make the situation worse, the "prosaic" character of everyday experience induces many artists to look for artifices of all kinds, from the slogan of "l'art pour l'art"[193] to various forms of "abstract art". This, again, makes the modern artist's thematic freedom appear an extremely problematic attainment, a Pyrrhic victory indeed.

(3) As to the public, the main effect of alienation in this regard is the appearance of a "public" which is barred from participating in the processes of artistic creation. The "free" modern artist presents this public with a ready-made *product*—a saleable commodity in fact. All that is left to the public is to assume the rôle of a *passive consumer*. In this impersonal relation—where the recipient "Public" is an abstract entity—there can be only one measure of approval and success: money. The term "bestseller" revealingly expresses the relationship from which personality—on both sides—has totally disappeared. All that is left behind is an empty "value-word" which can equally apply to the work of great artistic genius and the clever gimmick-seller. The depersonalization of this relationship thus inevitably carries with it the disappearance of aesthetic value, whose place is taken over by pseudo-values of the "bestseller" type.

4. *Production and Consumption and Their Relation to Art*

As we have already seen Marx criticizes private property because it has made us "so stupid and one-sided that an object is only o u r s when we have it—when it exists for us as capital, or when it is directly possessed, eaten, drunk, worn, inhabited, etc.—in short *when it is u t i l i z e d by us*" (106). Elsewhere he makes the point that "wherever the sensuous affirmation is the direct annulment of the object in its independent form (as in eating, drinking, working up the object, etc.), this is the affirmation of the object" (136).

These points are very important for the assessment of alienation in art. Art, just as much as any other activity, involves consumption, and the nature of every particular form of consumption reveals the specific character of the activity in question. If, therefore, a work of art is consumed as a mere object of utility, this shows that there is something wrong with its specific being as a work of art. As Marx says, *"consumption creates the drive for production".*[194] This puts into relief a relationship of interaction which is often forgotten. In view of such interaction it is clear that if the work of art is consumed as a commercial object, the "drive for production" which is created by this kind of consumption is one that produces commercial objects (i.e. commodity production).

In this context it is vital to keep in mind the enormous complexity of the problem of consumption, and oppose it to the one-sided views we encounter. It is customary to treat consumption as something *passive* and merely *individualistic*. In this picture man is represented as an isolated individual who confronts the ready-made objects of his consumption, whether on trees or in the baskets of supermarkets. Two different, but equally harmful practical attitudes follow from this conception.

The first subordinates all major functions of society—from industrial production to education and art—to the task of filling those baskets, ignoring the anti-human effects of this process. The much advertised "individual" of this relationship is "commodity-man" who is a slave of his consumption, and of the intricate institutions that enable him to be a passive commodity-man.

By contrast, the second practical attitude *minimizes* the importance of individual consumption and creates institutions capable of enforcing the laws that regulate the functioning of a system of production with restricted individual consumption. But, ironically, this approach of restricted individual consumption transforms the view formerly critical of alienated commodity-man into his (unintended) idealization. (Cf. the problematic measure of socialist achievements: "overtaking the leading capitalist country in *per capita* production".)

The contradictions of both approaches derive from a common source: the neglect of the profound structural implications of treating consumption as a passive entity to be manipulated. (The historical causes of such neglect are, of course, very different in the two cases). In the first case the contradictions become manifest in the form of "chronic *affluence*", in the second: of "chronic *scarcity*". Human relations of the first attitude are characterized by the paralysing flood of *impersonalization*, and of the second: by bureaucratization and direct *administrative interference* with all bodies and processes of decision-making. And a common feature is a tremendous waste of creative human energies that can be activated only be means of grasping the proper relationship between consumption and production in all spheres of human activity, from economy to art.

Consumption is neither merely individualistic, nor passive, even if this false appearance may be created by the temporary success of the above-mentioned efforts of manipulation. (The consequences of such efforts are far-reaching and, of course, self-perpetuating: i.e. they make the adoption of the correct approach increasingly more difficult.) The individual aspect of consumption is stressed by Marx in this way: *"in consumption the products become objects of pleasure, of individual appropriation."*[195] There would be no production without the need for consumption. (This need is related both to the existing products and to the powers and vital energies of man—a being of nature. The powers of man can only be experienced in the self-producing, self-consuming and self-reproducing act of production. Thus the need for consumption is at the same time also a need for production, and conversely the need for production is simultaneously also a need for consumption.)

One must, furthermore, emphasize that production is also a form of *social consumption* in the course of which man is "consumed" as a mere individual (the powers given to him by nature) and reproduced as a *social individual*, with all the powers that enable him to be engaged in a *human* form of production and consumption. Thus the social and individual factors are closely intertwined in both consumption and production. And it is precisely this dialectical interrelationship that saves consumption from being passive and makes it become something creative, even if—to take the extreme case—what is produced is an alienated system of human activities. One should not forget that together with such a system its conditions of supersession are also created.

The more production is conceived and carried on as subordinated to individual consumption, the poorer it is bound to become (moving in the narrow circle of, maybe, half a dozen "mass consumer-goods"). On the other hand the poorer production becomes the greater is human impoverishment which, in its turn, has its impoverishing effect again on production—and so on.

There seems to be no way out of this vicious circle, because of the extremely complex interaction of cause and effect in this dialectical interrelationship. One cannot introduce improvements on the production side without at the same time enriching (though not simply in terms of money) the individual consumer. But how can one succeed in this latter task without carrying out structural changes (not merely legal-institutional changes) in the whole complex of production?

Obviously neither side can be simply subordinated to the other without distortions to both, with the inevitable waste of creative human energies already mentioned. And this is the point where we can clearly see the overriding importance of *ideals* in efforts that aim at improving a given state of affairs. Since one cannot rely for a dynamic change in the structure of production on the impoverished needs of alienated commodity-man, one must turn to the ideal of a *"rich social individual"* (Marx) whose needs are capable of providing a new scope for production. But such an ideal must be firmly rooted in reality—unlike the "positive hero" of "revolutionary romanticism" whose distinctive feature is not a rich range of human needs but a *fictitious* overcoming of the needs of individual consumption—otherwise it remains an abstraction as incapable of solving the problems at stake as the easily manipulated "consumer-individual". Not only needs create ideals; ideals also create needs. But only those ideals have a chance of succeeding in this which are latent in the given human relationships, namely which already exist *potentially*. Only from the realization of these ideals may one hope for a solution of the contradiction between production and consumption.

The case of art is particularly illuminating in this respect. The work of art, because of its specific character, requires a specific mode of consumption. The main reason why art suffers in capitalistic society is that it is difficult, if not impossible, to secure in the prevailing circumstances the necessary conditions for the mode of consumption adequate to the true nature of the work of art. We have to keep in mind that :

(1) the work of art cannot be consumed simply as an *object of utility*, even if as a natural object it may serve a useful purpose (e.g. architecture, pottery, etc.);

(2) the *possession* of a work of art as one's exclusive property is completely irrelevant to its aesthetic consumption : the appropriation

of a work of art merely as one's private property is a pseudo-consumption;

(3) in the course of artistic creation the natural object itself which is reflected in the work of art is not changed; there is no "working up" of the object as a *natural* object;

(4) as consumers of the basic objects of utility we are motivated by direct natural needs (need for food and shelter, etc.). By contrast, it is a *pre-condition* of art that man should achieve a certain *distance* (freedom) from his direct natural needs. "Admittedly"—writes Marx—"animals also produce. They build themselves nests, dwellings, like the bees, beavers, ants, etc. But an animal only produces what it *immediately* needs for itself or its young. It produces *one-sidedly*, whilst man produces universally. It produces only under the *dominion of immediate physical need*, whilst man produces even when he is *free from physical need* and only truly produces in freedom therefrom. . . . An animal forms things in accordance with the standard and the need of the species to which it belongs, whilst man knows how to produce in accordance with the standard of every species, and knows how to apply everywhere the *inherent standard* to the object. Man therefore also forms things *in accordance with the laws of beauty*" (75–76). Thus, since the consumption of the work of art cannot be motivated by a direct natural need, artistic consumption will take place only if there is a need of some other kind;

(5) after consumption the work of art remains as it was before—but only in its physical being; its aesthetic substance is constantly recreated *in the activity of consumption*. The work of art has no strictly "independent" aesthetic being. Poison remains poison—in virtue of the testable effects of its chemical composition—even if no one is prepared to take it. But the work of art becomes a mere natural or utilitarian object if there is no artistically adequate consumer for it.

Considering points (1) and (2) it becomes clear that in the circumstances when an object is only ours "when it is directly possessed, eaten, drunk, worn, inhabited, etc., in short when it is u t i l i z e d by us", the work of art cannot be consumed as a work of art, but only as an object of utility. The proper human relationship underlying artistic production is thus disrupted, and the artist is forced to think of himself as the "omega and alpha"—or *producer and consumer*—of his own work.

210

This situation is further aggravated by the characteristics mentioned in points (3), (4) and (5). The fact that in artistic production there is no "working up" of the reflected natural objects may create—under certain circumstances: when the artist is socially isolated—the illusion that the artist's relationship to the outside world is confined to stone, metal, wood, paint, sound and word, whereas in every other respect the artist is absolutely free to do whatever he wants. From here can issue both the contempt for *mimesis* and the excessive preoccupation with the manipulation of dead matter. That *"nature fixed in isolation from man is n o t h i n g for man"* (169) remains a truth no matter how high a price the gimmicky nothing—dead matter fixed in its immediacy and isolation from man—will fetch on the art-market.

The crucial question in this context concerns the *organ* of artistic consumption. Nature takes care of the reproduction of our need for food, shelter, etc. When this fails to occur, we call the doctor or the psychiatrist. But we cannot resort to such help when the need for artistic consumption is absent, or, worse, when it is replaced by a need for the production of works of art as commercial objects: marketable commodities. And, of course, in the absence of the need for artistic consumption the necessary recreation of the work of art in its aesthetic being—referred to in point (5)—cannot take place.

5. *The Significance of Aesthetic Education*

The solution is hinted at when Marx writes: *"music alone awakens in man the sense of music . . . the most beautiful music has no sense for the unmusical ear—is no object for it, because my object can only be the confirmation of one of my essential powers and can therefore only be so for me as my essential power is present for itself as a subjective capacity, because the sense of an object for me goes only so far as m y senses go"* (108). This points to the great importance of "aesthetic education" without which one cannot create the organ of artistic consumption in man.

As we have already seen Marx objected to "direct, one-sided gratification", to mere "having" as abstract "possession", because in it man's manifold relations with his objects are impoverished in a twofold sense:

(1) only those relations are retained which are suitable to serve this kind of gratification;

(2) even these restricted relations are retained only to the extent

to which they can *directly* serve that one-sided gratification. In other words: impoverishment means both the narrowing down of the *range* of human objects of enjoyment and the loss of particular richness and *intensity* of the retained narrow range of objects.

It is not difficult to see that art particularly suffers as a result of these developments, because works of art are not suitable for one-sided gratification. The damage inflicted on art amounts to more than simply cancelling one item from the list of objects of gratification. Range and intensity—or, in other words, "extensive and intensive totality"—are dialectically interrelated concepts. The narrower the range the poorer will be the intensity of gratification, which in its turn results in a further narrowing down of the range. Thus the lack of adequate aesthetic consumption is revealing about human impoverishment in general, which manifests itself in the extreme poverty of gratification confined to the one-sidedly appropriated narrow range of objects of enjoyment.

Aesthetic education is crucial for changing this situation: for turning the narrow and one-sided gratification into the self-fulfilling enjoyment of the "extensive and intensive totality" of the human world. Without aesthetic education there can be no real consumer— only commercial agent—for works of art. And since the work of art cannot properly exist without being constantly recreated in the activity of consumption—the awareness of which must be embodied in the creation itself—aesthetic education, as the creator of the organ of aesthetic consumption, is a vital condition for the development of art in general.

Artistic creation, under suitable circumstances, is considered by Marx as free activity, as an adequate fulfilment of the rich human being. Only in relation to a natural being can the question of freedom be raised as fulfilment which is in harmony with this being's inner determination, and only in this relation can freedom be defined in positive terms.

Art, in this sense, is an "end in itself" and not a means to an end external to it. But art, conceived in such terms, is not one of the specialities among the many, preserved for the fortunate few, but an essential dimension of human life in general. In the form in which we know it, art is deeply affected by alienation, because the "exclusive concentration of artistic talent in some" is inseparably bound up with "its suppression in the masses as a result of the division of labour". As Marx puts it: "as soon as labour is distributed, each man has a particular, exclusive sphere of activity, which is forced upon him and from which he cannot escape. He is a hunter, a shepherd, or a critical critic, and must remain so if he does not want to lose his means of livelihood; while in communist society, where nobody has one exclusive sphere of activity but each can become accomplished in any branch he wishes, society regulates the general production and thus makes it possible for me to do one thing to-day and another to-morrow, to hunt in the morning, fish in the afternoon, rear cattle in the evening, criticize after dinner, just as I have a mind, without ever becoming hunter, fisherman, shepherd or critic".[190]

What matters here is to point out that art, insofar as it is negatively affected by the division of labour, must be superseded. Since "Religion, family, state, law, morality, science, art, etc., are only p a r t i c u l a r modes of production", and since production in general is under the spell of alienation, the positive transcendence of human self-estrangement can only be realized by means of a "return of man from religion, family, state, etc., to his h u m a n, i.e. s o c i a l mode of existence". (102–103; "etc." here clearly includes art that occurred in the previous enumeration to which this latter one refers.)

This passage does not mean that art, science etc. ought to be abolished—although this impression may be created by the references to religion, state and law. It goes without saying that in Marx's view mankind without art and science would be an enormously impoverished humanity, if conceivable at all in concrete historical terms. But just as he insisted that *alienated* science must be transformed into a *"human science"*, so he insists that art too must lose its *alienated* character.

The issue is, therefore, not that of "job-diversification". Even a capitalist society ought to be able to produce the latter, on an incomparably larger scale than we have experienced so far. (Of course under capitalism such programmes can only be realized within the narrow limits of the given social structure; i.e. by further extending the profitable operations of "leisure industry" to cover all the so-called "artistic activities" that are suitable for being marketed in some conveniently assembled kit-form.) Needless to say, what Marx had in mind has nothing to do with this kind of approach. What he was after was not a more extensive collection of hierarchically arranged functions in place of their presently more limited number. For it is simply inconceivable that the individuals could master even a small proportion of activities that characterize contemporary society, let alone all of them. And it is by no means self-evident why the exercise of half a dozen or so functions should be *in itself* inherently more rewarding than that of a smaller number of them.

If, as is obvious, one cannot aim in this regard at the realization of "extensive totality", other criteria than just numbers must be found for displaying the qualitative superiority of one system over the other. What Marx repeatedly emphasized was the necessity to liberate one's life-activities—no matter how many or how few—from the iron laws of capitalistic economy which affected art just as much as anything else. The limitation manifest in the numerical aspects of this issue—i.e. the exclusivistic distribution of functions: art for a privileged few and degrading mechanical work for the vast majority—is simply the *form* in which a basic contradiction of commodity-producing society appeared, but not the cause itself. It is the cause—commodity-production itself—that must be done away with, because it dehumanizes *every* activity—including, of course, artistic activity—degrading it to the status of mere *means* subordinated to the ends of capitalistic market economy.

Thus the utopian advocacy of a "redistribution" of the activities and functions recognizable in capitalistic society could not be further removed from the real issue which is the critical recognition of the inherent meaninglessness of every activity that accommodates itself to the narrow limits of commodity-production. And "job-diversification" cum prefabricated "hobbies"—subordinated to the needs of capitalism in general and to "leisure-industry" in particular—would only intensify the sense of meaninglessness people experience already. The true development of one's abilities and inclinations—in a social framework freed from the paralysing requirements of commodity-production which *apriori* determine the numbers admissible for the exercise of any particular activity, oppressing the *human* demand in favour of the *commercial* need—necessarily implies an inherent *meaning* to *all* functions and activities of the individual concerned. Why should he, otherwise, wish to enlarge the list of his activities? It is precisely this problematics of the meaningfulness of human activities—their liberation from being mere means to alienated ends—which is at stake in Marx's condemnation of the hierarchical social division of labour.

As far as art is directly concerned, Marx's message means that artistic creation has ultimately to be transformed into an activity the social individuals as readily engage in as in the production of the goods necessary for the reproduction of the conditions of their life. It means above all that the existing—alienated—relationship between production and consumption must be radically changed, so that the creative aspect of consumption enhances and intensifies the inherent creativity of artistic production. The only form in' which this can happen is a *reciprocal participation* of both sides in the various processes of artistic production and consumption.

Such a transformation of artistic creation and enjoyment—which implies, of course, a radical change in *all* human relations—is not conceivable without an aesthetic education of man. (Also it goes without saying that the problems of aesthetic education are inseparable from the various other aspects of education.) Marx's conception of art aims at adding a new dimension to human life, in order to transform it in its totality through the fusion of this new dimension with all the other human life-activities. In this conception artistic production and consumption become inseparable aspects of the same life-activity which can also be described as the *practical* aesthetic *self-education* of man.

PART III

CONTEMPORARY SIGNIFICANCE OF MARX'S THEORY OF ALIENATION

The realm of freedom actually begins only where labour which is determined by necessity and mundane considerations ceases; thus in the very nature of things it lies beyond the sphere of actual material production. Just as the savage must wrestle with Nature to satisfy his wants, to maintain and reproduce life, so must civilized man, and he must do so in all social formations and under all possible modes of production. With his development this realm of physical necessity expands as a result of his wants; but, at the same time, the forces of production which satisfy these wants also increase. Freedom in this field can only consist in socialized man, the associated producers, rationally regulating their interchange with Nature, bringing it under their common control, instead of being ruled by it as by the blind forces of Nature; and achieving this with the least expenditure of energy and under conditions most favourable to, and worthy of, their human nature. But it nonetheless still remains a realm of necessity. Beyond it begins that development of human energy which is an end in itself, the true realm of freedom, which, however, can blossom forth only with this realm of necessity as its basis. The shortening of the working-day is its basic prerequisite.

—Capital

VIII. *The Controversy about Marx*

1. *"Young Marx" versus "Mature Marx"*

IT is impossible to deal with the various interpretations of Marx's theory of alienation in a systematic way within the confines of this study. All we can do is to choose a few characteristic points which help to clarify some questions of importance, and thus carry a step forward the main arguments of this enquiry.

One of the most controversial issues is : what place ought to be assigned to the early works of Marx in his system as a whole?

Ever since the publication of the *Economic and Philosophic Manuscripts of 1844* many philosophers have maintained that the young Marx ought to be treated separately, because there is a *break* between the thinker who deals with problems of alienation and the "mature Marx" who aspires to a scientific socialism. And, strangely enough, the holders of this view belonged to politically opposite camps. Their differences amounted to this, that while the one camp idealized the young Marx and opposed his early manuscripts to his later works, the other only accepted these latter, and dismissed his earlier writings as idealistic.

In his study of *The Early Development of Marx's Thought* John Macmurray characterized these approaches in this way : "Communists are rather liable to misinterpret this early stage even if they do not entirely discount it. They are naturally apt to read these writings in order to find in them the reflection of their own theory as it stands today, and, thereiore, to dismiss as youthful aberrations those elements which do not square with the final outcome. This is, of course, highly undialectical. It would equally be a misunderstanding of Marx to separate the early stages of his thought from their conclusion, though not to the same extent. For they a r e earlier stages, and though they can only be fully understood in terms of the theory which is their final outcome, they are historically earlier and the conclusion was not explicitly in the mind of Marx when his earlier works were written."[197]

These words were published as far back as 1935, but the highly undialectical separation of the young Marx from the later Marx has not disappeared in the years that separate us from the early 'thirties. On the contrary, the assertion of a supposed break has become an accepted common-place in a considerable amount of current philosophical literature.

Is it true, as is often affirmed, that the notion of alienation "drops out" from the later writings of Marx; indeed, that he treats it ironically, thus detaching himself from his own philosophical past? Two references are usually given in support of this thesis: one to *The German Ideology* and the other to the *Communist Manifesto*. The question is, however, are the passages in question rightly interpreted?

Undoubtedly there are ironical sentences in *The German Ideology* which contain the words "estrangement" or "self-estrangement". There are actually two of them. The first says that "This 'estrangement' (to use a term which will be comprehensible to the philosophers) can, of course, only be abolished given two *practical* premises."[198] And the second adds: "The whole process was thus conceived as a process of the self-estrangement of 'man'."[199] The translator and Editor, Roy Pascal, comments in his notes on these passages: "In *The German Ideology* Marx makes his *final reckoning* with this concept of 'self-estrangement'." This "final reckoning" is supposed to be in sharp contrast to the earlier *Manuscripts of 1844* in which Marx still "*wrestles* with this concept, and charges it with a new content."[200]

This contraposition is highly misleading. "Final reckoning" following the previous "wresting" sounds pretty dramatic and is in keeping with the Marx-Engels-Lenin Institute's preface to the edition of *The German Ideology*. This preface greatly exaggerates the differences of this latter from the earlier writings and claims as radical innovations points that had, in fact, been worked out in the *Manuscripts of 1844*, or even earlier. Yet the simple, undramatic truth is that there is neither a "final reckoning" in *The German Ideology*, nor some kind of a "wrestling" in the Paris Manuscripts which could be interpreted as lagging behind the presumed mature reckoning. Indeed the position criticizing the idealistic philosophers— our first quotation—and referring the matter of alienation to *practice*, had been reached by Marx well *before* the *Manuscripts of 1844* (see especially his *Introduction to the Critique of the Hegelian Philosophy of Right*).

Marx made it explicit more than once in his *Manuscripts of 1844* that he sets out from the language of political economy in order to rescue its achievements, which remained hidden to the political economists themselves, as well as to criticize them in their own terms. He adopted exactly the same approach towards idealistic philosophy. This is why he could never "drop" the concept of alienation: it would have amounted to depriving himself of a *real* achievement (i.e. the "rational kernel" of the Hegelian philosophy) *notwithstanding* its mystifying setting. In the disputed passage Marx simply wants to point out—as he does on numerous occasions in the Paris Manuscripts—that the language of "estrangement" is mystifying *without* the necessary references to social *practice*.

As to the second quotation, a more careful reading will make it clear that it has nothing to do with the rejection of the term of "self-estrangement". The relevant passage reads as follows: "The individuals, who are no longer subject to the division of labour, have been conceived by the philosophers as an *ideal*, under the name '*man*'. They have conceived the whole process which we have outlined as the evolutionary process of 'man', so that at every historical stage 'man' was substituted for the *individuals* and shown as the motive force of history. The whole process was thus conceived as a process of the self-estrangement of '*man*', and this was essentially due to the fact that the average individual of the later stage was always foisted on to the earlier stage, and the consciousness of a later age on to the individuals of an earlier. Through this inversion, which from the first is an abstract image of the actual conditions, it was possible to transform the whole of history into an evolutionary process of *consciousness*."[201]

As we can see, there is nothing that even vaguely resembles a final reckoning, but only an argument quite familiar to us from the *Manuscripts of 1844*. What Marx is ironical about is not the concept of self-estrangement, but philosophical abstractionism which substitutes for the *real* (historically and socially concrete) *individual* the idealistic image of *abstract man*, and thus mystifies the *actual* estrangement of *real man* (the social individual) by representing it as the estrangement of *consciousness*. In other words, what he objects to is the identification of the concept of man with abstract, *generic consciousness*. This objection, well known to us also from his earlier writings, does not make the notion of "the self-estrangement of real man" obsolete in the least.

The reference to the *Communist Manifesto* is no more convincing. This is the passage in question: "It is well known how the monks wrote silly lives of Catholic Saints o v e r the manuscripts on which the classical works of ancient heathendom had been written. The German literati reversed this process with the profane French literature. They wrote their philosophical nonsense beneath the French original. For instance, beneath the French criticism of the economic functions of money, they wrote 'Alienation of Humanity', and beneath the French criticism of the bourgeois state they wrote 'Dethronement of the Category of the General', and so forth. The introduction of these philosophical phrases at the back of French historical criticism they dubbed 'Philosophy of Action', 'True Socialism', 'German Science of Socialism', 'Philosophical Foundations of Socialism', and so on. The French Socialist and Communist literature was thus completely emasculated. And, since it ceased in the hands of the German to express the struggle of one class with the other, he felt conscious of having overcome 'French one-sidedness' and of representing, not true requirements, but the requirements of Truth; not the interests of the proletariat, but the interests of Human Nature, of Man in general, who belongs to no class, has no reality, who exists only in the misty realm of philosophical phantasy."[202]

Again, we can see, the criticism is not directed against the concept of alienation, but the idealist use of it, because such a use "completely emasculates" it, deprives it of its concrete social content and power of practical criticism. Equally, what is attacked here is not the notion of man defined by Marx in 1844 as the social individual, but the abstraction "Human Nature" and "Man in general" as used by his opponents, because these only exist in the "misty realm of philosophical phantasy". Quite the opposite of a break : the most remarkable continuity. Every single point made in this passage can easily be found even in Marx's Introduction to the Critique of the Hegelian Philosophy of Right which preceded, as we all know, not only The German Ideology, but also the Manuscripts of 1844. Here are a few quotations to prove this assertion : "But man is no abstract being squatting outside the world. Man is the world of man, the state, society."; "If the speculative philosophy of right, that abstract extravagant thinking on the modern state, the reality of which remains a thing of the beyond, if only beyond the Rhine, was possible only in Germany, inversely the German thought-image of the modern state which makes abstraction of real man was possible only because and insofar as the modern state itself makes abstraction of real man or satisfies the whole of man only in imagination. In politics the

Germans t h o u g h t what other nations d i d."; "no class in civil society has any need or capacity for general emancipation until it is forced by its i m m e d i a t e condition, by m a t e r i a l neces- ity, by its v e r y c h a i n s. Where, then, is the p o s i t i v e possi- bility of a German emancipation? A n s w e r : In the formation of a class with r a d i c a l c h a i n s, a class of civil society which is not a class of civil society, an estate which is the dissolution of all estates, . . . This dissolution of society as a particular estate is the p r o l e t a r i a t."[203] In reading these passages, should not one be struck by the basic identity of the early Marx's approach with that of his later work?

Nothing could be further removed from the truth than to assert— no matter from which political point of view—that from 1845 onwards Marx is no longer interested in man and his alienation, because his critical attention is then diverted in another direction by the introduction of the concepts of "the classes" and "the prole- tariat". As we have seen, these concepts had acquired a crucial importance in his thought already in 1843. We must emphasize that if by "man" one means, as Marx's opponents did, "abstract man" or "Man in general" who is "abstracted from all social determina- tions", then this is completely beside the point. He was, in fact, *never* interested in this "Man", not even *before* 1843, let alone at the time of writing the *Economic and Philosophic Manuscripts of 1844*. On the other hand "real man", the "self-mediating being of nature", the "social individual" *never* disappeared from his horizon. Even towards the end of his life when he was working on the third volume of *Capital*, Marx advocated for human beings the "con- ditions most favourable to, and worthy of, their *human nature.*"[204] Thus his concern with classes and the proletariat in particular *always* remained to him identical with the concern for "the g e n e r a l h u m a n emancipation"[205]—a programme clearly laid down in the same early *Introduction to the Critique of the Hegelian Philosophy of Right.* And this programme, formulated in these words, is only another expression for what he called elsewhere the "transcendence of alienation".

But what about the concept of alienation in Marx's works which followed the *Manuscripts of 1844?* Why did he "drop" this concept (or why did he drop the "word", as others put it) if he remained faithful to his programme of transcending alienation? The simple answer is that he did *not* drop the word at all, let alone the concept. As a matter of fact there is *ample* evidence to show that Marx went on using the word "alienation" up to the very end of his life. So ample is this evidence that even if we confine ourselves to the word *Entfremdung*, taken—as in the Paris Manuscripts—with its predicative forms (leaving out, that is, *Entäusserung* and *Veräusserung*: i.e. two further words which mean "alienation", as well as *Verdinglichung, Verselbstständigung, Fetischismus*, etc.) we can' only give a very modest selection of the expressions in which the disputed word occurs. For a *complete* reproduction of all the relevant passages containing also these closely related terms, we would need to multiply the length of this chapter several times over. Here then is our limited sample, in chronological order. (For obvious reason we have to reproduce these passages in the original German. Translation is given in Note No.[200])

The Holy Family. We have already seen (Chapter III) that quite a few passages from the *Manuscripts of 1844* were incorporated into this later work. It was also shown that, contrary to some assertions, these presumably idealistic passages which dealt with the problem of "alienation" were known to, and approvingly quoted by, Lenin.

The German Ideology. "solange die Menschen sich in der naturwüchsigen Gesellschaft befinden, solange also die Spaltung zwischen dem besondern und gemeinsamen Interesse existiert, solange die Tätigkeit also nicht freiwillig, sondern naturwüchsig geteilt ist, *die eigne Tat des Menschen ihm zu einer Fremden, gegenüberstehenden Macht wird*, die ihn unterjocht, statt dass er sie beherrscht." (Just as in the good, or bad, old days, alienation is presented as the transformation of man's—the purists should notice: *man's* and not *men's* or the *classes'*—own activity into an *alien power that confronts him*; as such it is opposed to freedom, or free activity.) "Eben weil die Individuen n u r ihr besondres, für sie nicht mit ihrem gemeinschaftlichen Interesse zusammenfallendes suchen, überhaupt das Allgemeine illusorische Form der Gemeinschaftlinchkeit, wird dies als ein ihnen '*fremdes*' *und von ihnen* '*unabhängiges*', als ein selbst wieder besonderes und eigentümliches 'Allgemein'-Interesse geltend gemacht, oder sie selbst müssen sich in diesem Zwiespalt bewegen, wie in der Demokratie." (Two points should be noticed: 1.) Marx does not say that the particular interests of the individuals are *identical* with their communal interests, but that they should not follow *exclusively* their particular interests; doing this actually defeats their purpose, superimposing on them their real communal interests in an alienated form as abstract "General-Interest". 2) The illusory depiction of man's real communal interests as an abstract "General-Interest"—what he calls elsewhere "the legalistic illusion"—and its representation as something quite different from the actual human individual, hides a real alienation: man's *self-alienation* in the form of the *"Spaltung* zwischen dem *besondern und gemeinsamen Interesse"*. It is on this basis that real alienation can be mystified by the philosophers as the alienation of "Man", meaning by "Man", as Marx commented: "D e r Mensch = dem 'denkenden Menschengeist'." ("M a n = the 'thinking human spirit'.") In reality "General-Interest" is not a separate "essence" that should be contrasted with and opposed to the "individual essence" of Man; it is only an alienated expression of an actual state of alienation. Real man is the "wirklicher historischen Mensch" to whom his communal interest actually "belongs"—i.e. it is inseparable from his nature as a social individual being—even if in a given historical situation it confronts him in an alienated form. This is why one can think of alienation as capable of supersession.)

"mit der kommunistischen Regelung der Production und der darin liegenden *Vernichtung der Fremdheit, mit der sich die Menschen zu ihren eigenen Produkt verhalten,* die Macht des Verhältnisses von Nachfrage und Zufuhr sich in Nichts auflöst. . . ."

"In der bisherigen Geschichte . . . die einzelnen Individuen mit der Ausdehnung der Tätigkeit zur Weltgeschichtlichen immer mehr unter einer ihnen *fremden* Macht geknechtet worden sind. . . ."

". . . *Bedingungen,* die bisher dem Zufall überlassen waren und *sich gegen die einzelnen Individuen* eben durch ihre Trennung als Individuen . . . *zu einem ihnen fremden Bande* geworden war, *verselbständigt hatten.* . . . In der Vorstellung sind daher die Individuen unter der Bourgeoisieherrschaft *freier als früher, weil ihnen ihre Lebensbedingungen zufällig sind;* in der Wirklichkeit sind sie natürlich *unfreier, weil mehr unter sachliche Gewalt subsumiert."* (MEWE, Vol. 3, pages 33, 34, 49, 42, 35, 37, 75–76.)

Communist Manifesto. "der Macht über fremde Arbeit"; "Der Kommunismus nimmt keinen die Macht, sich gesellschaftliche Produkte anzueignen, er nimmt nur die Macht, sich durch diese *Aneignung fremde Arbeit* zu unterjochen." (MEWE, Vol. 4, pages 476, 477.)

Wage Labour and Capital. "Je rascher die Arbeiterklasse die ihr *feindliche Macht, den fremden, über sie gebietenden Reichtum* vermehrt und vergrössert, unter desto günstigeren Bedingungen wird ihr erlaubt, von neuem an der Vermehrung des bürgerlichen Reichtums, an der Vergrösserung der Macht des Kapitals zu arbeiten, zufrieden, sich selbst die goldenen Ketten zu schmieden, woran die Bourgeoisie sie hinter sich herschleift." (MEWE, Vol. 6, p. 416.)

Outlines of a Critique of Political Economy. (Rohentwurf.) This work contains *hundreds* of pages where the problems of alienation are analysed in a comprehensive way. The words "Entfremdung", "entfremdet" etc. occur on these pages *several hundred times.* I have chosen one passage only. It will show not only how wrong they are who assert that "alienation" has dropped out from Marx's later works, but also that his approach to the discussed problems is essentially the same as in the *Manuscripts of 1844.* This passage reads as follows: "Der Ton wird gelegt nicht auf das V e r g e g e n s t ä n d l i c h t s e i n, sondern das E n t f r e m d e t-, Entäussert-, Veräussertsein, das Nicht-dem-Arbeiter-, sondern den personifizierten Produktionsbedingungen-, i.e. dem-Kapital-Zugehören der ungeheuren gegenständlichen Macht, die die gesellschaftliche *Arbeit selbst sich* als eins ihrer Momente *gegenübergestellt hat.* Soweit auf dem Standpunkt des Kapitals und der Lohnarbeit die Erzeugung dieses gegenständlichen Leibes der Tätigkeit im Gegensatz zum unmittelbaren Arbeitsvermögen geschieht—dieser Prozess der Vergegenständlichung in fact als *Prozess der Entäusserung* vom Standpunkt der Arbeit aus oder der *Aneignung fremder Arbeit* vom Standpunkt des Kapitals aus erscheint—, ist diese Verdrehung und Verkehrung eine w i r k l i c h e, keine bloss g e m e i n t e, bloss in der Vorstellung der Arbeiter und Kapitalisten existierende. Aber offenbar ist dieser Verkehrungsprozess bloss h i s t o r i s c h e Notwendigkeit, bloss Notwendigkeit für die Entwicklung der Produktivkräfte von einem bestimmten historischen Ausgangspunkt aus, oder Basis aus, aber keineswegs eine a b s o l u t e Notwendigkeit der Produktion; vielmehre eine verschwindende, und das Resultat und der Zweck (immanente) dieses Prozesses ist diese Basis selbst aufzuheben, wie diese Form des Prozesses. Die bürgerlichen Ökonomen sind so eingepfercht in den Vorstellungen einer bestimmten historischen Entwicklungsstufe der Gesellschaft, dass die Notwendigkeit der V e r g e g e n s t ä n d l i c h u n g der gesellschaftlichen Mächte der Arbeit ihnen unzertrennbar erscheint von der Notwendigkeit der E n t f r e m d u n g derselben *gegenüber der lebendigen Arbeit.*

Mit der Aufhebung aber des u n m i t t e l b a r e n Charakters der
lebendigen Arbeit als bloss e i n z e l n e r, oder als bloss innerlich,
oder bloss äusserlich allgemeiner, mit dem Setzen der Tätigkeit der
Individuen als *unmittelbar allgemeiner oder g e s e l l s c h a f t-
l i c h e r*, wird den gegenständlichen 'Momenten der Produktion
diese *Form der Entfremdung* abgestreift; sie werden damit gesetzt
als Eigentum, als *der organische gesellschaftliche Leib*, worin die
Individuen sich reproduzieren als Einzelne, aber als *gesellschaftliche
Einzelne.*" (*Rohentwurf*, p. 716). (Here we have even the "anthropological" notions of the early Marx, together with the conception of the supersession of alienation as the transcendence of the
abstract *mediated* character of human activity.)

Theories of Surplus-Value. As one would expect from a critical
monograph on past theories of surplus-value, this monumental work,
(almost 2,000 pages long) has many references to "alienation". For
instance, dealing with Linguet's theories, Marx writes: "Die Reichen
haben sich aller Produktionsbedingungen bemächtigt; (dies führte
zur) *E n t f r e m d u n g   d e r   P r o d u k t i o n s b e d i n g u n g e n*, die
in ihrer einfachsten Form die Naturelemente selbst sind." But there
are places of a different kind too, where "Entfremdung" etc. do
not simply occur in the summary or quotation of someone else's
argument, but in the exposition of Marx's own ideas. For instance:
"Der Z i n s an sich drückt also grade das Dasein der Arbeitsbedingungen als K a p i t a l in ihrem gesellschaftlichen Gegensatz und
ihrer Metamorphose als persönliche Mächte gegenüber der Arbeit
und über die Arbeit aus. Er resümiert den *e n t f r e m d e t e n
Charakter der Arbeitsbedingungen* im Verhältnis zur Tätigkeit des
Subjekts. Er stellt das Eigentum des Kapitals oder das blosse Kapi-
taleigentum als Mittel dar, die *Produkte fremder Arbeit* sich
anzueignen als *Herrschaft über fremde Arbeit.* Aber er stellt diesen
Charakter des Kapitals dar als etwas, was ihm *ausser* dem Produk-
tionsprozess selbst zukommt und keineswegs das Resultat der spezi-
fischen Bestimmtheit dieses Produktionsprozesses selbst ist." One
could fill many pages with passages of this kind which can be found
in Marx's *Theories of Surplus-Value*. (For the reported two passages
cf. MEWE, Vol, 26. Part I., p. 321 and Part III. p. 485.)

Capital. "Die verselbständigte und *entfremdete Gestalt*"; "Da
vor seinem Eintritt in den Prozess seine eigne Arbeit *ihm selbst
entfremdet*, dem Kapitalisten angeeignet und dem Kapital einverleibt ist, vergegenständlicht sie sich während des Prozesses beständig

in fremden Produkt. . . . Der Arbeiter selbst produziert daher beständig den objektiven Reichtum als Kapital, *ihm fremde*, ihn beherrschende und ausbeutende Macht, und der Kapitalist produziert ebenso beständig die Arbeitskraft als subjektive, von ihren eignen Vergegenständlichungs- und Verwirklichungsmitteln getrennte, abstrakte, in der blossen Leiblichkeit des Arbeiters existierende Reichtumsquelle, *kurz den arbeiter als Lohnarbeiter.*"; "alle Mittel zur Entwicklung der Produktion . . . verstümmeln den Arbeiter in einen Teilmenschen, entwürdigen ihn zum Anhängsel der Maschine, vernichten mit der Qual seiner Arbeit ihren Inhalt, *entfremden ihm die geistigen Potenzen* des Arbeitsprozesses im selben Masse, worin letzterem die *Wissenschaft als selbständige Potenz* einverleibt wird; . . ."; "diese Produktionsmittel treten dem Besitzer der Arbeitskraft gegenüber als *fremdes Eigentum*. Andererseits steht der Verkäufer der Arbeit ihrem Kaufer gegenüber als *fremde Arbeitskraft*, . . ."; "Diese Vorstellungsweise ist um so weniger befremdlich, als ihr der Schein der Tatsachen entspricht, und als das Kapitalverhältnis in der Tat den innern Zusammenhang verbirgt in der vollständigen *Gleichgültigkeit, Äusserlichkeit und Entfremdung*, worin es den Arbeiter versetzt gegenüber den Bedingungen der Verwirklichung seiner eignen Arbeit."; "Es bleibt jedoch nicht bei der *Entfremdung* und Gleichgütigkeit zwischen dem Arbeiter, dem Träger der lebendigen Arbeit hier, und der ökononiischen, d.h. rationellen und sparsamen Anwendung seiner Arbeitsbedingingen dort."; "Das Kapital zeigt sich immer mehr als gessellschaftliche Macht, . . .- aber als *entfremdete, verselbständigte gesellschaftliche Macht, die als Sache*, und als Macht des Kapitalisten durch diese Sache, *der Gesellschaft gegenübertritt*."; "Dieser *Entfremdung* der Produktionsbedingung vom Produzenten entspricht hier aber eine wirkliche Umwälzung in der Produktionsweise selbst."; "die wirklichen Produktionsagenten in diesen *entfremdeten und irrationellen Formen* von Kapital—Zins, Boden— Rente, Arbeit—Arbeitslohn, sich völlig zu Hause fühlen, denn es sind eben die Gestaltungen des Scheins, in welchem sie sich bewegen und womit sie täglich zu tun haben." (MEWE, Vol. 23; Vol. I of *Capital*—pp. 455, 596, 674; Vol. 24; Vol. II of *Capital*—p. 37; Vol. 25; Vol III of *Capital*—pp. 95, 96, 274, 610, 838.)

Reading these quotations will, perhaps, suffice to suggest an answer to the question: just how much attention should be paid to the "drop-out" theory. It should be clear by now that *none* of the meanings of alienation as used by Marx in the *Manuscripts of 1844* dropped out from his later writings. And no wonder. For the concept of alienation, as grasped by Marx in 1844, with all its complex ramifications, is not a concept which could be dropped, or one-sidedly "translated". As we have seen in various parts of this study, the concept of alienation is a vitally important pillar of the Marxian system as a whole, and not merely one brick of it. To drop it, or to translate it one-sidedly, would, therefore, amount to nothing short of the complete demolition of the building itself and the re-erection, perhaps, of its chimney only. That some people have been—or are still—engaged in such operations, trying to build their "scientific" theories on chimney-tops decorated with Marxist terminology, is not in doubt here. The point is that their efforts should not be confused with the Marxian theory itself.

2. *"Philosophy" versus "Political Economy"*

The numerous versions of the "young Marx versus mature Marx" (or the other way round) approach have something in common. This is: an effort to oppose political economy to philosophy or philosophy to political economy and use Marx as a supporting authority in favour of such pseudo-alternative. Broadly speaking those who want to evade or reject the vital—and by no means speculative—philosophical problems of freedom and the individual, side with the "mature political economist" or "scientific" Marx, whereas those who wish the practical power of Marxism (which is inseparable from its demystification of capitalist economy) never existed exalt the "young philosopher Marx".

Needless to say, there is something extremely artificial and arbitrary in this contraposition. It is, therefore, not surprising at all to find that the constructions based on this prefabricated opposition do not stand up to examination. Thus, for instance, we can read from the pen of Daniel Bell about a presumed transmutation in Marx's *Economic and Philosophic Manuscripts*: "The title itself is both literal and *symbolic*. Beginning as an *anthropology*, it ends as a *political economy*."[207] What should we think of this statement? What is the title "symbolic" of? It cannot be of anything in Marx because he never gave these manuscripts a title himself. (As is made explicit in a footnote, the title was given by the editors of the Moscow Institute of Marxism-Leninism.) And what about the assertion that this work *begins* as an anthropology and *ends* as a political economy? For this is how it *actually* begins: *"Wages* are determined through the *antagonistic struggle* between *capitalist* and *worker.* Victory goes necessarily to the capitalist." This means that the *Manuscripts of 1844* begin as full-blooded "mature Marx" with the notions of political economy. True, there is a short *Introduction* to the volume in which there are references to Feuerbach which might, perhaps, be construed as beginning as an anthropology. But this *Introduction*—as the same footnote tells the reader—was written *after the completion* of the rest of the Manuscripts. Thus if one said that the Manuscripts begin with political economy and finish with philosophy, this would reflect a simple chronological fact. This, however, could not fit into a construction which seeks to assert the exact opposite and make something terribly significant out of it.

It would be a waste of the reader's time to analyse these constructions were they not significant *ideologically.* Daniel Bell borrows his grotesque ideas on young Marx from R. W. Tucker to whom, in his own words, he is "indebted for many insights".[208] Now Tucker's efforts, expressed in his book *Philosophy and Myth in Karl Marx,* are directed at a complete emasculation of the Marxian ideas so that the unsuspecting reader would be led into believing that *"Marx's concept of communism is more nearly applicable to present-day America, for example, than his concept of capitalism".*[209] The object of such exercises is to "demonstrate" the meaninglessness of the Marxian "abstractions", and Daniel Bell willingly contributes his share of hot air to keep Tucker's balloon flying. Talking about the revival of interest in young Marx he writes:

> "To the extent that this is an effort to find a new, radical critique of society, the effort is an encouraging one. But to the extent—and this seems as much to be the case—that it is a form of new myth-making, in order to cling to the symbol of Marx, it is wrong. For while it is *the early Marx,* it is *not the historical Marx.* The historical Marx had, in effect, *repudiated the idea of alienation. . . .* The irony, however, is that in moving from 'philosophy' to 'reality', from phenomenology to political economy, Marx himself had moved *from one kind of abstraction to another.* For in his system, self-alienation becomes transformed: man as 'generic man' (i.e. Man writ large) becomes divided into classes of men. The only social reality is not Man, not the individual, but *economic classes. Individuals, and their motives, count for nought."*[210]

Here the ideological motivations, despite all the efforts to keep them in the background, come out into the open. For so long as there is some hope that young Marx would be used against the economic "abstractions" of the "historical Marx", the effort is hailed as an encouraging radical critique of society. If, however, people do not fall for this anti-Marxist separation but recognize the essential continuity of the Marxian thought, this must be condemned as "a form of myth-making, in order to cling to the symbol of Marx". The construction opposing the "young philosopher" to the "mature political economist Marx" must be maintained at all costs, even if the evidence to the contrary is overwhelming.[211] The mystifying—and crudely falsifying—interpretation according to which the "original philosophical expression" of Marx's ideas embodied a timeless *"socio-psychological condition"*[212] (with no reference to capitalism, classes, exploitation, social antagonisms, etc.) must be maintained so that "the historical Marx" and those who pay attention to him could be dismissed as guilty of "myth-making".

Thus in Bell's view the Marxian "abstractions" ought to be distributed between two classes: (1) the young Marx's categories, allegedly related to those timeless, philosophically respectable "socio-psychological" conditions, and (2) the "economic abstractions" of the mature Marx which, *horribile dictu*, criticize capitalism. And of course one is welcome to toy with the philosophico-psychological categories of "the human condition"[213]—thus earning the praise: "a radical critique of society"—provided that (a) *capitalism* is never mentioned in this "radical critique" of "society", and that (b) the Marxian "economic abstractions" are condemned by our "radicals", because such "abstractions" do not lend themselves to mystifying twists and falsifications.

This "detached", "non-ideological" analysis of Marxism is taken a stage further—to the point of personal vilification :

> "Although Marx drew most of his ideas from his peers—self-consciousness from Bauer, alienation from Feuerbach, communism from Moses Hess, the stages of property from Proudhon—he was not content, simply, to synthesize these ideas, but had to attack, and usually viciously, all these individuals *in the determined effort to appear wholly original.*"[214]

No further comments are required. Our quotations, reproducing Daniel Bell's own words, set alongside the title of his book—THE END OF IDEOLOGY—speak loudly enough for themselves.

Admittedly, in the *Economic and Philosophic Manuscripts of 1844* Marx spoke about the task of superseding political economy. But in the same breath he also spoke about the practical abolition of philosophy. These propositions stand or fall together because they are related to one and the same historical task as seen by Marx. It is, therefore, quite arbitrary to pick one of them and to use it against the other.

When Marx referred to the task of superseding philosophy and political economy, he did not mean superseding the one by "vulgar economism" and the other by "anthropology", or a "philosophico-psychological" analysis of the "human condition", etc. As we have seen in chapter III, the point he was making was that philosophy and political economy apply a *"different* and *opposite* yard-stick to man", both of them in an equally *exclusivistic* manner, standing "in an estranged relation to the other", since their points of reference are basically different. And he wanted to supersede them by something that is neither traditional philosophy nor traditional political economy.

He realized that the different and opposite yardsticks as ordering criteria of the particular theoretical fields inevitably result in "in-tegralistic" attempts that embrace only those aspects of the complex problems of reality which can be easily fitted into the isolated, special schemes, arbitrarily excluding all the other aspects and antagonistically opposing those disciplines which work out their generalizations on the basis of these excluded aspects. This is why Marx opposed to the arbitrary integralism of the particular theoretical fields—which he explained as a necessarily alienated reflection of practical alienation—the ideal of a "human science", i.e. the non-alienated *synthesis* of *all* aspects. A "human science" oriented by a non-artificial and all-inclusive measure : man himself. (Marx's own expressions were : "there will be o n e science", "the science of man".)

The supersession of philosophy and political economy in this conception does not mean the abolition of the problems of either traditional philosophy or those of political economy, nor indeed a running away from them. Marx is convinced that philosophical etc. problems cannot be "abolished" (or "dissolved") in thought, only in *social practice*, because they are expressions of reality, how-ever mystified and alienated they may be. Equally, he is convinced that one must not evade them, or simply declare that they are mystifications and leave everything at that, but face up to them

and meet them at the level where they present themselves. Therefore the critique of traditional philosophy or political economy
implies the positive elaboration of alternatives to the persistent old
questions.

It goes without saying that, in Marx's view, such a task cannot
be accomplished within the limits of either philosophy or political
economy. To turn political economy into a "super-science" to which
everything else should be subordinated would certainly amount to
"economic determinism". And, as we have seen, nothing is further
removed from Marx than that. He knows very well that political
economy is just as one-sidedly integralistic as philosophy, and more
dangerous in the sense that its representatives often have direct
access to power.

Thus when he develops his criticism of political economy—no
matter in how great a detail or how many highly technical problems
are taken into account—he is not the "political economist mature
Marx". Nor is he indeed the "young philosopher" or "anthropolo-
gist" Marx when he criticizes Hegel. The earliest comprehensive
idea of young Marx was the unification of philosophy with practical
human reality, and this went far beyond the horizon of traditional
philosophy. Whenever Marx analyses philosophical problems, in his
youth or in his old age, he always tries to do this in the form of
synthesizing—in an "aufgehoben" sense—the most general philosophical formulations with the insights gained from actual human
experience as well as from its theoretical and artistic reflections:
from history to political economy, and from Shakespeare and Goethe
to Balzac. And, of course, he proceeds in the same way when he
discusses the problems of political economy : by mobilizing the whole
range of human experience known to him—e.g. Shakespeare on
money in the Paris Manuscripts as well as in *Capital*—and synthesizing it with the fundamental insights he gained from the critical study
of the most comprehensive general formulations of philosophy.

It is, therefore, simply not true that the mature Marx had no
time for or interest in the problems of philosophy. His interest in
philosophy was *never* "philosophical" : it was always practical-
human. Nor was his interest in political economy "scientific-
economical" : it was also practical-human. Thus for him both
philosophy and political economy were from the beginning merged
in a practical-human concern. In the *Economic and Philosophic
Manuscripts of 1844* Marx was not less interested in "political
economy" than in his *Rohentwurf* or in *Capital*. Or, to put it the

other way round, in these latter he was not less doing "philosophy"—
of course *his* kind of philosophy, just as in the early works—than
in the Paris Manuscripts. The people who deny this tend to be
either those who crudely identify "human" with "economic", or
those who, in the name of mystifying psychological abstractions,
treat with extreme scepticism the relevance of social-economic
measures to the solution of human problems. To assert, however,
the radical break in Marx's development, undisturbed by the
evidence of his work as a whole, is to deduce a little too much from
a mere title Marx himself never gave to an unfinished manuscript.

3. *Marx's Intellectual Development*

The rejection of the "young Marx versus mature Marx" dichotomy does not mean the denial of Marx's intellectual development.
What is turned down is the dramatized idea of a radical reversal of
his position in the aftermath of the *Manuscripts of 1844*.

This is not the place to discuss in detail the complex problems
of Marx's intellectual development. There are, however, a few
aspects of it—those directly related to the problems raised in the
previous section—which ought to be touched upon, if only briefly,
in this context.

(1) As we have seen in chapter II., the concept of alienation
played a minor rôle in Marx's thought prior to 1843. Even in 1843
its importance was relatively small as compared with the *Manuscripts of 1844*. The point of really significant change is not between
1844 and 1845 but between 1843 and 1844. (And even this change
is far more complex than the vulgarizers—who can only operate
with crude schemes like "idealism" versus "materialism" etc.—
imagine.)

To see the contrast, it is enough to read a short passage from
Marx's *Introduction to the Critique of the Hegelian Philosophy of
Right*. It says: "the criticism of heaven turns into the criticism of
the earth, the criticism of religion into the criticism
of right and the criticism of theology into the
criticism of politics."[215] Unquestionably, Marx's insight concerning the task of unifying philosophy with practice can be perceived here. Yet at this stage of his development it is expressed in
a rather generic form. If we are able to recognize the genius of this
Marxian insight it is because we are aware of its later elaborated,

immensely far-reaching implications, thanks to the keys we were given by Marx himself, in the works that followed this *Introduction*. Had Marx remained at the abstract programmatic level of generalization which characterizes this *Introduction* he could hardly have exercised the sort of influence he did on later intellectual and social developments.

Marx of the *Manuscripts of 1844* made a great step forward, as we have seen in several contexts. By recognizing that the key to all alienation—religious, juridicial, moral, artistic, political, etc.—is "alienated labour", the alienated form of man's practical productive activity, he was able to base his whole conception on a sure footing. Now it became possible for him to elaborate his ideas in a most concrete form, indicating the strategic points of the necessary practical activity. Since the concept of "labour's self-alienation" pinpointed the ultimate cause of all forms of alienation, the criticism of economics—i.e. an adequate understanding of its laws and mechanisms—acquired a crucial importance: it became the vital link in the programme of gaining mastery over the various causal factors involved, serving the purpose of practically superseding alienation in all spheres of life. While the earlier *Introduction* went only as far as emphasizing that the criticism of theology must be transformed into the criticism of *politics*, the *Manuscripts of 1844* accomplished the structurally vital step of turning the criticism of politics into the criticism of *economics*. Thus the earlier abstractly-programmatic character of the Marxian ideas had been effectively superseded. Marx did not have to stop any longer at the point of *postulating* the unity of theory and practice (see chapter II on Marx's own references to a "categorical imperative" in the *Introduction*), he could now concretely demonstrate *how* to realize in social practice this revolutionary programme.

And this is how the concept of alienation became the central concept of Marx's whole theory. It is, therefore, not only not true that when Marx acquired an interest in the problems of political economy he turned his back on the concept of alienation: the exact opposite is true. For as soon as he realized that economic alienation was the common link of all forms of alienation and dehumanization, it was impossible for him *not* to adopt the concept of alienation—this structural common denominator—as the centre of reference of his entire conception. The *Manuscripts of 1844* provide massive evidence in support of this view. They also show that, enriched by the insights he gained from his critical study of political economy, his philosophical criticism became more profound and comprehensive than ever before.

(2) There can be no doubt about Feuerbach's influence on Marx : he himself acknowledged this on more than one occasion. The question is, however, what did this influence really amount to in 1844, or indeed towards the end of 1843? Greatly exaggerated claims are made in this regard which, if true, would reduce Marx— up to the time he jotted down his *Theses on Feuerbach*—into a mere follower of the latter.

We possess two important letters addressed by Marx to Feuerbach which help to dispel this legend. Already the first of them—written on the 3rd of October 1843—reveals a substantial difference of approach. In the spirit of Marx's general line of thought at that time, it advocates the criticism of society in the form of the criticism of politics. Marx would like to see Feuerbach actively involved in this effort and asks for his contribution accordingly :

> "Schelling succeeded in uniting not only Philosophy and Theology but also Philosophy and Diplomacy. He turned Philosophy into the general science of Diplomacy, into a Diplomacy for all. An attack on Schelling would, therefore, be an indirect attack on our whole, namely Prussian, political system. Schelling's philosophy is Prussian Politics *sub specie philosophiae*."[216]

Perhaps Marx had illusions about Feuerbach's willingness or ability to engage in such battles against the existing order, perhaps he only wanted to enlist the support of a powerful ally and at the same time, as a good editor, push his would-be collaborator forward in radicalism, bringing him into line with *his own* conception of the journal's tasks. It does not matter which way we look at the issue. What matters, however, is that Feuerbach could not possibly supply what Marx expected or hoped to get from him.

The other letter is even more important in this respect. Written on the 11th of August 1844—i.e. approximately at the time of the completion of the *Economic and Philosophic Manuscripts of 1844*— it directly raises the question of the meaning of "man", the "unity of men with other men" and "the human species" (Menschengattung). This is how Marx looks on these concepts, not *after* his *Theses on Feuerbach*, not at the time of the *Communist Manifesto*, not in the course of the elaboration of his *Capital*, but right in the middle of 1844 :

"In your writings you have given—*I do not know whether consciously or not*—a philosophical foundation to socialism, and we communists at once have *understood your works in this sense*. The unity of men with other men, which is based on the real differences between men, *the concept of the human species* brought down from the sky of abstraction to the real ground of earth, *what else is it if not the concept of s o c i e t y*."[217]

These considerations are in full agreement with *Marx's* own use of the discussed terms in the Paris Manuscripts, but they could hardly be further removed from *Feuerbach's* concepts. Marx puts *his* interpretation of these concepts to Feuerbach—on the occasion of posting to him a published copy of the *Introduction to the Critique of the Hegelian Philosophy of Right*—in the hope of starting a fruitful exchange of ideas with him. The distance was, as Feuerbach realized reading Marx's letter and the *Introduction*, far too great to be bridged, and he never followed up the offer.

As a matter of fact Marx himself was well aware of the qualitative difference between his own aspirations and Feuerbach's actual achievements. Already in the *Introduction* he made it clear that the Feuerbachian criticism is only a *necessary preliminary* to the fundamental task, the "criticism of earth" as he put it. In the *Manuscripts of 1844* he was fully engaged in the theoretical realization of this task which necessarily implied a radical departure from Feuerbach's sphere to its real socio-economic basis. (Only in his criticism of the Hegelian philosophy could Marx use Feuerbach more extensively, as a positively superseded "moment" of his own incomparably more comprehensive general conception.)

Also, almost every single point Marx made in his *Theses on Feuerbach*, in the first months of 1845, can be found in the *Manuscripts of 1844*, even though without explicit critical references to Feuerbach himself. That he made efforts to take Feuerbach with him in carrying out an enterprise he considered to be the logical continuation of Feuerbach's necessary preliminaries, was thoroughly consistent with his general outlook; these efforts, therefore, should not be considered as merely tactical steps. Equally, the next logical step for Marx was—after seeing the failure of his efforts to enlist Feuerbach's active help in the cause of a radical practical criticism of society—to make the formerly implicit criticism explicit on Feuerbach as well, all the more because Marx's adversaries made great use of the Feuerbachian line of reasoning. (Marx's attitude towards some of his other contemporaries was very similar, but this did not make him share their views and illusions. He always tried to carry them with him on the road *he* had chosen, but did not hesitate to take the criticism to its utmost once this proved impossible when his former friends ideologically lined themselves up with his political adversaries.)

Thus the point of contact between Marx and Feuerbach at the time of writing the *Manuscripts of 1844* is more *terminological* than anything else. Terminological in Marx's sense, of course : i.e. implying that even a mystified terminology reflects a problem of reality that ought to be grasped in its proper setting. In other words, this kind of terminological contact should not be crudely simplified as "lip-service" or mere "tactics". It follows from Marx's historical-structural principle that one's method of setting out from the available, to greater or lesser extent mystified, terms is not only admissible but also necessary. It is, in fact, the only way in which it is possible to grasp the dialectical movement of ideas as concrete genesis, provided they are related to their real basis in the course of their concrete demystification.

In *The German Ideology* Marx identified the reason why his efforts at enlisting Feuerbach's support had to fail :

> "in reality and for the *p r a c t i c a l materialist*, i.e. the c o m-
> m u n i s t, it is a question of revolutionizing the *existing world*,
> of *practically attacking* and changing *existing things*. When
> *occasionally* we find such views with Feuerbach, they are never
> more than *isolated surmises* and have much too little influence on
> his general outlook to be considered here as anything else than
> *embryos capable of development*."[218]

At the time of writing the *Economic and Philosophic Manuscripts of 1844* Marx did not realize that these "embryos" were not capable of development by Feuerbach himself. But who could deduce from this fact the conclusion that in 1844 Marx himself was not a "*practical* materialist" engaged in realizing his programme of "revolutionizing the existing world, of practically attacking and changing existing things"? He did not realize, in 1844, that the *occasional* remarks in Feuerbach's philosophy concerning the "practical criticism of the existing world" were only "*isolated surmises*" leading to no practical consequence whatsoever. But who could deduce from this fact the conclusion that consequently for Marx too the idea of a "practical criticism of earth" was nothing but an "isolated surmise"? Feuerbach could not possibly accept

Marx's offers precisely because in his philosophy the idea of a practical attack on existing things was peripheral and partial : never embracing the totality of the socio-political system, for he simply did not have the concept of the social relations of production. To find out about the real limits of the Feuerbachian philosophy, to find out how far he himself was capable of developing the isolated "embryos" of his system, it was necessary to try to enlist his active support for the practical task of radically attacking the existing order of society and its supporters, like old Schelling. That Feuerbach could not meet Marx's expectations is not surprising in the light of these limitations of which we are all now aware. But to suggest that Marx shared in the least the same limitations in 1844—or indeed in 1843 when he first wrote to Feuerbach—means to take no notice whatsoever of the young Marx's efforts at radicalizing this "contemplative materialist", not to speak of ignoring the evidence of Marx's philosophical works themselves.

It may be argued that Marx had illusions about Feuerbach in 1844. It would be, however, an elementary logical error to equate Marx's illusions *about* Feuerbach with *Feuerbach's own* illusions. Yet it is precisely this error which we encounter when we are told that Marx's concept of man in the *Economic and Philosophic Manuscripts of 1844* is the Feuerbachian "generic man".

(3) The concept of alienation is eminently a concept of synthesis. This means, among other things, that the word "alienation" is not necessarily required when the complex problematics covered by it is presented or developed in a detailed form. To take an example, let us consider the following passage from *Wage-Labour and Capital* (Lohnarbeit und Kapital) :

"But the exercise of labour power, labour, is the worker's own life-activity, the manifestation of his own life. And this l i f e- a c t i v i t y he sells to another person in order to secure the necessary m e a n s o f s u b s i s t e n c e. Thus this life-activity is for him only a means to enable him to exist. He works in order to live. He does not even reckon labour as part of his life, it is rather a sacrifice of his life. It is a commodity which he has made over to another. Hence, also, the product of his activity is not the object of his activity. What he produces for himself is not the silk that he weaves, not the gold that he draws from the mine, not the palace that he builds. What he produces for himself is w a g e s, and silk,

gold, palace resolve themselves for him into a definite quantity of
the means of subsistence, perhaps into a cotton jacket, some copper
coins and a lodging in a cellar. And the worker, who for twelve
hours weaves, spins, drills, turns, builds, shovels, breaks stones,
carries loads, etc.—does he consider this twelve hours' weaving,
spinning, drilling, turning, building, shovelling, stone breaking as a
manifestation of his life, as life? On the contrary, life begins for
him where this activity ceases, at table, in the public house, in bed.
The twelve hours' labour, on the other hand, has no meaning for
him as weaving, spinning, drilling, etc., but as e a r n i n g s, which
bring him to the table, to the public house, into bed. If the silk
worm were to spin in order to continue its existence as a caterpillar,
it would be a complete wage-worker."[219]

Here we have some of the most fundamental aspects of alienation
as seen in the *Manuscripts of 1844*—from "selling one's life-
activity" to asserting that "life-activity becomes a mere means of
existence" and to saying that the perceptible world, because of the
external character of labour, is not appropriated by man in a direct
sensuous form which would be ontologically appropriate, but is
mediated by abstract "wages", as a result of the transformation of
labour power into a commodity—and yet, the *word* "alienation"
is never mentioned.

There may have been a number of particular reasons for this,
such as (a) Marx's deliberate policy of avoiding any resemblance
to "true socialism" which abused the word; (b) the fact that the
public to which *Wage-Labour and Capital* was presented—first as
a series of lectures in the Workers' Club in Brussels and later in the
form of newspaper articles in the "Neue Rheinische Zeitung"—
was not at all familiar with the extremely complex philosophical
problematics of "Entfremdung" and "Entäusserung".

Nevertheless what keeps the various phenomena conceptually
together in this analysis is the underlying concept of alienation as
their focal point or common denominator. One must distinguish
between *conception* and *presentation*. It is simply unthinkable to
conceive the Marxian vision without this fundamental concept of
alienation. But once it is conceived in its broadest outlines—in the
Manuscripts of 1844—it becomes possible to let the general term
"recede" in the *presentation*. Moreover, in order to work out in the
most concrete form the manifold specific aspects of this comprehensive vision, it becomes also imperative to find those particular terms
which adequately express the specific features of the particular

spheres, levels, mediations, etc. of the overall problematics. The concrete articulation of the comprehensive vision cannot possibly be carried out by using always the same general term : doing this would not only result in endless repetitions but, ultimately, in a colossal tautology as well. Thus the receding of the general term in the course of the concrete elaboration of the complex problematics of alienation should not be mistaken for abandoning the concept itself.

The notion of alienation has something about it that could be described as a *"shorthand"* character. It can, legitimately, comprehend a great deal and, therefore, it is eminently suitable to serve the purposes of quickly surveying and summarizing for one's own use a broad synthesis. But formulating the broad outlines of a synthesis is not the end of the task, only its real beginning. This outline or preliminary synthesis must be rendered specific enough in every respect, otherwise the practical realization of the philosophical programme inherent in this synthesis cannot be seriously contemplated for a moment. It is in the course of this articulation or "rendering concrete" of the broad preliminary synthesis that the term "alienation" must be replaced in numerous contexts. This is why it is not at all surprising to find that the works which followed the *Manuscripts of 1844*, up to about 1856—and written for publication—are far less densely populated with the word "alienation" than the first broad synthesis.

If, however, the reader has doubts about this interpretation, he should consult Marx's *Grundrisse der Kritik der politischen Ökonomie—Rohentwurf* (Outlines of the Critique of Political Economy—Rough Draft)—a work written between 1857 and 1858—and he should compare this work with its incomplete articulation in the three volumes of *Capital*. The *Rohentwurf* is Marx's second broad synthesis whose conception was made necessary by the enormous wealth of material he had accumulated between 1844 and 1856. When he was trying to integrate this material into a coherent whole, the notion of alienation again pushed itself into the foreground and maintained its massive presence throughout the whole manuscript. (The length of this *Rohentwurf* is many times that of the *Manuscripts of 1844*.) While in the *Rohentwurf* the term "alienation" occurs in *innumerable* contexts, in *Capital* it occupies a *relatively* modest place. This second broad synthesis—it must be made explicit, in order to avoid misunderstandings—is in no way *opposed* to the *Manuscripts of 1844* : it is only incomparably richer and more concretely comprehensive. In fact the *Rohentwurf* is the fully articulated equivalent of the early system *in statu nascendi*. It is probably the greatest single theoretical monument of Marx's life.

(4) One of the striking features of Marx's work is that, despite the immense labour that went into them, *all* his major works remained unfinished. Not only the *Manuscripts of 1844* but also the *Theories of Surplus-Value*; not only the *Rohentwurf* but also— as is sometimes forgotten—his *Capital*. This cannot be explained simply by the circumstances of his life, however hard these might have been.

The cause lies deeper, in the innermost nature of his work, inseparable from his conception of superseding philosophy, political economy, etc. by a comprehensively integrated, empirically founded and practically tested and realized "science of man". There is something subjectively self-defeating about this ideal of comprehensiveness. In its origins it goes back to Hegel who not only formulated it as a programme but also carried it out in his monumental— though of course speculative—philosophical synthesis. However, to achieve such a synthesis in an idealistic form is a task radically different from Marx's aim of elaborating the general framework of a unified human science which integrates all the real accomplishments of human knowledge with the practical requirements of human life. If, in the idealistic system, there are gaps, the "World Spirit" is always at hand to fill them in : the more congenially so the bigger these gaps and cleavages are. In Marx's vision, however, according to which the whole enterprise must be carried out "on earth", with means that can be put to practical tests, the realization of the programme requires, among other things, the highest degree of development in all fields of science. If, therefore, some of the necessary conditions of the non-speculative generalizations are absent, the thinker cannot legitimately resort to a new speculative device but has to sit down and work out the problems for himself, no matter how much time-wasting research is involved in this effort. Besides : the more comprehensive his grasp becomes the more he must realize the inevitable gaps due to the always larger and more comprehensive interconnections. Also : every new fundamental achievement in the particular fields requires the thorough revision of the picture as a whole which in its turn again enlarges the previous limits of particular research. And this mutual interaction and reciprocal enrichment goes on indefinitely, for only ideally can the two poles merge into each other.

The task, in this Marxian vision, is clearly beyond the power of any particular individual, no matter how great he might be. The unfinished character of the work of synthesis thus inevitably follows from this new vision of synthesis itself, and in this sense it may be called subjectively self-defeating. In another sense, however, this vision provides a challenging task for generations to follow. A task of coming nearer, in the course of the reciprocal integration of theory and practice, to the Marxian ideal : through constant reformulations and supersessions of previous efforts, even though—by the very nature of the whole enterprise which implies a constantly renewed practical interchange with a constantly changing practice—never definitively realizing it.

4. Theory of Alienation and Philosophy of History

Marx's theory of alienation is his "philosophy of history". Not in the sense of a specialized branch of philosophy that operates with concepts which are of no relevance to any other sphere, but as the reflection of a dynamic movement which is at the basis of all of them.

The concepts of "alienation" and "transcendence" are closely interrelated and thus if someone speaks of history in terms of alienation, he cannot justifiably forget about the problem of its transcendence. As soon as one realizes this, a vital issue arises : what does one mean by the supersession or transcendence of alienation?

Nowhere is the danger of misunderstanding and misinterpretation greater than precisely in this context. Especially if there are—and where are there not?—social contingencies that could tempt people to adopt a self-complacently distorted view. The dream of the "golden age" did not originate yesterday and is most unlikely to disappear tomorrow.

It would go against the spirit of Marx's general conception to settle the problem of "Aufhebung", once and forever, in the fairy-tale form of a utopian golden age. In Marx's vision—which cannot recognize anything as *absolutely final*—there can be no place for a utopian golden age, neither "round the corner" nor astronomical distances away. Such a golden age would be an end of history, and thus the end of man himself.

Yet the fact remains that not only Marx's enemies but also many

of his followers and vulgarizers identified him with the prophet of
a promised land, and some even have claimed to have realized—or
of being very near to the realization of—his alleged idea of a
promised land. There are, of course, sentences in Marx which, if
taken in isolation, can be construed as supporting such claims.
Moreover there is the additional, and more serious, difficulty that
Marx—despising the occupation of day-dreaming about the future
—did not anticipate in explicit form the rejection of these
approaches.

Because of this lack of explicitness the answer to the question of
a transcendence of alienation must be "worked out" from some of
Marx's fundamental concepts. To mention just two of them :

(1) *"Aufhebung"* necessarily implies not only the supersession of
any given form of alienation but also the "preservation" of some
of its "moments";

(2) *"historische* Notwendigkeit" means not only that social
phenomena are established historically and cannot be fictitiously
dreamed away from the historical stage but also that all particular
stages of human history *necessarily disappear*, because to be a
historical necessity is to be a necessarily disappearing necessity (*eine
verschwindende Notwendigkeit*). It is not difficult to see, therefore,
that to posit a utopian "golden age" as a "verschwindende
Notwendigkeit" is a contradiction in terms.

Nevertheless this does not mean that, with a summary reference
to these and similar concepts, one could consider settled the
complicated problems that arise in connection with the "Aufhebung" of alienation. What is important is to separate the genuine
difficulties from their mystifications in bourgeois philosophy.

As we have seen Hegel, representing "the standpoint of political
economy", identified *alienation* with *objectification*, thus precluding
the possibility of an *actual*, practical transcendence of alienation.
Understandably, therefore, this is the one and only Hegelian idea
which has met with the wholehearted approval of all trends of
bourgeois philosophy in the twentieth century. Since this was the
crucial point of difference between Marx and Hegel, the modern
irrationalistic re-edition of the Hegelian idea could be eminently
used against Marx, or indeed sometimes in support of an existen-
tialistically mystified interpretation of Marx. In the twentieth
century Marx could not be ignored any longer. The best way to
neutralize his intellectual impact was, therefore, an existentialistic
interpretation of his thought which consisted basically in the

mystification of the historically specific—anticapitalist—conception of alienation. Accordingly, the concept of alienation gained an incomparably greater significance in the writings of twentieth century existentialists than in those of their forefather, Kierkegaard himself.[220] Heidegger, for instance, defines Marx's importance like this: "Because Marx, through his experience of the *alienation of modern man*, is aware of a *fundamental dimension of history*, the Marxist view of history is superior to all other views".[221] Needless to say, Marx did not experience alienation as "the alienation of modern man", but as the alienation of man in capitalist society. Nor did he look upon alienation as a "fundamental dimension of history", but as the central issue of a given *phase* of history. Heidegger's interpretation of Marx's conception of alienation is thus revealing not about Marx, but about his own very different approach to the same issue.

The same attempt is expressed, in a less subtle form, in Jean Hyppolite's discussion of the relationship between alienation and history. He writes, with direct reference to Marx's criticism of the Hegelian identification of alienation and objectification: "L'auteur de la *Phénoménologie*, de *l'Encyclopédie*, de la *Philosophie de l'histoire*, n'a pas confondu l'aliénation de l'esprit humain dans l'histoire avec l'objectivation sans quelques raisons valables, autres que celles qu'on peut découvrir dans la structure économique de l'époque et dans l'état du système capitaliste. Que l'homme, en s'objectivant dans la culture, dans l'Etat, dans l'oeuvre humaine en général, en même temps s'aliène, se fasse autre et découvre dans cette objectivation une altérité insurmontable et qu'il faut pourtant tenter de surmonter, c'est là une t e n s i o n i n s é p a r a b l e d e l ' e x i s t e n c e, et le mérite de Hegel est d'avoir insisté sur cette tension, de l'avoir conservée au centre même de la conscience de soi humaine. Une des grandes difficultés du marxisme est par contre de prétendre supprimer cette tension dans un avenir plus ou moins proche, de l'expliquer trop rapidement par une phase particulière de l'histoire. . . . Tel quel, ce concept ne nous paraît pas réductible au seul concept d'aliénation de l'homme dans le capital comme l'interprète Marx. Ce n'est là qu'un cas particulier d'un problème plus universel qui est celui de la conscience de soi humaine, qui, incapable de se penser comme un cogito séparé, ne se trouve que dans le monde qu'elle édifie, dans les autres moi qu'elle reconnaît et où parfois elle se méconnaît. Mais cette façon de se trouver dans l'autre, cette objectivation est toujours plus ou moins une aliénation,

244   MARX'S THEORY OF ALIENATION

une perte de soi en même temps qu'une découverte
de soi. Ainsi objectivation et aliénation sont inséparables et leur
unité ne peut être que l'expression d'une tension dialectique qu'on
aperçoit dans le mouvement même de l'histoire."[222]

Thus Hyppolite interprets alienation as a "tension inséparable
de l'existence" and as necessarily inherent in the very nature of
"human self-consciousness" ("la conscience de soi humaine"). This
is an idealistic mystification which condemns all attempts directed
at a practical transcendence of alienation to the fate of a Quixotic
enterprise. Hyppolite's ultimate premise is the arbitrarily assumed
anti-dialectical concept of a so-called "altérité insurmontable"
(insurmountable otherness) which he couples with an equally
arbitrary, irrational *"Sollen"*: *"qu'il faut* pourtant *tenter* de
surmonter"* ("one *ought*, nevertheless, to *try* and surmount it").
Such an enterprise is no more meaningful than "trying" to rewrite
—in the very last second of one's life—Tolstoy's *War and Peace*.
Attempts make no sense whatsoever if they are *apriori* condemned
to failure. As we have seen, "ought" played a major rôle also in
Rousseau's concept of alienation. The difference, however, could
not be more radical. Rousseau's "ought", expressing an objective
contradiction of which the philosopher himself was not aware, was
meant to have an actual impact on reality, in order to remove the
existing alienations. Here, by contrast, the basic premise is a willing
acceptance and glorification of an alleged "altérité insurmontable"
as a "tension inséparable de l'existence". Consequently the "ought"
which is brought into this picture cannot be other than an absurd,
irrationalistic, empty "ought" whose only function is to give a "moral
respectability" to a crude apology for the capitalistically alienated
social relations of production. What is at fault here is not the *use* of
a moral category but its mystifying *abuse* in support of the existing,
dehumanized order of society.

It goes without saying, there is a grain of truth in these interpretations, otherwise they could hardly succeed in their mystificatory
function. Their methodology is characterized by the exaggeration
of this element of truth out of all proportion, so that—by suppressing
the complex dialectical interconnections as well as by removing the
concrete socio-historical references—it is turned into a grave
distortion. The main effort is directed at obscuring even the visible
lines of demarcation, instead of aiming at the elaboration of those
specific concepts which could highlight the objective differences

that are veiled by the reification of the existing social relations of production.

There is some truth in asserting that alienation and objectification are "plus ou moins inséparables". But the validity of statements of this kind depends entirely on the philosopher's ability to specify, both conceptually and socio-historically, his terms of reference. Here, however, we are not given any concretization whatsoever. On the contrary, the vague generality of "plus ou moins" serves the purpose of both exempting the philosopher from the task of concretization and at the same time of creating the semblance of a proper assessment.

Moreover, inseparability of alienation and objectification only applies if one treats "objectification" as a homogeneous category which it is not. One must distinguish, at least, between objectification manifesting itself in the form of objects such as tables, chairs, etc., and objectification taking the form of human institutions. There is no reason why tables etc. should be considered as inseparable from alienation. Objects of this kind can certainly assume institutional functions—when, e.g. the solemn managerial desk also helps to carry out the function of keeping the distance from the man who is ceremoniously shown in to sit down behind it. But the "alienation" involved is not due to the existence of desks as human objectifications but to their *institutional functions* which can be changed.

It is different with objectification as *institutionalization*. Totally and definitively to abolish alienation in this respect would imply the total abolition of human institutions, while we do not need to abolish desks to remove their alienated institutional functions. But what the total abolition of human institutions would amount to is, paradoxically, not the abolition of alienation but its *maximization* in the form of total anarchy, and thus the abolition of *humanness*. "Humanness" implies the opposite of anarchy: *order* which, in human society, is inseparable from some *organization*. Even "conscious association"—no matter how conscious it might be—is inconceivable without having some specific form, and this form, for human beings, cannot be other than some kind of institution set up on the basis of some guiding principles. And even if we take the ideal case—when the underlying guiding principle is conscious guarding against any possible petrification or "reification"—the fact still remains that the specific form of association has to deal with specific tasks which will also determine the character of the institution in question. But this last—inescapable—fact means that the given new form of institution which has just superseded a reified structure contains—from the first moment of its existence and not merely in its dying-out stages—an element of reification, insofar as it is *necessarily biased* against the tasks it is *incapable* of fulfilling. To do away completely with this difficulty one would have to postulate either the absolute finality of certain tasks (i.e. "ideal tasks"—that is, the end of history or a utopian "golden age") or the absolute finality of an institution (i.e. the "ideal institution" which could ideally solve all possible tasks—such an ideal institution would not and could not have any specific form and, of course, it could not solve any specific task whatsoever). For such postulates, however, one would also have to invent a being to fit in them : a being whose needs, tasks, functions, etc., never change, or a being who has no needs, tasks, functions, etc. at all.

Another important aspect of this problem is that, no matter how conscious human efforts to eliminate all possible contradictions between the individual and the given form of society may be, an element of potential alienation is always involved. In this connection we can only briefly refer to two aspects of this complex problematics: (1) A necessary precondition for any individual to acquire *his* personality is to be in a multiplicity of relations with *other* people, using, for self-development, the means and tools he is *given* (at least up to a certain point of independence and maturity), and trying out his *own* forces insofar as he is capable of identifying them in a reciprocal interchange with others, provided that they are noticeably present in some form in his fellow-men. To abolish, absolutely and definitively, all elements of alienation and reification in this respect would, again, be only possible by idealizing these relations to such an extent that they would sharply contradict all possible relations between the real individual and society. (2) One of the striking features of this problem is that for the individual—whether he is conscious of it or not—his own self-realization is, in the first place, necessarily a task of fitting into the existing and available (but of course not created specifically for him) rôles and functions. Later he may be able to enlarge their limits or to break out of them if they are incapable of adaptation and if his strength to break out encounters no defeating resistance. Nevertheless the problem remains that the individual can realize his own powers only if he has outlets for them, if, that is, his fellow-men are able and willing to take what he has to offer.

Also, the relationship between society and technology is not free from problems with serious implications. In a letter to Annenkov (28 Dec. 1846) Marx made the important distinction between technology and its socially determined application. This distinction, however, cannot mean that technology itself is *totally* neutral in this respect, for all determinants are also themselves determined.[223] Technology is neutral *in principle*, but a given form of *established* technology is not. Every form of technology has its limits not only in the quantity of its products but also—and this is the relevant point here—in the *quality* of human needs it is best suited to satisfy. This implies the danger of distorting the whole range of human needs in the direction of the "minimum resistance", or the "optimal allocation of human resources" etc., which in its turn—since consumption reaches back to production—can again enhance those potentials of the given technology which in the first place tended to produce seriously distorting effects. Evidently against this danger one has to appeal to social priorities, involving a most thorough examination of the whole complexity of human needs. In this sort of examination and assessment the tasks facing any form of society must be formulated also in terms of a constant struggle against the alienating potentials of technology.

All these problems, nevertheless, are capable of a solution, though of course only of a dialectical one. In our assessment of the transcendence of alienation it is vitally important to keep the "timeless" aspects of this problematics in their proper perspectives. Otherwise they can easily become ammunition for those who want to glorify capitalist alienation as a "tension inséparable de l'existence".

What the problems described above really amount to can be summed up as follows:

(1) that no *apriori* safeguards and assurances can be given for a practical supersession of alienation, since the issues involved are themselves inherently socio-historical;

(2) that there are some *dangers* of alienation which are inherent in the reifying *potential* of certain instruments and institutions of human interchange;

(3) and that no achievement in this respect (however radical and important) can be considered an *absolutely definitive* (permanent) "Aufhebung" of all possible forms of alienation.

Dangers, nevertheless, can be controlled, at least in principle. And this is precisely what is denied by the mystifiers who first make history stop arbitrarily at its capitalist phase, characterized by an actual lack of control, and then conclude that human "objectifications" are uncontrollable in principle. They misrepresent *dangers* and alienating *potentials* as *metaphysical necessities* (by calling alienation a "tension inséparable de l'existence", a "fundamental dimension of history", etc.) in order to justify the existing, socio-historically specific and transcendable *actuality* of capitalist alienation as an inescapable, *absolute necessity*. Thus in opposition to the dynamic, socio-historically concrete, dialectical ontology of Marx they offer a frozen, metaphysical, antihistorical, "phenomenological" pseudo-ontology. To say that "alienation is a fundamental dimension of history" is to negate history altogether. An "ontology" based on the foundations of such a negation is nothing but a mystifying projection of capitalist alienation and reification on a "timeless" scale.

The alienating potentials inherent in the instruments and institutions of human intercourse can be controlled provided that they are recognized *as* instruments and consciously brought into relation with *human ends*. And this is where we can identify what is really at stake and in what way and form is the socio-historically specific, capitalist, alienation involved in the matter. For it is not in the "ontological" nature of the instruments themselves that they get "out of control" and turn from *means* into self-sustaining *ends*. It is not the ontologically fundamental first order mediation between man and nature that is at stake here (i.e. not the fact that human beings have to produce in order to survive, and that no production is conceivable without instruments of some kind) but the *capitalist* form of *second order mediations*. Human instruments are not uncontrollable under capitalism because they are *instruments* (it is a sheer mystification to say that they represent an "altérité insurmontable" because they are distinct from "human self-consciousness", "la conscience de soi humaine") but because they are the instruments—specific, reified second order mediations—of *capitalism*. As such they cannot possibly function, except in a "reified" form; if, that is, they *control* man instead of being controlled by him. It is, therefore, not their *universal* characteristic of being instruments that is directly involved in alienation but their *specificity* of being instruments of a certain *type*. It is indeed one of the *diferentia specifica* of capitalistic instruments that they represent an "altérité insurmontable" to the "conscience de soi humaine" which is incapable of controlling them. Precisely because they are capitalistic second order mediations—the fetish character of commodity, exchange and money; wage-labour; antagonistic competition; internal contradictions mediated by the bourgeois state; the market; the reification of culture; etc.—it is necessarily inherent in their "essence" of being "mechanisms of control" that they must elude human control. This is why they must be *radically* superseded : the "expropriators must be expropriated"; "the bourgeois state must be overthrown"; antagonistic competition, commodity-production, wage-labour, the market, money-fetishism must be eliminated; the bourgeois hegemony of culture must be broken, etc. Consequently the programme of superseding capitalist alienation can be concretized as the replacement of the uncontrollable, reified instruments of capitalism by controllable instruments of human interchange. For in the very moment in which man succeeds in consciously subordinating his instruments to the realization of *his own ends* their "altérité insurmontable" *is surmounted.*

It goes without saying, a radical transformation of this magnitude cannot happen overnight. The "expropriation of the expropriators" is no more than the first act of a long and immensely complex process of change, characterized by the dialectic of "continuity in discontinuity" and "discontinuity in continuity". Granting that it is unthinkable to supersede alienation in a form that could be considered as absolutely and definitely superseding all possible dangers and potentials of reification, is fully compatible with conceiving "Aufhebung" as a succession of social enterprises of which the later is *less* (indeed *qualitatively* less) alienation-ridden than the preceding one. What matters is not only the given amount and extent of something you fight against—as criminologists know all too well—but also the general *trend* of development of the phenomenon in question. Capitalism is not characterized simply by alienation and reification but, at the same time, also by the *maximization* of the *trend* of alienation, to the point where the very existence of mankind is now at stake.

What gives sense to human enterprise in socialism is not the fictitious promise of a fictitious absolute (a world from which all possible contradiction is eliminated for ever) but the *real* possibility of turning a menacingly *increasing* trend of alienation into a reassuringly *decreasing* one. This itself would already be a *qualitative* achievement on the road to an effective, practical supersession of alienation and reification. But further qualitative achievements are possible which can be pinpointed not only in terms of the *reversal* of the general trend itself but also as regards the substantially different—self-fulfilling—character of specific forms of human activity which are freed from their subjection to alienated means serving the purpose of the perpetuation of the reified social relations of production.

The substitution of consciously controlled instruments and means of human interchange for the existing, capitalistically alienated and reified "second order mediations" is the socio-historically concrete programme of this transcendence. As to the "timeless" aspects of the dangers inherent in the instruments themselves, as we have seen they are not timeless at all because mere *potentialities* cannot become *realities* without the practical intervention of socio-historically *always* specific forms of human agency. Whether or not such potentialities remain mere potentialities or become dehumanizing realities depends entirely on the specific nature of the intervening human agency. If, therefore, the capitalistically alienated second order mediations—which are *apriori*, by their "essence", incompatible with human control—are abolished and replaced by instruments devised for the realization of consciously adopted human aims, then whatever dangers and potentials of alienation may present themselves at any stage of history, they must, in principle, be capable of human mastery and control.

History, therefore, in the Marxian conception remains history, which means simply that the instruments and forms of human interchange are conceived by Marx as inherently historical, changing, socio-historically specific,—at *any* stage whatsoever of human development.[224] And this is the point where we can clearly see the *practical* implications of the difference between an "open" and a "closed system" discussed in general terms at the end of chapter III.

Marx opposes to the actual, practical mystification of capitalism—which is only *reflected* in an alienated form in the various philosophical rationalizations of the *practical* negation of history by capitalism—the openness of his conception: the assertion of a "historicité insurmontable" of human existence. By contrast the Hegelian categories were mere concepts, logical abstractions;—therefore their "historicity", too, was a "speculative" one, i.e. "*terminable*" at the point which represented the socio-historical limits of the philosopher's standpoint. ("The standpoint of political economy.") Indeed, since Hegel was operating with logical abstractions as his categories, his category of historicity too had to be introduced into his conception in the form of a logical abstraction, a

mere concept. And just as easily—and arbitrarily—as one speculatively *introduces* the category of historicity into such a system,
just as easily one can bring to an end the whole "abstract, speculative, logical" process. This is why in the end the Hegelian conception of teleology must turn out to be a peculiar version of *theological teleology*. And a "historical ontology" which is based on a
theological theology is not only a closed, speculative, pseudo-
historical system but also a *metaphysical* ontology.

By contrast the Marxian ontology is dynamically historical and
objectively dynamic. Marx does not "deduce" human society from
the "categories" but, on the contrary, sees the latter as specific modes
of existence of the social being. He does not "add" historicity to an
originally *static* vision; for if historicity is merely added at a certain
point it can be also taken away at another. Instead he defines the
ontological substance of his conception as "the *self-mediating* being
of *nature*", i.e. as an *objective* being who cannot help being *inherently historical*.

Man, in the Marxian conception, is not a "dimension of history"
but, on the contrary, human *history* is a dimension of man as a self-
mediating objective being of nature. Only an objective being can
be historical, and an objective being can only be historical. History
is a meaningless abstraction unless it is related to an objective being.
In this dual sense history is, therefore, a dimension of man as an
objective, self-mediating being of nature.

If, however, history is a dimension of man, alienation cannot be
"a fundamental dimension of history". Being a dimension of an
objective being, history cannot have any dimension of its own—let
alone one which is the direct *negation* of all historicity. By turning
alienation into "a fundamental dimension of history", Heidegger
liquidates the historicity of an inherently historical, objective being.
Insofar as alienation is a negation of humanness, it is characteristic
of a certain *phase* of history, of a certain *stage* of development of the
social ontology of the objective "self-mediating being of nature".
A phase which *perpetuates* itself through the reification of the
social relations of production and, insofar as it succeeds in this self-
perpetuation, it *practically negates* history, by opposing the power
of the reified institutions of human interchange to all human efforts
which aim at the replacement of the uncontrollable instruments of
capitalism. This actual, *practical negation* of history by the capitalistically reified social relations of production is mystified by Heidegger
and others, in their effort to transfer the socio-historically specific

phenomena of capitalist alienation and reification to the eternal, "fundamental", metaphysical plane of an anti-historical, frozen ontology. This is why time and history must be "substantified" and given some fictitious "fundamental dimensions" : so that man should be deprived of *his* historical dimension and confronted, instead, with the uncontrollable power of a mythical "history" equated with an alleged metaphysical "eternality" and "fundamentality" of alienation in the pseudo-historical "Geworfenheit" (thrownness) of human existence.

In the Marxian conception—against which all these mystifications are directed—both alienation and its transcendence must be defined in terms of the objective necessities that characterize the *objective social ontology* of the "self-mediating being of nature". The necessity of alienation is defined as a necessity inherent in the objective teleology of human "self-development and self-mediation" at a certain stage of development of human productive activity which requires such alienation and reification for the—however alienated—self-realization of human potentialities. Since this necessity of alienation is a *historical* necessity, it is bound to be superseded (aufgehoben) through the concrete historical development of the same productive activity, provided that :

(1) the development of the productive forces *allows* the radical negation of capitalistic alienation;

(2) that the ripening of the social contradictions of capitalism (in the closest interchange with the development of the productive forces) *compels* man to move in the direction of an "Aufhebung";

(3) that the insights of human beings into the objective characteristics of their instruments *enable* them to elaborate those forms of control and interchange which prevent the reproduction of the old contradictions in some new form;

(4) and that the radical transformation of education from being a mere instrument of bourgeois hegemony into an organ of self-development and conscious self-mediation *inspires* the individuals to produce "according to their real human capabilities",—*unifying* knowledge and ideals, design and execution, theory and practice, as well as *integrating* the particular aspirations of the social individuals into the consciously adopted general aims of society as a whole.

The transcendence of alienation thus cannot be measured merely in terms of production *per capita,* or anything like that. Since the whole process directly involves the individual, the "measure" of success can hardly be other than the real human individual himself. In terms of such a measure, the transcendence of alienation—its decreasing hold over men—is in an inverse ratio to the increasingly fuller self-realization of the social individual. Since, however, the individual's self-realization cannot be abstracted from the society in which he lives, this question is inseparable from that of the concrete interrelations between individual and society or the types and forms of social institutions in which the individual may be able to integrate himself.

IX. *Individual and Society*

1. *Capitalist Development and the Cult of the Individual*

MODERN philosophers continue to insist on the "natural rights of the individual" : a concept that would have been unintelligible to Aristotle who wrote : "When several villages are united in a single complete community, large enough to be nearly self-sufficing, the state comes into existence, originating in the bare needs of life, and continuing for the sake of a good life. And therefore, if the earlier forms of society are natural, so is the state, for it is the end of them, and the nature of a thing is its end. For what each thing is when fully developed, we call its nature, whether we are speaking of a man, a horse or a family. Besides, the final cause and end of a thing is the best, and to be self-sufficing is the end and the best. Hence it is evident that the state is a creation of nature, and that *man is by nature a political animal.* . . . The proof that the state is a creation of nature and *prior to the individual* is that the individual, when isolated, is not self-sufficing; and therefore he is like a part in relation to the whole. But he who is unable to live in society, or who has no need because he is sufficient for himself, must be either a beast or a god : he is no part of a state. *A social instinct is implanted in all men by nature.*"[225]

As a result of capitalistic developments the notion of a social instinct "implanted in all men by nature" disappears completely. Now *individual* liberties appear to belong to the realm of "nature" and *social* links, by contrast, seem to be artificial and imposed, as it were, "from outside" upon the self-sufficient individual.

In Aristotle's conception there is a *harmonious* relationship between individual and community. This is formulated in the Aristotelian ethical principle according to which ". . . it is evident that the same life is best for each individual, and for states and for mankind collectively".[226] And this is by no means a mere "ought". On the contrary, it is an adequate philosophical expression of a certain stage of historical development at which the individual is organically integrated in the community to which he belongs.

254

The Aristotelian conception of a natural cohesion and harmony between the individual and society disappears from modern theories and its place is taken by picturing this relationship in terms of conflicts and contradictions. Expressions like "the lonely crowd" and "enforced privatization" have become catchphrases in recent sociological literature. We must read them, however, in their proper perspectives: against the historical background of this century. In fact "loneliness", for the past fifty years, has been a central theme in artistic works as well as in many theoretical discussions.[227]

From the seventeenth century onwards philosophers had paid an increasingly greater attention to the problem of "individual freedom". This contrasted sharply with the prevailing view of even the late Middle Ages when, as Burckhardt emphasizes, "Man was conscious of himself only as a member of a race, people, party, family, or corporation—only through some general category."[228] D. G. Ritchie makes the same point and adds: "The Aristotelian doctrine that 'man is by nature a political animal', had acquired the sanctity of a dogma, and kept the medieval thinker from imagining man's rights in abstraction from any particular political society."[229]

It goes without saying, Ritchie's depiction of the actual causal relations is idealistic. The medieval thinkers did not hold the views correctly described by Ritchie because the Aristotelian doctrine that man is by nature a political animal "had acquired the sanctity of a dogma", but because the social conditions of life induced them to do so. Indeed if the Aristotelian doctrine could acquire the sanctity of a dogma, it was due to the same causal factors. Similarly, when this "dogma" had lost its appeal, and philosophers started to be intensively preoccupied with the problems of "individual freedom", this was due—as we have already seen—to the dynamic development of the capitalistic relations of production which required the universal extension of "liberty" to every single individual so that he could enter into "free contractual relations" with other individuals, for the purpose of selling and alienating everything that belongs to him, including his own labour power.

By the time we reach the twentieth century, what acquires the "sanctity of a dogma" is the belief that "liberty" is inherent—as if it were a "natural right"—in the isolated individual. Political and social references tend to disappear, and the socio-historically conditioned circumstances of the individual's atomized, privatized life are characterized, ahistorically, as "the human condition". This

trend is graphically expressed in T. S. Eliot's dramatized philosophical meditations, *The Cocktail Party*. At a certain point the
heroine, Celia, is frightened by "an awareness of *solitude*" and
even more frightened by the temptation to seek explanations *outside*
herself, which would mean putting the blame on the world in which
she happens to live. She says thereafter :

> I mean that what has happened has made me aware
> that I've always been alone. That *one always is alone.*
>
> . . . it isn't that I want to be alone,
> But that everyone's alone—or it seems to me.
> They make noises, and think they are talking to each other;
> They make faces, and think they understand each other.
> And I'm sure that they don't.

The alternative to isolated individuality is described as "an illusory
new person : *us*", and when this latter vanishes what remains is
the paralyzing feeling that "the dreamer is no more real than his
dreams". Under similar conditions alienation that assumes the form
of a "real loneliness", opposed to the hallucinatory or "illusory us",
appears as a remedy. "The human condition" seems to be to live
with the inescapable alienation of human existence, to reconcile
oneself to it. As expressed in the words of the poet's mouthpiece,
the mysterious Dr. Reilly :

> I can reconcile you to *the human condition,*
> The condition to which some who have gone as far as you
> Have succeeded in returning. They may remember
> The vision they have had, but they cease to regret it,
> Maintain themselves by the common routine,
> Learn to avoid excessive expectation,
> Become tolerant of themselves and others,
> Giving and taking, in the usual actions
> What there is to give and take. They do not repine;
> Are contented with the morning that separates
> And with the evening that brings together
> For casual talk before the fire
> Two people who know they do not understand each other,
> Breeding children whom they do not understand
> And who will never understand them.
>
> Celia
> Is that the best life?
> Reilly

It is a good life.

A fitting description indeed of the alienated routine of bourgeois life. However, if this is "the human condition", nothing can be done about alienation in reality. In Eliot's mystical and aristocratic conception the transcendence of alienation belongs to the sphere of "beyond", and only the elected few can gain insight into it. The "other way" of living, contrasted by Eliot with "the human condition", might in the end, "transcend" alienation—in a mysterious way. A way which is:

> . . . unknown, and so requires faith—
> The kind of faith that issues from despair.
> The destination cannot be described;
> You will know very little until you get there;
> You will journey blind. But the way leads towards possession
> Of what you have sought for in the wrong place.

The difference between the two ways consists in two different kinds of awareness. The first supersedes the world of "hallucination" by an awareness of the "human condition", that is by an unquestioning resignation to the blind necessity of this condition of alienation. This way enables those who follow Dr. Reilly's first rules to "forget their loneliness". The second way is a kind of "awareness of the awareness"—a continuous awareness of the human condition being loneliness—wherefore one can never forget one's loneliness. But it is precisely this higher degree of awareness that "liberates" man from alienation. If we ask, how can one *live* the first way, Eliot can still point to the alienated routine of the fireside chats of resignation. But if we ask the same question about the second way, he can only invite us to a revealing mysticism: to share a faith whose point of departure is the unhesitating, conscious acceptance of dehumanization in reality.

It is by no means accidental that individual liberty as a political and moral ideal is absent from the ancient world, and appears only with the High Renaissance. When direct "dependence on nature" is a general concern of a particular community, aspirations to a distinct form of individual liberty can only be expressed marginally.

As we all know, this direct "dependence on nature" is overcome by the development of the capitalistic productive forces, implying the realization of individual liberty in its formal universality. The victorious advance of the capitalistic productive forces produces a way of life with an increasingly stronger accent on *privacy*. As the capitalistic liberation of man from his direct dependence on nature progresses, so human enslavement by the new "natural law" manifest in the alienation and reification of the social relations of production intensifies. Facing the uncontrollable forces and instruments of capitalistically alienated productive activity, the individual takes refuge in his "autonomous" private world. This he *can* do, because the hostile power of direct natural necessity which formerly united him with his fellow men now seems to be under control. And this is not all. The "übergreifendes Moment" (overriding factor) is that he is also *induced*, even *compelled* to withdraw into his little private realm—not only *enabled* to do so by the capitalistic development of the productive forces—insofar as with the extension of *commodity-production* his rôle as a *private consumer* acquires an increasingly greater significance for the perpetuation of the capitalist system of production.

In this realm of *privacy*—where the individual asserts his illusory "Sovereignty" (heavily mortgaged but grotesquely glorified by naive wishful thinking, expressed in slogans like "the Englishman's home is his Castle")—liberty may appear to be complete; for the aims and limits of action and the means and powers of execution seem to coincide, to be in perfect harmony. Yet, the underlying contradiction is striking. The relative liberation of man from his direct dependence on nature is achieved by means of a *social* action. Nevertheless, because of the reification of the social relations of production, this achievement appears in an alienated form : not as a relative independence from *natural* necessity but as a freedom from the constraints of *social* ties and relations, as an ever intensifying cult of "individual *autonomy*". This sort of alienation and reification, by producing the deceiving appearance of the individual's independence, self-sufficiency and autonomy, confers a value *per se* on the world of the individual, in abstraction from its relationships with society, with the "outside world". Now the fictitious "individual autonomy" represents the positive pole of morality and social relations count only as "interference",[230] as mere negativity. Self-seeking egoistic fulfilment is the straitjacket imposed by capitalist development on man, and the values of "individual autonomy" represent its ethical glorification. "Individualethik" is the sublimated expression of crude bourgeois egoism that prevails as a result of the reification of the social relations of production. Even if it takes notice of the links of men with each other, it can only do so in the form of a mere "ought" : the alleged manifestation of a "transcendental sphere", an "absolute sphere", a sphere radically opposed to the "contingency" of social relations. In such an ethical theory the concept of "human nature"—a mystified, desocialized reflection of the "natural law" of capitalism in the human relations of privatized, fragmented, isolated, self-seeking, "autonomous individuality"—serves to absolutize, as a metaphysical inescapability, a social order which "keeps men in their crude solitariness", antagonistically opposed to each other, in subjection to their "artificial appetites" and to the "rule of the dead thing over man".

By contrast, prior to capitalistic developments it was inconceivable to abstract, in the name of the individual's autonomous scale of values, from an objective order of nature and society. We need not go back as far as Aristotle to see how fundamentally modern conceptions differ from earlier ones and to what extent this change was due to the capitalist form of supersession of man's direct dependence on nature. We find this clearly expressed, at the dawn of the modern age, in Paracelsus' works. He simply cannot, as yet, conceive man and human activity except in the closest organic relationship with nature: "Was ist das Glück anderst denn *Ordnung halten mit der Wissenheit der Natur*? Die Natur, gehet sie recht, so ist das ein Glück, gehet sie unrecht, so ist das ein Unglück. Denn *wir haben unser verordnet Wesen in der Natur*."[231] And thus to be active, in order to find out "die Heimlichkeit der Natur" (nature's secret) and "das Licht der Natur" (the light of nature)—expressions frequently used by Paracelsus—is not only physically necessary but also *morally* the only adequate form of human life. *Vita activa* occupies the highest point on the human scale of values. Paracelsus speaks of "the inner man", man proper, "the man of the second creation", who was created by labour to which man was compelled when he was driven out of Paradise. "We received all members of our body at the first creation, after all other things had been created. But the knowledge that man needs was not yet in Adam but was given him only when he was expelled from Paradise. Then he received 'knowledge' through the angel; but not all knowledge. For he and his children must learn one thing after another in the light of nature, in order to bring to light that which lies hidden in all things. For although man was created whole as regards his body, he was not so created as regards his 'art'. All the arts have been given him, but not in an immediately recognizable form; he must discover them by learning."[232] And elsewhere: "*Happiness* does not consist in laziness, or sensual pleasure, or riches, or chattering, or gluttony.

In labour and in sweat must each man use the gifts that God conferred upon him on earth, either as a peasant in the fields, as a workman in the smithy, in the mines, on the seas, in medicine, or as one who proclaims the word of God. *The proper way resides in work and action, in doing and producing*; the perverse man does nothing, but talks a great deal. We must not judge a man by his words, but by his heart. The heart speaks through words only when they are *confirmed by deeds.*"[233] The human essence can only become manifest through labour: "No one sees what is hidden in him [in man], but only *what his works reveal.* Therefore *man should work continually* to discover what God has given him."[234] This is why, according to Paracelsus, labour (Arbeit) must serve as the ordering principle of society: he advocates even the expropriation of the wealth of the idle rich, in order to compel them to lead a productive life.[235]

We can understand now why Goethe was so attached to Paracelsus: an actual, historical model of the "Faustian spirit". Paracelsus, standing at the gates of the modern age, was not only singing the swansong of an outgoing world but also anticipating a far-distant future—well beyond the bourgeois horizon—insisting on the great potentialities of mankind inherent in his labour. By the time, however, when Goethe was completing his Faust, "self-fulfilment in labour"—as a result of capitalistic dehumanization of labour—had become an extremely problematic concept. But Goethe mastered, with supreme artistry, the tragic dilemma: whether one should give up with scepticism the ideal or resign oneself, in the spirit of "uncritical positivism", to its violation and alienated realization in capitalism. He asserted the universal (perspectival) validity of the Paracelsian ethos in spite of its temporal devaluation in existing reality. To assert this dialectical duality of perspectives, without rhetorics, he had to find a situation in which the necessary distance from Faust's illusions does not suggest in the slightest way a sceptical negativity, nor indeed some form of resigning accommodation. He succeeded in achieving this through the wonderfully subtle irony of the scene in which Faust—blinded by *Sorge* (Anxiety) for refusing to yield to her—greets the noise of the Lemurs who dig his grave as the welcome noise of canal-digging, in realization of his great project:

> A swamp along the mountains' flank
> Makes all my previous gains contaminate;
> My deeds, if I could drain this sink,

Would culminate as well as terminate :
To open to the millions living space,
Not danger-proof but free to run their race.
Green fields and fruitful; men and cattle hiving
Upon this newest earth at once and thriving,
Settled at once beneath this sheltering hill
Heaped by the masses' brave and busy skill.
With such a heavenly land behind this hedge,
The sea beyond may bluster to its edge
And, as it gnaws to swamp the work of masons,
To stop the gap one common impulse hastens.
Aye! Wedded to this concept like a wife,
I find this wisdom's final form :
He only earns his freedom and his life
Who takes them every day by storm.
And so a man, beset by dangers here,
As child, man, old man, spends his manly year.
Oh to see such activity,
Treading free ground with people that are free!
Then could I bid the passing moment :
'Linger a while, thou art so fair!'
The traces of my earthly days can never
Sink in the aeons unaware.
And I, who feel ahead such heights of bliss,
At last enjoy my highest moment—this.
(Faust dies.) (Translated by Louis MacNeice)

Thus the tormenting dilemma is resolved by Goethe in a form that reasserts the validity of the Faustian ideal and intensifies it by the tragic pathos of this "divina tragoedia" of mankind. Notwithstanding the striking contrast between the existing reality and the Faustian ideal the ethos of *vita activa* triumphs in the comprehensive perspectives of human development as a whole.

However, eleven years before Goethe completes his *Faust* Schopenhauer publishes his main work : *The World as Will and Idea*. This work announces a radically different orientation which becomes increasingly more dominating in modern bourgeois philosophy. Schopenhauer and his followers treat the ethos of *vita activa* with aristocratic contempt, idealizing "withdrawal" and "contemplative" idleness. The line of this philosophical approach goes from Schopenhauer and Kierkegaard, through Unamuno, Ortega y Gasset, Huizinga, Berdyaev, Gabriel Marcel and others down to their present-day epigons like Hannah Arendt. The last named characteristically closes her book, *The Human Condition* (!), with these words: "how right Cato was when he said: *Numquam se plus agere quam nihil cum ageret, numquam minus solum esse quam cum solus esset*—'Never is he more active than when he does nothing, never is he less alone than when he is by himself'."[236] The idealization of individual autonomy, carried to its extreme, leads inevitably not only to the acceptance of inactivity but also to conferring on it the highest moral praise.

The devaluation of *vita activa* and the idealization of "individual autonomy"—to the point of opposing it to "liberty"—belong to the same process of alienation. As we have seen, the development of capitalism necessarily carries with it the abolition of feudal privileges and the adoption of the contractual prerequisite of "civil society": the principle of "universal and equal liberty". At the early stages of capitalist development the accent is, inevitably, on the *universal* aspect of liberty. The adoption of "equal liberty" as the guiding principle of "economic society" is the *common concern* of the "Third Estate", in opposition to the interests of the ruling Estates of feudal society. Furthermore, in order to strengthen the moral claims of the advocated principle, it is stressed that "liberty" is the *universal* concern of all men. No sign, therefore, of a conception of freedom as "individual autonomy" opposed to "universal and equal liberty".

Later, however, when the "equality" involved in "universal liberty" turns out to be hollow—a merely *formal* equality—and the principle of liberty is realized in the form of both crying economic and social inequality and the universalization of "commodity-slavery" (i.e. the complete negation of human freedom by the reified social relations of production; the domination of men by a blindly prevailing "natural law" of their own making) then, but only then, the concept of "individual autonomy" is pushed into the foreground. Now that the power relations of society are solidified and structurally safeguarded by the capitalist reification of the social relations of production, the concept of "universal and equal liberty" can only represent a challenge and a menace of "subversion". The conduct of "public affairs" is, therefore, best assigned to the specialists of established, bureaucratic bodies of repression—in Kierkegaard's view to the Church and to the Monarchy: the "bulwarks" of society against the "rabble"—and "withdrawal" is glorified as the only "authentic" way of life. The cult of "privacy" and of "individual autonomy" thus fulfils the dual function of *objectively* protecting the established order against "challenge by the rabble", and *sub-*

jectively providing a spurious fulfilment in an escapist withdrawal
to the isolated and powerless individual who is mystified by the
mechanisms of capitalist society which manipulate him.

Needless to say, in this situation "outer-directed" human activity
cannot bring fulfilment to the individual. *Vita 'activa* cannot acquire
a moral significance unless it is recognized—as by Paracelsus or
Faust—that its accomplishments are of a "common concern". Such
an activity necessarily involves "the other" and therefore it cannot
be conceived in terms of "individual autonomy", in isolation from
the given social relations. When, however, work is dehumanized
and subordinated as a mere means to the end of perpetuating the
reified social relations of production, "common concern" becomes
an empty word, and self-fulfilment achieved through labour as
man's life-activity is unthinkable. What remains after the capitalist
"devaluation of the world of man" is merely the dehumanized
illusion of a fulfilment through "withdrawal", through "contemplative" idleness, through the cult of "privacy", "irrationality", and
"mysticism"—in short through the idealization of "individual
autonomy" as openly or implicitly opposed to "universal liberty".

Gabriel Marcel tries to resolve this contradiction between liberty
and autonomy by saying that *"non-autonomy"* is *"liberty
itself"*[237]. It seems, then, as if the accent were now on "universal
liberty". But if we examine more closely Marcel's argument, we
find that this "liberty itself" as opposed to "autonomy" (to autonomy
conceived as the sphere of activity necessarily integrated with alienation : the world of "having" interconnected with an "autonomous"
activity) is nothing but a fictitious direct connection between the
abstract individual ("ego") and the *abstract universal* ("being"). The
only possible way to achieve in full this "liberty of non-autonomy"
("non-autonomy" because of the advocated direct connection of
individual "ego" with universal "being")—transcending thus, in
Marcel's view, the world of alienation—is by means of "contemplation" and "adoration". In other words, the remedy is found, again,
within the confines of the *speculative* world of the *actually* isolated
individual. The problem then at the end is reduced to a mere matter
of terminology and "liberty" conceived in these terms covers in fact
only a limited part of the sphere designated elsewhere as "individual
autonomy". The capitalist dehumanization of activity—its subordination to "having" etc.—is mystified as a metaphysical absolute
which can only be opposed by the mysticism of "another sphere".
And, just as in Eliot, even this form of fictitious transcendence of

alienation is not open to everybody. The philosopher is "less autonomous" (and, of course, "more free") than the scientist who is, again,
"less autonomous" than the technician, and so on. This kind of
solution is in full agreement with the general aristocratic character
of Gabriel Marcel's philosophy. He denounces the democratic conception of epistemology as something that "takes us to ruin" and
in this spirit he turns his back on *"le on"*, the contemptuously designated "man in the street".

Similarly in Heidegger, *das Man* (the neuter "one", rendered in
English as "the they") gets all the blame. "One belongs to the
Others oneself and enhances their power. 'The Others' whom one
thus designates in order to cover up the fact of one's belonging to
them essentially oneself, are those who proximally and for the most
part 'a r e t h e r e' in everyday Being-with-one-another. The 'who'
is not this one, not that one, not oneself (man selbst), not some
people (einige), and not the sum of them all. The 'who' is the neuter,
t h e 'they' (das Man). . . . This Being-with-one-another dissolves
one's own Dasein completely into the kind of Being of 'the Others',
in such a way, indeed, that the Others, as distinguishable and
explicit, vanish more and more. In this inconspicuousness and un-
ascertainability, the real dictatorship of the 'they' is unfolded. . . .
Everyone is the other, and no one is himself. The 't h e y', which
supplies the answer to the question of the 'w h o' of everyday
Dasein, is the 'n o b o d y' to whom every Dasein has already sur-
rendered itself in Being-among-one-another (Untereinandersein). . . .
In these modes one's way of being is that of *inauthenticity* and failure to *stand by one's Self*. . . . The Self of everyday Dasein is the
t h e y - s e l f, which we distinguish from the a u t h e n t i c Self—
that is, from the Self which has been taken hold of in its own way
(eigens ergriffenen). As they-self, the particular Dasein has been
d i s p e r s e d into the 'they', and must first find itself. This dis-
persal characterizes the 'subject' of that kind of Being which we
know as *concernful absorption in the world* we encounter as closest
to us."[238] Thus some specific socio-historical phenomena of
modern capitalism are inflated into the "cosmic" proportions of an
irrationalist, timeless, metaphysical ontology. At the same time the
diagnosis of negative phenomena is carefully mixed up with a denunciation of the only possible antidote: the individual's' "concernful
absorption in the world", in a common effort with "Others", so
that they should gain control over their own life now ruled and
manipulated by the complex mechanisms of capitalist "everyday-

ness". The Heideggerian mystification which labels "inauthentic" Being-with-one-another as such and *opposes* to one's "concernful absorption in the world" the irrationality of "the Self's own way", successfully manipulates and disarms the individuals' spontaneous anticapitalist protest. And he is by no means alone in these efforts. Their common methodology is the mystifying fusion of the *negative* reality of capitalist routine and the *positive* potentiality of its supersession in a deceiving form of negation which leaves the existing order unchallenged, indeed fortified. The unveiling of their methodology reveals the ideological substance of their "timeless", frozen ontology.

But the cult of the individual's "autonomy" is not confined to these aristocratic sermons on the metaphysical inescapability of capitalistic alienation and reification. Surprising as it might sound at first, liberal intellectuals often fall for the same mystification. A typical example is David Riesman. He admits that "It is difficult enough to consider how we may remove the barriers of false personalization and enforced privatization. It is enormously more difficult to descry, after these barriers are overcome, what in man may lead him to *autonomy*, or to invent and create means that will help him to *autonomy*. In the end our few suggestions are paltry ones, and we can only conclude our discussion by saying that a vastly greater stream of creative, utopian thinking is needed before we can see more clearly the goal we dimly suggest by the word *'autonomy'*."[239] But if we ask what is this "autonomy", we find that it amounts to very little, if anything at all. On the closing page of the book we read: ". . . of one thing I am sure: the enormous potentialities for diversity in nature's bounty and men's capacity to differentiate their experience *can become valued by the individual himself*, so that he will not be tempted and coerced into adjustment or, failing adjustment, into anomie. The idea that men are created free and equal is both true and misleading: *men are created different*; they lose their social freedom and individual autonomy in seeking to become like each other."[240]

The questions that badly need answering are all left unanswered, or not even asked. What is the guarantee that "differentiation" can become "valued" by the individual himself in the conditions in which he lives? It is of little comfort, if any, that it "can" become valued, in abstraction. What matters is whether or not it can become valued in the *actual* conditions of life to which the analysis refers.

Furthermore it is by no means self-evident that this "differentiation" constitutes a value in itself. That "men are created different" is either resounding rhetoric or the shallowest of platitudes. Man can be *humanly* different only to the extent to which any given form of society allows or can afford to allow genuine differentiation. Thus actual differentiation, far from equalling *"autonomy"*, can only acquire a sense and value if it is conceived as *social reciprocity*. To be different for the sake of being different, is worthless. The murderer is, admittedly, "different" from his victim, but no one would praise him for this. It is the actual *content* of differentiation that matters. Only that kind of differentiation can become a value which can be socially integrated, thus contributing to the enrichment and positive development of the social individual.

Consequently if one sees—as Riesman does—that society interferes with the desired differentiation, one should raise the question of how to change the given society in order to realize the values which are at the focal point of one's criticism. But Riesman fails to raise this question too. What he asks, instead, is this : "Is it conceivable that these economically privileged Americans will some day wake up to the fact that they overconform?" And he answers, rather pessimistically : "Since *character structure* is, if anything, even more tenacious than *social structure*, such an awakening is *exceedingly unlikely*. . . . But to put the question *may* at least raise *doubts* in the minds of *some*. Occasionally *city planners* put such questions."[241]

The trouble with Riesman's question is that it does not matter which way you answer it. For, suppose those privileged Americans did "wake up" one day to the fact that they overconform—then what? Could they close the next day the factories that *overproduce*, in an uncontrollable fashion, all those goods which are inseparably linked to this "overconformity"? Hardly. So even the miracle, if it happened, would make no difference as to the realizability of the desired differentiation. If it is true that "character structure" is as tenacious as Riesman claims it to be (*opposing* the tenacity of this "character structure" to that of the social structure, instead of linking it to the latter), then there must be some mysterious power which radically transforms those who are "created different" into overconforming individuals. And if the opposition between character structure and social structure is tenable, there remains only one thing to do : to wait for the miracle of universal awakening, and for the further miracle of obtaining the desired change without transforming in depth that tenacious social structure as well. (As to the likely fruits of city planning, it is naive, to say the least, to expect anything from it under capitalism. The more so because—as even Riesman admits—the few imaginative city planners meet with sustained resistence from extremely powerful groups and vested interests. The sobering truth is that the "doubts" that might be raised "in the minds of some" can only produce significant results if the defeating resistence of the reified social relations of production is first overcome.)

To seek the remedy in "autonomy" is to be on the wrong track. Our troubles are not due to a lack of "autonomy" but, on the contrary, to a social structure—a mode of production—that forces on men a *cult* of it, isolating them from each other. The vital question that must be asked about autonomy is: what can one *do* with it? If one just "has" it, as a "psychological faculty", a feature of "character structure", or as a hollow right confined to the realm of "privacy", for all practical purposes this comes to the same thing as *not* to have it at all.

To be able to do something by means of one's "autonomy" necessarily involves "the other". Consequently the only form of autonomy which is worth considering is *non-autonomous "autonomy"*. In other words: humanly meaningful "autonomy" is really no different from *social reciprocity* in the course of which the individuals involved with each other *mutually* adapt themselves to the conditions of the given interchange and at the same time retain the power of new initiative. Whether or not such a reciprocity exists, depends on the character of the given social structure. It is therefore highly misleading to reduce this problem—which involves many social, economic, political, educational, etc. factors—to the hollow psychological slogan of the "dimly suggested word 'autonomy'."

Clearly, the cult of the individual—itself a product of alienation—cannot offer any remedy against alienation and reification. It can only widen the gulf that separates man under capitalism from his social integration.

2. *Individual and Collectivity*

When Attila József asked: "How is it possible that *homo moralis* or *homo ideologicus* finds himself in conflict with *homo oeconomicus*? Or, to put it otherwise, what prevents the economic judgment from functioning as it should?"—he was trying to find an explanation for the tragic events of the period when Fascism triumphed—a triumph that would have been impossible if man's "economic judgment" had been as effective as the protagonists had thought. In the circumstances he could only conclude that "So long as man's emotional powers—little as we know about them—are strong enough to enrol men in camps opposed to their human interest, how can we believe that, motivated by their economic judgment, they will devote themselves to the building of a new world?!"[242]

The criticism implied in the words of this supremely great socialist poet was directed against Stalin's antidialectical and bureaucratic conception. For according to Stalin the overthrow of capitalism is *ipso facto* a solution of the whole social problem, and any internal difficulties that remain are to be attributed to the "survivals of capitalism". Thus the very possibility of a socialist criticism of postrevolutionary society is denied. It is not surprising, therefore, that socialist aspirations which appeal to the Marxian programme of "human self-realization" are condemned as mere "moralizations". (This is why even some of Marx's most fundamental works must be rejected as "idealist".)

The first thing to note is that the social standpoint which *apriori* condemns the very idea of a socialist criticism of postrevolutionary society as mere "moralization" is bound to be *abstract*. It does not take into account the most important factor of the given historical situation: the actual human beings who constitute society after the revolution just as before. It voluntaristically superimposes over the "real, human individual" (Lenin) the generic categories of an idealistically anticipated social-historical *phase*. The "rightness" of human conduct is measured—positively or negatively—by its alleged approximation to (or distance from) one of the arbitrarily invented stereotypes like "positive hero", "the waverer", "the enemy", etc., regardless of the concrete socio-historical circumstances in which the individual is acting.

Particularly revealing is in this respect the concept of "revolutionary romanticism" which demonstrates the bureaucratically "moralizing" character of Stalinist dogmatism. The slogans of "revolutionary romanticism" constitute in fact a far from revolutionary ethico-juridical code that categorically repudiates any criticism of the *present* from the standpoint of a bureaucratically manipulated society whose social and moral superiority is asserted in the name of the *presumed future* of *homo oeconomicus*. Naturally, if value judgments are formulated from the standpoint of a *desired future*, in striking opposition to the objective characteristics of the *actual present*, those judgments which do not follow the rules of "revolutionary romantic" (i.e. conservative-bureaucratic) wishful thinking but are based on *present* actualities must appear to the wishful thinkers as "moralizing" survivals from the *past*. They must be, therefore, condemned *apriori*. Thus the complex objective contradictions of a great social transformation are voluntaristically reduced to convenient subjective terms and become the simple problem of how to deal administratively with the "resisting individual" who is a "survival from the past". The issues are raised one-sidedly and bureaucratically—so that they should be amenable to an administrative solution, in keeping with the Stalinist institutional framework of post-revolutionary society. The individual is confronted with bureaucratic bodies which pour romantic sermons upon him. He can either behave, sincerely or not, as if he lived in accordance with the abstract subjectivist models expressed in those sermons, or else suffer the administrative consequences.

Here we have to recall one passage in the *Grundrisse der Kritik der politischen Ökonomie* in which the "mature Marx" analyses the relation between the individual and his social environment. He concludes that alienation is transcended only if *"the individuals reproduce themselves as individuals, but as social individuals"*. Thus in Marx's view the individual in a socialist society does not dissolve his individuality within the general social determinations. On the contrary, he must find an outlet for the full realization of his own personality (Gesamtpersönlichkeit). In a capitalist society the individuals can only reproduce themselves as *isolated* individuals. In a bureaucratically collectivized society, on the other hand, they cannot reproduce themselves as *individuals*, let alone as *social individuals*. In both of them the *public* sphere is divorced from the *private* one and opposed to it, however different the forms of such opposition might be. According to Marx, by contrast, the realization of "Gesamtpersönlichkeit" necessarily implies the reintegration of *individuality* and *sociality* in the tangible human reality of the *social individual*.

When Marx referred to a positive transcendence of alienation, he uttered a warning against "re-establishing 'Society' as an abstraction *vis-à-vis* the individual" (104). Such an opposition of "Society" to the individual—in the shape of bureaucratized collective bodies—

makes impossible the *self-mediation* of the social individual. For the claimed "universality" of bureaucratic collectivity is not a directly human universality but, on the contrary, an *abstraction* from the actual conditions of life of the "real, human individual". Thus instead of enabling the particular individuals to transcend their limitations through a reciprocal social integration with each other, abstract collectivity dissolves them within its own *generic* framework in which there can be no room for the *specific* characteristics of the real individuals. In place of the *isolated individual* is now put an *abstract universal* ("abstrakt Allgemeine"—e.g. "member of the Socialist State", "Positive Hero", etc.) and not the truly *social individual* who has become a "concrete universal" by self-mediation within a real *community*.

The problematic character of these developments can be clearly seen in the fate of the socialist principle : "from everyone according to his abilities, to everyone according to his work". Viewed from the abstract standpoint of bureaucratic collectivity, the sole obstacle to the realization of this principle is that the individuals who are asked to contribute "according to their abilities" resist the natural tendency to become "positive heroes" because of the "survival of capitalism" in them. What this amounts to is the assertion that the individual's contribution to "the whole" (by which is meant "Society" set in abstract opposition to the individual) must consist in *conforming to a predetermined norm*. In this imposed act of conformity the ideal is divorced from the individual (it is conceived as something *above* him) and obliterates the particular personality of the individual. That working "according to one's ability" means above all the realization of conditions in which the real human individual's manifold abilities are not pressed into the Procrustean bed of narrowly predetermined bureaucratic requirements is not visible, of course, from the standpoint of abstract collectivity.

Needless to say, the apologists of capitalism dismiss the Marxian idea of a "positive transcendence of alienation" as an "utopian dream" and exploit the historically conditioned failures of the Stalin era as a timeless "proof" that the capitalistically reified conditions of life are "the best that men can obtain". On the other hand Stalinist self-complacency also puts the blame for its own failures on the continued survival of capitalism. Both these approaches are untenable. Unfortunately for the adversaries of socialism, this century has produced different *types* of post-capitalist society—i.e. China, Cuba and Vietnam, in addition to Yugoslavia and the Peoples

Democracies—which, if they can help it, are far from repeating the Soviet pattern of development. As to Stalinist self-complacency, it is clear that complex historical developments cannot be reduced to a single cause. Obviously the continued existence of world-capitalism played an important part in the Stalinist distortions of the original revolutionary potentials of October 1917. But the real pattern of socio-historical causality is dialectical *reciprocity*, not mechanical one-sidedness. There were many internal and external factors which all contributed, by their reciprocal interplay with each other, to the final outcome, within the general framework of a *global* situation. Here we must confine ourselves—in comparing three different types of postrevolutionary developments: the Soviet, the Chinese and the Cuban—to a very brief discussion of some, particularly important, historical factors.

We must remember that Soviet development suffered two major reversals before Stalin's line of policy had finally triumphed. The first was the long civil war when the urgent tasks of laying the foundations of a socialist economy in a most backward country had to be subordinated to the even more urgent task of defending the revolution against foreign intervention. (Some of the institutional germs of a potential socialist democracy, generated in the course of the revolution, were the obvious casualties of this phase.) The second was when, in the interest of bare survival, the New Economic Policy (NEP) had to be introduced: a policy that made serious concessions to private gain as a powerful motivational force, trying to counteract its far-reaching negative effects by *judiciary* means. This we can see in a letter Lenin sent to D. I. Kursky, Procurator General of the People's Comissariat for Justice: "Under the Tsar, the procurators were sacked or promoted on the strength of the percentage of cases they won. We managed to adopt the worst of tsarist Russia—red tape and sluggishness—and this is virtually stifling us, but we failed to adopt its *good practices*. . . . I find that the P.C.J. is 'swimming with the tide'. But its task is to swim against the tide. . . . If the P.C.J. fails to prove by a series of *model trials* that it knows how to trap offenders against this rule and *chastise . . . with shooting*, then the P.C.J. is good for nothing and I shall deem it my duty to get the Central Committee to agree to a total replacement of all senior workers of the P.C.J."[243] Thus when the NEP period was over, nothing was easier for Stalin than establishing a continuity between his own authoritarian methods and the NEP trials. The desperate situation which forced upon Lenin the method of trying to cope with the grave economic and political problems by means of "model trials" could only strengthen the bureaucratic central authorities which anyway enjoyed a "built-in" supremacy thanks to their power of control over the distribution of the extremely scarce material resources. Since both justice and the distribution of the available economic resources was being administered *from above*, a dual standard of living could be increasingly adopted: one for the specialists and party functionaries, and another for the vast majority of the population. And, of course, parallel to the intensification of inequalities, the ideological forms had become increasingly dominated by the false perspectives of "communism round the corner" cultivated by "revolutionary romanticism" that fictitiously "transcended" the existing inequalities by substituting an imaginary *future* for the actual *present*.

The contrast between the Stalinist perspectives and those of Mao Tse-tung is striking. Mao Tse-tung insists that even *after* several decades of hardship and self-denial—i.e. even at the turn of the twenty-first century—one must still economize, since, as he says, frugality is a basic principle of socialist economics in general. One must add here that the underlying general philosophical conception is also a highly realistic one. In Mao Tse-tung's view "The history of mankind is one of continuous development from the realm of necessity to the realm of freedom. This process is *never-ending*."[244]

The contrast here with China is not simply ideological. Rather: the greater realism in the Chinese ideological perspective reflects a very different historical situation. In China not only was there no NEP. More significant: a NEP-type reversal was simply unthinkable: the revolution was *peasant-based*. Also, *before* the revolution could become victorious, it had to solve in practice many social, political, economic and administrative problems which in the Soviet Union have only arisen *after* a politically successful revolution. So the Soviet revolutionaries almost overnight found themselves in a situation in which they had to provide an answer to everything *at once*, and when they made mistakes they have made them on a *massive* scale, involving the whole state, whereas the Chinese could work out a strategy of success while correcting errors committed in more localized conflicts, extending the scope of their influence in the process of learning to cope with increasingly greater problems of social administration.

A crucial issue, singled out by Lenin himself, was the relationship between the new organs of the revolution and the old state appar-

atus. Lenin's analysis of this problem in his stock-taking speech on
the NEP is most revealing. "We took over the old machinery of
state, and *that was our misfortune*. Very often this machinery
operates against us. In 1917, after we seized power, the government
officials sabotaged us. This frightened us very much and we pleaded :
'Please come back.' They all came back but *that was our misfortune*.
We now have a vast army of government employees, but lack
sufficiently educated forces *to exercise real control over them*. In
practice it often happens that here at the top, where we exercise
political power, the machine functions somehow; but down below
government employees have *arbitrary control* and they often
exercise it in such a way as to *counteract our measures*. At the top,
we have, I don't know how many, but at all events, I think, no more
than a few thousand, at the outside several tens of thousands of
our own people. Down below, however, there are hundreds of
thousands of old officials whom we got from the Tsar and from
bourgeois society and who, partly deliberately and partly unwittingly,
work against us."[245] The urgency and magnitude of the suddenly
acquired tasks forced Lenin and his comrades to resign themselves
to the idea of heavily relying on a massive old bureaucratic state
machinery : a mill-stone around the neck of the revolution. The
subjective attitude of the officials towards the revolution was
secondary. The massive bureaucratic machinery as such, with its
own institutional inertia, was *objectively* opposed to revolutionary
measures, engulfing in an "unwitting" hostility even those officials
who subjectively happened to sympathize with the revolution. The
old heritage with its massive inertia was a factor that weighed
heavily on successive stages of Soviet development.

Chinese development was historically much more fortunate in
this respect. Partly because the old state machinery was of a very
different kind, and partly because the organizational and administrative problems themselves have arisen in quite a different way.
Though the numbers involved were much greater, the margin of
manœuvre and the possibility of retreat was greater too. The organizational framework was worked out on an enormously wide popular
basis. If there was to be a successful revolution at all, it had to be
peasant-based, even though the original ideology was urban working class oriented. Mao Tse-tung prophesied at the beginning of
1927 : "The present upsurge of the peasant movement is a colossal
event. In a very short time, in China's central, southern and northern provinces, several hundred million peasants will rise like a mighty

storm, like a hurricane, a force so swift and violent that no power, however great, will be able to hold it back. They will smash all the trammels that bind them and rush forward along the road to liberation."[246] This conception of the revolution—as a colossal peasant movement of elemental force—carried with it the principle that *"The people, and the people alone, are the motive force in the making of world history"*[247] and in practice the task of developing grass-root democracy to set free the "boundless creative power of the masses." (The revolutionary intellectual is seen as a vitally important instrument to set free this creative power.) The emerging state machinery is organized—including the army in a war situation— to minimize friction between the people and the government bodies, and to further self-reliance and reciprocal help. This is well illustrated by the following example: "In recent years our army units in the Border Region have undertaken production on a big scale to provide themselves with ample food and clothing and have simultaneously done their training and conducted their political studies and literacy and other courses much more successfully than before, and there is *greater unity than ever within the army and between the army and the people.*"[248] In the same spirit the recent *Cultural Revolution* reasserted, in a practical form, the validity of the principle that "the people alone are the motive force", in opposition to bureaucratization, with the active participation of virtually hundreds of millions.

The Cuban leadership had been repeatedly attacked, from various sectarian quarters, for its "heresy". So much so in fact that Fidel Castro had to emphasize in the clearest possible terms: *"We don't belong to any sect; we don't belong to an international Masonic order; we don't belong to any church."*[249] Admittedly, in Cuba's survival in face of the massive naked power of American imperialism, Soviet help, both military and economic, played an enormously important rôle. But no country can survive on outside help alone. Cuba's continued existence and advance are irrefutable evidence of the great positive vitality of her own type of development. The foundations were laid in the days of the armed revolution which extended its sphere of influence in the form of activating the *repressed spontaneity* of the masses in the fight against the Batista regime. If the revolution was to survive in the "American hemisphere", such foundations not only had to be maintained but also deepened and further extended at the same time. And this is precisely what is being attempted in Cuba today: it is enough to think of the programmes of popular participation in developing economy, politics and culture alike, of the conscious efforts to keep bureaucracy at bay, and last but not least of the ethos of *equality* which characterizes the emerging human relations, in all spheres of life. Within the framework of these perspectives there can be no room for the dogmas of an "international Masonic order". The stakes are high, since Cuba lives permanently in the shadow of a mortal menace. In such a situation when "the moment of truth" is not a fleeting moment but a cathartic permanence, the essentials easily sort themselves out from the dogmatic inessentials. The "cunning of history" can only help those who are capable of helping themselves. In a socialist framework of genuine reciprocity even the obvious military weakness can be overcome and turned to positive use: for the only form of military operation which could conceivably contain the aggressor in the event of another U.S. invasion is one which is the elemental, spontaneous, total effort of the people as a whole: disciplined *from within* and capable of the ultimate sacrifice as a matter of course. Thus military disadvantage is turned into a powerfully dynamic factor of social cohesion and development. Also, there can be no question of waiting for the establishment of socialist human relations until *after* some predetermined economic targets are reached: educational aims and economic programmes must be realized in a reciprocal integration with each other. Significantly enough the Cuban leadership is characterized by a "heretic" economic thinking, not only as regards the programme of industrialization. More radical are the efforts—affecting the general perspectives of development in a most fundamental way—which aim at reducing the rôle of exchange and money in running the economy. Thus what is directly challenged by means of these measures, however tentative they may—indeed must—be at this stage, is the system of "second order mediations" which is the heaviest of all the millstones inherited from the capitalist past. And no postcapitalist society can hope to fully realize the *social individual* without demolishing this system of second order mediations and replacing it by adequate instruments of human interchange.

Needless to say, the different types of development towards socialism cannot be understood simply in terms of the local conditions but only if the latter are inserted into the general framework of a *global* situation of which they are an integral part. The Soviet Union, being the "first broken link of the chain of imperialism", had to constitute herself right in the middle of capitalist-interventionist assaults: it was imperative for her to build up a military power capable of withstanding a total confrontation with world capitalism. By the time Cuba was embarking on the road of her development, the shrinking world of capitalism was being successfully challenged not only by the existence of the Soviet system but also by the victorious Chinese revolution. The emancipation of man from capitalist alienation is a global process of immense complexity, necessarily implying the *objective complementarity*—which should not be confused with some central coordination—of all socialist movements confronting the world system of capitalism. As Lenin emphasized more than half a century ago:

"it would be a fatal mistake to declare that since there is a dis-crepancy between our economic 'forces' and our political strength, it 'follows' that we should not have seized power. Such an argument can be advanced only by a 'man in a muffler' [a narrow-minded, conservative philistine], who forgets that there will always be such a 'discrepancy', that it always exists in the development of nature as well as in the development of society, that only by *a series of attempts*—each of which, taken by itself, will be *one-sided* and will suffer from certain *inconsistencies*—will *complete socialism* be created by the revolutionary co-operation of the proletarians of *a l l* countries."[250]

Thus there can be no universally valid "models", nor indeed univers-ally compulsory measures and moves centrally directed by some "international Masonic order". The full realization of the social individual concerns the "real, human individual", with all his specific problems, needs and aspirations. Only if—"in accordance with the actual capabilities of the real human individual"—these problems, needs and aspirations are made into the comprehensive regulative principle of all social efforts, reciprocally integrating the real individuals within the broad educational framework of the social body as a whole, only then may one speak of a "positive trans-cendence of alienation".

3. *Self-mediation of the Social Individual*

Marx defines communism as "the g e n u i n e resolution of the *conflict* between man and nature and between man and man— the true resolution of the strife between existence and essence, between objectification and self-confirmation, between freedom and necessity, between the *individual and the species*" (102). This utterance should not be interpreted to mean that now "individual" and "mankind" become the same concept. (As we have seen, Marx repeatedly stressed that the individual never merges directly with his social determinations.) On the contrary, when the possibility of resolving the age-old conflict between individual and mankind is in sight, only then it becomes possible to draw adequately the line of demarcation between the ontological sphere of the individual and that of mankind. Prior to this historical stage the two concepts are vaguely defined, if at all, and within the framework of moral discourse their basic differences remain, as a rule, hidden from sight.

There is no space here for a detailed discussion of this problematics: we can merely hint at some of its most important aspects. A quotation from Paracelsus well illustrates our point of departure:

> "you should not judge people according to their stature, but *honour them all equally*. What is in you is in all. *Each* has what you also have within you; and the poor grows the same plants in his garden as the rich. In *man*, the ability to practise all crafts and arts is innate, but not all these arts have been brought to the light of day. Those which are to become manifest in him must first be awakened. . . . The child is still an uncertain being, and he receives his form according to the *potentialities* that you awaken in him. If you awaken his ability to make shoes, he will be a shoemaker; if you awaken the stonecutter in him, he will be a stonecutter; and if you summon forth the scholar in him, he will be a scholar. And this can be so because *all potentialities are inherent in him*; what you awaken in him comes forth from him; the rest remains unawakened, absorbed in sleep!"[261]

Thus Paracelsus invites us to honour *mankind* in *each* particular individual. This is a splendid assertion of the principle of *equality*—at the beginning of the sixteenth century—within moral discourse which, however, appears through the identification of two fundamentally different modes of being as an assertion about an actual state of affairs. The *actual* potentialities of *particular individuals* must, nevertheless, be distinguished from their *ideal* potentialities, i.e. from those capabilities which can be considered *actual* only in relation to *mankind* as a whole. Traditional moral discourse, however, cannot possibly make this distinction, as we shall see in a moment.

What would need here a close examination is the extremely complex involvement of the real individuals in moral situations;

their manifold obligations and commitments and their complicated links with the dynamically changing community in which they happen to live. There is a great deal to be disentangled here since moral discourse, inevitably, blurs the lines of objective demarcation and applies to the individual its own categories and distinctions which tend to abolish, in thought, the vital distinction between individual' and mankind in order to measure the efforts and failures of the individual with a yardstick applicable to mankind only. Of course there is something great and positive in all this. The categorical absoluteness of the moral rule forces upon the individual—in an unconscious form—the consciousness of his *objective sociality*. Or, to put the same thing in a different way : the objective sociality of the individual enables him to have the dimension of morality in his dialectical self-transcending relation to his limitations. But unless one keeps constantly in mind that morality is an organ of self-development of mankind as a whole, the assessment of the actual relations of interpersonal situations gets inevitably distorted.

In Kant's philosophy "Ought implies (moral) Can" served to establish the realm of *noumena* which in its turn established the *absolute validity* of the *Moral Rule*. The "noumenal world" to which Kant's moral agent belongs corresponds in reality to the individuals' objective sociality whose intricacies cannot be explained simply in terms of "natural causality". *Social causation*, both vertically and horizontally—i.e. both historically and in its structural functioning at any given moment—is unintelligible without fully taking into account the enormous power of that *relatively autonomous* organ of humanity's self-development : morality. But since we are dealing with an organ of mankind as a whole, it is necessary to draw the lines of distinction when it comes to assessing the individuals' rôle and responsibility.

Even though morality is an organ of self-development of mankind as a whole, it cannot, of course, work except through the more or less selfconscious actions of particular individuals. It is, therefore, inevitable that in the consciousness of the individuals the differences be blurred or suppressed altogether. The individual "takes upon himself" the full weight of representing the capabilities of mankind in the given moral situation, whether he is individually capable of living up to the moral expectations or not. If this were not so, if, that is, the objective difference between his greatly limited capabilities and the virtually limitless powers of mankind were not blurred in his consciousness through the categorical language of moral discourse, OUGHT could not fulfil its function: the awareness of one's objective limitations—which cannot be divorced from one's own, often inaccurate, assessment of those selfsame limitations—would tend to strengthen the claims of "CANNOT be done" and undermine those of "OUGHT to be done". Consequently, traditional morality can only work if OUGHT overrules and blurs in the individual's self-consciousness all those objective differences which could weaken its categorical claims.

It must be added, however, that the extent to which the individual can be emancipated from the interference—in some situations nothing short of absolute tyranny—of this organ of self-development of mankind, is a historical question. The form of consciousness in which the individuals take note of their moral predicament changes from age to age and from society to society. (We shall return to this problem in a moment.)

Nevertheless, the question of "transcendence" cannot be properly assessed if the ontological foundation of the differences between individual and mankind are ignored. The most important difference is that while the individual is *inserted* into his ontological sphere and sets out from the *given* forms of human interchange which function as axiomatic premises of his end-positing activity, mankind as a whole—the "self-transcending" and "self-mediating being of nature"—is *"author"* of its own ontological sphere. The temporal scales are, of course, also basically different. While the individual's actions are strictly circumscribed by his limited life-span—and furthermore by a host of other limiting factors of his cycle of life— mankind as a whole transcends such time-limitations. Consequently very different yardsticks and measures are adequate to the assessment of "human potentiality"—a term applicable, strictly speaking, only to mankind as a whole—and to the evaluation of the actions of the limited individual.

Under a different aspect and using terminology familiar to us from traditional moral philosophy, one might describe the isolated individual's ontological predicament as "phenomenality" in sharp contrast to the "noumenality" of the social sphere. For only a social-interpersonal activity can be *end-positing* activity in which "things"—i.e. "mere phenomenality"—acquire their "essence" in relation to and in terms of the activity in question. As Lukács puts it: "Only in productive activity [Arbeit] originates necessarily *the concept of the things*".[252] Only if the individual is considered in total isolation can he be characterized as "mere phenomenality". The real individual, however, who finds himself in the ontological sphere into which he is inserted, is a "noumenal being", insofar as his *sociality* is inseparable from him in principle. But in practice the separation occurs: through the alienation and reification of the social relations of production which isolate the individual in his "crude phenomenality" and superimpose on him, in a mystified form, his own actual nature as a "transcendental noumenal essence". Thus originates the contradiction between "existence and essence, between the individual and the species". And it is this hostile contradiction—this unconscious transcendentalism—which Marx seeks to resolve through the transcendence of alienation.

The resolution of the *hostile contradiction*, however, does not mean the suppression of the real *differences*. Such an endeavour could only succeed in fiction, through *merging* individual and mankind in a mythical Collective Subject. For no matter how strongly one stresses the sociality ("noumenality") of the individual, one cannot eliminate the objective lines of demarcation without gravely distorting the fundamental relations. The existing basic ontological differences make it idle to attribute to the individual powers which he could not conceivably possess. For only the abstract individual of speculative philosophy lives in the realm of "possibilities"—the real individual has to content himself with the field of "probabilities" within which he must move, consciously or not, gratified or not. The opposition between the categories of OUGHT (Sollen) and IS (Sein) can only be solved in relation to the ontological level of mankind. What appear as "Oughts", addressed to the individual in the specific terms of moral discourse, express in fact some *objective* "projects" and *actual historical tasks* which exist in the complex structures of human society as *needs* and *trends* of development: needs, however, which are practically *negated* by some prevailing necessity (e.g. "scarcity") and therefore must be strengthened by the power of "Ought" against such negation. In the course of human development these conflicting needs are resolved and "needs", "tasks", and "trends" of development become realities, whereby the imperative form is *practically* superseded. As far as the particular individual is concerned, however, these "needs", "tasks" and "trends" preserve their axiological character in relation to him—he can "choose" them as his positive or negative "values" by acting for or against their realization—and moral imperatives remain "norms" or "rules" to him. The particular individual can but live in accordance with such rules and norms or break them—

within limits—and thus contribute to the constitution of a new set
of rules and norms.

By contrast, mankind as a whole tends to supersede not only the
historically given, particular sets of rules but moral discourse—i.e.
the expression of a separate moral consciousness—altogether. This
supersession, nevertheless, can be grasped only as a *limiting* concept
since the situation to which it applies is not a particular *historical
stage* (which would be an ahistorical conception, postulating an "end
of history") but the virtually boundless development and continued
self-transcendence of mankind. The conceptual limit of this kind
of transcendence can only be infinity. The conditions of "absolute
truth" apply—*mutatis mutandis*—in the field of morality as well:

> "The sovereignty of thought is realized in a series of extremely un-
> sovereignly-thinking human beings; the knowledge which has an
> unconditional claim to truth is realised in a series of relative errors;
> neither the one nor the other can be *fully* realised except *through
> an unending duration of human existence.* . . . This is a contra-
> diction which can be resolved only in the course of *infinite* progress,
> in what is—at least practically for us—an *endless succession of
> generations of mankind.* . . . [Human thought] is sovereign and *un-
> limited* in its disposition [Anlage], its vocation, its *possibilities* and its
> historical ultimate goal; it is not sovereign and it is limited in its
> individual realisation and *in reality* at each *particular moment*."[253]

Similarly with moral discourse: it is an ideal possibility of mankind
to supersede it altogether "through an *unending* duration of human
existence", through an "*endless* succession of generations of mankind". But these "unlimited *possibilities*" cannot be realized "*in
reality*" (i.e. at any "*particular moment*") except in the form of
relative, *limited* achievements succeeding each other *ad infinitum.*
All the more so because the power of moral discourse which is
conceived as being superseded in *infinity* is an elementary condition
of human advancement itself. Consequently those bureaucratic dogmatists who reject the moral ideas of Marx as "ideological concepts",
as "humanism" and "youthful idealism", fictitiously postulating a
"scientific theory" which is supposed to have definitively superseded
all this, negate some fundamentals of Marxist dialectics.

It goes without saying, even if moral discourse itself is being
transcended only "through an *unending* duration of human existence", the supersession of capitalist alienation represents a radical,
qualitative achievement in the realization of this dialectical process.
The "unconscious condition of mankind" is a form of society whose

moral consciousness can be but *unconscious* as well. The system of capitalist second order mediations carries with it a fundamental contradiction: that between the *"potentialities"* of mankind and the narrowly circumscribed field of *"probabilities"* of the particular individuals who have to operate in subjection to the blindly prevailing mechanisms of capitalist instrumentality.

This contradiction, nevertheless, is not the manifestation of a timeless, metaphysical, untranscendable "falling" (*Verfallen*) and "thrownness" (*Geworfenheit*), as in Heidegger's frozen ontology, but the characteristic of historically changing reality. Here we can identify a typical feature of the Heideggerian methodology of mystification: blurring the distinction between the particular individual and mankind so that a desocialized, fictitious existential subject would take the place of both historically developing mankind and the real social individual. If Heidegger asserted that the particular *individual* is "thrown" into an alienated "world", this could be accepted, provided that the necessary socio-historical qualifications—specifying the capitalistic nature of the alienation in question —were made first. But such socio-historical concretization is precisely what Heidegger wants to avoid, indeed to label as "alienation". This is why he "sublimates" the specifically alienated relationships of the historically and socially specific individuals of capitalist society and turns them into metaphysical "ontological dimensions" of "Existence" itself. He speaks of the "falling" and "thrownness" of *Dasein* (Existence, or Being-there), insisting that:

> "Falling is a definite *existential characteristic of Dasein itself*. . . . We would misunderstand the *ontologico-existential structure* of falling if we were to ascribe to it the sense of a *bad and deplorable* property of which, perhaps, more advanced stages of human culture *might be able to rid themselves*."[254]
> "Dasein's facticity is such that *as long as it is what it is*, Dasein *remains in the throw*, and is sucked into the turbulence of *the 'they's' inauthenticity*. Thrownness, in which facticity lets itself be seen phenomenally, belongs to Dasein, for which, in its Being, that very being is an issue."[255]

In these perverted perspectives alienation is not "what it is" in reality but any attempt whatsoever at doing something against actual alienation, even if it takes only the form of critically reflecting upon the conditions of alienation in specific comparative terms:

> "*alienation* cannot mean that Dasein gets factically torn away from itself. On the contrary, this alienation drives it into a kind of Being

which borders on the most *exaggerated 'self-dissection', tempting itself with all possibilities of explanation,* so that the very 'character-ologies' and 'typologies' which it has brought about are themselves already becoming something that cannot be surveyed at a glance. This alienation c l o s e s o f f from Dasein its *authenticity and possibility,* even if only *the possibility of genuinely foundering.*"[256]

Thus the socio-historical characteristics of capitalist alienation are safely "transcended" through the agile mystifications of the Heideggerian ontology that glorifies the "unconscious condition of mankind" as "the ontologico-existential structure of Dasein itself".

In reality the contradiction between mankind's "potentialities" and the narrowly determined "probabilities" of the individual's cycle of life, is by no means an eternal ontological contradiction inherent in the very nature of two different ontological spheres : one "universal" and the other "particular". To say this is to beg the question, and to disregard at the same time the socio-historical conditions. For the fully realized *social individual* is a *"concrete universal"*; if however his dimension of universality (sociality) is negated by the capitalistically reified social relations of production, his "ontological sphere" is, evidently, that of mere particularity. But this is not because his ontological sphere *as such* is so limited but it is so limited because under capitalism his universality is necessarily divorced from man and confronts him in a hostile manner in the form of the alienated social relations of production.

The contradiction mentioned above is not merely a formal opposition between two different ontological spheres but an *internal* contradiction of the dynamic, historically changing, social ontology of mankind. Only because this contradiction is inherent in the ontological sphere of mankind under capitalism can we perceive the contradictory and transcendable character of the relations in question. As has been mentioned already, when the relationship between individual and mankind assumes the character of a natural order— and not only when man is directly dependent upon nature but also when the cohesion is due to some social cause, such as a common effort to secure the survival of a particular community against enemy attack—the contradiction is merely formal, not actual. Not so under capitalism, once the relative historical justification of private property as the, however alienated, "unfolding of human essence" had disappeared. Now, since all further development must be contained—because of the paralysing inertia of the established order—within the extremely narrow limits of capitalistic instrumentality, mankind itself is *divorced* from its *actual potentialities* and only its *alienated potentialities*—or potentialities for *universal self-alienation*—can be realized. "Human potentialities" become a hollow word—an *abstract ideal*—for the real individual not because they are potentialities of mankind but because they are effectively *negated* by capitalist second order mediations in social practice. The individual's *"ideal potentialities"* become an empty abstraction not because they are "ideal" but because they are *apriori nullified* by capitalistic instrumentality which *necessarily* subordinates human life-activity as a mere *means* to the alienated ends of these second order mediations. Thus instead of extending the individual's range of *actual capabilities*, capitalist development ends up with restricting and negating the potentialities of mankind as well. (This is why Goethe had to conclude his *Faust* the way he did.)

The "resolution of the strife between *existence and essence*, between *objectification and self-confirmation*, between *freedom and necessity*, between *the individual and the species*" (102) necessarily implies the supersession of the *unconscious* character of moral discourse. This process does not mean, however, the abolition of moral discourse itself but the qualitative transformation of its structure and framework of reference: its supersession as a form of *false consciousness*. In traditional moral discourse the necessities that give rise to OUGHT remain hidden, as a rule, from man. The OUGHT-form itself is largely responsible for this, insofar as it represents itself as an *apriori* opposition to the realm of necessity and not as its specific expression. In this necessary misrepresentation of the actual relations OUGHT displays its character of "false consciousness". To get to the actual terms of relations it is always necessary to go beyond the immediacy of the OUGHT-form of discourse towards the comprehension of the underlying objective necessities, however deeply hidden they may be under the intricate layers of normative crust. In the course of such "de-mystification" it becomes possible to separate the "genuine Oughts" which sustain some actual necessity of the development of mankind from the "reified Oughts" which have become independent of man and oppose him in the form of blind, unquestionable *apriori prescriptions*. (The latter represent a "direct negation of the human essence", according to Marx.) Thus the questioning examination of the underlying necessities of OUGHT enables us to draw the necessary line of demarcation between the objective, positive functions of moral discourse and its reified myths.

Needless to say, the supersession of the *unconscious* character of moral discourse cannot make the objective differences and conflicts disappear. It can only help to contribute (1) *negatively* to the removal of their hostile power (which manifests itself in the form of social determinations blindly prevailing over the aims and efforts of the individuals) and (2) *positively* to the genuine appropriation of "human potentialities" by sustaining a type of development which *objectively* narrows the gap between the individual's "*ideal* potentialities" and his "*actual* capabilities". And since actual human ontology is a dynamically changing social ontology—in sharp contrast to its Heideggerian mystification as "the ontologico-existential structure of Dasein"—this narrowing of the gap, through the *practical* extension of the range of the individual's actual capabilities, is a real potentiality of human development.

This process is inseparable from the realization of the "truly *social individual*". The more the individual is able to "reproduce himself as a social individual", the less intense is the conflict between individual and society, individual and mankind—i.e. in Marx's words, the less intense is "the strife between existence and essence, freedom and necessity, the individual and the species". But the individual cannot reproduce himself as a social individual unless he takes an increasingly active part in determining all aspects of his own life, from the most immediate concerns to the broadest general issues of politics, socio-economic organization and culture.

Thus the practical issue at stake is the specific nature of the effective instruments and processes of human self-mediation. If the social individual reproduces himself as a "social *individual*"—i.e. if he does not merge directly with his general social determinations—this amounts to saying that the relationship between individual and society, individual and mankind always remains a *mediated* one. To do away with all mediation is the most naive of all anarchist dreams. As has been repeatedly stressed, it is not mediation itself which is at fault but the capitalistic form of reified second order mediations. According to Marx non-alienated human relations are characterized by *self-mediation* and not by some fictitious direct identity with, or dissolution in, some generic Collective Subject. The problem for socialist theory and practice is the concrete practical elaboration of *adequate* intermediaries which enable the social individual to "mediate himself with himself", instead of being mediated by reified institutions. In other words, according to Marx, the task is to bring the instruments of human interchange in line with the objective *sociality* of human beings. What is really implied by the concept of an adequate "self-mediation of the social individual" is not the disappearance of all instrumentality but the establishment of consciously controlled socialist forms of mediation in place of the capitalistically reified social relations of production.

This raises the vitally important question of the relationship between *means* and *ends*. The contradiction between means and ends appears in moral discourse in the highly problematical pure postulate that "no man should be used as a means to an end". This is a moralistic reduction of a much broader issue. For the point is not only that all ends require their means of realization which they dictate, even if it necessarily carries with it human sacrifices, but also that the adopted ends, whose realization required the *institution* of certain types of means, create an "unwanted result": the *institutionalization* of the instituted means. Thus in actual social practice the original relations are overturned and the means become an end in themselves in the very course of realization of the original end, i.e. in the course of this "self-instituting institution" and self-institutionalization. Thus success (the realization of a particular task) turns into defeat with far-reaching consequences, for institutionalized instrumentality prevails over the actions of the particular individuals who become instruments of instrumentality.

No wonder, therefore, that the sour point of Ideology is the concrete definition of the relationship between the chosen means and the envisaged ends. Simply to postulate that in the anticipated future form of society there can be no contradiction whatsoever between means and ends would be an utopian evasion of the problem. Nor is this problem adequately resolved by the very formulation of what might be termed "fused concepts", such as *"revolution"*, *"self-realization"*, *"self-mediation"*, *"self-transcendence"*, *"participation"*, *"direct democracy"*, *"permanent revolution"*, *"cultural revolution"*, etc., however vitally important such concepts might be as far as the *general* perspectives of socialist development are concerned. They do not resolve the problem mentioned above although *means and end* appear in them in a *unity*. ("Revolution" is both an end and its own general means and mode of realization at the same time; and so are the others as well.) What is remarkable about these "fused concepts" is that the *normative* substance assumes in them an *instrumental* image, thus indicating a certain *type* of action to follow. Nevertheless they remain essentially *norms* and *ends*—indicative of the general framework of society aimed at—

whose *actual* realization necessarily requires the "de-fusion" of these general concepts and their articulation in terms of *concrete* tasks and means. But as soon as such a specific "de-fusion" takes place, the original dilemma reappears on the horizon and the danger of institutionalization of instrumentality reproduces itself. ("Cultural revolution", "anti-bureaucracy", etc. are not simply the reassertion of the general validity of the originally adopted "fused concepts" but also a new assertion : namely that the established framework of post-capitalist society itself must be "periodically" or "constantly" subjected to a radical "re-fusion" and searching reexamination in the light of the overall ideals of socialism.)

Nevertheless ideals themselves, even if they are genuinely socialist, are not enough on their own. Vitally important though they are for determining the general orientation of social efforts, they require for their practical realization the objective power of *specific institutions of self-realization*. The type of institution which is capable of fulfilling this task is one that functions on the basis of the *reciprocal self-determination* of the individuals involved. An example is the institution of *Workers' Councils*, analysed by Lukács some fifty years ago in these terms :

> "The Workers' Council is the politico-social conquest of capitalist reification. In the situation after the dictatorship, it ought to overcome the bourgeois separation of legislative, executive and judiciary; similarly, in the struggle for power it is called upon to end the spatio-temporal fragmentation of the proletariat, and also to bring together economics and politics into the true unity of proletarian activity, and in this way to help reconcile the dialectical opposition of immediate interest and ultimate aim".[257]

But this is only one example, however important it is in a strategic sense. Capitalistically reified second order mediations embrace the totality of—hierarchically structured—society, from the economic and political spheres to the cultural and ideological manifestations of life. Consequently no socialist strategy can hope to succeed unless its general principles of orientation are adequately translated into socio-historically specific, dynamic and flexible, instruments and institutions capable of *restructuring* the *whole* of society, in accordance with the constantly changing realities of world-situation.

It is not enough to overthrow the bourgeois state : its actual functions must be redesigned—in the framework of the general guideline (not to be illusorily mistaken for what it is not : namely a

historically concrete organizational form) of the "fused concept" :
"Direct Democracy"—in accordance with the *global* strategic task
of *radically restructuring* the totality of society inherited from capitalism. Similarly, in the field of economics, it is not enough to
nationalize the instruments of production. The strategic task is the
radical restructuring of the social relations of production : the
abolition of commodity-production, the gradual elimination of
money as "the universal galvano-chemical power of society" (139),
and, above all, the generation of a radically new ethos of work,
motivated by self-confirmation in work as the positive life-activity
of the social individual. And, last but not least, it is not enough to
change the control of the traditional instruments and institutions
of culture and education : the strategic task is their *radical restructuring* in accordance with the comprehensive tasks of a socialist
transformation of society as a whole which is inconceivable without
the great educational achievement whereby the "real human individuals" acquire a consciousness adequate to their *social individuality*.

Needless to say, the problems involved in the realization of these
strategic tasks are immensely complex, requiring the greatest sense
of reality and concretization at any particular stage and in all
specific situations. As Marx had repeatedly emphasized, the "negation of the negation"—i.e. the socialist negation of capitalist mediations which practically negate "the human essence" : the realization
of the actual potentialities of human beings—is still conditioned by
what it negates. It is, therefore, inconceivable to achieve this radical
restructuring of society in one sweep, however broad and elemental
it might be. One can realistically set out only from the available
instruments and institutions which must be restructured *en route*,
through manifold *transitions* and *mediations*. To pretend otherwise
is nothing but dangerous, self-disarming *"maximalism"* which in
reality turns out to be not only *"minimalism"* but, more often than
not, also directly responsible for disarray and defeat. Strategic tasks
are vitally important because they can give direction and a framework of reciprocal integration to the multifarious specific—mediated,
transitory—efforts of self-mediating social individuals, and not because they are (since they are not) suitable for being *directly* translated into particular measures, forms and "models" of social organization.

X. *Alienation and the Crisis of Education*

No society can persist without its own system of education. To point to the mechanisms of production and exchange alone in order to explain the actual functioning of capitalist society is quite inadequate. Societies exist in and through the actions of particular individuals who seek to realize their own ends. Consequently the crucial issue for any established society is the successful reproduction of such individuals whose "own ends" do not negate the potentialities of the prevailing system of production. This is the real size of the educational problem: "formal education" is but a small segment of it. As Gramsci emphasized:

> "There is no human activity from which all intellectual intervention can be excluded—*homo faber* cannot be separated from *homo sapiens*. Also every man, outside his own job, develops some intellectual activity; he is, in other words, a 'philosopher', an artist, a man of taste, he shares a conception of the world, he has a conscious line of moral conduct, and so *contributes towards maintaining or changing a conception of the world*, that is, towards encouraging new modes of thought."[258]

Thus in addition to reproducing, on an enlarging scale, the manifold *skills* without which productive activity could not be carried on, the complex educational system of society is also responsible for producing and reproducing the framework of *values* within which the particular individuals define their own specific aims and ends. The capitalistically reified social relations of production do not perpetuate themselves *automatically*. They succeed in this only because the particular individuals *"interiorize"* the outside pressures: they adopt the overall perspectives of commodity-society as the unquestionable limits of their own aspirations. It is by doing so that the particular individuals "contribute towards maintaining a conception of the world" and towards maintaining a specific form of social intercourse which corresponds to that conception of the world.

Thus the positive transcendence of alienation is, in the last analysis,

289

an educational task, requiring a radical "cultural revolution" for its realization. The issue at stake is not simply the political modification of the institutions of formal education. As we have seen, Marx strongly stressed the objective ontological continuity of the development of capital, embodied in *all* forms and institutions of social interchange, and not merely in the directly economic second order mediations of capitalism. This is why the task of transcending the capitalistically alienated social relations of production must be conceived in the global framework of a socialist educational strategy. The latter, however, should not be confused with some form of educational utopianism.

1. *Educational Utopias*

The concept of "aesthetic education" was made famous by Schiller's *Letters upon the Aesthetical Education of Man*,[259] written in 1793–4 and published in 1795. Needless to say, Schiller's idea—formulated as a possible antidote to the harmful "rationality" of capitalistic developments—remained a mere idea: it could not find a significant place in the prevailing systems of educational practices.

In his essay *On Schiller's Aesthetic* Lukács emphasizes that the Schillerian conception of aesthetic education was meant to offer an aesthetic model that would enable Germany to realize the social achievements of the French Revolution without a revolution. According to Lukács "Schiller stresses *above all* the inner transformation of the spiritual life of man".[260] But a few years after the publication of his *Letters upon the Aesthetical Education of Man* Schiller's self-criticism concerning his youthful revolutionary period—expressed in the ethico-aesthetic principle of his idea of an aesthetic education, in place of more immediate social concerns—becomes even more radical. If earlier he insisted *"above all"* (vor allem) on the *inner* transformation of the spiritual life of man, now he makes the same point with categoric *exclusiveness*, rejecting all possible alternatives to this absolutization of the inner world of the individual. With this step the pessimistic utopianism of his original concept of an aesthetic education of man becomes an extreme form of pessimism. There is no more room for a genuine educational ideal in Schiller's conception. Man is no longer considered as a member of a community. "Man" becomes synonymous with the isolated "individual" who is confronted with the "spirit" (Geist) and with

his own "soul" (Seele). We can see this in the tragic pessimism of
Die Worte des Wahns (The Words of Folly)—written in 1799 :

> Three words of significant meaning there are
> In the mouths of the wisest and best,
> Yet vainly they echo, like tones from afar,
> And yield no assistance or rest.
> Man forfeits the fruits he could lightly attain
> If after impalpable shadows he strain.

> So long as he pictures a glorious age,
> Rejoicing in honour and right—
> Those gifts will assuredly combat engage
> With a foe who for ever will fight.
> Thou must at him in air, for a contact with earth
> Supplies to his force a regenerate birth.

> So long as he thinks that success will attend
> On nobility's conduct and aims—
> He will find that she looks upon wrong as a friend,
> That the world what is worthy disclaims.
> A wanderer he, and his duty to roam
> To discover elsewhere an immutable home.

> So long as he dreams that the reason of man
> Can with absolute verities close—
> He will find an abyss which no mortal can span;
> We can but assume and suppose.
> In a word, it is true, thou canst prison the mind,
> But it surges away on the wings of the wind.

> Then hasten thy soul from illusions [Wahn] to wean,
> And a higher religion endue !
> What the ear never heard, and the eye has not seen
> Remains what is lovely [das Schöne] and true [das Wahre]!
> It is not abroad [draussen], as the foolish contends,
> 'Tis within [in dir], and upon thine own ardour depends.[261]

If, then, it is "folly" and "delusion" to seek the solutions "outside",
i.e. in human interrelations, what sense can have an "aesthetic
education" which necessarily presupposes such interrelations? Significantly, in the final synthesis only two of the "three words of folly"
appear : "das Wahre" (true) and "das Schöne" (beautiful). The
third—"das Rechte" (right): an inherently "public" term—cannot

be inserted into the imaginary "inner world" of the absolutized individual. Not that "das Wahre" and "das Schöne" were not indicative of objective relationships; indeed they are. This is why Schiller has to redefine them as : "What the ear never heard, and the eye has not seen". (Their difference from "das Rechte" is that the latter resists this kind of quasi-mystical redefinition.) But such a redefinition carries with it the end of the "aesthetic ideal" as a possible educational programme, shortly after its original conception in the turmoil created by the French Revolution.

It would have been nothing short of a miracle if this idea of an "aesthetic education of man" had a different fate, in a world dominated by capitalistic alienation. For "the s e n s e caught up in crude practical need has only a r e s t r i c t e d sense. . . . The care-burdened man in need has no sense for the finest play; the dealer in mineral sees only the mercantile value but not the beauty and the unique nature of the mineral : he has no mineralogical sense" (108–9). And "crudity" is not a fatality of *nature*; on the contrary, under the conditions of capitalism this crudity is *artificially* produced by superimposing on all physical and mental senses "the sheer estrangement of a l l the senses—the sense of h a v i n g" (106). Consequently the remedies cannot be found in some fictitious "inner world", divorced from, and opposed to, the actual world of men. The traditional philosophical opposites : "subjectivism and objectivism, spiritualism and materialism, activity and suffering, only lose their antithetical character, and thus their existence, as such antitheses *in the social condition*; . . . the resolution of the t h e o r e t i c a l antitheses is o n l y possible i n a p r a c t i c a l way, by virtue of the practical energy of men. Their resolution is therefore by no means merely a problem of knowledge, but a r e a l problem of life, which p h i l o s o p h y could not solve precisely because it conceived this problem as m e r e l y a theoretical one" (109). Aesthetic education is therefore only possible in a genuine socialist society which—in the global framework of a socialist educational strategy—transcended the capitalist "alienation of all the senses", and thus produces man in the "entire richness of his being— *produces the r i c h man p r o f o u n d l y e n d o w e d with all t h e s e n s e s—as its enduring reality*" (109). Thus an adequate aesthetic education of man cannot be confined to an imaginary "inner world" of the isolated individual, nor indeed to some remote utopian haven of alienated society. Its realization necessarily involves the totality of social processes in their complex dialectical reciprocity with each other. This is why the separate programme of an "aesthetic education of man", as an antidote to the spread of capitalistic "rationality", is condemned to a hopeless utopianism under conditions when the uncontrollable second order mediations of the reified social relations of production determine—in a narrowly utilitarian framework—the educational processes just as much as all the other aspects of commodity society.

Indeed, considering the problems closely connected with the failure of the efforts which aimed at an "aesthetic education of man", we find that this failure cannot be understood except as an aspect of a more fundamental issue : the inherently problematic character of education under capitalism. The concept of "aesthetic education" is, in fact, a specific attempt at dealing with the dehumanization of the educational processes in capitalist society, and as such it is an aspect of an ever intensifying crisis. It is necessary, therefore, to inquire, very briefly, into the nature of this crisis which goes back a long way in the past.

At the dawn of the modern age Paracelsus spoke in these terms about education: "*Learning is our very life,* from youth to old age, indeed to the brink of death; no one lives for ten hours without learning."[262] By the middle of the eighteenth century, however, things have significantly changed. Adam Smith, though himself a great champion of the "commercial spirit", strongly emphasizes that the division of labour is doubly damaging for education. On the one hand, it impoverishes man to such an extent that one would need a special educational effort to put things right. But no such effort is forthcoming. On the contrary—and this is the second aspect of the negative impact of the "commercial spirit" on education—since the division of labour simplifies in an extreme form the work-processes, it largely diminishes the need for a proper education, instead of intensifying it. Thus in accordance with the needs of the prevailing system of production, the general level of education is not raised but lowered instead : the extremely simplified work-processes make possible the spread of child-labour, and consequently the children are denied the possibility of a balanced education. The "commercial spirit"—i.e. the victoriously advancing spirit of capitalism—"confines the views of men. Where the division of labour is brought to perfection, every man has only a simple operation to perform; to this his whole attention is confined, and few ideas pass in his mind but what have an *immediate* connection with it. When the mind is employed about a variety of objects, it is some-

294   small caps

how expanded and enlarged, and on this account a country artist is generally acknowledged to have a range of thoughts much above a city one. The former is perhaps a joiner, a house carpenter, and a cabinetmaker, all in one, and his attention must of course be employed about a number of objects of very different kinds. The latter is perhaps only a cabinetmaker; that particular kind of work employs all of his thoughts, and as he had not an opportunity of comparing a number of objects, his views of things beyond his own trade are by no means so extensive as those of the former. This must be much more the case when *a person's whole attention is bestowed on the seventeenth part of a pin or the eightieth part of a button*, so far divided are these manufactures. . . . The rule is general; in towns they are not so intelligent as in the country, nor in a rich country as in a poor one. Another inconvenience attending commerce is that *education is greatly neglected*."[263] And a few pages later Adam Smith concludes: "These are the disadvantages of a commercial spirit. The minds of men are *contracted*, and rendered incapable of elevation. *Education is despised, or at least neglected*, and heroic spirit is almost utterly extinguished. *To remedy these defects would be an object worthy of serious attention*."[264]

It goes without saying, Adam Smith can only identify the problem, without being able to find an adequate remedy to it. He notices that the authority of money undermines the traditional authority of the father in the family, but he draws one-sided conclusions from his observation: "But, besides this want of education, there is another great loss which attends the putting boys too soon to work. The boy begins to find that his father is obliged to him, and therefore throws off his authority. When he is grown up he has no ideas with which he can amuse himself. When he is away from his work, he must therefore betake himself to drunkenness and riot. Accordingly we find that, in the commercial parts of England, the tradesmen are for the most part in this despicable condition; their work through half the week is sufficient to maintain them, and through want of education they have no amusement for the other but riot and debauchery. So it may very justly be said that the people who clothe the whole world are in rags themselves."[265] We can disregard here the total unreality of the suggestion that if the people who clothe the world are in rags they have only to blame their own lack of education for it. More important is in this context that the educational ideal appears as a mere *means* to the end of "having *ideas* with which the grown up boy can *amuse himself*" (in his "leisure time", of course)—so that he should keep away from "drunkenness and riot" and, above all, from wasting all that precious money which could be put to the productive use of capitalist accumulation. The fact that economic factors are at work not only in "the putting boys too soon to work" but also in exploiting the worker's "drunkenness and debauchery", is one that must escape, of course, the moralist Adam Smith's attention. The "standpoint of political economy" turns out to be self-defeating in this respect as well. Since Adam Smith cannot question the economic framework of capitalism whose standpoint he represents, he must look for remedies to the negative effects of the "commercial spirit" outside the economic sphere. And thus he ends up with a moralizing advocacy of an unrealistic educational antidote. (As we have seen he is by no means alone in this among his contemporaries, or indeed in the line of bourgeois thinkers and writers who came after him.)

And here an inner contradiction comes to the fore. For if Adam Smith's diagnosis is correct that "neglecting and despising education" etc. are *due* to the power of the advancing "commercial spirit," how can one expect then an effective *remedy* to all the observed negative effects from a mere appeal to an "ought-to-be aducation"? But precisely because this is an *inner* contradiction of the bourgeois standpoint—necessarily involving both the negation and the uncritical affirmation of the fundamental causal factors—the "transcendence" of the criticized phenomena can only be envisaged in the form of an utopian "ought".

Robert Owen, at a later date, describes with graphic realism the way in which everything becomes dominated by the power of money: "Man so circumscribed sees all around him hurrying forward, at a mail-coach speed, to acquire *individual wealth*, regardless of him, his comforts, his wants, or even his sufferings, except by way of a d e g r a d i n g p a r i s h c h a r i t y, fitted only to steel the heart of man against his fellows, or to form the tyrant and the slave. To-day he labours for one master, to-morrow for a second, then for a third, and a fourth, until all ties between employers and employed are frittered down to the consideration of what *immediate gain* each can derive from the other. The employer regards the employed as *mere instruments of gain*".[266] It would be difficult to find a more fitting description of how all human relations become subordinated to the impersonal authority of money and profit-seeking. And yet, even Owen, though more practical in his efforts at setting up an educational experiment, expects the cure of the denounced ills from the impact of "reason" and "enlightenment" :

> "Shall we then longer withhold national instruction from our fellow-men, who, it has been shown, might easily be trained to be industrious, intelligent, virtuous, and valuable members of the State? True, indeed, it is, that all the measures now proposed are only a compromise with the errors of the present system; but as these errors now almost universally exist, and *must be overcome solely by the force of reason*; and as reason, to affect the most beneficial purposes, makes her advance *by slow degrees*, and progressively substantiates one truth of high import after another, it will be evident, to minds of comprehensive and accurate thought, that *by these and similar compromises alone can success be rationally expected in practice*. For such compromises bring *truth and error* before the public; and whenever they are fairly exhibited together, *truth must ultimately prevail*. . . . it is confidently expected that the period is at hand, when man, *through ignorance*, shall not much longer inflict unnecessary misery on man; because *the mass of mankind will become enlightened*, and will clearly discern that by so acting they will inevitably create misery to themselves."[267]

This quotation is highly significant in another respect as well. For it reveals the close interrelationship between utopianism and the advocacy of proceeding "by slow degrees", "by compromises alone", of overcoming the existing problems "solely by the force of reason" (today one would say : by "social engineering", by "human engineering", and, of course, "by compromises worked out around the negotiating table", etc.). Indeed the necessary limitations of the bourgeois horizon prescribe the methodology of "gradualism" and "compromises" as an axiom of "critical reasoning". Since, however, the problems at stake are comprehensive ones, the contradiction between the *global* character of the criticized social phenomena and the *partiality* and *gradualism* of the remedies which alone are compatible with "the standpoint of political economy" must be fictitiously reconciled by the sweeping generality of some utopian "ought". And thus the earlier acutely observed *specific social phenomenon* (the dehumanizing impact of the "commercial spirit", turning men into "mere instruments of gain", etc.)—now considered from the angle of the envisaged imaginary—intellectual remedy—loses its specific *social* character and becomes vague and timeless "error" and "ignorance". So that in the end the social philosopher can conclude with triumphant circularity that the problem of "truth versus error and ignorance"—which is a problem of "reason" and "enlightenment"—can be solved "solely by the force of reason". (Needless to say, the only assurance he can give for the success of his educational remedy is, again, a circular one: the assertion that "truth must ultimately prevail, because the mass of mankind will become enlightened".)

Contemporary opponents of Marx often denounce the alleged "utopian" and "ideological" character of his thought—in the name of a "social engineering", of "proceeding by compromises", "by slow degrees", etc. Criticisms of this kind, however, cannot be taken seriously. For the fact is that utopianism is incompatible with the dialectical comprehensiveness of the Marxian approach which does not assign an exclusive power to any particular social factor since it presupposes the dialectical reciprocity of them all. Utopianism is, by contrast, necessarily inherent in all attempts which offer merely *partial* remedies to *global* problems—in accordance with the socio-historical limitations of the bourgeois horizon—bridging the gap between the partiality of the advocated ad hoc measures and the overall results by arbitrarily anticipating an outcome of their own liking. And this is precisely what characterizes the ideological efforts of "social engineering". Since the latter, by definition, cannot have an overall strategy, it has no right to anticipate the overall impact of the particular measures. Yet it does so, by advocating its own approach in opposition to the comprehensive alternatives, confidently expecting that the established social system will be able to cope with its problems by means of the gradualism of "social engineering". The veiled utopianism of this approach consists in the arbitrary postulation of the given, capitalist, form of society as the necessary framework of all conceivable—at any rate all "reasonable"—change, and it presupposes a completely unfounded, utopian faith in the capability of the admissible partial measures to achieve the anticipated overall result. The "rational" measures of "gradual social engineering" are put forward as representing reality ("Is"), firmly rooted in the ground, in opposition to the normative ("ought") character of the denounced comprehensive "utopias" and "ideologies". In fact, however, the advocacy of "gradualism" and "partial measures" is nothing but a *negative form of normativity*, in defence of the established positions of power against the growing socio-historical challenge of socialist forces. No wonder, therefore, that the ideologists of "social engineering" dismiss the Marxian challenge of their wishful perspectives as "utopianism" and "ideology".

It goes without saying, there are very substantial differences between the "heroic utopianism" of the early bourgeoisie—whose representatives: the Rousseaus, Kants, Goethes, Schillers, Adam Smiths and Owens are truly "Titanenartig" as compared to the present-day defenders of the bourgeois order—and the *apologetic*, "veiled utopianism" of the various contemporary trends of "social engineering". Nevertheless the structure of bourgeois thought in general is inherently utopian and gradualist. Since the foundations of capitalist society must be axiomatically taken for granted, the dehumanizing effects of the "commercial spirit" can only be "transcended" in the form of a utopian "ought" which, as soon as translated into some practical measure, invariably turns out to be a miscarriage : some kind of "gradual measure" which—in its practical defence of the capitalist order of society—can only intensify the contradictions inherent in the alienated social relations of production, instead of superseding them. Hence the tragic irony of Faust's death : the noise of grave-digging avidly greeted, in wishfulfilment, as the actual realization of the great Faustian dream. For the capitalist alienation and reification of all humanness "must be overcome solely by the force of reason"—by a "reason" constricted by the necessary premises of bourgeois society—and reason is, clearly, not enough. All the more because an actual social force—practically challenging the "reason" of utopian gradualism—appears on the horizon. Hence the fright and despair of a Schiller who, in the sister poem of *The Words of Folly*, written in 1797 and entitled *The Words of Faith*, turns his back on "the rabble" which showed its power in the French Revolution, and deeply entrenches himself in the *inner* realm of a *transcendental "ought"* :

> Let the cry of the rabble pass over thee,
> And the howl of extravagant swains !
> Of no free man stand thou in fear,
> Nor of slave who conquered a free career.
>
> And a God there is, whose will compels
> The wavering mind of men,
> And thought of the loftiest order swells
> *Beyond time's wildest ken.*
> *Though the world in eternal vicissitude roll,*
> *There is ever repose for the peaceable soul.*[268]

The utopian gradualism of Owen is also motivated by a fear of the emerging socio-historical alternative. He insists that under the conditions in which they live the workers "acquire a gross ferocity of character, which, if legislative measures shall not be judiciously devised to prevent its increase, and ameliorate the condition of this class, *will sooner or later plunge the country into a formidable and perhaps inextricable state of danger.* The direct object of these observations is to effect the amelioration and *avert the danger.*"[269]

Given this background, it can be no surprise to us that the great educational utopias of the past—which were originally intended as a countervailing force to the alienating and dehumanizing power of the "commercial spirit"—had to remain completely ineffective against the diffusion of alienation and reification in all spheres of life. Even in the field of higher education, which for a long time could shelter behind the glorified façade of its own irrelevance to the direct needs of a "spontaneously" expanding "laissez faire" capitalism, the erstwhile ideal of creating a "harmonious" and "many-sided individual" has been gradually abandoned and the narrowest of specialization prevailed in its place, feeding with "advisers", "experts", and "experts in expertise" the cancerously growing bureaucratic machinery of modern capitalism. "We are well aware of the disintegration of thought and knowledge into an increasing number of separate systems, each more or less self-contained, with its own language, and recognizing no responsibility for knowing or caring about what is going on across its frontiers. . . . The story of the Tower of Babel might have been a prophetic vision of the modern university; and the fragmentation which is spotlighted there affects the whole of society."[270] "Commercial spirit", for its full realization, required the fragmentation, mechanization and reification of all human relations. This is why the fate of the ideal of "universality" expressed in the great educational utopias of the past had to be settled in the way we are all familiar with. What decided the fate of these utopias at the very moment of their conception was the fact that they aimed at producing the desired effects *in place* of the necessary social changes, and not *through* them.

2. *The Crisis of Education*

No sane person would deny that education is in crisis today.[271] Nevertheless the nature of this crisis is, quite understandably, far from being generally agreed upon. Professional cold-war ideologists are mystified. As Chomsky observes: "Having settled the issue of the political irrelevance of the protest movement, Kristol turns to the question of what motivates it—more generally, what has made students and junior faculty 'go left', as he sees it, amid general prosperity and under liberal, Welfare State administrations. This, he notes, 'is *a riddle to which no sociologist has as yet come up with an answer*'. Since these young people are well-off, have good futures, etc., their protest must be *irrational*. It must be the result of boredom, of too much security, or something of this sort."[272]

Others, while willing to concede some minor points (related to "research facilities", the "size of the classes", and the like) insist that only "a handful of troublemakers" and "academic thugs" are responsible for the disturbances. The persistence and the growing intensity of the crisis of education in the leading capitalist countries, without a single exception, point, however, towards a very different conclusion. To anticipate it in one sentence: today's crisis is not simply that of some educational institution but the structural crisis of the whole system of capitalist "interiorization" mentioned at the beginning of this chapter.

Such an "interiorization", needless to say, cannot take place without the concerted effort of the various forms of "false consciousness" which represent the alienated social relations of commodity-production as the direct, "natural" expression of the individuals' aims and desires. "Normally"—i.e. when commodity-production has its undisturbed run, backed by expanding individual demand—"consumer-ideology", reflecting the material framework of society, prevails in the form of generating the necessary "consensus": the easy acceptance of the pseudo-alternatives, as genuine choices, with which the manipulated individual is confronted on both the economic and the political markets. Serious complications arise, however, at the time of economic crises. In the United States, for instance, at the time of the last economic recession a few years ago, newspaper articles and advertising slogans were full of references to one's alleged "patriotic duty" to buy even the most unwanted objects, with the implicit admission—a clear departure from the normal practice of everyday advertising based on the "non-ideological" axiom of the "naturalness" of capitalism—that such goods are indeed *unwanted* and bear no relation to the individuals' "spontaneous" appetites. What the public was asked to buy were unredeemable "patriotic bonds" of the American system of capitalism. The main function of Vietnam-type operations in the American system of incentives is that the direct military involvement provides the framework of "patriotic" advertising and the multimilliard boost to the economy magnifies the appetite of the *system*—in the self-consuming way of war production—without needing to expand the heavily saturated appetite of the stuffed consumer-individual.[273]

Indeed, due to the economic contradictions of capitalism, the structure of the economy has significantly changed a long time ago as regards the relationship between the consumer and the non-consumer branches of industry. As Robert Heilbroner writes:

> ". . . a central aspect of our growth experience of the past two decades is one which few spokesmen for the future candidly discuss. This is the fact that our great boom did not begin until the onset of World War II, and that its continuance since then has consistently been tied to a military rather than to a purely civilian economic demand."[274]

And S. M. Rosen correctly adds: *"The arms economy has been the major Keynesian instrument of our times. But its use has been cloaked as 'national interest'."*[275] Yet, so long as the share of consumer-industries did not appear again as the vital factor in maintaining the overall balance, there was no crying need to modify the traditional consumer-ideology. Not only because this ideology of consumerism had acquired an added significance as a measure of the system's "superiority" over the post-capitalist economies (which had to embark on the hard road of a "socialist accumulation" at a very backward level) but also because the claims to representing the "national interest" have always been an integral part of bourgeois ideology. Nevertheless as the complications of the economic system multiply, so grows the need for a significant "de-materialization" of the system of individual incentives, necessarily requiring a major readjustment of the mechanisms of "interiorization" as well. All the more because the "technological gap" between the United States and the other leading capitalist countries is getting narrower, intensifying competition and endangering the high rate of profit, under the pressure of relatively high wage-costs.[276] To this we have to add another factor which is perspectively of the greatest significance: the blocking of the road of seeking a solution to the grave structural crisis of society through a third world war. The potential impact of this blockage can be grasped by remembering that the "Great Wars" of the past had (1) automatically "de-materialized" the system of incentives, adjusting, accordingly, the mechanisms of "interiorization" as well; (2) suddenly imposed a radically lower standard of living on the masses of people, which they willingly accepted, given the circumstances; (3) with equal suddenness (in close interrelation with the previous point, of course) they had radically widened the margin of profit; (4) introduced a vital element of rationalization and coordination into the system; and, last but not least, (5) they had given an immense technological boost to the economy as a whole, on a wide front. Current military demand, however massive, simply cannot be compared to this set of both economic and moral-educational-ideological factors whose removal may well prove too much for the system of world capitalism.

The need to readjust the mechanisms of "interiorization" is great and growing. There is, however, no acceptable ideology at hand to back it up. The traditional "authorities" of bourgeois democracy are in the middle of a crisis today which dwarfs "the crisis of democracy" that once brought Fascism to the fore as a "solution" in keeping with the needs of commodity-production. (Today, however, the capitalist power groups cannot readily opt for the Fascist solution; not only because such a choice would necessarily imply a third world war but also because the present structure of commodity-production—which requires an ever-intensifying *overconsumption* of largely *unwanted* goods—does not allow it. For it is just not feasible to induce overconsumption at the point of a gun. The countries—from Spain and Portugal to Greece and to various Latin American regimes—which, under American tutelage, could get away with a Fascist type solution to their problems are all, without one single exception, not only economically underdeveloped but also powerless to assert an independent foreign policy which could carry with it the danger of starting a third world war.) The monstrous *bureaucratization* of society, in accordance with the needs of an increasingly more complex system of commodity-production, succeeded in emptying the "democratic institutions" of all their erstwhile significance, reducing even Parliament—this "pinnacle of democratic institutions"—to the status of a second-rate debating society, thanks to the "consensus" (amounting in fact, if not necessarily in intention, to sheer "collusion") which prevails on all major issues of policy. Also, the various *hierarchical* structures of society which in the past were vitally important in determining the orientation of the younger generation, now, for a number of reasons to which we shall return in a moment, turn out to be not only ineffective in their value-orienting and stabilizing function but also prove to be definite targets for active dissent and radical opposition.

One must consider the crisis of formal education within the framework of this broader picture. For—as a Paracelsus still knew very well—education is "our very life, from youth to old age, indeed up to the brink of death", and therefore its proper assessment cannot be confined to contemplating merely a fraction of the complex phenomena involved. Formal education is closely integrated in the totality of the social processes, and even as regards the particular individual's consciousness, its functions are judged in accordance with its identifiable *raison d'être* in society as a whole. In this sense the present-day crisis of formal education is but the "tip of the iceberg". For the *formal* educational system of the society cannot function undisturbed unless it is *in accord* with the *comprehensive* educational structure—i.e. the specific system of effective *"interiorization"*—of the given society. Thus the crisis of educational institutions is indicative of the totality of processes of which formal education is an *integral* part. The central issue of the current "contestation" of the established educational institutions is not simply the "size of the classes", the "inadequacy of research facilities", etc., but the *raison d'être* of education itself. It goes without saying: such an issue inevitably involves not only the totality of educational processes, "from youth to old age", but also the *raison d'être* of the instruments and institutions of human interchange in general. Are such institutions—including the educational ones—made for men, or should men continue to serve the alienated social relations of production—this is the real subject of the debate. Thus the "contestation" of education, in this wider sense, is the greatest challenge to capitalism in general, for it directly affects the very processes of "interiorization" through which alienation and reification could so far prevail over the consciousness of the individuals.

Education has two main functions in a capitalist society: (1) the production of the skills necessary to running the *economy*, and (2) the formation of the cadres, and the elaboration of the methods, of *political* control. As Gramsci had emphasized: "In the modern world the category of the intellectuals . . . has been inordinately enlarged. They have been produced in imposing numbers by the *democratico-bureaucratic social system*, beyond what is justified by the social needs of *production*, even if justified by the *political needs* of the fundamental ruling class."[277] Accordingly, the crisis of education also manifests itself primarily on the economic and the political plane. Robert Owen had noticed already that his educational programmes met with the resistance of both political and economic interests. He tried to reassure them that the measures he had been advocating "when influenced by no *party feelings* or narrow mistaken notions of *immediate self-interest*, but considered *solely in a national view*, will be found to be beneficial to the child, to the parent, to the employer, and to the country. Yet, as we are now trained, many individuals cannot detach general subjects from *party considerations*, while others can see them only through the medium of present *pecuniary gain*."[278]

These economic and political factors do not stand, of course, in a harmonious relation to each other. On the contrary, they are manifestations of an antagonistic structure of society, and the attempted syntheses—e.g. in Owen's "rational" appeal to the "national view"—can only bring temporary remedies, and the proposed measures are acceptable only in so far as they are in agreement with the *partial* interests of the bourgeoisie. The issues are, however, further complicated by a contradiction *within* this partiality. Namely: the contradiction between the particular interests of the *individual* capitalists (in Owen's words: "the narrow mistaken notions of *immediate* self-interest") and the wider interests of the bourgeoisie *as a class*. (It is this latter which is presented as "the national interest".) Generally speaking, the "*political* needs of the fundamental ruling class" are the interests of the bourgeoisie as a whole, whereas the *economic* needs of production are much more directly related to the interests of the individual capitalists.

Needless to say, we are not talking about a *static* relationship: the various sets of political and economic needs interplay with each other. Also, it must be stressed, the impact of one set or the other is not always the same in the system of overall social determinations. In Gramsci's life-time the *overproduction* of intellectuals he had noticed was due primarily to the "political needs of the fundamental ruling class". The situation is very different today. The principal cause of intellectual overproduction is now *economic* not *political*; indeed it prevails *despite* the political instability necessarily associated with it.

This is a very important issue because it displays the limits within which capitalism is capable of mastering its inner contradictions. The so-called "national aims"—the overall interests of the ruling class as a whole, worked out through the much idealized political machinery of "compromises"—are determined in agreement with the immediate interests of the majority of individual capitalists. (The term "majority" does not mean, of course, a simple numerical majority of individual shareholders, but the representatives of the most powerful economic interest-groups.) Accordingly, the immediate economic interests always prevail in capitalism, and the ultimate rationalization of capitalism, operating on the basis of the *general* interests of capital, in full transcendence of the particular interests of the *individual* capitalists, necessarily implies the effective liquidation of the bourgeoisie as a social force, which is conceivable only through the overthrow of the bourgeois state.[279] Thus no matter how acute the political dangers involved in some trends of economic development, capitalism is in principle incapable of finding a radical remedy to them.

As regards the structural overproduction of intellectuals, the fact of the matter is that an increasing amount of the economic machinery is being tied to the educational field, producing not only a growing number of graduates and postgraduates etc., but also a whole network of companies directly interested in the expansion of "culture". The fact that in the production of intellectuals—unlike that of motor-cars—the upper limit is not the sky but the availability of meaningful employment-opportunities (which depends, of course, on the structure of society as a whole), is one that cannot be inserted into the system of calculations of commodity-production. Economic expansion requires an expanding intellectual production (whatever its quality and overall effects), and this is enough to keep the wheels turning. (Of course the Quixotic "Black-paper writers" who want to solve this problem by restrictive political and economic measures have no idea what kind of a capitalist society they live in.)

The problem is rendered increasingly grave by another contradiction of the system : the multiplication of "leisure" as a result of the spectacular technological advances we witness today. It goes without saying, up to a point the system is capable not only of absorbing the newly produced "free time" and the unemployment that potentially goes with it, but also of turning them into instruments of further economic expansion and boom. (The growing "industry of culture", the expansion of parasitic services, etc.) But here, again, the limits should not be overestimated. Not only because the pace of technological advance is precipitous, and not only because the capitalist power groups cannot escape in the long run from the consequences of the structural weakening of their competitive position (due to the increasing share of the parasitic factors in the economy as a whole) as regards the emerging post-capitalist systems, but also because a trouble-free expansion of "leisure" is inconceivable without a radical overcoming of its sense-less present-day character.

It would be illusory to expect significant changes in this respect. The only form of accountancy known to capitalism is a narrow *monetary* accountancy, while seriously tackling the problems of "free time" (not idle "leisure") requires a radically different approach : the institution of a *social accountancy* in a society which succeeded in emancipating itself from the crippling pressures of the alienated second order mediations of commodity-production. As we have seen, bourgeois ideology, ever since Adam Smith, could only tackle the problem of education and leisure in a narrowly utilitarian framework : as "amusement of the mind", destined partly to restore the worker's energies for the next day's soulless routine, and partly to keep him away from wasteful "debauchery". The conception of "free time" as the vehicle of transcending the opposition between mental labour and physical labour, between theory and practice, between creativity and mechanical routine, and between ends and means, had to remain far beyond the bourgeois horizon. Even Goethe insisted in his *Faust*, with profound ambiguity, that "to accomplish the Great Work, One spirit is enough for a thousand hands" :

> *"Dass sich das grösste Werk vollende,*
> *Genügt Ein Geist für tausend Hände."*

The Marxian view, in sharp contrast to "leisure" blindly subordin-ated to the needs of commodity-production, implies not only the replacement of "piecemeal" monetary accountancy by a compre-hensive social accountancy, but at the same time also the practical realization of the culture, acquired through "free time", in the form of integrating "execution" with policy- and decision-making which alone can give it a sense of purpose—thanks to the positive trans-cendence of the existing social hierarchies.

As to the crisis of present-day bourgeois ideology, we can observe the maturation and the sharpening of an old contradiction. We have seen that *"utopianism"* and *"gradualism"* were but two sides of the same coin. Another aspect of this problem concerns the opposition between *specialization* and *comprehensiveness.* Neo-positivistically oriented specialization in ideology could only prevail in the social framework of a relative capitalist stability—achieved through the establishment of the Keynesian monetary mechanisms and their massive economic supporter: the arms industry of monopoly capital—which had as its immediate ideological needs the production of the necessary *manipulatory techniques* of "social engineering", "communications", "human engineering", "public relations", "market research", "opinion polls", "job-structuring", etc. Indirectly this cult of "sound specialization" also served as a form of ideological self-advertising in opposition to "utopianism", "ideology", "metaphysics", "messianism", "holism", the "millenium", etc.—all overwhelmingly directed against Marxism, even if the "scientific" and "objective meta-ideological" pretences often did not allow the authors concerned to make this explicit. When the ideologists who traded in "the end of ideology" accused Marxism of promising the millenium, they were in fact hiding their own rejection of all historicity, thus hiding a perverted and hypocritical cult of a capitalist millenium. As Marx observed, the champion of "democracy":

> "sees the *millenium* in the democratic republic and has no suspicion that it is precisely in this last form of state of bourgeois society that the class struggle has to be fought out to a conclusion."[260]

The difference with the present-day apologists of bourgeois "democracy" is that they cannot help having at least some suspicion as to the reality of the class struggle. However, in the recent period of expansion and relative internal stability of capitalism, the glorification of manipulative expertise as "social science" and "political science" (and who knows what not: in some American Universities there are even Departments of "Apiary Science" and "Mortuary Science", teaching bee-keeping and undertaking) was for them a convenient way of both "objectively" dealing with the ideological adversary and at the same time also of creating the "scientifically founded" impression of the absolute permanence of capitalist society. Nevertheless, as S. M. Rosen rightly puts it: "The stress on scientism is itself a kind of ideology; it suggests that the central values of the economic tradition in the West—free markets, efficiency, growth—are sufficiently valid for our time to require no further serious scrutiny. Rather, they are the accepted base on which to build more effective techniques for achieving them."[261]

At a time of instability and crisis, nevertheless, the manipulative techniques, no matter how "scientific" they are supposed to be,

308   MARX'S THEORY OF ALIENATION

are not enough. Thus new efforts have to be made to work out "general theories", "comprehensive models", "flexible metaphors", etc.—through the "President's Commission on National Goals", through institutions of "Strategic Studies", through agencies like the "Rand Corporation", and so forth. And significantly enough there are even attempts at "rehabilitating", and thus rescuing for "objective" use, a respectable form of "utopia" as well. In the revised edition of his book Daniel Bell writes :

> "The end of ideology is not—should not be—the end of utopia as well. If anything, one can begin anew the discussion of utopia only by being aware of the trap of ideology. [the new, *empirical* utopia] has to specify w h e r e one wants to go, h o w to get there, the costs of the enterprise, and some realization of, and justification for the determination of w h o is to pay. . . . The problems which confront us at home and in the world are resistant to the old terms of ideological debate between 'left' and 'right', and if 'ideology' by now, and with good reason, is an irretrievably fallen word, it is not necessary that 'utopia' suffer the same fate."[282]

Thus the sort of "utopia" which can be semantically rescued from the state of "irretrievable fallenness of ideology" is the "cost-effective, empirical utopia" of American capitalism. (We have seen how loudly he applauded Tucker's self-reassuring assertion that Marx's concept of communism is being realized in "present-day America".) The criteria which he puts forward for telling the "empirical utopias" from the "ideological" ones are equally revealing : (1) the rejection of the "rhetoric of revolution" of the New Left (the "old" is supposed to be irretrievably buried, together with its fallen "ideological concepts") : (2) the condemnation of "Pan-Africanism or some other ideology" of the independent African States; and (3) the denunciation of the "hatred, intolerance and the wiping out of the middle ground" which is supposed to characterize Cuba's development. One criterion is more "objectively-scientifically meta-ideological" than the other ! Indeed, one worthier than the other of "The Great Society" and of "The New Frontiers" of the splendidly cost-effective empirical utopia of monopoly capital which demonstrates its superiority to all ideology every day not only in Vietnam but in forty-eight other countries as well.[283]

However, when it comes to working out concretely the "general theories", not just denouncing the "ideologically trapped" adversary for offering "little definition of the future",[284] the results are very meagre indeed. As Chomsky writes about a much advertised "classic" of this new wave of "strategic thinking", Herman Kahn's book *On Thermonuclear War* (hailed by some as "one of the great works of our time"): "this is surely one of the emptiest works of our time. . . . Kahn proposes no theories, no explanations, no factual assumptions that can be tested against their consequences, as do the sciences he is attempting to mimic. He simply suggests a terminology and provides a façade of rationality. When particular policy conclusions are drawn, they are supported only by *ex cathedra* remarks for which no support is even suggested. . . . What is remarkable is that serious people actually pay attention to these absurdities, no doubt because of the façade of toughmindedness and pseudoscience."[285]

Indeed it would be very surprising if the results were different from what they actually are. For the contradictions determining the partiality of the bourgeois ideological standpoint are much more acute today—when monopoly capital is powerfully challenged both internally and internationally—than at the time of the failure of the great "heroic utopias". A comprehensive and dynamic sociohistorical theory is inconceivable without a force, positively interested in social transformation, as its practical ground. The partiality of bourgeois self-interest which is evidently not interested in such a transformation can offer nothing more than variations on a *static* model: the projection of the established order of society as a kind of "empirical millenium" subject to "gradual improvements" and "piecemeal reforms" as applied to its minor details.

The present-day ideological crisis is only a specific expression of the general structural crisis of capitalistic institutions. There is no space here to enter into a detailed discussion of this complex matter. We have to content ourselves with merely pointing to some of its more important aspects. The main issue is that the institutions of capitalism are inherently violent and aggressive; they are built on the premise of: "war if the 'normal' methods fail". The blind "natural law" of the market mechanism, the realization of the principle of *bellum omnium contra omnes* carries with it that the social problems are never *solved*, only *postponed*, or indeed—since postponement cannot work indefinitely—transferred to the *military* plane. Thus the "sense" of the hierarchically structured institutions of capitalism is given in this ultimate reference to the violent "fighting out" of the issues, in the international arena, for the socioeconomic units—following the inner logic of their development—

grow bigger and bigger, and their problems and contradictions increasingly more intense and grave. Growth and expansion are inner
necessities of the capitalist system of production and when the local
limits are reached there is no other way out except by violently
readjusting the existing relation of forces. The relative internal
stability of the leading capitalist countries—Britain, France, and the
United States—was in the past inseparable from their ability to
export the aggressiveness and the violence internally generated by
their systems. Their weaker partners—Germany, Italy, and others—
after the first world war found themselves in the middle of a grave
social crisis and only the Fascist promise of a radical readjustment
of the established relation of forces could bring a temporary solution
acceptable to the bourgeoisie, through diverting the pressures of
internal aggressiveness and violence into the channels of a massive
preparation for a new world war. The small capitalist countries, on
the other hand, simply had to subordinate themselves to one of
the great powers and follow the policies dictated by them, even at
the price of chronic instability.

However "irrational" may seem to be this mechanism of postponement inevitably leading to periodical collisions, it was a model
of "rationality" as compared to the present situation. For it was
rational in the limited senses of (1) offering to the individuals some
specific objectives to achieve, no matter how monstruous they may
have been (e.g. Fascist policies); (2) structuring the various institutions of capitalism in a hierarchical functional pattern, assigning to
them definite tasks in pursuing the overall objectives of growth and
expansion. Today—since the system has been decapitated through
the removal of its ultimate sanction—an all-out war on its real
or potential adversaries—even the semblance of rationality has disappeared. Exporting internal violence is no longer possible on the
required massive scale. (Attempts at doing so on a limited scale—
e.g. the Vietnam war—not only are no substitutes for the old
mechanism but even accelerate the inevitable internal explosions,
by aggravating the inner contradictions of the system.) Nor is it
possible to get away indefinitely with the ideological mystifications
which represented the *internal* challenge of socialism : the only
possible solution to the present crisis, as an *external* confrontation :
a "subversion" directed from abroad by a "monolithic" enemy. For
the first time in history capitalism is globally confronted with its
own problems which cannot be "postponed" much longer, nor
can they be indeed transferred to the military plane in order to be

"exported" in the form of an all-out war.[286] But both the institutions and the ideology of monopoly capital are *structurally* incapable of solving such a radically new problem. The intensity and the gravity of the educational-ideological crisis of present-day capitalism is inseparable from this great historical challenge.

NOTES

1 E.g., R. C. Tucker, *Philosophy and Myth in Karl Marx* (Cambridge University Press, 1961). A detailed discussion of this book can be found in Note No. 209.

2 Louis Althusser, *Pour Marx* (Maspéro, Paris, 1967), p. 18.

3 In German the terms "Entäusserung", "Entfremdung", and "Veräusserung" are used to render "alienation" or "estrangement". "Entäusserung" and "Entfremdung" are much more frequently used by Marx than "Veräusserung" which is, as Marx defines it, "die Praxis der Entäusserung" (the practice of alienation—Marx-Engels, *Werke* (henceforth abbreviated to, MEWE), Vol. 1, p. 376), or, elsewhere, "Tat der Entäusserung" (the act of alienation—MEWE, Supplementary Volume I, p. 531). Thus "Veräusserung" is the act of translating into practice (in the form of selling something) the principle of "Entäusserung". In Marx's use of the term, "Veräusserung" can be interchanged with "Entäusserung" when a specific "act" or "practice" is referred to. (See MEWE, Vol. 26, Part I, pp. 7–8— on Sir James Steuart's doctrine concerning "profit upon alienation". Alienation in this context is rendered by Marx both with "Veräusserung" and "Entäusserung".) Both "Entäusserung" and "Entfremdung" have a threefold conceptual function : (1) referring to a *general principle*; (2) expressing a given *state of affairs*; and (3) designating a *process* which leads to that state. When the accent is on "externalization" or "objectification", Marx uses the term "Entäusserung" (or terms like "Vergegenständlichung"), whereas "Entfremdung" is used when the author's intention is to emphasize the fact that man is being *opposed* by a *hostile* power of his own making, so that he defeats his own purpose.

4 See CHAPTER VIII, on *The Controversy about Marx*.

5 Not all of them to the same degree. CHAPTER VII, which deals with the *Aesthetic Aspects* of alienation, is the easiest to read on its own. By contrast CHAPTER V, which discusses the *Political Aspects*, is heavily dependent not only on CHAPTER IV, *(Economic Aspects)* but also on CHAPTER VI. *(Ontological and Moral Aspects)*.

6 Ancient solutions to problems of this kind played an extremely important rôle in their modern reformulations. See the importance of Greek thought for the school of "Natural Law", for instance.

7 Milton, *Paradise Lost*, Bk. I.
8 "Combien voyons-nous de chrétiens aliénés de la vie de Dieu!" Fénélon, *Oeuvres* (Versailles, 1820), Vol. XVII, p. 328.
9 *Epistle to the Ephesians*, Ch. II.
10 "the dispensation of the grace of God" as "the mystery of Christ". Ibid., Ch. III.
11 *On the Jewish Question*, in Karl Marx, *Early Writings*, Translated and Edited by T. B. Bottomore, (C. A. Watts & Co. Ltd., London, 1963), p. 39.
12 *Deuteronomy*, XV, 11.
13 *Isaiah*, LXI, 5.
14 Marx, *On the Jewish Question*, op. cit., pp. 38–9.
15 *Deuteronomy*, XIV, 21.
16 *Exodus*, XXII, 25.
17 Marx, *On the Jewish Question*, op. cit., p. 38.
18 Ibid., p. 38.
19 Ibid., p. 40.
20 Ibid., p. 40
21 Ibid., p. 35.
22 See Martin Luther, *Werke* (Kritische Gesamtausgabe, Hermann Böhlau, Weimar, 1883), Vol. I, p. 677. See also Luther, *Freiheit eines Christenmenschen* (1520), in *M. Luther: Reformatorische Schriften* (Reclam Verlag, Leipzig, 1945), pp. 98–108.
23 Thomas Münzer, *Hochverursachte Schutzrede und Antwort wider das geistlose, sanftlebende Fleisch zu Wittenberg, welches mit verkehrter Weise durch den Diebstahl der heiligen Schrift die erbärmliche Christenheit also ganz jämmerlich besudelt hat*, (1524). Quoted by Marx in his essay *On the Jewish Question*, Vol. cit., p. 37.
24 Adam Smith, *An Inquiry into the Nature and Causes of the Wealth of Nations*, (1776), Everyman edition, Vol. II, p. 342.
25 "Le Bourgois ne peut pas aliener la chose de la commune sanz le commendement de roi." In *Livre de jostice et de plait*. Edited by P. N. Rapetti (Paris, 1850), p. 47.
26 "Chascun peut le sien doner et aliener par sa volenté." In *Assises de Jérusalem*, Edited by A. A. Beugnot (Paris, 1841), Vol. I, p. 183.
27 Hobbes, *Philosophical Rudiments Concerning Government and Society* (Royston, London, 1651), Chapter VIII, § 6. See also Hobbes, *The Elements of Law* (1640, first published in London, 1650). New edition, with a Preface and critical notes by Ferdinand Tönnies (Cambridge University Press, 1928) : "And seeing both the servant and all that is committed to him, is the property of the master, and every man may dispose of his own, and transfer the same at his pleasure, *the master may therefore alienate his dominion over them*, or give the same, by his last will, to whom he list." pp. 100–101.
28 "To make earth an object of huckstering—the earth which is our one and all, the first condition of our existence—was the last

step towards making oneself an object of huckstering. It was and is to this very day an immorality surpassed only by the immorality of self-alienation." Engels, *Outlines of a Critique of Political Economy*, p. 190 of Moscow edition of Marx's *Manuscripts of 1844*.

29 Kant, *Werke* (Akademische Ausgabe, Berlin, 1902f), Vol. VI, p. 360. Kant sees clearly that "Besitz (p h y s i s c h e r) aber ist die Bedingung der Möglichkeit der H a n d h a b u n g *(manipulatio) eines Dinges als eine Sache;* wenn dieses gleich, *in einer anderen Beziehung,* zugleich als *Person* behandelt werden muss." (Ibid., p. 358.) In this sense, speaking of the various forms of V e r d i n g u n g s v e r t r a g" (Reifying Contract) he writes about the *wage-labourer*: "Der L o h n v e r t r a g (locatio operae), d. i. die Bewilligung des *Gebrauchs meiner Kräfte* an einen anderen für einen bestimmten Preis (merces). Der *Arbeiter* nach diesem Vertrage ist der *Lohndiener (mercenarius).*" (Ibid., p. 285.) Relations of this kind belong to the "d i n g l i c h - p e r s ö n - l i c h e s Recht (ius realiter personale) des *Besitzes* (obzwar nicht des Gebrauchs) *einer anderen Person als einer Sache.*" (Ibid., p. 285.)

30 "Die Übertragung seines E i g e n t u m s an einen anderen ist die V e r ä u s s e r u n g." Ibid., p. 271. Kant was greatly influenced by Adam Smith and assigned to the latter's ideas a very high place in his own philosophy of Right. We can see this from the following quotation: " 'Geld ist also (nach Adam Smith) derjenige Körper, dessen *Veräusserung* das *Mittel* und zugleich *der Maszstab* des Fleisses ist, mit welchem Menschen und Völker unter einander Verkehr treiben.'—Diese Erklärung führt den *empirischen* Begriff des Geldes dadurch auf *intellektuellen* hinaus, dass sie *nur auf die F o r m* der wechselseitigen Leistungen im belästigten Vertrage sieht (und *von dieser ihrer Materie abstrahiert*), und so auf Rechtsbegriff in der Umsetzung des Mein und Dein (commutatio late sic dicta) überhaupt, um die obige Tafel einer dogmatischen Einleitung a priori, mithin der Metaphysik des Rechts, als eines Systems, angemessen vorzustellen." Ibid., p. 289.

31 Homer, *Odyssey* (Penguin Edition, Translated by E. V. Rieu), p. 285.

32 Marx, *On the Jewish Question*, Vol. cit., p. 39. "*Selling* is the practice of alienation"—("Die *Veräusserung* ist die Praxis der Entäusserung", MEWE, Vol. 1, p. 276)—in Bottomore's translation reads: "*Objectification* is the practice of alienation". This is incorrect. For Marx specified in the, previous sentence that "*zu veräussern = verkäuflichen*", and "verkäuflichen" means unambiguously "selling". This meaning of "Veräusserung" as "selling" or "alienation through selling" can be found also in othef works of Marx. See Note No. 3 for references.

33 MEWE, Vol. 1, p. 376.

34 See CHAPTER IX of this study.

35   Goethe, *Dichtung und Wahrheit*, in Goethes *Sämtliche Werke* (Cottasche Jub. Ausg., Stuttgart u. Berlin, 1902f), Vol. 24, p. 81.

36   "nicht etwa selbstisch vereinzelt, nur in Verbindung mit seinesgleichen macht er Fronte gegen die Welt", Goethe, *Wilhelm Meisters Wanderjahre*, (Jub. Ausg.), Vol. 19, p. 181.

37   See Adam Ferguson, *Essay on the History of Civil Society* (Edinburgh, 1767). New edition, edited with an introduction by Duncan Forbes, (University Press, Edinburgh, 1966).

38   Aristotle, *Politics*, Book I, Chapter 2. (Translated by Benjamin Jowett).

39   Ibid., Book VII, Chapter 2.

40   Feuerbach, *Das Wesen des Christentums* (first published in 1841). Part I bears the title: "Das wahre, d.i. anthropologische Wesen der Religion", and Part II is entitled: "Das unwahre, d.i. theologische Wesen der Religion".

41   Giambattista Vico, *The New Science*, Translated from the third edition (1744) by T. G. Bergin and M. H. Fisch (Doubleday & Co. Inc., New York, 1961), p. 3.

42   "personifizierte Natur, oder eingekleidete Weisheit". Herder, *Vom neuern Gebrauch der Mythologie* (first published in 1767), in Herder's *Sämtliche Werke*, Abt. "Zur Schönen Literatur und Kunst", Vol. 2, (Carlsruhe, 1821), p. 251.

43   Ibid., pp. 252-3.

44   "La première attaque contre la superstition a été violente, sans mesure. Une fois que les hommes ont osé d'une manière quelconque donner l'assaut à la barrière de la religion, cette barrière la plus formidable qui existe, comme la plus respectée, il est impossible de s'arrêter. Dès qu'ils ont tourné des regards menaçants *contre la majesté du ciel*, ils ne manqueront pas, le moment d'après, de les diriger *contre la souveraineté de la terre*. La câble qui tient et comprime l'humanité est formé de deux cordes; *l'une ne peut céder sans que l'autre vienne à rompre*." (*Lettre à la Princesse Dashkoff*, 3 April 1771) in Diderot, *Correspondance*, edited by Georges Roth (Éditions de Minuit, Paris, 1955f), Vol. XI, p. 20.

45   "Si le journalier est misérable la nation est misérable." Diderot's entry on *Journalier* in the *Encyclopédie*.

46   Diderot, *Supplément au Voyage de Bougainville*, in *Oeuvres Philosophiques*, edited by Paul Vernière (Garnier, Paris, 1956), p. 482.

47   Ibid., p. 468.

48   Ibid., p. 468.

49   Marx, *Capital*, Translated by Samuel Moore and Edward Aveling (Moscow, 1958), Vol. I, p. 288.

50   Ibid., p. 486.

51   Henry Home (Lord Kames), *Loose Hints upon Education, chiefly concerning the Culture of the Heart*, (Edinburgh & London, 1781), p. 257.

52 Ibid., p. 284.
53 Ibid., pp. 306–7.
54 Ibid., p. 307.
55 Rousseau, *A Discourse on Political Economy*, Everyman Edition, Translated by G. D. H. Cole, pp. 262–4.
56 Rousseau, *The Social Contract or Principles of Political Right*, Everyman Edition, Translated by G. D. H. Cole, pp. 35–7.
57 Rousseau, *Troisième Dialogue*, in *Oeuvres Complètes*, (Éditions du Seuil, Paris, 1967), Vol. I, p. 474.
58 Rousseau, *Émile*, Everyman Edition, Translated by Barbara Foxley, p. 20.
59 Rousseau, *The Social Contract*, Ed., cit., p. 7.
60 Ibid., p. 12.
61 Ibid., p. 13.
62 Ibid., p. 16.
63 Ibid., p. 16. The last sentence reappears, almost word by word, as a fundamental principle of the Kantian philosophy.
64 Hume's rather cynical rejection of Rousseau's conception—see his essay entitled : *Of the Original Contract*—is extremely problematical. Nevertheless it puts in sharp focus the crude reality of the established system which does not bear any resemblance to Rousseau's moral construction. Yet, Hume's criticism was to a large extent beside the point. For, as Kant realized, Rousseau's conception does not apply to *questio facti* but to *questio iuris*. In the spirit of Rousseau's approach Kant emphasized that the state *ought* to be run *as if* it were founded on a Social Contract.
65 Rousseau, *The Social Contract*, Ed., cit., p. 20.
66 Ibid., p. 20.
67 "Tout est bien sortant des mains de l'Auteur des choses, tout dégénère entre les mains de l'homme." Rousseau, *Émile ou de l'éducation* (Garnier-Flammarion, Paris, 1966), p. 35.
68 "la nature a fait l'homme hereux et bon mais . . . la société le déprave et le rend misérable. L'*Émile* en particulier, ce livre tant lu, si peu entendu et si mal apprécié, n'est qu'un *traité de la bonté originelle de l'homme*, destiné à montrer comment le vice et l'erreur, *étrangers à sa constitution*, s'y introduisent *du dehors* et l'altèrent insensiblement. . . . Partout il nous fait voir l'espèce humaine meilleure, plus sage et plus hereuse dans sa constitution primitive, aveugle, misérable et méchante à mesure qu'elle s'en éloigne." Rousseau, *Troisième Dialogue*, ed. cit., p. 474.
69 "une marche aussi rapide vers la perfection de la société et vers la détérioration de l'espèce." Ibid., p. 474.
70 "L'homme civil naît, vit et meurt dans *l'esclavage* : . . . il est *enchaîné par nos institutions*." *Émile ou de l'éducation*, ed. cit., p. 43.
71 *A Discourse on Political Economy*, ed. cit., p. 265.
72 Ibid., p. 259.

73   *Émile ou de l'éducation*, ed. cit., p. 51.

74   Ibid., p. 614.

75   "Je pense que chacun doit sa vie et son sang à la patrie; qu'il n'est pas permis de *s'aliénér* à des princes auxquelles on ne doit rien, moins encore de *se vendre*, et de faire du plus noble métier du monde celui d'un *vil mercenaire*." Rousseau, *Julie ou la Nouvelle Héloïse*, (Garnier-Flammarion, Paris, 1967), p. 68.

76   Rousseau, *A Discourse on Political Economy*, ed. cit., p. 260.

77   "On raisonne beaucoup sur les qualités d'un bon gouverneur. La première que j'en exigerais, et celle-là seule en suppose beaucoup d'autres, c'est de n'être point *un homme à vendre*." "Voilà la fonction que vous confiez tranquillement à des *mercenaires*." *Émile ou de l'éducation*, ed. cit., pp. 52 & 53. (The English translation—Everyman edition—consistently waters down Rousseau's points. The sentence about the mercenary tutor—this "man for sale"—is rendered like this : "he should not take up his task *for reward*". p. 17).

78   "L'instruction qu'on retire des voyages se rapporte à l'objet qui les fait entreprendre. Quand cet objet est un système de philosophie, le voyageur ne voit jamais que ce qu'il veut voir; quand cet objet est l'intérêt, il absorbe toute l'attention de ceux qui s'y livrent. Le commerce et les arts, qui mêlent et confondent les peuples, les empêchent aussi de s'étudier. *Quand ils savent le profit qu'ils peuvent faire l'un avec l'autre, qu'ont-ils de plus à savoir?*" Ibid., pp. 594–5.

79   Rousseau, *The Social Contract*, ed. cit., p. 19.

80   Ibid., p. 19.

81   "Mais supposons ce prodige trouvé. C'est en considérant ce qu'il doit faire que nous verrons ce qu'il doit être." Rousseau, *Émile ou de l'éducation*, ed. cit., p. 53.

82   Rousseau, *The Social Contract*, ed. cit., p. 36.

83   Equally problematical is Rousseau's analysis of the "body politic as a moral being", conceived on the basis of an anthropological model. See pp. 4 & 24 of his *Social Contract*, and pp. 236–7 of *A Discourse on Political Economy*.

84   Rousseau, *A Discourse on Political Economy*, ed. cit., p. 254.

85   Ibid., p. 234.

86   Ibid., p. 268.

87   Ibid., p. 255.

88   Rousseau, *A Discourse on the Origin of Inequality: Appendix*, Everyman edition, translated by G. D. H. Cole, p. 228.

89   In a *historically limited* sense this is valid, of course, in so far as capitalist society, in the last analysis, cannot admit any other law than "contractual law", i.e. "might turned into right", upholding this legitimized "might" by its own terms of "right". As Rousseau puts it : "The peculiar fact about *this alienation* is that, in taking over the goods of individuals, the community, so far from despoiling them, only assures them *legitimate* possession,

and *changes usurpation into a true right and enjoyment into proprietorship.*" (*The Social Contract*, ed. cit., p. 18.) Consequently, respect for such a law can only be generated by considering the loss of what it provides; i.e. ultimately the loss of proprietorship and all the rights built on this fundamental right of proprietorship. But this is no argument in favour of private property. Since the latter, in its "non-legitimized" form—i.e. as usurpation—is the necessary premise of the *kind* of legal system to which it gives rise, Rousseau's ahistorical assertion about the rôle of property, in generating respect for the law, in reality means that *private property* (as sanction) *is for the benefit of private property* (i.e. for the perpetuation of a specific legal system which sustains and defends private property).

90 "Ce sont les grandes villes qui épuisent un État et font sa faiblesse : *la richesse qu'elles produisent est une richesse apparente et illusoire; c'est beaucoup d'argent et peu d'effet.*" *Émile ou de l'éducation*, ed. cit., p. 614.

91 Rousseau, *The Social Contract*, ed. cit., p. 10.

92 Ibid., p. 26.

93 Rousseau, *A Discourse on the Origin of Inequality*, pp. 144 & 229.

94 An important epistemological aspect of "alienation" we can see in Diderot's words : "Je sais aussi *m'aliéner*, talent sans lequel on ne fait rien qui vaille." (*Lettre à Madame Riccobini*, 27 Nov. 1758, *Correspondance*, ed. cit., Vol. II, p. 97.) In this sense "to alienate" means to achieve the required level of *abstraction* and *generalization* in thought. This idea, in a somewhat different form, appeared in fact a long time before Diderot, in Campanella's works. In his *Metaphysica* Campanella wrote : "Sapere è *straniarsi da se stessi*, straniarsi da se stessi è diventare pazzi, perdere la propria *identità* e assumerne una *straniera*." (Pt. I, Lib. I, § I, Art. 9.) Fichte, much later, explored this problematics in more than one of his works. (See in particular his *Grundlagen der gesamten Wissenschaftslehre*, 1794; *Darstellung der Wissenschaftslehre*, 1801; *Nachgelassene Werke*, Vol. 2). An important passage from Fichte reads as follows : "habe ich nun das Ich vollkommen *entäussert* durch Denken aus der unmittelbaren Anschauung heraus und in die Region der äussern Wahrnehmung, gestellt." (*Die Thatsachen des Bewusstseyns*, 1810–11, publ. 1817, p. 91.)

95 For a penetrating analysis of Hegel's economic insights and their rôle in his philosophical development see G. Lukács, *Der junge Hegel. Über die Beziehungen von Dialektik und Ökonomie*, (Luchterhand, Neuwied & Berlin, 1967, 3rd edition.)

96 Marx, *Grundrisse der Kritik der politischen Ökonomie* (Rohentwurf, 1857–1858) (Dietz Verlag, Berlin, 1953), p. 716.

97 MEWE, Supplementary Vol. I, p. 171.

98 Marx-Engels, *The German Ideology* (Lawrence & Wishart, London, 1965), p. 533.

99 MEWE, Suppl. Vol. I, p. 286.
100 Ibid., p. 296.
101 Ibid., p. 304–5.
102 Marx, *The Leading Article of No. 179 of KÖLNISCHE ZEIT-UNG* (written at the beginning of July 1842), in Marx-Engels, *On Religion* (Moscow, 1957), p. 38.
103 Ibid., p. 23.
104 Ibid., p. 23.
105 Speaking of the "estates of civil society" (Stände der Bürgerlichen Gesellschaft) Marx writes in the same work: "die bürgerliche Gesellschaft war durch ihre. Trennung von der politischen eine andere geworden. . . . Der Ständeunterschied ist hier nicht mehr ein Unterschied des B e d ü r f n i s s e s und der A r b e i t als selbständige Körper. . . . Innerhalb der Gesellschaft selbst aber bildete sich der Unterschied aus in beweglichen, nicht festen Kreisen, deren Prinzip die W i l l k ü r ist. G e l d und B i l d u n g sind die Hauptkriterien. . . . Das Characteristische ist nur, dass die B e s i t z l o s i g k e i t und *der S t a n d d e r u n-m i t t e l b a r e n Arbeit, der konkreten Arbeit, weniger einen Stand der bürgerlichen Gesellschaft als den Boden bilden, auf dem ihre Kreise ruhen und sich bewegen.*" (MEWE, Vol. I, p. 284.) Here we have in a nutshell Marx's earliest theory of the classes, though his terminology is still rather vague, in so far as he holds on to the terms inherited primarily from Hegel. It is clear, none the less, that he considers "labour" not so much a "class in itself" (or an estate proper) as the necessary foundation of bourgeois society as such, as the condition of existence of the bourgeois order.
106 MEWE, Vol. I, pp. 284–5.
107 see Marx, *On the Jewish Question*, ed. cit., p. 39.
108 Ibid., p. 5.
109 Marx has written two articles on the subject, reviewing Bruno Bauer's works: *Die Judenfrage* (The Jewish Question) and *Die Fähigkeit der heutigen Juden und Christen, frei zu werden* (The Capacity of the Present-day Jews and Christians to Become Free). First published in the "Deutsch-Französichen Jahrbücher", (edited by Marx and Arnold Ruge), in February 1844.
110 See MEWE, Vol. I, pp. 374–7.
111 Marx, *Zur Kritik der Hegelschen Rechtsphilosophie. Einleitung.* (MEWE, Vol. I, pp. 378–91.) First published in the same issue of "Deutsch-Französischen Jahrbücher" as the articles *On the Jewish Question*. For an English translation see pp. 41–58 of Marx-Engels *On Religion* (Moscow, 1957), and pp. 43–59 of K. Marx, *Early Writings*, translated by T. B. Bottomore (London, 1963).
112 p. 44 of T. B. Bottomore's translation.
113 Ibid., pp. 44–5.
114 Ibid., pp. 52 & 57–9.

115 MEWE, Vol. I, p. 391.
116 p. 55 of T. B. Bottomore's translation.
117 Ibid., p. 57.
118 Ibid., p. 48.
119 Ibid., p. 49.
120 Ibid., p. 52.
121 Ibid., p. 46.
122 Quoted from the appendix of the volume containing Marx's *Economic and Philosophic Manuscripts of 1844*, pp. 175–209, translated by Martin Milligan.
123 See, for instance, *Capital* (Moscow, 1958), Vol. I, p. 75.
124 See Marx's *VIth Thesis on Feuerbach.*
125 It is worth noting here that Hegel criticized Solger—the only romantic philosopher with whom he otherwise sympathized—precisely because of Solger's failure to overcome *dualism*. ("Solger fängt mit einen *unversöhnten Dualismus* an, obwohl seine ausdrückliche Bestimmung der Philosophie ist, nicht in einem Dualismus befangen zu sein." Hegel, *Sämmtliche Werke*, Jub. Ausgabe, Vol. 20, p. 169.)
126 Marx, *Theses on Feuerbach*, ed. cit., p. 69.
127 Goethe, *Sämtliche Werke* (Cottasche Jub. Ausgabe) Vol. 39. One of its most important passages reads as follows: "In der lebendigen Natur geschieht nichts, was nicht in einer Verbindung mit dem Ganzen stehe, und wenn uns die Erfahrungen nur isoliert erscheinen, wenn wir die Versuche nur als isolierte Fakta anzusehen haben, so wird dadurch nicht gesagt, dass sie isoliert s e i e n; . . . Da alles in der Natur, besonders aber die allgemeine Kräfte und Elemente in einer ewigen Wirkung und Gegenwirkung sind, so kann man von einem jeden Phänomene sagen, dass es mit unzähligen andern in Verbindung stehe, wie wir von einen frei schwebenden Punkte sagen, dass er seine Strahlen nach allen Seiten ausende." (p. 23.) Many philosophers, including Feuerbach, because of their failure to elaborate the category of *mediation* (Vermittlung, or *mediator*: Vermittler) remained trapped by dualism, notwithstanding their efforts to overcome it.
128 Marx, *Theses on Feuerbach*, ed. cit., p. 70.
129 Ibid., p. 70.
130 Such a partial cure is advocated, for instance, by Adam Smith who idealizes man's "propensity to exchange and barter", and who wants to neutralize the negative effects of the "commercial spirit" through education. (For a further discussion of these problems see CHAPTER X.)
131 MEWE, Suppl. Vol. I, p. 463. (Marx's Comments on James Mill's *Elements of Political Economy* were written approximately at the same time as his *Economic and Philosophic Manuscripts of 1844*.)
132 Ibid., p. 446.
133 "The meaning of private property—*liberated from its estrange-*

ment—is the existence of essential objects for man, both as *objects of enjoyment* and *as objects of activity*" (137).

134 Lenin, *Collected Works*, Vol. 38, p. 30.
135 Ibid., pp. 29–30.
136 Ibid., p. 564.
137 See Lenin, *Collected Works*, Vol. 38, pp. 27, 39, 40 & 48.
138 Both quotations in this sentence are from Lenin, *Coll. Works*, Vol. 2, p. 23.
139 Ibid., p. 23.
140 Quoted by Lenin in his *Conspectus of The Holy Family*.
141 See MEWE, Suppl. Vol. 1, pp. 445–463.
142 Marx-Engels, *The German Ideology*, ed. cit., p. 40.
143 Rousseau, *Émile ou de l'éducation*, ed. cit., p. 40.
144 See, for instance, a few pages after this criticism of the "bourgeois . . . a nothing", p. 51 of the Garnier-Flammarion edition.
145 Ibid., p. 53.
146 See Marx, *Economic and Philosophic Manuscripts of 1844*, ed. cit., pp. 61–3.
147 Ibid., pp. 118–9.
148 In : *Georg Lukács : Schriften zur Ideologie und Politik*, ed. by Peter Ludz (Luchterhand, Neuwied & Berlin, 1967), p. 286. (Quotation translated by G. H. R. Parkinson.)
149 Marx, *Grundrisse der Kritik der politischen Ökonomie*, ed. cit., p. 716.
150 See on these points CHAPTERS VI–X.
151 See in particular MEWE, Vol. II, pp. 32, 34 & 44.
152 For a general evaluation of Marx's relation to Proudhon see his letter to J. B. von Schweitzer, 24 January 1865, MEWE, Vol. XVI, p. 25.
153 Ibid, p. 28.
154 Marx often compares the political economists to the theologians. In his *Capital*, for instance, he quotes the following passage from the original French edition of his work; *Misère de la philosophie* (Paris, 1847) : "Les économistes ont une singulière manière de procéder. Il n'y a pour eux que deux sortes d'institutions, celles de l'art et celles de la nature. Les institutions de la féodalité sont des institutions artificielles, celles de la bourgeoisie sont des institutions naturelles. Ils ressemblent en ceci aux théologiens, qui eux aussi établissent deux sortes de réligions. Toute réligion qui n'est pas la leur, est une invention des hommes, tandis que leur propre réligion est une émanation de Dieu—Ainsi il y a eu de l'histoire, mais il n'y en a plus." Vol. I, p. 81).
155 Marx, *Capital*, ed. cit., Vol. III, p. 804.
156 See Marx, *Economic and Philosophic Manuscripts of 1844*, pp. 109–10. Though Feuerbach's name is not mentioned here, the implicit criticism applies to his work as well.
157 See Marx, *Capital*, Vol. III, pp. 799–800.
158 Ibid., Vol. I, p. 76.

159 "C'est d'après ce point de vue que je hasarde d'entrer ici dans une discussion assez étendue, pour faire voir le peu de fondement des opinions de ceux qui ont *condemné l'intérêt du prêt fait sans aliénation du capital,* et la fixation de cet intérêt par la seule convention." Turgot, *Oeuvres* (Paris, 1844) Vol. I, p. 118.

160 See Marx, *Capital,* Vol. III, p. 766.

161 Political economy deals "the deathblow to r e n t—the last, i n d i v i d u a l, n a t u r a l mode of private property and source of wealth existing independently of the movement of labour, that expression of feudal property, an expression which has already become wholly economic in character and therefore incapable of resisting political economy. (The Ricardo school.)" *Economic and Philosophic Manuscripts of 1844,* p. 95.

162 Ibid., p. 133.

163 "Die Individuen sind immer von sich ausgegangen, gehen immer von sich aus. Ihre Verhältnisse sind Verhältnisse ihres wirklichen Lebensprozesses. Woher kömmt es, dass *ihre Verhältnisse sich gegen sie verselbständigen?* dass *die Mächte ihres eignen Lebens übermächtig gegen sie werden?* Mit einem Wort: d i e T e i l-u n g d e r A r b e i t, deren Stufe von der jedesmal entwickelten Produktivkraft abhängt." MEWE, Vol. III, p. 540. (From a notebook of the young Marx.)

164 See Marx, *Economic and Philosophic Manuscripts of 1844,* pp. 133–4.

165 In opposition to such a system the young Engels writes about a future socialist society: "The truth of the relationship of competition is *the relationship of the power of consumption to the power of production.* In a world worthy of mankind there will be no other competition than this. The community will have to calculate what it can produce with the means at its disposal; and in the light of the relationship of this productive power to the mass of consumers it will determine how far it has to raise or lower production, how far it has to give way to, or curtail, luxury." *(Outlines of a Critique of Political Economy,* ed. cit., p. 197.) Only some elements of this conception are tenable. The influence of the English and French utopian socialists can be detected in this assessment of competition and Engels himself invites the reader, on the same page, to "consult the writings of the English Socialists, and partly also those of Fourier", in order to see how great an increase in productivity can be expected "from a rational state of affairs within the community".

166 See Marx, *Economic and Philosophic Manuscripts of 1844,* p. 132.

167 One of the most important passages of this work reads as follows: "The immediate consequence of private property was *the split of production into two opposing sides—the natural and the human sides,* the soil which without fertilization by man is dead and sterile, and human activity, whose first condition is that

very soil. Furthermore we have seen how human activity in its turn was dissolved into labour and capital, and how these two sides antagonistically confronted each other. Thus already we had the struggle of the three elements against one another, instead of their mutual support; and to make matters worse, private property brings in its wake the splintering of each of these elements. One *estate* stands confronted by another, one piece of *capital* by another, one unit of *labour-power* by another. In other words, because *private property isolates everyone in his own crude solitariness*, and because, nevertheless, everyone has the same interest as his neighbour, one landowner stands antagonistically confronted by another, one capitalist by another, one worker by another. In this discord of identical interests resulting precisely from this identity, is consummated the immorality of mankind's condition hitherto; and this consummation is competition. The opposite of competition is monopoly. Monopoly was the war-cry of the mercantilists; competition the battle-cry of the liberal economists. It is easy to see that this antithesis is again a quite *hollow antithesis.* . . . Competition is based on self-interest, and self-interest in turn breeds monopoly. In short, competition passes over into monopoly. . . . Moreover, competition already presupposes monopoly—namely, *the monopoly of property* (and here the *hypocrisy of the liberals* comes once more to light)." Ed. cit., pp. 193–4.

168 See Marx, *Capital*, Vol. I, pp. 77–8.
169 We should recall that Marx objects to Hegel because of the "uncritical positivism and the equally uncritical idealism" of his later works, finding elements of this uncritical attitude already in the *Phenomenology*. (See p. 149 of the 1844 Manuscripts.) As regards the *Phenomenology* Marx's criticism concerns mainly the Hegelian method of treating problems as "thought-entities", whereas in the criticism of Hegel's later works the evaluation of the state is directly involved.
170 See Marx, *Economic and Philosophic Manuscripts of 1844*, pp. 104–5.
171 Engels, *Outlines of a Critique of Political Economy*, ed. cit., p. 193.
172 "Free will" is, strictly speaking, a contradiction in terms. This concept simultaneously *posits* an object (by defining itself as "will" to which some object must be necessarily related) and also *negates* this necessary relationship (by calling the will "free") in order to be able to envisage a—fictitious—exercise of this "free will".
173 Some modern theologians, under the impact of the "scientific revolution", have introduced an ambiguously "rehabilitated" concept of reason into their works. Here is a quotation to show this trend : "Nicht die *Vernunft als solche* steht in Gegensatz zum Glauben, sondern nur die in sich geschlossene Vernunft, die

sich an die Stelle Gottes setzt, die Vernunft, die Gott in sich statt *sich in Gott verstehen* will, die anmasslich-selbstherrliche Vernunft. Nicht zwischen Glauben und Vernunft, sondern zwischen Glauben und Rationalismus besteht der Krieg auf Leben und Tod, wobei unter Rationalismus nicht bloss das flache Denken des *18. Jahrhunderts* verstanden wird, sondern ebensogut das titanische Vernunftdenken, das *deutscher Idealismus* heisst, und jenes, das wir aus der *griechischen Philosophie* als Erbe übernommen haben." (Emil Brunner, *Gott und sein Rebell*, Rowohlt, Hamburg, 1958, pp. 61–2.) One might ask : what is left standing if all this is knocked down? The "reason" of the mystics? The circularity of this kind of reasoning is striking. For if *"Reason as such"* (Vernunft als solche) is defined as *"to grasp itself in God"* (sich in Gott verstehen), everything that does not conform to this idea is excluded from "reason" not by means of concrete arguments but through an unestablished definitional assumption.

174 See in particular his views on our "duty to promote the *summum bonum*" which leads to postulating the existence of God, etc.

175 Hume, *A Treatise of Human Nature*, Book III, Part II, Section I.

176 "Hunger ist Hunger"—writes Marx later—"aber Hunger der sich durch gekochtes, mit Gabeln und Messer gegessnes Fleisch befriedigt, ist ein andrer Hunger als der rohes Fleisch mit Hilfe von Hand, Nagel und Zahn verschlingt. Nicht nur der Gegenstand der Konsumtion, sondern *auch die Weise der Konsumtion* wird daher durch die Produktion produziert, nicht nur objektiv, sondern auch subjektiv. *Die Produktion schafft also den Konsumenten.* Die Produktion liefert dem Bedürfnis nicht nur ein Material, sondern sie liefert dem Material auch ein Bedürfnis. Wenn die Konsumtion aus ihrer ersten Naturroheit und Unmittelbarkeit heraustritt—und das Verweilen in derselben wäre selbst noch das Resultat einer in der Naturroheit steckenden Produktion—so ist sie selbst als Trieb *vermittelt* durch den Gegenstand. Das Bedürfnis, das sie nach ihm fühlt, ist durch die Wahrnehmung desselben geschaffen. Der Kunstgegenstand—ebenso jedes andre Produkt—schafft ein kunstsinniges und schönheitsgenussfähiges Publikum. Die Produktion produziert daher nicht nur einen *Gegenstand für das Subjekt*, sondern auch ein *Subjekt für den Gegenstand*." (*Grundrisse der Kritik der politischen Ökonomie*, ed. cit., pp. 13–4.)

177 Anatole France, in his novel *Les dieux ont soif*, represents "Evariste Gamelin, peintre, élève de David," who, as a "citoyen d'un peuple libre, il charbonnait d'un trait vigoureux des Libertés, des Droits de l'Homme, des Constitutions Françaises, des Vertues républicaines, des Hercules populaires terrassant l'Hydre de la Tyrannie, et mettait dans toutes ces compositions toute l'ardeur de son patriotisme." France shows with great power not only that this painter becomes one of the most bloodthirsty leaders

of the Terror, but also that such a practical outcome is organically connected with the *inhuman abstractness* of Gamelin's ideals, with *"l'irrémédiable chasteté du peintre."* The number of similar examples from modern history is virtually endless, from the Inquisition to our own times.

178 "durch die Sozietät geschaffene Bedürfnisse", *Grundrisse der Kritik der politischen Ökonomie,* ed. cit., p. 15.

179 But not *necessarily* unconsciously. Under certain conditions this opposition may very well become a conscious one which asserts itself in the form of the cult of the senses, as "the only sensible thing to do". This, however, would not change the fact that such an alienated-self-consciousness is "being at home in unreason as unreason". (We are all familiar with attitudes of this kind in our own society.) If human development takes place in an alienated form, this cannot alter the alienated character of the negation of human development as such. It can only provide an explanation for the appearance of specific forms of alienated opposition to alienation.

180 The roots of this development reach back to the least into the eighteenth century.

181 Hume, Op. cit., Book III, Part II, Section II.

182 Kant's incorporation of the notion of scarcity into his philosophical system is not less problematic. In his reflections on philosophy of history he makes the moral improvement of mankind depend on the fictitious expectation that since, because of scarcity, the increasingly complex and expanding natural needs of man cannot be gratified, he will turn to morality.

183 Marx, *Economic and Philosophic Manuscripts of 1844,* p. 141. See also p. 140 on the power of money to turn things into their opposites.

184 "The difference between effective demand based on money and ineffective demand based on my need, my passion, my wish etc., is the difference between b e i n g and t h i n k i n g, between the imagined which e x i s t s merely within me and the imagined as it is for me outside me as a r e a l o b j e c t." Ibid., p. 140.

185 "Man makes *his life-activity itself the object of his will and of his consciousness.* He has conscious life-activity . . . it is only because he is a *species-being* that he is a *conscious-being,* i.e. that his own life is an object for him. Only because of that is *his* activity *free activity.*" Ibid., p. 74.

186 Ibid., p. 38. Elsewhere : "Whilst labour is man's active property . . . the landowner and the capitalist, who *qua* landowner and capitalist are merely privileged and idle goods, are everywhere superior to the worker and lay down the law to him." (Ibid., p. 28.) "In labour all the natural, spiritual and social variety of individual activity is manifested and is variously rewarded, whilst dead capital always shows the same face and is *indifferent to the r e a l individual activity.*" (Ibid., p. 23.)

187 Marx only objects to "direct, one-sided gratification"; to mere "having" as abstract *"possession"*, i.e. to a relation in which an object is *"ours"* only if it is an object of direct consumption, of mere *utilization*. In this kind of (one-sided), gratification man's manifold relations with the objects of his experience are extremely *impoverished* : only those relations are retained which are suitable to serve this kind of narrow, utilitarian, capitalistically motivated gratification. See also Section 5 of CHAPTER VI.

188 "Recognition of necessity" in its abstract form can be easily opposed to the actual needs of the real individual, and thus it can become a façade for the worst violations of freedom, in so far as the idea of "freedom" is postulated as a "conscious" acceptance of a (bureaucratic) necessity which is totally external to the "real human individual".

189 Keats, *Letter to Richard Woodhouse*, 27 October 1818.

190 See in particular two volumes : *K. Marx und F. Engels als Literaturhistoriker.* (Aufbau Verlag, Berlin, 1952) & *Probleme des Realismus* (Aufbau Verlag, Berlin, 1955).

191 Another aspect of this problem appears in the following criticism of Hegel : "my true religious existence is my existence in the philosophy of religion; my true political existence is my existence within the philosophy of right; my true natural existence, existence in the philosophy of nature; my true artistic existence, existence in the philosophy of art; my true human existence, my existence in philosophy. Likewise the true existence of religion, the state, nature, art, is the philosophy of religion, of nature, of the state and of art." *Economic and Philosophic Manuscripts of 1844*, p. 162.

192 "Only through the objectively unfolded richness of man's essential being is the richness of subjective human sensibility (a musical ear, an eye for beauty of form—in short, senses capable of human gratifications, senses confirming themselves as essential powers of man) either cultivated or brought into being. For not only the five senses but also the so-called mental senses—the practical senses (will, love, etc.)—in a word, human sense—the humanness of the senses—comes to be by virtue of its object, by virtue of humanized nature. The forming of the five senses is a labour of the entire history of the world down to the present." Ibid., p. 108.

193 The young Lukács strongly emphasized the contradictory character of such programme : "The admirers of 'form' have killed the form; the high priests of 'l'art pour l'art' have paralyzed art." (*Aesthetic Culture*, 1910).

194 "Die Konsumtion schafft den Trieb der Production". *Grundrisse der Kritik der politischen Ökonomie*, ed. cit., p. 13.

195 "in der Konsumtion werden die Produkte Gegenstände des Genusses, der individuellen Aneignung". Ibid., p. 10.

196 Marx-Engels, *The German Ideology* (International Publishers Co., New York, 1947), p. 22.

197 John Macmurray, "The Early Development of Karl Marx's Thought", in *Christianity and the Social Revolution*, edited by John Lewis, Karl Polányi, Donald K. Kitchin (Victor Gollancz Ltd., London, 1935), pp. 209–10.

198 Marx-Engels, *The German Ideology*, Edited with an Introduction by Roy Pascal (International Publishers Co., New York, 1947), p. 24.

199 Ibid., p. 68.

200 Ibid., p. 202.

201 Ibid., p. 68.

202 Marx-Engels, *Manifesto of the Communist Party*, In: *Selected Works*, ed. cit., Vol. I, p. 58.

203 Marx, Introduction to a *Critique of the Hegelian Philosophy of Right*, In: Marx-Engels *On Religion* (Moscow, 1957), pp. 41, 49 & 56–7.

204 Marx, *Capital*, ed. cit., Vol. III, p. 800.

205 Marx-Engels *On Religion*, ed. cit., p. 53.

206 THE GERMAN IDEOLOGY. "as long as man remains in natural society, that is, as long as a cleavage exists between the particular and the common interest, as long, therefore, as activity is not voluntarily, but naturally, divided, *man's own deed becomes an alien power opposed to him, which enslaves him instead of being controlled by him.*" (pp. 44–5.) "Just because individuals seek o n l y their particular interest, which for them does not coincide with their communal interest (in fact the general is the illusory form of communal life), the latter will be imposed on them as an interest *'alien' to them, and 'independent' of them,* as in its turn a particular, peculiar 'general' interest; or they themselves must remain within this discord, as in democracy." (p. 46) "with the communistic regulation of production (and, implicit in this, *the destruction of the alien relation between men and what they themselves produce*), the power of the relation of supply and demand is dissolved into nothing" (p. 47.) "In history up to the present it is certainly an empirical fact that separate individuals have, with the broadening of their activity into world-historical activity, become *more and more enslaved under a power alien to them*" (p. 49). "*conditions* which were previously abandoned to chance and *had won an independent existence over against the separate individuals* just because of their separation as individuals, and because of the necessity of their combination which had been determined by the division of labour, and through their separation *had become a bond alien to them*. . . . Thus, in imagination, individuals seem freer under the dominance of the bourgeoisie than before, because their conditions of life seem accidental; in reality, of course, *they are less free, because they are more subjected to the violence of things.*" (pp. 95–6.)

MANIFESTO OF THE COMMUNIST PARTY. "to command the labour of others" (i.e. to rule over alienated labour, ed. cit., p. 48.) "Communism deprives no man of the power to appropriate the products of society; all that it does is to deprive him of *the power to subjugate the labour of others* by means of such appropriation." (p. 49.)

WAGE-LABOUR AND CAPITAL. "To say that the most favourable condition for wage labour is the most rapid possible growth of productive capital is only to say that the more rapidly the working class increases and enlarges *the power that is hostile to it, the wealth that does not belong to it and that rules over it*, the more favourable will be the conditions under which it is allowed to labour anew at increasing bourgeois wealth, at enlarging the power of capital, content with forging for itself the golden chains by which the bourgeoisie drags it in its train." (*Selected Works*, Vol. I, p. 98.)

OUTLINES OF A CRITIQUE OF POLITICAL ECONOMY. (Grundrisse . . . Rohentwurf.) "The stress is not on being o b j e c t i f i e d, but on being *a l i e n a t e d*, externalized, estranged : on the fact that the immense objective power *set up by social labour*, as one of its moments, *over against itself*, does not belong to the worker but to the personified conditions of production, i.e. to capital. Inasmuch as at the standpoint of capital and wage-labour the production of this objective body of activity unfolds in opposition to direct labour-power—this process of objectification appears in fact as a *process of alienation* from the standpoint of labour and as *appropriation of alien labour* from the standpoint of capital—this perversion and overturning is r e a l, not i m a g i n e d : it does not merely exist in the mind of workers and capitalists. But obviously this process of overturning is only a h i s t o r i c a l necessity; it is a necessity for the development of the productive forces from a certain point of departure, or basis, but by no means an a b s o l u t e necessity of production as such; rather it is a disappearing necessity, and the result and end which is immanent in this process is the supersession of this basis and of this particular form of objectification. Bourgeois economists are so tied to the representations of a determinate historical stage of social development that in their eyes the necessary o b j e c t i f i c a t i o n of labour's social powers is inseparable from the latter's necessary *a l i e n a t i o n from living labour*. However, with the supersession of the d i r e c t character of living labour as merely i n d i v i d u a l—or as merely internally, or only externally universal—labour, with the constitution of the individuals' activity as *directly universal, i.e. s o c i a l activity*, the objective moments of production will be freed of this *form of alienation*; they will be constituted as property, as the *organic body of society* in which the individuals reproduce themselves as individuals, but *as social individuals*."

THEORIES OF SURPLUS VALUE. "The rich have taken possession of
all the conditions of production; [hence] the *a l i e n a t i o n
o f   t h e   c o n d i t i o n s   o f   p r o d u c t i o n,* which in their
simplest form are the natural elements themselves." (Part I,
Translated by Emile Burns, Moscow, without date, p. 335.)
"I n t e r e s t in itself expresses precisely the being of the conditions of labour as c a p i t a l in its social opposition to labour,
and its metamorphoses as personal powers over against labour.
It sums up the *a l i e n a t e d character of the conditions of
labour* in relation to the activity of the subject. It represents
the property of capital—i.e. mere capital-ownership—as a means
to appropriate the products of alien labour, as rule over alien
labour. But it represents this character of capital as something
that comes from *outside* the process of production, and not as
the result of the specific determination of this process of production itself."

CAPITAL. "the character of *independence and estrangement* which
the capitalist mode of production as a whole gives to the instruments of labour and to the product, as against the workman"
(Vol. I, p. 432.) "Since, before entering on the process, his own
labour has already been *alienated from himself* by the sale
of his labour-power, has been appropriated by the capitalist
and incorporated with capital, it must, during the process, be
realized in a product that does not belong to him. . . . The
labourer therefore constantly produces material, objective wealth,
but in the form of capital, of *an alien power that dominates
him;* and the capitalist as constantly produces labour-power, but
in the form of a subjective source of wealth, separated from the
objects in and by which it can alone be realized; in short
he produces the labourer, but as a wage-labourer." (Vol. I, pp.
570–71.) "within the capitalist system all methods for raising
the social productiveness of labour are brought about at the cost
of the individual labourer; all means for the development of production transform themselves into means of domination over,
and exploitation of, the producers; they mutilate the labourer
into a *fragment of a man,* degrade him to the level of an *appendage of a machine,* destroy every remnant of charm in his work
and turn it into a hated toil; they *estrange from him the intellectual potentialities* of the labour-process in the same proportion
as *science* is incorporated in it as an *independent power.*" (Vol. I,
p. 645.) "These means of production are in opposition to the
owner of the labour-power, being *property of another* (fremdes
Eigentum). On the other hand the seller of labour faces its
buyer as *labour-power of another* (fremde Arbeitskraft)" (Vol. II,
p. 29.) "This conception is so much the less surprising since it
appears to accord with fact, and since the relationship of capital
actually conceals the inner connection behind the *utter indifference, isolation and alienation* in which they place the labourer

vis-à-vis the means incorporating his labour." (Vol. III, p. 84.) "However, it is not only the *alienation* and indifference that arise between the labourer, the bearer of living labour, and the economical, i.e., rational and thrifty, use of the material conditions of his labour." (Vol. III, p. 86.) "Capital comes more and more to the fore as a social power . . . It becomes *an alienated, independent social power, which stands opposed to society as an object* (Sache), and as an object that is the capitalist's source of power." (Vol. III, p. 259.) "But under this system *separation of the producer from the means of production* (Entfremdung der Produktionsbedingung vom Produzenten) reflects an actual revolution in the mode of production itself." (Vol. III, p. 583.) "On the other hand, it is just as natural for the actual agents of production to feel completely at home in these *estranged and irrational forms* of capital—interest, land—rent, labour—wages, since these are precisely the forms of illusion in which they move about and find their daily occupation." (Vol. III, pp. 809–10.)

207 In *Revisionism, Essays on the History of Marxist Ideas*, Edited by L. Labedz (Allen & Unwin Ltd., London, 1962), p. 201.

208 See Daniel Bell, *The End of Ideology*, Revised Edition (The Free Press, New York, 1965), p. 433.

209 R. C. Tucker, *Philosophy and Myth in Karl Marx* (Cambridge University Press, 1961), p. 235. Tucker's book is worth a closer look as a characteristic ideological effort. His line of argument runs as follows. It is quite wrong to pay attention to Marx as an economist, sociologist or political thinker. His philosophy must be understood as a "moralism of the religious kind" (p. 21). As such it ought to be traced back to German philosophy—notably Kant, Hegel and Feuerbach—which displays a compulsive drive for "self-aggrandizement" and "self-infinitizing", i.e. a psychopathological aspiration of man to become God. We are told by Tucker that "What made Hegelianism irresistibly compelling to young Marx was the theme of man's soaring into the unlimited. *His own darkly proud and ambitious nature*, in which his worried father Heinrich discerned what he called a 'Faust-like spirit', was *the key to his response*" (p. 74). All this is said quite seriously. If Heinrich Marx discovers in his son a "Faust-like spirit", there must be something deeply wrong with the Faust-like spirit. "*The Faust-theme is pride* in the sense of *self-glorification* and the resulting search for *self-aggrandizement*." (p. 31.) "Marx's main work is an *inner drama projected as a social drama*." (p. 221)—but Marx deceives himself about its real nature. Just like Feuerbach—as Hegel before him—who did not realize that when he analysed religion he was in fact talking about "*the neurotic phenomenon of human self-glorification or pride*, and the estrangement of the self that results from it" (p. 93), Marx had no idea that in his presumed analysis of capitalism he unconsciously painted something resembling

Robert Louis Stevenson's *Dr. Jekyll and Mr. Hyde* : a purely psychological problem, related to an entirely "individual matter" (p. 240). "Being a suffering individual himself, who had *projected upon the outer world an inner drama of oppression*, he saw suffering everywhere" (p. 237); "*the inner conflict* of alienated man with himself became, *in Marx's mind*, a social conflict between 'labour' and 'capital', and the alienated species-self became the class-divided society. Self-alienation was *projected as a social phenomenon*, and Marx's *psychological original system* turned into his *apparently* sociological mature one," (p. 175).

All this can be summed up in one sentence : Marx was a neurotic who—after experiencing the inner drama of his own darkly proud and ambitious personality and after expressing it in his original psychological system—succumbed to total self-deception and mythically projected his inner drama on the outside world, misleading people into believing that alienation was not an entirely individual matter but primarily a social problem with possible social solutions to it.

Tucker's book is full of inconsistencies and self-contradictions. One of them concerns the question : "Two Marxisms or One". We get contradictory answers to this question : (1) there are two Marxisms : "Original Marxism" and "Mature Marxism"; (2) there is one Marxism only; the differences are merely terminological; e.g. " 'division of labour' becomes the comprehensive category of mature Marxism corresponding to the category 'self-alienation' in original Marxism" (p. 185).

The so-called "Original Marxism" is supposed to be an "openly-subjectivistic, psychological original system". The most conspicuous difference between the "original" and the "mature system" is, we are told, that "self-alienated man, who was the central subject of original Marxism, disappears from view in the later version" (p. 165). As regards the time of this alleged transformation we are given, again, contradictory answers. First we learn that it began "approximately with the statement of the Materialist Conception of History by Marx in *The German Ideology* (1845–6)" (p. 165) and that "Marx put forward this thoroughly 'socialized' version of Marxism in the immediate *aftermath* of his work on the manuscripts of 1844" (p. 166). A few pages later, however, we are surprised with this statement : "The transition to the seemingly 'dehumanized' mature Marxism actually occurred at that point *in the manuscripts of 1844* where Marx decided, uncertainly but irrevocably, that man's self-alienation could and should be grasped as a social relation 'of man to man' " (p. 175). This statement contradicts not only the previous assertions but also an earlier reference to Marx's essay *On the Jewish Question* (1843). There, after quoting Marx, Tucker added : "Marx concludes that the liberation of man from alienation in the state, unlike his liberation from religion, will require *a real social revolution*" (p. 105). Now he wants us to believe that *one year later*, in his "psychological system" of 1844, Marx's concern with alienation was not at all social but merely psychological, having in mind *"the conflict of an alienated generic man with himself"* (p. 173).

The only place where Tucker makes an attempt at substantiating with quotations from Marx his own assertion that "man" means non-social "generic man" in the *Manuscripts of 1844* is this : "Marx says that man is a natural being and must, *like any other natural being*, undergo a developmental process or act of becoming. This self-development process of man is the 'act of world history'. By 'man', moreover, Marx *following Feuerbach*, means mankind or the human species. The act of world history is the self-realization of man in this collective or generic sense. Marx, of course, does not overlook (any more than Hegel did) the existence of individuals as parts of and participants in the *collective life of the species*. But the self-developing being of whom he speaks in his system is *man writ large in the species*. 'The individual life and species-life of man are *not distinct*', he says, for 'the determinate individual is only a d e t e r m i n a t e species being'. The life of the individual is a microcosm of *the life of man on the generic scale*. Accordingly, the 'man' of whom Marx speaks in his manuscripts is *understood as man in general*." (pp. 129–30.)

Understood by whom? Certainly not by Marx, for he maintains, on every single point of this quotation, the exact opposite of Tucker's assertions. He does not think that man must "undergo" a developmental process *"like* any other natural being". On the contrary, he says that *unlike* all the other natural beings man develops himself—creates himself—through his labour in society, and thus he is the *only* being who has a *history* of his own. Also, as we have already seen, Marx does not *follow* Feuerbach in understanding by man "generic man" but, on the contrary, he radically departs from this abstraction and the dualism implicit in it. Nor does he believe that there is such a thing as the separate "collective life of the species" or "the life of man on the generic scale" (whatever that may mean). On the contrary, he insists that the difference amounts only to that of a "mode of existence" as reflected in human consciousness, and that the centre of reference of the essential unity between the individual and the species is the *"real i n d i v i d u a l* social being".

The passage from which Tucker quotes is full of expressions like "real community", "social fabric", "social being", "social life" and "social existence", but they are all carefully avoided by our learned author, in order to give a semblance of authenticity to the assertion according to which man means "generic man" in Marx's "psychological" and "openly subjectivistic original system". What Marx was actually concerned with in this passage (see *MSS of 1844*, pp. 104–5, and T. B. Bottomore's translation, pp. 158–9) was to point, in a direct criticism of abstract philosophizing, to the unity of thinking and being, the species and the individual, finding this unity, as we have seen, in the "real i n d i v i d u a l social being" who is at the same time "a determinate species being". He did not say that they are not *"distinct"*—otherwise how could they possibly form a dialectical *unity* : the lack of distinctness would amount to a simple *identity*. He only insisted that, since they are *not "different things"* (Bottomore's translation, p. 158), they should not be *opposed* to each other. In other words, this is a rejection of the Hegelian solution which declares that the individual has to accept alienation in his actual life, for the supersession of alienation (i.e. the realization of species-life) is to be achieved merely in *thought*, not in *being* : in a fictitious "transcendence" of alienation which leaves the real existence of the particular individual as alienated as before. This is what Marx was talking about, fully engaged in formulating the question of superseding alienation as a *social programme* centred around man as a *"real individual social being"*, in *opposition* to the generic character of abstract philosophizing on the one hand and to "the re-establishing of 'Society' as an abstraction vis-à-vis the individual" on the other.

There is no space to go on much longer with the discussion of the numerous inconsistencies and misinterpretations we find in Tucker's book. To the examples discussed so far we can only add his treatment of the problems of (1) the division of labour; and (2) "egoistic need" and "competition".

(1) We are told that Marx's concept of the division of labour is nothing but a "translation of the original psychological term : self-alienation" into the mystified "apparently sociological" terms of "mature Marxism". This interpretation is untenable not only because "self-alienation" for Marx has never been a merely phychological term but also because "division of labour" played an extremely important part, as we have seen, in the *Economic and Philosophic Manuscripts of 1844*.

(2) The concepts of "money worship" and "egoistic need" are treated as unconscious projections of the psychological urge for "self-aggrandizement", and it is stated that in *Capital*—as a *reversal* of Marx's earlier position—competition is introduced as the source of the "acquisitive mania". But, we are told, this is a big mistake because "The whole system instantly collapses without the werewolf hunger for surplus value as a primary underlying postulate" (pp. 216–7).

One might ask : whose system? Marx's system or Tucker's psychiatric caricature of it? To get the answer we should read the footnote on p. 217 : "As mentioned earlier (p. 138), Marx stated in the manuscripts of 1844, that the only wheels that set political economy in motion are greed and the war among the greedy—competition. *Now* he suggests that the latter sets the former in motion, or that the war is the cause of the greed. He must have been uneasily aware that *the whole structure rested on the postulate of infinite greed* as the driving force of capitalist production. To suggest that this could be derived from the competitive mechanism itself was a way of minimizing the total dependence of the system upon a highly questionable postulate, and at the same time of reinforcing the postulate." As a matter of fact at the place referred to by Tucker, Marx is talking about the inability of bourgeois political economy to go beyond external appearances and get to the causes. (See *MSS of 1844*, p. 68. In Bottomore's even clearer version : "The only moving forces which political economy recognizes are a v a r i c e and the w a r b e t w e e n the a v a r i c i o u s, c o m p e t i t i o n." p. 121.) And there are many places in the *Manuscripts of 1844* where Marx makes it amply clear that the accumulation of capital (and thus "greed" coupled with it) is the *necessary result* of competition, not its cause.

The alleged contradiction, therefore, simply does not exist in Marx. He is not concerned in the disputed passage with the *"competitive mechanism"* of capitalism but with its *distorted reflection* in the writings of bourgeois political economy. There is no trace of a psychologistic treatment of greed and competition in the *Manuscripts of 1844* but, on the contrary, the clearest possible statement of Marx's rejection of the bourgeois notion of "egoistic man" (who is supposed to be selfish "by nature"). Thus the *whole structure* of Tucker's argument rests on a *complete misunderstanding* of the passage which is supposed to establish his whole case. Without *his* postulate of *"infinite greed"* (of which even in his own mistranslated version of Marx's words there is no trace) this whole amateurish psychiatry-centred construction collapses.

To sum up : reading the evidence presented by Tucker in support of his psychiatric hypothesis, we find that the whole construction is based on distortions, mistranslations, and sometimes even on a complete misunderstanding of the passages referred to. Moreover, this book is full of inconsistencies and self-contradictions. Thus the conclusion is inescapable : Marx's non-social, openly subjectivistic, psychological system is a myth which exists only in Tucker's imagination. *Philosophy and Myth in Karl Marx* is constructed around the dogmatic assertion according to which the fundamental human relationship is the individual's *"intra*-personal" relation to himself, and the relations of *men to men* are secondary, derivative, etc. No attempt is made to prove this assertion, or even to put forward a single argument in its favour. It is simply assumed by Tucker as self-evident and as the absolute standard of all evaluation. Accordingly, alienation is a merely individual matter : *"No matter how many in-*

dividual men may belong to this category, it is always an *individual matter.*" (p. 240.) Thus the "supersession" of alienation must also be confined to the individual's imagination : "Only so long as an alienated man can *find in himself* the courage to recognize that the 'alien power' against which he rebels is *a power within him,* that the inhuman force which makes his life a *forced labour* is *a force of the self,* that the 'alien, hostile, powerful man' is an *inner man,* the absolute being of his *imagination,* has he hope of transcending his alienation" (pp. 241–2). Here we can also see why this book is, despite its almost unbelievable intellectual standard, a favourite of men like Daniel Bell : for in this kind of a "radical critique of society" no mention is ever made of capitalism in a negative sense. The "radical critique of society" turns out to be a critique of the "inner man" of the isolated individual who finds in himself alone the (merely psychological) causes of his own "self-alienation", insisting that even the "forced labour" to which he is subjected under the capitalistically reified social relations of production is only "a force of the self", a feature of his own "imagination".

210 D. Bell, *The End of Ideology,* ed. cit., pp. 365–6.
211 Overwhelming in *all* works of Marx, including the tendentiously misrepresented *Economic and Philosophic Manuscripts of 1844.*
212 D. Bell, *The End of Ideology,* ed. cit., p. 362.
213 Characteristically enough we read in Bell's book : "The most interesting discussion of the thought of young Marx can be found in the recent study by Hannah Arendt, *The Human Condition.*" (ed. cit., p. 433.)
214 Ibid., p. 364.
215 In Marx-Engels *On Religion,* ed. cit., p. 42.
216 MEWE, Vol. 27, p. 420.
217 MEWE, Vol. 27, p. 425.
218 Marx-Engels, *The German Ideology* (Lawrence & Wishart, London, 1965), p. 57.
219 Marx, *Wage-Labour and Capital,* In Marx-Engels, *Selected Works,* ed. cit., Vol. I, pp. 82–3.
220 This is why we have to read with caution Heinemann's assertion that "Existentialism is in all its forms a philosophy of crisis. It expresses the crisis of man openly and directly, whereas other schools, like that of the Logical Positivists, express it indirectly and unconsciously. For this reason, the fact of estrangement in its enormous complexity and manysidedness became central with them." (F. H. Heinemann, *Existentialism and the Modern Predicament,* Adam & Charles Black, London, 1953, p. 167.) That existentialism is a philosophy of crisis may be true, abstractly speaking. However, the "crisis of man" is always historically specific. In existentialism itself, it was the changing nature of this crisis that gave rise to the very different forms of the movement. It is highly inaccurate to say that the category of aliena-

tion is *central* in existentialism as a whole. E. Mounier is much
more accurate when he writes: "One cannot discuss fundamental estrangement from a Christian standpoint. . . . This concept of estrangement, which, from the Christian standpoint so categorically denies the Incarnation of the Transcendent Being in
human being, is, by contrast, a prominent feature of the Atheist
branch of existentialism." (*Existentialist Philosophies. An Introduction.* Translated by Eric Blow, Rockliff, London, 1948,
pp. 35–6. Mounier distinguishes between "fundamental estrangement" and "accidental estrangement". This latter is present, in
various degrees, in the different forms of Christian existentialism
as well.) The general conceptual framework of a philosophical
trend is modified according to the particular socio-historical situations in which the philosophers conceive their works. There
are very great differences in this respect among the various trends
of existentialism. In Kierkegaard's writings "alienation" is rather
peripheral, as compared to those of Sartre; and there are existentialists—like Jaspers and Gabriel Marcel, for instance—who are
situated somewhere between the two extremes. Besides, even
when the notion of alienation plays an important part in the
philosopher's system, one should not ignore the differences in the
social significance of its various interpretations. In the 'thirties
and after the war the concept of alienation started to play a
greater rôle in the various existentialist approaches to contemporary problems, reflecting a more dynamic socio-historical
situation. Mounier himself—the principal figure of existential
"personalism"—reformulated in this sense the programme of his
movement shortly after the war, insisting that "Le personnalisme
est un effort continu pour chercher les zones où une victoire
décisive sur toutes les formes d'oppression et d'aliénation,
économique, sociale ou idéologique, peut déboucher sur une
véritable libération de l'homme." (In "L'Esprit", January 1946,
p. 13.)

221 See Iring Fetscher, *Marxismusstudien.* In "Soviet Survey", No.
33 (July-September, 1960), p. 88.

222 Jean Hyppolite, *Études sur Marx et Hegel* (Librairie Marcel
Rivière & Cie., Paris, 1955), pp. 101–2.

223 "It is superfluous to add that men are not free to choose their
productive forces—which are the basis of all their history—for every productive force is an acquired force, the product of former activity. The productive forces are therefore
the result of practical human energy; but this energy is itself
conditioned by the circumstances in which men find themselves,
by the productive forces already won, by the *social form* which
exists before they do, which they do not create, which is the
product of the former generation. Because of this simple fact
that every succeeding generation finds itself in possession of the
productive forces won by the previous generation, which serve

it as the *raw material* for new production, an *inter-connection* arises in human history, there is a history of humanity which has become all the more a history of humanity since the productive forces of man and therefore his social relations have been extended. Hence it necessarily follows : the *social* history of men is never anything but the history of their *individual development*, whether they are conscious of it or not. Their material relations are the basis of all their relations. These material relations are only the *necessary forms* in which their *material* and *individual* activity is realised." *Letter to Annenkov*, (28 Dec. 1846), in Marx *The Poverty of Philosophy* (Martin Lawrence Ltd., without date), Appendix, pp. 152-3.

224   See the Marxian expressions : "the beginning of *real history*"— i.e. a form of society in which human beings are in control of their life—in contrast to *"prehistory"* characterized by the subjection of men to the alienated social relations of production.

225   Aristotle, *Ethics*, Book I, Chapter 2.

226   Ibid., Book VII, Chapter 3.

227   We should remember in this connection not only the countless works which explicitly refer to "man's alienation" but also the more mediated expressions of this problematics—in particular the "inwardness" of the greater part of the artistic creeds in the twentieth century. The latter is well illustrated by Max Jacob's words : *"Le monde dans un homme; tel est le poète moderne"* ("the world in one man; that is the modern poet"—*L'art poètique*). And Pierre Reverdy's words are equally significant; according to him "Le poète est poussé à créer par le besoin constant et obsédant de *sonder le mystère de son être intérieur"* *(Le gant de crin)*.

228   Jacob Burckhardt, *The Civilization of the Reniassance in Italy* (Phaidon Press, London, 1965), p. 81.

229   D. G. Ritchie, *Natural Rights* (London, 1916), p. 7.

230   Even when this process of reification is accomplished, the "natural liberty" of the individual is willingly suspended from time to time : for instance in the case of wars in which the physical or civic survival of a whole community is at stake. In such situations the individual's social relations acquire the cohesive force of a "natural order". Individual liberty and "autonomy" then does not seem to be violated even by the most drastic interference of society, or it seems entirely justified that individual liberty *should* be so violated. The fiction of a "natural right" is shelved for a while, to be brought into play again when the war is over and "consumer society" newly embarks on its "natural course".

231   Paracelsus, *Leben und Lebensweisheit in Selbstzeugnissen* (Reclam Verlag, Leipzig, 1956), p. 132.

232   Paracelsus, *Selected Writings* (Translated by Norbert Guterman, Routledge & Kegan Paul, London, 1951), pp. 176-7.

233   Ibid., p. 189.

234 Ibid., p. 183.
235 "Der selig Weg der Nahrung des Wirtschaftslebens steht allein in der Arbeit und nit in müssig gehn. So wird hiermit all die Nahrung, so nit mit Arbeit gewunnen wird, verworfen und entsetzt. . . . Und unser Arbeit soll gewunnen sein je eins dem andern, und dem der nit arbeitet soll auch genommen werden, was er hat, uff dass er arbeite." Paracelsus, *Leben und Lebensweisheit in Selbstzeugnissen*, ed. cit., p. 134.
236 Hannah Arendt, *The Human Condition*, 2nd ed., (Doubleday Anchor Books, New York, 1959), p. 297.
237 Gabriel Marcel, *Être et avoir* (Paris, 1935), p. 254.
238 Martin Heidegger, *Being and Time* (Translated by John Macquarrie and Edward Robinson, Basil Blackwell, Oxford, 1967), pp. 164–7.
239 David Riesman (with Nathan Glazer and Reuel Denney), *The Lonely Crowd. A Study of the Changing American Character.* (Doubleday Anchor Books, New York, 1953), p. 346.
240 Ibid., p. 349.
241 Ibid., p. 348.
242 Attila József, *A szocializmus bölcselete* (The Philosophy of Socialism), 1934.
243 Lenin, *On the tasks of the People's Commissariat for Justice under the New Economic Policy*, In *Collected Works*, Vol. 36, pp. 562–4.
244 *Quotations from Chairman Mao Tse-tung* (Peking, 1967), p. 203.
245 Lenin, *Collected Works*, Vol. 33, pp. 428–9.
246 Mao Tse-tung, *Report on an Investigation of the Peasant Movement in Hunan*, In *Selected Works*, Vol. I, p. 23.
247 Mao Tse-tung, *On Coalition Government*, In *Selected Works*, Vol. III, p. 257.
248 Mao Tse-tung, *We must Learn to Do Economic Work*, In *Selected Works*, Vol. III, p. 243.
249 Quoted in *Revolution in a Revolution* by Régis Debray (Penguin ed.), p. 125.
250 Lenin, *Collected Works*, Vol. 27, pp. 345–6.
251 Paracelsus, *Selected Writings*, ed. cit., p. 179.
252 Hans Heinz Holz, Leo Kofler, Wolfgang Abendroth, Theo Pinkus (editor), *Gespräche mit Georg Lukács* (Rowohlt Verlag, Hamburg, 1967), p. 21.
253 Engels, *Anti Dühring* (Moscow, 1959), pp. 435–8. Quoted by Lenin in his *Materialism and Empirio-Criticism*, In *Collected Works*, Vol. 14, pp. 133–4.
254 Heidegger, op. cit., p. 220.
255 Ibid., p. 223.
256 Ibid., p. 222.
257 Lukács, *Geschichte und Klassenbewusstsein*, ed. cit., p. 93. (Quotation translated by G. H. R. Parkinson.)
258 Antonio Gramsci, *The Formation of Intellectuals*, In *The Modern*

Prince and Other Writings (Translated by Louis Marks, Lawrence and Wishart, London, 1957), p. 121.

259 *Über die ästhetische Erziehung des Menschen, in einer Reihe von Briefen*, English edition in the volume *Schiller: Essays, Aesthetical and Philosophical* (G. Bell & Sons, London, 1884).

260 Lukács. *Zur Ästhetik Schillers*, In G. L. *Werke*, Vol. 10, (Luchterhand, Neuwied u. Berlin, 1969), p. 47.

261 Translated by E. P. Arnold-Forster.

262 Paracelsus, *Selected Writings*, ed. cit., p. 181.

263 Adam Smith, *Lectures on Justice, Police, Revenue, and Arms* (1763). In *A. Smith's Moral and Political Philosophy*, edited by Herbert W. Schneider (Hafner Publishing Co., New York, 1948), pp. 318–9.

264 Ibid., p. 321.

265 Ibid., pp. 319–20.

266 Robert Owen, *A New View of Society and Other Writings*, Introduction by G. D. H. Cole, Everyman Edition, p. 124.

267 Ibid., pp. 88–9.

268 Translated by E. P. Arnold-Forster.

269 R. Owen, op. cit., p. 124.

270 M. V. C. Jeffreys, *Personal Values in the Modern World* (Penguin, 1962), p. 79.

271 The extent of this crisis is well illustrated by the fact that hundreds of volumes have been published on this subject within the last few years all over the world.

272 Noam Chomsky, *The Responsibility of Intellectuals*, In *The Dissenting Academy*, Edited by Theodore Roszak (Penguin, 1969, First published in the USA by Random House, 1967), p. 240.

273 There are, of course, various other methods of "absorption of surplus". See Chapters 4–7 of *Monopoly Capital* by Paul A. Baran and Paul M. Sweezy (Monthly Review Press, New York and London, 1966).

274 R. Heilbroner, *The Future as History* (Harper & Row, New York, 1960), p. 133. Quoted in S. M. Rosen, *Keynes Without Gadflies*, in *The Dissenting Academy*, p. 79.

275 Ibid., p. 81.

276 See E. Mandel, *Where is America Going?* "New Left Review", No. 54, pp. 3–15.

277 Gramsci, op. cit., p. 125.

278 R. Owen, op. cit., p. 125.

279 In *principle* it should be feasible to rationalize capitalist production to the point at which *all* individual bourgeois interests are *completely* subordinated to the interests of the class as a whole, in the framework of a "comprehensively planned" capitalist system of production. In reality, however, such a "rationalization" is a mere wishful thinking, although some people—e.g. J. K. Galbraith—insist that it is being accomplished and thus the "two systems" effectively "converge" into a "techno-

structure", leaving merely some anachronistic "ideological differences" to be disposed of. (See J. K. Galbraith, *The New Industrial State*—Hamish Hamilton, London, 1967—and Ralph Miliband's critical review of it in "The Socialist Register", 1968, pp. 215–29.) Significantly enough the "President's Commission on National Goals" in its conclusion could come up only with the bombastically inflated platitudes of bourgeois liberalism. E.g. : "Our deepest convictions impel us to foster individual fulfilment. We wish each one to achieve the promise that is in him. We wish each one to be worthy of a free society, and capable of strengthening a free society." (*Goals for Americans*, p. 81. Quoted in Baran & Sweezy, *Monopoly Capital*, ed. cit., p. 306.) Reading between the lines of this hypocritical rhetoric one can see that the ideal of "individual fulfilment" is circumscribed by the aim of "strengthening a free society" (i.e. capitalism), and the "promise in each individual" is recognized as legitimate only if it is "worthy of a free society", i.e. only if it is "capable of strengthening" capitalism. Thus the "national goals" in a capitalist society cannot be other than *immediate individual fulfilment* in agreement with the requirements of the capitalist system of production. In other words the capitalist system of production cannot function unless it can supply immediate individual fulfilment to the members of the dominating interest groups. It is this factor that circumscribes the powers of the bourgeois state as well. For no matter what kind of ideas John F. Kennedy might have had in mind at the time when he assembled his "Brains-Trust"—for the purpose of elaborating "national goals" and "national policies" capable of furthering the interests of U.S. capitalism *in general*—in reality only those policies could be adopted which were in close agreement with the *immediate interests* of the "individual fulfilment" of the members of the dominating capitalist groups. The bourgeois state watches carefully over a specific structure of relations in which the immediate economic interests of the most powerful groups predominate. To postulate a "comprehensively planned and rationalized" capitalist society is therefore out of the question. (Apart from being a contradiction in terms economically speaking.) Only the *community as a whole* is capable of assuming the functions of *"the universal capitalist"*. Such a form of society presupposes *"l a b o u r as a state in which every person is put and c a p i t a l as the acknowledged universality and power of the community."* (Marx, *Economic and Philosophic Manuscripts of 1844*, p. 100.) No bourgeois state is compatible with a system of relations of this kind. To imagine that the "universality" of capitalist "rationalization" can be achieved merely by eliminating competition among the capitalists by means of some kind of a "super techno-structure" is elementary muddle-headedness grown out of the soil of wishful thinking. Those who are guilty of it forget (or ignore) that the *basic contradiction* of capitalist society is not between capitalists and capitalists but between *capital and labour*.

280　Marx, *Critique of the Gotha Program*, in *Selected Works*, (ed. cit.,) Vol. II, p. 31.

281　S. M. Rosen, op. cit., p. 83.

282　D. Bell, op. cit., pp. 405–6.

283　"The power of American fighting men is visible in forty-eight countries, the power of our investors is felt in several dozen more." Paul Booth, *The Crisis of Cold War Ideology*, in *The New Student Left*, ed. by Mitchell Cohen & Dennis Hale (Beacon Press, Boston, 1967), p. 323.

284　Bell, op. cit., p. 405.

285　Chomsky, op. cit., pp. 241–2.

286　Of course such a war can *happen*, but its actual planning and active preparation in the open cannot function as a vital internal stabilizer.

BIBLIOGRAPHY

Abbagnano, Nicola (et al.), *Studi sulla dialettica*, Torino, 1958.
Acton, H. B., *The Illusion of the Epoch*, London, 1955.
Adams, H. P., *Karl Marx in His Earlier Writings*, London, 1940.
Adorno, T. W., Horkheimer, Max, *Dialektik der Aufklärung*, Amsterdam, 1947.
Adorno, T. W., *Prismen. Kulturkritik und Gesellschaft*, Frankfurt/M., 1955.
Adorno, T. W., *Aspekte der Hegelschen Philosophie*, Berlin-Frankfurt/M., 1957.
Adorno, T. W., *Drei Studien zu Hegel*, Frankfurt/M., 1963.
Adorno, T. W., *Negative Dialektik*, Frankfurt/M., 1966.
Althusser, Louis, *Pour Marx*, Paris, 1965.
Althusser, Louis (et al.), *Lire le Capital*, Paris, 1965.
Annali dell'Istituto Feltrinelli, Milano 1963. (Dedicated to the analysis of "Left Hegelianism" and of Marx's intellectual development. Studies by Pierre Aycoberry, Bronislaw Baczko, Emile Bottigelli, Gian Mario Bravo, Claudio Cesa, Auguste Cornu, Jacques Droz, Kurt Koszyk, Sergio Carlo Landucci, Vera Macháčková, Alexandre Malych, Wolfgang Mönke, Karl Obermann, Guido Oldrini, Edmund Silberner, Jerzy Szacky, G. A. van den Bergh van Eysinga, Andrej Walicki.) Edited by Giuseppe Del Bo.
Annali dell'Istituto Feltrinelli, Milano 1965. (Dedicated to the young Marx, with studies and bibliographies by Bert Andréas, Rolf Bauermann, Gerhard Drekonja, Camillo Dresner, Ivan Dubský, Walter Euchner, Iring Fetscher, Roger Garaudy, Lucien Goldmann, Enrique Gonzalez Pedrero, Veljko Korać, Henri Lefèbvre, L. M. Lombardi Satriani, György Márkus, István Mészáros, Ambrus Oltványi, John O'Neill, Titos Patrikios, Adam Schaff, Rudolf Schlesinger, Andrija B. Stojković, Shiro Tohara, Predrag Vranicki.) Edited by Giuseppe Del Bo.
Antoni, Carlo, *Considerazioni su Hegel e Marx*, Napoli, 1946.
Arendt, Hannah, *The Human Condition*, Chicago, 1958.
Aron, Raymond, *Dix-huit leçons sur la société industrielle*, Paris, 1962.
Asveld, Paul, *La pensée religieuse du jeune Hegel. Liberté et aliénation*, Louvain-Paris, 1953.
Avineri, Shlomo, *The Social and Political Thought of Karl Marx*, Cambridge, 1968.

Axelos, Kostas, *Marx penseur de la technique. De l'aliénation de l'homme à la conquête du monde*, Paris, 1961.

Baas, Emile, *L'humanisme marxiste. Essai d'analyse critique*, Colmar, 1947.

Badaloni, Nicola, *Marxismo come storicismo*, Milano, 1962.

Banfi, Antonio, *L'uomo copernicano*, Milano, 1950.

Barth, Hans, *Wahrheit und Ideologie*, Zürich, 1945.

Bell, Daniel, *The End of Ideology*, New York, 1961.

Bekker, Konrad, *Marx' philosophische Entwicklung, sein Verhältnis zu Hegel*, Zürich, 1940.

Benjamin, Walter, *Das Kunstwerk im Zeitalter seiner technischen Reproduzierbarkeit*, Frankfurt/M., 1955.

Berlin, Isaiah, *Karl Marx: His Life and Environment*, London, 1960.

Bigo, Pierre, *Marxisme et humanisme. Introduction à l'oeuvre économique de Karl Marx*, Paris, 1953.

Bloch, Ernst, *Subjekt-Objekt*, I-III., Berlin, 1952-1959.

Bloch, Ernst, *Das Prinzip Hoffnung*, Berlin, 1954.

Bloch, Ernst, *Naturrecht und menschliche Würde*, Frankfurt/M., 1961.

Bobbio, Norberto, *Prefazione* a K. Marx *Manoscritti economico-filosofici del 1844*, Torino, 1949.

Bockmühl, K., *Leiblichkeit und Gesellschaft. Studien zur Religions-kritik und Anthropologie von Feuerbach und Marx*, Göttingen, 1961.

Bottigelli, Emile, *Présentation* à K. Marx *Manuscrits de 1844*, Paris, 1962.

Bottomore, T. B., *Introduction* to Karl Marx *Early Writings*, London, 1963.

Buber, Martin, *Le problème de l'homme*, Paris, 1962.

Caire, Guy, *L'aliénation dans les oeuvres de jeunesse de Karl Marx*, Aix-En-Provence, 1957.

Calvez, Jean-Yves, *La pensée de Karl Marx*, Paris, 1956.

Cantimori, Delio, *Interpretazioni e studi intorno al pensiero di Marx e di Engels, 1919-1939*, Pisa, 1947.

Carbonara, Cleto, *Materialismo storico e idealismo critico*, Napoli, 1947.

Cases, Cesare, *Marxismo e neopositivismo*, Torino, 1958.

Caute, David, *Essential Writings of Karl Marx*, London, 1967.

Cerroni, Umberto, *Marx e il diritto moderno*, Roma, 1962.

Chatelet, Fr., *Logos et Praxis. Recherches sur la signification théorique du marxisme*, Paris, 1962.

Chiodi, Pietro, *Sartre e il marxismo*, Milano, 1965.

Colletti, Lucio, *Il marxismo e Hegel*, Bari, 1969.

Cooper, David (ed.), *The Dialectics of Liberation*, London, 1968.

Cornforth, Maurice, *Dialectical Materialism*, London, 1954.

Cornu, Auguste, *Karl Marx. De l'hégélianisme au matérialisme historique*, Paris, 1934.

Cornu, Auguste, *Karl Marx et la pensée moderne*, Paris, 1948.

Cornu, Auguste, *Essai de critique marxiste*, Paris, 1951.

Cottier, Georges M., *L'athéisme du jeune Marx. Ses origins hégéliennes*, Paris, 1956.

Dahrendorf, Ralf, *Marx in Perspektive. Die Idee des Gerechten im Denken von Karl Marx*, Hannover, 1952.

Dal Pra, Mario, *Il pensiero filosofico di Marx dal 1835 al 1848*, Milano, 1959.

Dal Pra, Mario, *La dialettica in Marx*, Bari, 1965.

Dawydow, J. N., *Freiheit und Entfremdung*, Berlin, 1964.

Della Volpe, Galvano, *La teoria marxista dell'emancipazione umana. Saggio sulla trasmutazione marxista dei valori*, Messina, 1945.

Della Volpe, Galvano, *Per la teoria di un umanismo positivo. Studi e documenti sulla dialettica materialistica*, Bologna, 1949.

Della Volpe, Galvano, *Rousseau e Marx e altri saggi di critica materialistica*, Roma, 1957.

Della Volpe, Galvano, *Logica come scienza positiva*, Messina-Firenze, 1956.

Dunayevskaya, Raya, *Marxism and Freedom from 1776 until Today*, New York, 1958.

Dupré, Louis, *The Philosophical Foundations of Marxism*, New York, 1966.

Easton, L. D., and Guddat, K. H., *Introduction to Writings of the Young Marx on Philosophy and Society*, New York, 1967.

Fallot, Jean, *Marx et le machinisme*, Paris, 1966.

Fetscher, Iring, *Von Marx zur Sowietideologie*, Frankfurt/M.-Berlin-Bonn, 1957.

Fortini, Franco, *La verifica dei poteri*, Milano, 1965.

Friedrich, Manfred, *Philosophie und Ökonomie bei jungem Marx*, Berlin, 1960.

Fromm, Erich, *Marx's Concept of Man*, New York, 1961.

Fromm, Erich (ed.), *Socialist Humanism*, Garden City, 1965.

Gabel, Joseph, *La fausse conscience*, Paris, 1962.

Garaudy, Roger, *Humanisme marxiste*, Paris, 1957.

Garaudy, Roger, *Perspectives de l'homme. Existentialisme, pensée catholique, marxisme*, Paris, 1959.

Garaudy, Roger, *Qu'est-ce que la morale marxiste*, Paris, 1963.

Garaudy, Roger, *Karl Marx*, Paris, 1964.

Godelier, Maurice, *Rationalité et irrationalité en economie*, Paris, 1966.

Goldmann, Lucien, *Sciences humaines et philosophie*, Paris, 1952

Goldmann, Lucien, *Recherches dialectiques*, Paris, 1959.

Gorz, André, *La morale de l'histoire*, Paris, 1959.

Gorz, André, *Stratégie ouvrière et néocapitalisme*, Paris, 1964.

Gorz, André, *Le socialisme difficile*, Paris, 1967.

Gramsci, Antonio, *La formazione dell'uomo* (ed. by G. Urbani), Roma, 1967.

Grégoire, Franz, *Aux sources de la pensée de Marx: Hegel, Feuerbach*, Paris, 1947.

Gurvitch, Georges, *La vocation actuelle de la sociologie*, Paris, 1950.

Gurvitch, Georges, *Dialectique et sociologie*, Paris, 1962.

Habermas, Jürgen, *Theorie und Praxis*, Neuwied/Rhein, 1963.

Hauser, Arnold, *Philosophie der Kunstgeschichte*, München, 1958.

Hauser, Arnold, *Der Manierismus. Die Krise der Renaissance und der Ursprung der modernen Kunst*, München, 1964.

Havadtöy, Alexander, *Arbeit und Eigentum in den Schriften des jungen Marx*, Basel, 1951.

Heinemann, F. H., *Existentialism and the Modern Predicament*, London, 1953.

Heiss, Robert, *Wesen und Formen der Dialektik*, Köln-Berlin, 1959.

Heiss, Robert, *Die grossen Dialektiker des 19. Jahrhunderts: Hegel, Kierkegaard, Marx*, Köln-Berlin, 1963.

Hillman, G., *Marx und Hegel. Von der Spekulation zur Dialektik*, Frankfurt/M., 1966.

Hobsbawm, Eric, *Introduction* to Karl Marx *Pre-Capitalist Economic Formations*, London, 1964.

Hommes, Jakob, *Der technische Eros. Das Wesen der materialistischen Geschichtsauffassung*, Freiburg, 1955.

Hook, Sidney, *From Hegel to Marx: Studies in the Intellectual Development of Karl Marx*, New York, 1936.

Hyppolite, Jean, *Introduction à la philosophie de l'histoire de Hegel*, Paris, 1948.

Hyppolite, Jean, *Etudes sur Marx et Hegel*, Paris, 1955.

Kaegi, Paul, *Genesis des historischen Materialismus*, Zürich-Wien, 1965.

Kamenka, Eugene, *The Ethical Foundations of Marxism*, London, 1962.

Klages, Helmut, *Technischer Humanismus. Philosophie und Soziologie der Arbeit bei Marx*, Stuttgart, 1964.

Kofler, Leo, *Geschichte und Dialektik. Zur Methodenlehre der dialektischen Geschichtsbetrachtung*, Hamburg, 1955.

Kofler, Leo, *Marxistischer oder ethischer Sozialismus*, Bovenden, 1955.
Korsch, Karl, *Marxismus und Philosophie*, 2nd ed., Leipzig, 1930.
Korsch, Karl, *Karl Marx*, London, 1938.

Labedz, Leopold (ed.), *Revisionism*, London, 1962.
Lacroix, Jean, *Marxisme, existentialisme, personnalisme*, Paris, 1949.
Landshut, Siegfried, *Kritik der Soziologie*, Neuwied-Berlin, 1969.
Lapin, N. J., *Der junge Marx im Spiegel der Literatur*, Berlin, 1965.
Lefèbvre, Henri, *Pour connaître la pensée de Karl Marx*, Paris, 1956.
Lefèbvre, Henri, *Sociologie de Marx*, Paris, 1966.
Leff, Gordon, *The Tyranny of Concepts: a Critique of Marxism*, London, 1961.
Lewis, John, *The Life and Teaching of Karl Marx*, London, 1965.
Lichtheim, George, *Marxism: An Historical and Critical Study*, London, 1961.
Lichtheim, George, *Marxism in Modern France*, London, 1966.
Lobkovicz, Nicholas, *Theory and Practice from Aristotle to Marx*, Notre Dame, 1967.
Löwith, Karl, *Von Hegel zu Nietzsche. Der Revolutionäre Bruch im Denken des 19. Jehrhunderts. Marx und Kierkegaard*, Stuttgart, 1950.
Lukács, Georg, *Geschichte und Klassenbewusstsein*, Berlin, 1923.
Lukács, Georg, *Moses Hess und die Probleme der idealistischen Dialektik*, Leipzig, 1926.
Lukács, Georg, *Der junge Hegel. Über die Beziehungen von Dialektik und Ökonomie*, Zürich-Wien, 1948.
Lukács, Georg, *Die Zerstörung der Vernunft*, Berlin, 1954.
Lukács, Georg, *Zur philosophischen Entwicklung des jungen Marx*, in : "Deutsche Zeitschrift für Philosophie", 1954.
Lukács, Georg, *Gespräche mit Georg Lukács*, Hamburg, 1967.

MacIntyre, Alasdair, *Marxism: an Interpretation*, London, 1953.
Macmurray, John, *The Early Development of Karl Marx's Thought*, in : "Christianity and the Social Revolution" (ed. by John Lewis, Karl Polányi, Donald Kitchin), London, 1935.
Maihofer, Werner, *Demokratie im Sozialismus. Recht und Staat im Denken des jungen Marx*, Frankfurt/M., 1968.
Mallet, Serge, *La nouvelle classe ouvrière*, Paris, 1963.
Mandel, Ernest, *La formation de la pensée économique de Karl Marx*, Paris, 1967.
Mannucci, Cesare, *La società di massa. Analisi di moderne teorie sociopolitiche*, Milano, 1967.
Marcuse, Herbert, *Transzendentaler Marxismus*, in : "Die Gesellschaft", 1930.

Marcuse, Herbert, *Neue Quellen zur Grundlegung des historischen Materialismus*, in : "Die Gesellschaft", 1932.

Marcuse, Herbert, *Reason and Revolution*, Oxford, 1941.

Marcuse, Herbert, *Eros and Civilization*, Boston, 1955.

Marcuse, Herbert, *One-Dimensional Man*, London, 1964.

Marcuse, Herbert, *An Essay on Liberation*, London, 1969.

Marek, Franz, *Philosophie der Weltrevolution*, Wien, 1966.

Mascolo, Denys, *Le communisme. Révolution et communication ou la dialectique des valeurs et des besoins*, Paris, 1953.

Mayo, Elton, *The Human Problems of an Industrial Civilization*, New York, 1960.

McLellan, David, *The Young Hegelians and Karl Marx*, London, 1969.

Mende, Georg, *Karl Marx' Entwicklung vom revolutionären Demokraten zum Kommunisten*, Berlin, 1960.

Merleau-Ponty, Maurice, *Les aventures de la dialectique*, Paris, 1955.

Mésaventures de l'anti-marxisme, (Contributions by M. Caveing, G. Cogniot, J. T. Desanti, R. Garaudy, J. Kanapa, V. Leduc, H. Lefèbvre), Paris, 1956.

Mészáros, István, *Il problema dell'alienazione*, (in : "Nuova Presenza", 1961); *L'individuo e l'alienazione*, (ibid., 1961); *Collettività e l'alienazione*, (ibid., 1962); *Attualità e problematicità dell'educazione estetica*, (ibid., 1963); *Alienazione ed educazione moderna*, (ibid., 1963).

Miliband, Ralph, *The State in Capitalist Society*, London, 1969.

Miller, Alexander, *The Christian Significance of Marx*, London, 1946.

Mills, C. Wright, *The Marxists*, New York, 1962.

Mondolfo, Rodolfo, *Sulle orme di Marx*, Bologna, 1948.

Mondolfo, Rodolfo, *Il materialismo storico di F. Engels*, Firenze, 1952.

Mondolfo, Rodolfo, *Umanismo di Marx. Studi filosofici 1908-1966*, Torino, 1968.

Morf, Otto, *Das Verhältnis von Wirtschaftstheorie und Wirtschaftsgeschichte bei Karl Marx*, Bern, 1951.

Naville, Pierre, *De l'aliénation à la juissance*, Paris, 1957.

Neri, Guido D., *Prassi e conoscenza*, Milano, 1967.

Nizan, Paul, *Ecrits et correspondance 1926-1940*, Paris, 1967.

Oisermann, T. I., *Die Entfremdung als historische Kategorie*, Berlin, 1965.

Paci, Enzo, *Funzione delle scienze e significato dell'uomo*, Milano, 1963.

Pappenheim, Fritz, *The Alienation of Modern Man*, New York, 1959.

Pascal, Roy, *Karl Marx: His Apprenticeship to Politics*, London, 1943.

Pascal, Roy, *Karl Marx: Political Foundations*, London, 1943.

Pennati, Eugenio, *L'etica e il marxismo*, Firenze, 1948.
Peperzak, Adrien T. B., *Le jeune Hegel et la vision morale du monde*, La Haye, 1960.
Petrović, Gajo, *Marx in the Mid-Twentieth Century*, New York, 1967.
Piettre, André, *Marx et le marxisme*, Paris, 1957,
Pischel, Giuliano, *Marx giovane (1818-1849)*, Milano, 1948.
Polányi, Karl, *Origins of Our Time. The Great Transformation*, London, 1945.
Popitz, Heinrich, *Der Entfremdete Mensch. Zeitkritik und Geschichtsphilosophie des jungen Marx*, Basel, 1953.
Poulantzas, Nicos, *Pouvoir politique et classes sociales*, Paris, 1968.
Prestipino, Giuseppe, *La dialettica materialistica e le categorie della prassi*, Messina-Firenze, 1957.
Preti, Giulio, *Praxis e empirismo*, Torino, 1957.

Quarta, Giuseppe, Cipriano, Luigi, *Karl Marx e il concetto di classe sociale*, Roma, 1961.

Raphael, Max, *Zur Erkenntnistheorie der konkreten Dialektik*, Paris, 1934.
Riesman, David (et al.), *The Lonely Crowd*, New Haven, 1950.
Rosdolsky, Roman, *Zur Entstehungsgeschichte des Marxschen Kapitals*, Frankfurt/M., 1968.
Rosenberg, D. I., *Die Entwicklung der ökonomischen Lehre von Marx und Engels in den 40er Jahren des 19. Jahrhunderts*, Berlin, 1958.
Rossi, Mario, *Introduzione alla storia delle interpretazioni di Hegel*, Messina, 1959.
Rossi, Mario, *Marx e la dialettica Hegeliana*, I-II, Roma, 1960-1963.
Rubel, Maximilien, *Karl Marx. Essai de biographie intellectuelle*, Paris, 1957.

Sabetti, Alfredo, *Sulla fondazione del materialismo storico*, Firenze, 1962.
Sartre, Jean-Paul, *L'Etre et le néant*, Paris, 1943.
Sartre, Jean-Paul, *Critique de la raison dialectique*, Précédé de *Questions de méthode*, Paris, 1960.
Schaff, Adam, *Marxismus und das menschliche Individuum*, Wien, 1966.
Schlawin, H., *Grundzüge der Philosophie des jungen Marx*, Basel, 1957.
Schlesinger, Rudolf, *Marx: His Time and Ours*, London, 1950.
Schmidt, Alfred, *Der Begriff der Natur in der Lehre von Marx*, Frankfurt/M., 1962.
Schuffenhauer, Werner, *Feuerbach und der junge Marx*, Berlin, 1965.

Schwarz, J., *Die anthropologische Metaphysik des jungen Hegel*, Hildesheim, 1931.

Schwarz, J., *Hegels philosophische Entwicklung*, Frankfurt/M., 1938.

Sebag, Lucien, *Marxisme et structuralisme*, Paris, 1964.

Somerhausen, Luc, *L'humanisme agissant de Karl Marx*, Paris, 1946.

Thao, Tran Duc, *Phénoménologie et matérialisme dialectique*, Paris, 1951.

Thier, Erich, *Die Anthropologie des jungen Marx nach den Pariser ökonomisch-philosophischen Manuscripten*, Köln-Berlin, 1950

Thier, Erich, *Das Menschenbild des jungen Marx*, Göttingen, 1957.

Tillich, Paul, *Der Mensch im Christentum und im Marxismus*, Stuttgart, 1953.

Tucker, Robert C., *Philosophy and Myth in Karl Marx*, Cambridge, 1961.

Venable, Vernon, *Human Nature: The Marxian View*, New York, 1945.

Vranicki, Predrag, *The Development of Karl Marx's Thought* (in Croat), Zagreb, 1954.

Wackenheim, C., *La faillite de la religion d'après Karl Marx*, Paris, 1963.

Weinstock, Heinrich, *Arbeit und Bildung. Die Rolle der Arbeit im Prozess um unsere Menschenwerdung*, Heidelberg, 1954.

Wetter, G. A., *Der dialektische Materialismus. Sein Geschichte und sein System in der Sovietunion*, Freiburg/Br., 1952.

APPENDIX

To page 67:

"Through the qualities the atom acquires an existence which contradicts its idea; it is posited as an alienated being, separated from its essence."

> Marx, *Differenz der demokritischen und epikureischen Naturphilosophie*, (Doctoral Dissertation), cf. Note No. [99]

"Firstly, Epicurus makes the *contradiction* between matter and form inherent in the character of nature as appearance; the latter thus becomes the counterpart of the essential, i.e. of the atom. This happens in that time is being opposed to space, the active form of appearance to the passive form. Secondly, it is only with Epicurus that appearance is grasped as appearance, i.e. as an *alienation of the essence* which *gives practical proof of its reality through such an alienation.*"

> *Ibid.,* cf. Note No. [100]

To pages 243–4:

"The author of the *Phenomenology*, the *Encyclopaedia*, and the *Philosophy of History* cannot have confused the historical alienation of the human spirit with objectification without some valid reasons, other than those one might find in the economic structure of the period and the stage reached by the capitalist system. By objectifying himself in culture, the State, and human labour in general, man at the same time alienates himself, becomes other than himself, and discovers in this objectification an insurmountable degeneration which he must nevertheless try to overcome. This is a tension inseparable from existence, and it is Hegel's merit to have drawn attention to it and to have preserved it in the very center of human self-consciousness. On the other hand, one of the great difficulties of Marxism is its claim to overcome this tension in the more or less near future and hastily to attribute it to a particular phase of history. . . . As such, this notion does not seem to be reducible solely to the concept of the alienation of man under capitalism, as Marx understands it. The latter is only a particular case of a more universal problem of human self-consciousness which, being unable to conceive itself as an isolated *cogito*, can only recognize itself in a world which it constructs, in the other selves which it recognizes and by whom it is occasionally disowned. But this manner of self-discovery through the Other, this objectification, is always more or less an alienation, a loss of self and a simultaneous self-discovery. Thus objectification and alienation are inseparable, and their union is simply the expression of a dialectical tension observed in the very movement of history."

Jean Hyppolite, *Studies on Marx and Hegel.* (Translated by John O'Neill, Heinemann, London 1969), pp 86–88.

To page 259:

"What else could fortune be than *living in conformity to nature's wisdom*? If nature goes well, that is fortune; if it does not, that is misfortune. For *our essence is ordained in nature*."

Paracelsus, *Leben und Lebensweisheit in Selbstzeugnissen,* cf. Note No. [231]

Index

353

INDEX

354

INDEX

INDEX

Lightning Source UK Ltd.
Milton Keynes UK
06 November 2009

145890UK00001B/48/A